RC 553 .D5 P48 1995
Phillips, Maggie.
     Healing the divided self
: clinical and Ericksonian

DATE DUE

OCT 10 1996	Richmond Public
OCT 2 4 1996	due Feb 9/02
NOV 2 1 1996	Greater Victoria Pub. Lib
DEC 0 5 1996	due May 4/02
JAN 2 2 1997	NOV 1 2 2002
Feb. 5/97	NOV 1 2 2002
FEB 2 4 1997	DEC 0 7 2002
MAR - 7 1997	
DEC - 8 1997	
FEB 27 1998	
APR 1 5 1998	
MAR 4 1999	
MAR 1 8 1999	
APR - 1 1999	
Victoria Public	
due May 29/0	
AUG 1 4 2001	

BRODART   Cat. No. 23-221

HEALING THE DIVIDED SELF

CLINICAL AND ERICKSONIAN
HYPNOTHERAPY FOR
POST-TRAUMATIC AND
DISSOCIATIVE CONDITIONS

HEALING THE DIVIDED SELF

CLINICAL AND ERICKSONIAN
HYPNOTHERAPY FOR
POST-TRAUMATIC AND
DISSOCIATIVE CONDITIONS

Maggie Phillips, Ph.D.
and
Claire Frederick, M.D.

W.W. NORTON & COMPANY • New York • London

Printed in the United States of America

First Edition

Composition by Bytheway Typesetting Services, Inc.
Manufacturing by Haddon Craftsman, Inc.
Book design by P.J. Nolan

Library of Congress Cataloging-in-Publication Data

Phillips, Maggie.
    Healing the divided self : clinical and Ericksonian hypnotherapy
for post-traumatic and dissociative conditions / Maggie Phillips and
Claire Frederick.
        p.   cm.
    "A Norton professional book".
    Includes bibliographical references and index.
    ISBN 0-393-70184-0
    1. Dissociative disorders–Treatment. 2. Hypnotism–Therapeutic
use. 3. Post-traumatic stress disorder–Treatment. I. Frederick,
Claire. II. Title.
    RC553.D5P48   1995
    616.85′21–dc20   94-40282 CIP

W. W. Norton & Company, Inc., 500 Fifth Avenue, New York, NY 10110
W. W. Norton & Company, Ltd., 10 Coptic Street, London WC1A 1PU

1 2 3 4 5 6 7 8 9 0

We dedicate this book to our teachers, who have inspired us in the practice of hypnotherapy; to our students, who have provoked important questions we were compelled to answer; to our patients, without whom this book would never have been written; and to our parents and families, who first taught us about the healing power of love.

FOREWORD

The topic of dissociation is no stranger to me. From my early days of growing up in a violent Irish Catholic alcoholic family, through being educated by Catholic nuns and Jesuits, to studying with Milton Erickson, to living in a state (and later in a country) governed by Ronald Reagan, to practicing hypnotic psychotherapy for 20 years, I learned a lot about dissociation, both good and bad. It served important purposes over the years: allowing me to separate, to examine experiences and relationships in certain ways, and to find refuge in internal worlds. Most of all, dissociation insulated me from further pain.

As a lifestyle, it worked reasonably well. Until, of course, the day I got married and was forced into facing the incompatibility of dissociation with human intimacy. The painful limitations of dissociation were revealed further when I became a parent and realized my growing commitment to staying connected in relationship. It is a long and difficult road to reassociate with community and the world, one that requires learning, as the Beatles once sang, "to get by with a little help from my friends."

Maggie Phillips and Claire Frederick are the sort of friends who make the journey possible. As writers and therapists, they have addressed the topic of recovering from dissociative retreats from life in a humane, articulate, and enormously insightful way. In reading their book, I was reminded of James Joyce's theory of aesthetics,[1] in which he makes the distinction between proper art and improper art. Using advertising as an example of improper art, Joyce asserts that its purpose is to draw consciousness away from a person, fixating it within the frame of art. The person is left with a feeling of agitation

---

[1] James Joyce, (1916), *A Portrait of the Artist as a Young Man*, London: Jonathen Cape. Cited by Joseph Campbell in D. K. Osbon (Ed.), *Reflections of the Art of Living: A Joseph Campbell Companion*, 1991, New York: HarperCollins.

and a compulsive drive to do something (e.g., buy the product) to reduce the agitation. In this sense, therapists or writers create improper art when one is left fixated on their theory and feeling a compulsion to use it to change clients, rather than seeing through it to something more important, i.e., the human beings it can illuminate or help. This idea echoes William Blake's observation that Satan has many names, Opacity being the most common.

In proper art, according to Joyce, consciousness is extended and expanded rather than projected. The viewer or listener experiences the art and feels a state of quiescent centering, one in which an expanded sense of possibility is felt. Proper art allows one to see through the frame to a deeper, more basic experience or meaning, and in doing so activates new life in the imagination of the viewer.

Maggie Phillips and Claire Frederick clearly engage in the practice of proper art. Like any good artists, they have a sound method, an impressive rigor, and a clear commitment to communication. In seeking to be warmly illuminative rather than blindingly brilliant, they offer coherent methods and practical techniques. One is left with a deeper compassion, a greater hope, and an expanded understanding of how to help clients struggling with dissociative processes. It is hard to imagine a book more helpful than this for therapists working with such clients. I hope you will enjoy it as much as I have.

Stephen Gilligan, Ph.D.
Encinitas,CA

FOREWORD

Even when they are augmented by insight, therapies that fail to access unconscious material may leave patients vulnerable to a return of their problems. What is needed today is a psychodynamically-oriented treatment approach, involving insights into unconscious conflicts, that can achieve the significant changes aimed at by psychoanalysis. It is in this area that the present work, *Healing the Divided Self,* makes its contribution.

Psychoanalysts over the past decades have learned much about the interactions of resistance and defensive processes, yet they have failed to improve their therapeutic *techniques*. Recent clinicians have utilized these understandings within the modality of hypnosis, and have made considerable progress through the development of *hypnoanalysis*—which has considerably shortened treatment time.

Other approaches toward incisive therapeutic intervention have stemmed from the innovative and intuitive methods of Milton Erickson. Yet his treatment was such a personal art that it has been difficult to teach.

With the recent increased attention to multiple personality, now termed dissociative identity disorder, we are learning more about the fragmentation of personality as it affects all normal and abnormal behavior. Findings from the study of dissociation, plus the techniques of hypnoanalysis, have been brought together into what is now called *Ego-State Therapy*, defined as the use of group, family and individual treatment techniques to resolve conflicts between the various "ego states" within a "family of self." Ego-State Therapy has been shown to effect significant personality reorganization even within short periods of time. And it is around this modality that Phillips and Frederick have focused the emphasis of their book.

However, *Healing the Divided Self* is not simply another publication on Ego-State Therapy. It is an attempt at integration, a bringing together of findings and methods drawn from psychoanalysis, hypnotherapy, Ericksonian methodology, and the work of MPD therapists, as well as our own experience in the development of Ego-State Therapy. The authors have also added to the original discoveries in this approach, through many innovative procedures of their own.

Drawing from a wealth of personal clinical experience, Phillips and Frederick report their use of ego-state methods in a systematic and scholarly way. They often review the ego-state theory involved, describe their techniques, and illustrate them with specific case examples, showing how this approach has achieved rapid therapeutic change.

The result is a significant treatise which will contribute substantially to an in-depth understanding of many difficult cases. Psychotherapists will find in *Healing the Divided Self* a broad psychodynamic approach devoted to dealing not only with dissociated conditions such as multiple personalities but also with many other neurotic and behavior disorders.

John G. Watkins, Ph.D.   *Helen H. Watkins, M.A.*
Professor Emeritus   Clinical Psychologist, Retired
University of Montana   University of Montana

ACKNOWLEDGMENTS

There are many people who have helped us in the creation of this book. Although the names are too numerous to list here, we wish to give special thanks to:

Jack and Helen Watkins, our friends and teachers, who introduced us to Ego-State Therapy and the great traditions of hypnoanalysis, and who have opened so many doors;

Stephen Gilligan, who introduced us to the genius of Milton Erickson and, with his gifts of heart and mind, has greatly influenced our styles as hypnotherapists;

John O. Beahrs, Christine Courtois, Yvonne Dolan, Judith Fleiss, Eliana Gil, Jack and Bev Gorsuch, Helge Jacobsen, Larz Jesperson, Shirley McNeal, Virginia Scott, David Steindl-Rast, and Michael Yapko for their insightful and enthusiastic critical comments;

Elgan Baker, Erika Fromm, Marlene Hunter, Moshe Torem, and Jeffrey K. Zeig for their support and encouragement;

Gerry Edelstien, who graciously introduced us to Susan Barrows Munro, our capable editor at W. W. Norton;

Andrea Bryck, who gave so generously of her time, talents, and humor in guiding our creative process, and who designed the cover and the illustrations;

Francie Kendall, for her discovery of Helen Hardin, whose painting illustrates the jacket;

Janice L. Stamm, for her invaluable legal advice;

Jean Wing, for her tireless efforts to make our manuscript perfect;

Louise Bettner, Dorann Boulian, Seena Frost, Marsha King, Nancy Norris,

Daniel Peterson, Beth St. John, Judy Stenovich, and members of our supervision groups, whose ideas and unqualified support sustained us through this process;

Bill Touchet and Carol Ann Wachner, for their artistic suggestions in the early stages of this project;

Our loving circle of friends, neighbors, family, and colleagues, who kept on telling us we could do it;

Ginger, Jennie, Samantha, and Seurat, our loyal animal friends, who sat patiently at our feet as we wrote and rewrote this book.

CONTENTS

INTRODUCTION

In recent years, books about trauma, abuse, and dissociative disorders, including multiple personality disorder, have proliferated within the mental health field. Most of them have devoted well over half their pages to the diagnosis and etiology of patient symptoms, a few more of their chapters to the specifics of treatment, and the rest to various issues that affect the treatment process.

Relatively few authors have attempted to present a step-by-step, practical guide to the difficult business of constructing and implementing a plan of action that can actually heal and integrate the effects of dissociated experiences and help to create new identity beyond that of "survivor" or victim of childhood traumas. Fewer still have ventured out into the lesser-known waters of hypnotherapy as a primary treatment modality for these conditions, presuming that hypnosis may be too "dangerous" for patients who are already dramatically dissociated from their internal, and sometimes external, realities, or that this approach is inappropriate for individuals who can only be helped by years of methodical insight therapy. At best, most authors include a chapter on hypnotic treatment approaches, even though many of the professional journals in recent years have presented evidence that points to hypnosis as the treatment of choice for problems of a dissociative nature. Still others do a credible job of presenting methods of achieving the strategic hypnotherapeutic resolution of trauma-based symptoms in a few well-planned sessions.

This is not a book about how to learn hypnosis. There are many excellent sourcebooks which introduce the practice of clinical and Ericksonian hypnotherapy. Of course, there are no substitutes for experiential hypnosis training, personal hypnotherapy experiences, and commitment to ongoing hypnosis study and practice. Rather, *Healing the Divided Self* is designed for the professional reader who already has some working knowledge of hypnosis and wants to expand skills in applying hypnotic approaches to the challenging array of dissociative symptoms that are seen in clinical practice today. Throughout this book, we attempt to make accessible numerous references to stimulate additional learning in various areas of applied hypnosis. We hope our readers will find help in what we have learned from and with our patients. More importantly, we hope you will be inspired to apply these concepts in ways that enhance your own style of skillful, creative therapy.

This is a challenging time for the mental health profession, as the issue of "false memory" brings lawsuits, debate, and confusion about how to work effectively and appropriately with clinical material and symptoms related to experiences of abuse, assault, neglect, and other traumas. We know that traumatic memory always includes deletions, mutations, distortions, and other inaccuracies because this is true of *all* memory. What is also clear is that it is not possible to go through psychotherapy without retrieving some kinds of false memories, because all memory contains some degree of falsehood (Ross, 1994). What is not yet clear is how best to educate clinicians, patients, and the general public about these issues so that the clinical experience results in patients' genuinely taking responsibility for "finding their own truth" during the course of therapy experiences.

Our view is that each patient is different. Much as each human being has a unique set of fingerprints, each patient who comes to therapy has a unique story of how past experiences have affected the evolution of current strengths and difficulties. Because we have been well trained in the uses of hypnosis and have found it uniquely helpful in liberating many of the missing details of our patients' life stories, we have written this book as a partial answer to the question, "How do you work responsibly and effectively with known and unknown traumatic experiences that can create a divided self?"

The clinical information and case material contained within these pages is designed to be used by trained mental health professionals in a clinical setting; this is *not* intended in any way as a self-help book. Readers are cautioned to note that none of the concepts, approaches, or case examples we provide can be understood or considered properly outside of the full context we have presented. In most cases, case examples and patient presentations are composites of our work with several patients, in order to ensure confidentiality.

Healing the Divided Self is intended to provide the clinician with a systematic guide to the whole spectrum of dissociative symptoms and disorders and their hypnotic treatment, ranging from a several-session perspective to one of more long-term hypnoanalytic therapy with severely dissociated individuals. Our approach offers a synthesis of both classical and Ericksonian styles of hypnosis, drawing from the most effective aspects of these traditions to find practical methods that seem to work consistently with these challenging patients. Because we work in outpatient private practice settings, this treatment mileu is featured throughout. In order to provide a balanced gender perspective, we have alternated general pronoun references to "she" and "he" on a chapter-by-chapter basis.

To the extent possible, the voice of this book reflects the many voices of our patients who have identified in diverse ways the most valuable aspects of healing in their therapy experiences. A second voice line reverberates from therapists who have worked with us in supervision and training contexts and have raised important clinical questions:

- How do I present hypnosis to patients I have already been working with from a psychodynamic (or other) orientation?
- How do I help create an atmosphere of safety for individuals who want to explore traumatic memories but are clearly terrified?
- What do I do when hypnotized or non-hypnotized patients experience such intense feeling states that they cannot communicate with me and seem to lose contact with the immediate reality?
- Most of my patients seem "stuck" in their roles as survivors of past horrors, as if that is their only identity. How can I help them create a new integrated identity that is not based on pain from the past?
- How can I handle my own feelings of fear, denial, outrage, or disgust when my patients are exploring hypnotic material related to extreme sexual and ritual abuse?
- How can I use hypnosis in such a way that I will not create or be accused of creating "false" memories?

Our primary goal is to present ways of introducing and implementing hypnotic interventions at every stage of treatment within the context of the therapeutic relationship, which we view as the single most important tool for developing and using hypnotic communication. Numerous clinical examples spanning the entire treatment process and a variety of transcribed excerpts from therapy sessions provide specific applications of the concepts we discuss.

HEALING THE DIVIDED SELF

CLINICAL AND ERICKSONIAN
HYPNOTHERAPY FOR
POST-TRAUMATIC AND
DISSOCIATIVE CONDITIONS

1

WHAT IS THE DIVIDED SELF?

We believe that an understanding of the nature of the divided self is essential for the clinician who is practicing psychotherapy today. Far too often we consult with patients who have seen numbers of therapists but have received no substantive results for their efforts. A major reason for this is that their therapy overlooked problems of self-division and failed to identify what was most central to the patient. It is not surprising, in view of this, that their previous therapy was unable to reach the depth of discovery necessary for healing.

Early Clinical Evidence for Personality Division

Until the 19th century, shamans, prophets, and medicine men attempted to help individuals afflicted with dissociative conditions by casting out demons. Exorcisms for these conditions has been featured in many cultures around the world; in fact, until relatively recent times, dissociative phenomena were deemed the proper domain of the church. For centuries exorcism was the recommended form of treatment in Western culture (Ellenberger, 1970), and even today several contemporary traditions exist for such treatment of MPD (DID) (Friesen, 1991; Hill & Goodwin, 1993).

In the late 19th and early 20th centuries clinicians began to treat and to write about dissociative disorders; these disorders, then called the "hysterias," included multiple personality disorder. Pierre Janet (1907), William James (1890), and Morton Prince (1906) published case studies about their work.

The most renowned theorizer of the time was Pierre Janet (1907, 1926), a philosopher turned physician. According to Janet, the conditions he and other clinicians were treating were caused by a process he called "dissociation." Dissociation was a separation of the thoughts, feelings, and perceptions associated with a particular event from the greater body of mental content.

1

Janet believed that dissociation occurred when a biologically susceptible individual underwent trauma. He postulated dissociation as the mechanism lying behind many clinical phenomena, such as the hysterias, obsessive compulsive disorders, and psychasthenia, as well as multiple personality disorder. For Janet the cure occurred when the trauma was discovered (Janet, 1907; Frankel, 1990).

Breuer's work with Anna O. (Breuer & Freud, 1893–1895) launched another way of viewing division in the human mind. He and his collaborator, a young physician named Sigmund Freud, used their work with hysterical patients as material from which they introduced their concept of the unconscious mind and a form of treatment, psychoanalysis. Initially, Freud shared Janet's view about psychopathology. He thought that it was produced by trauma, and that remembering and catharsis provided the cure. Freud even had specific ideas that the nature of the trauma in the case of the hysterias was childhood sexual abuse (Freud, 1896). However, as he continued to elaborate his thinking, he found it necessary to repudiate this seduction theory. A preponderance of his patients, predominantly female, were reporting that sexual molestation by their relatives had occurred when they were children. A number of these accused perpetrators were Freud's colleagues and members of his social and academic circle. He concluded that such frequency of child sexual abuse was unlikely and turned to his theories of infantile sexuality and unconscious oedipal conflict and fantasy to explain the material he heard from his patients (Ellenberger, 1970). Freud's struggle about the meaning of the memory material he retrieved from his patients, often under hypnosis, continues to be echoed in vociferous debate within the professional community today.

The work of the other 19th-century dynamic clinicians, as well as the therapeutic use of hypnosis, was eventually swept into temporary oblivion by a number of historical developments. Among them were the proposed psychoanalytic theories of Freud, which involved an unconscious mind, repression, and the mental mechanisms of defense, and Pavlov's work with the conditioned reflex, which heralded the dawn of behaviorism. These important trends, together with the tremendous advances taking place in physiological and biochemical understandings of the human organism, turned the tide of psychological theory away from the work the 19th-century clinicians and dissociative theory.

Therapeutic work with soldiers suffering from "battle fatigue" or "war neurosis" began during World War II, and it was amplified and studied further during the Korean and Vietnam conflicts. This work involved a revival of hypnosis as a therapeutic tool and paved the way for some exacting scientific work concerning the nature of hypnosis and of hypnotic susceptibility (Frankel, 1990; Hilgard, 1965; Orne, 1959).

Starting in the late 1960s, the women's movement brought a new freedom to reveal the prevalence of child sexual abuse. While astute clinicians had always been aware of its presence as a significant factor in the lives of many patients, the opening of the closet door on this social phenomenon made it clear that this kind of childhood trauma was widespread and cut across economic and social categories.

The publication of Ellenberger's vital and scholarly book, *The Discovery of the Unconscious*, in 1970 was a powerful factor in a revival of interest in the work of the early clinicians and their views concerning dissociation (Frankel, 1990). Clinicians were finding themselves in the position of having to reconsider some of the earlier ideas of the 19th- and early 20th-century clinicians and to refocus attention upon dissociation and the role of trauma in the production of human psychopathology (Ross, 1989). Some of the experimental evidence accrued in the past two centuries was also helpful in setting the stage for renewed interest in these topics.

The Emergence of Experimental Evidence for Division of Personality

THE DISSOCIATION THEORY

The idea that the human personality is naturally divided or segmented was commonly held in the late 19th and early 20th centuries. Janet was the first investigator to use the term "subconscious" (Ellenberger, 1970; Janet, 1907). He (Janet, 1907) clearly described aspects of personality that had patterns of feeling and cognition, and which, unlike the alters of the patient with multiple personality disorder, could only be activated by hypnosis. This was very much like Jung's concept of the "complex" (Jung, 1969).

One early clinician, the experimental and clinical psychologist Alfred Binet (1977a, 1977b), conducted a number of fascinating experiments in the field of hypnosis. Some of them had to do with the experimental creation of alter personalities. In a significant experiment with a highly hypnotizable subject he demonstrated that the subject could respond to visual stimuli without even being aware of them on a conscious level. Binet believed that a doubling of consciousness was a causative mechanism for the symptoms we might call dissociative. Similar phenomena were demonstrated by the American psychologist William James (1889), who also concluded that the mind operated under the control of several subpersonalities.

THE NEODISSOCIATION THEORY

Many years later Ernest Hilgard (1965–84) conducted careful experiments involving the perception of sound and pain under hypnosis. He also measured bodily responses in order to discover whether the body was responding physiologically to pain even when the hypnotized subject had anesthesia for it. Hilgard's experiments led him to the conclusion that cognitive functioning is the result of the interaction of many "subordinate control systems" (1973, p. 406). Hilgard posited the neodissociation theory to account for his experimental findings. This theory was completely compatible with Freudian theory. He hypothesized was that there were two kinds of defense mechanisms, with two different kinds of splits that could develop within the psyche. A horizontal split represented the Freudian topographical map, which separates conscious from unconscious repressed material, and a vertical split placed within the realm of the conscious mind separates dissociated material from the rest of conscious content into the preconscious (Figure 1). Hilgard named the main manifesting consciousness the "executive ego." Covert observing aspects of the mind activated experimentally under hypnosis were known as "hidden observers."

According to Spiegel (1986), dissociation can be distinguished from repression "in terms of the relationships among the material which is kept out of conscious awareness" (p. 124). Repressed material does not necessarily exclude other types of intrapsychic material.

In comparing repression with dissociation, Terr (1990) reminds us that the American Psychiatric Association (1994) has classified repression and

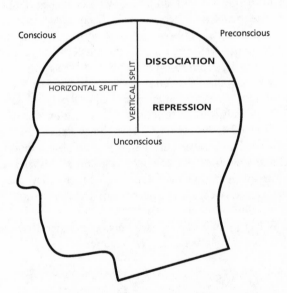

Figure 1. Neodissociation Theory:
Dissociation and Repression

dissociation as different unconscious mental mechanisms of defense (Appendix B, DSM-IV). Repression is a concept used by Freud to account for the individual's pushing significant painful material into the unconscious mind where, although completely forgotten, it continues to affect mental processes such as thought, feeling and behavior, and may produce symptoms. The defense of repression is present in normal as well as abnormal human psychology. Dissociation, on the other hand, was Janet's concept of a "sidewise slippage from consciousness, with a partition between the dissociated event and the mental component that knows and remembers" (Terr, 1990, p. 66).

The Dissociative Spectrum

Normal dissociative phenomena appear during the course of everyday life. Hilgard's (1973) example of a tune that runs, unbidden, through one's head is an excellent one. Ordinary daydreaming belongs on the dissociative spectrum, as does getting lost in an absorbing book or an exciting movie. Perfectly normal daily activities are probably dissociative whenever they involve automatic functioning, such as typing a paper or taking a trip by car. Some individuals have a greater capacity to dissociate. Here we find the "absent-minded professor" and many creative people who appear to be a little dreamy when they are involved in the creative process. Ross (1989) has cited not remembering getting up in the middle of the night to go to the bathroom as an example of normal organic dissociation.

Somewhere a little farther along the scale but for many still within the normal realm are certain dissociative reactions to traumatic situations. Among these are isolation of emotions during war situations, forgetting details of a hurricane or earthquake, or being paralyzed in the presence of a real physical threat. According to Ross (1989), amnesia after a concussion is normal biological dissociation. It should be located in this part of the spectrum. There is a defensive borderland where dissociation is being used to escape reality. For example, a child might lose herself in *Star Trek* or in video games to escape the noise and static of a dysfunctional family. The "forgetting" of an unpleasant conversation also belongs here.

Acute dissociative disorders, such as somnambulism, the conversion disorders (e.g., hysterical paralysis or blindness), and fugue states, can be found further along the spectrum, as can depersonalization disorder, derealization, and not feeling or experiencing one's own body, as well as amnesia; also in this area of the more pathological part of the spectrum can be found profound and chronic dissociative disorders. Certain clinical syndromes that have not traditionally been placed within the dissociative spectrum are often the result of chronic dissociation. These include eating disorders, depression, obsessive compulsive disorder, phobias, and panic disorder. Multiple personality disorder (now renamed dissociative identity disorder by the American Psychiatric Association in DSM-IV) and similar dissociative disorders (not otherwise specified) are, of course, the extreme result of chronic dissociation. A schema of the dissociative spectrum can be seen in Figure 2.

Trauma, Hypnosis, and Memory

THE LASTING EFFECTS OF TRAUMA

Significant information about the relationship of trauma and dissociation can be found in reports from clinicians who have treated patients with pathological dissociation that is the result of trauma, usually experienced in childhood. Terr (1991) has reported four characteristics that can be identified in anyone who has been subjected to extreme childhood trauma: "They include repeated visualizations or other returning perceptions, repeated behaviors and bodily responses, trauma-specific fears, and revised ideas about people, life, and the future" (p. 19). She regards Type I trauma, the unanticipated single traumatic event, as the kind of trauma that is extremely common in childhood and of the type typically described by Anna Freud (1969). Type II traumata are repeated and longstanding, and a massive array of defense mechanisms is brought into play to help the child endure these unendurable events. Among the defenses are denial (often massive) and psychic numbing, self-hypnosis and dissociation, repression with subsequent identification with the aggressor, and aggression turned against the self (Terr, 1991).

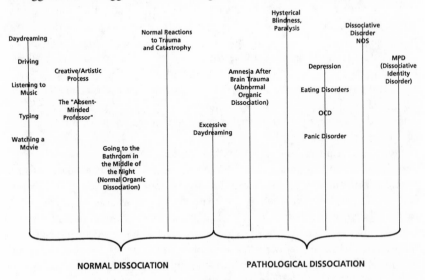

Figure 2. The Continuum of Dissociation

True psychological trauma is an event of the greatest magnitude, beyond the minor traumata of everyday experience. When it occurs, it will profoundly affect the future and the actual course of the life of its recipient. Beahrs (1990) has noted the prominent feature of increased arousal in post-traumatic stress behaviors. Like Terr (1991), he has observed phenomena associated with a return or reliving of the trauma, numbing and dissociation, and some degree of splitting as defensive reactions to overwhelming trauma. Trauma leaves individuals with marked vulnerabilities and damage (van der Kolk, 1987c). Even when they appear "normal," there may be fluctuation between an arousal of active PTSD symptoms and periods of emotional constriction.

That victims of trauma dissociate in order to protect themselves from the overwhelming pain of the situation has been well-known since the 19th century (Ellenberger, 1970). This phenomenon has been noted with war neuroses (Fisher, 1945; Watkins, 1949), in concentration inmates (Jaffe, 1968), and in MPD patients. Kluft (1985b) has observed that the trauma of childhood abuse is the causative factor for the development of childhood MPD, and that its cessation is necessary if the child is to recover. Coons (1980), Putnam (1989), and Ross (1989) have also identified childhood trauma as the causative agent in adult MPD patients. It is hypothesized that trauma produces spontaneous trance reactions, and that the resultant hypnotic dissociation is adaptive (Beahrs, 1990). Certainly, post-traumatic patients can often be observed to enter trance spontaneously (Kluft, 1985c; Spiegel & Fink, 1979; Stutman & Bliss, 1985) during their therapy sessions.

Spontaneous trance and dissociation are both adaptive (Beahrs, 1990; Braun & Sachs, 1985; Kluft, 1984b; Putnam, 1989; Spiegel, 1986) and damaging (Hilgard, 1973; Spiegel, 1986). Hilgard (1973) was able to demonstrate experimentally that subjects maintaining dissociation under hypnosis could not perform certain motor tasks as well as subjects who were not maintaining dissociation. Understanding both these aspects of dissociation allows the therapist to work effectively with dissociative disorder patients.

STATE-DEPENDENT LEARNING AND THE PSYCHOBIOLOGY OF MEMORY

State-dependent learning (Overton, 1978) is a concept that refers to the connection between the learning experience and the biochemical and physiological state of the central nervous system at the time the learning is taking place. It has been a subject of investigation for over forty years (Rossi & Cheek, 1988). It has been noted repeatedly that certain drugs have profound effects on the retention and reinstatement of memory. For example, an individual under the influence of alcohol may not be able to remember the details of her "important philosophical conversation" until she falls into a similar state of inebriation. Hilgard (1977), aware of this, postulated that divided consciousness was in itself "the paradigm of state dependent learning." He noted, "The concept of dissociation employed by Overton is consonant with neodissociation theory. That is, two types of behavior may be isolated from one another because of different available information" (pp. 244–245).

An awareness of state-dependent learning and the role of informational substances released by the nervous system (Pert, 1981) makes way for an understanding of why hypnotherapeutic approaches can be so valuable in the treatment of dissociative disorders. Rossi (1993a) has postulated that hypnotic states allow informational substances within the nervous system to approximate their situations in earlier times. Thus memories can be revived and relived.

HYPNOSIS AND MEMORY

One of the more heated topics of debate among mental health and research professionals is whether memories obtained under hypnosis are valid. Age regression for the purpose of uncovering and reconstructing traumatic memories is a time-honored hypnotic technique frequently used with dissociative patients. However, there have been considerable objections to the validity of material obtained in this fashion both from scientific investigators (Pettinati, 1988) and from a group called the False Memory Syndrome Foundation, which is composed of professionals, family members who claim they have been falsely accused of perpetrating abuse, and others who are interested in the topic.

The Nature of Memory

Memory is an extremely complex subject (Bowers & Hilgard, 1988). There are three stages of memory, each of which offers possibilities for distortion. The first is the *acquisition stage*. Memory can be encoded in a number of ways in this phase. For example, the encoding may be superficial or it may be deep; it may be holistic or detail-oriented (Orne, Whitehouse, Dinges, & Orne, 1988). Material that is encoded through deep processing can usually be recalled and recognized more easily (Craik & Lockhart, 1972). Distortions can occur here for a variety of reasons, such as poor illumination, distance, expectation, etc.

After memory is acquired, it is stored during the *retention phase*. Within this phase additional possibilities for distortion are present, as memories may lose their intensity or "fade," or be reworked, embellished, changed, or transformed by the unconscious mind for a variety of reasons.

Finally, distortions may occur during the *stage of memory retrieval*. The circumstances surrounding the retrieval can be extremely important. For example, false information supplied after an event can be accessed better than material previously remembered about the event. Thus an individual's version of an event can be revised in the light of information obtained after the details of the event have been stored in memory (Loftus, 1979; Loftus, Miller, & Burns, 1978). One form of information after the fact consists of leading questions; even when they are quite subtle (Loftus & Zanni, 1975), they are notorious for their ability to produce distortions that affect the validity of the retrieved memory (Bowers & Hilgard, 1988).

Memory can be long-term or short-term; also, there are thought to be two kinds of memory, *episodic* and *semantic* (Tulving, 1972). Episodic memory consists of events recalled by an individual within his life, whereas semantic memory is the memory of a general fund of information and techniques, such as how to brush one's teeth or ride a bicycle or what sugar is used for.

The way an individual thinks and feels about the nature of what he produces as a recalled memory or mnemonic experience may bear some, little, or no correspondence to the accuracy of the material recalled. Thus, an individual may recall quite accurate material without realizing that there is any connection to its corresponding memory source of origin. This kind of memory is not perceived as something remembered, but rather as one's own original thinking (*cryptamnesia*). Memory material that emerges in this way can lead to accusations of plagiarism for the person who claims it as his own creative production. The other side of the coin is the situation in which a person may experience a "memory" with great confidence when there has been no corresponding experience in her history (*confabulation*). This "memory" is based on the person's inner life, associations, fantasies, wishes, etc. (Bowers & Hilgard, 1988). There is no doubt that memory can be the subject of many vicissitudes in each of its stages.

The Effects of Hypnosis on Memory

Adding the element of hypnosis to memory opens possibilities for enhancing recall (*hypnotic hypermnesia*). Foundations for hypnotic hypermnesia are based on the work of such 19th-century clinicians as Janet, Freud, and Breuer, who used hypnosis for memory retrieval, and such contemporary researchers as Orne, Whitehouse, Dinges, and Orne (1988), who have noted that several experiments of a pioneering nature (Hull, 1933) appeared to confirm the clinical tradition. However, the use of hypnosis to improve recall is fraught with many possibilities for distortion. Orne et al. (1988) have reviewed a number of effects hypnosis has upon memory. Some the effects which must be taken into consideration are:

1. "Normal reality-monitoring activities . . . " (Orne et al., 1988, p. 23) are relinquished within a calm and peaceful environment, as is immediate responsibility for one's actions. Material produced under hypnosis could be the result of the subject's feeling freer to report material she previously felt too uncertain to report in the waking state.

2. Essential to the hypnotic situation is the involvement of imagination and fantasy; consequently, in hypnosis there is an enhanced opportunity for fantasy and historically valid memory to become enmeshed.

3. Hypnosis increases suggestibility; consequently, there is a greater opportunity for hypnotically accessed memories to be intentionally or unintentionally contaminated through the nature of the questions, how they are asked, and many other potentially extremely subtle cues. The subject may not be able to distinguish between the details of her own memory and the material thus "implanted" by the questioner.

4. Critical judgment is reduced in hypnosis, while fantasy increases. This makes it much easier for the subject, especially if she believes that hypnosis can retrieve accurate memories, to be certain that particular visualizations or imaginations about what happened are indeed accurate when there is no objective basis for this.

5. Subjects may convincingly feign hypnosis and distort and lie; subjects who are truly hypnotized may also lie. Hypnosis is not a truth serum.

6. Confidence is increased in hypnosis. This, coupled with the heightened proneness to fantasy and the reduction in critical judgment also characteristic of hypnosis, can lead to firm belief that experiences without veridicality are truly being remembered.

Orne et al. (1988) have suggested that hypnotic age regression may facilitate the retrieval of memories by reinstating the encoding context and cues. Since hypnosis is a powerful tool for the mobilization of affect, it can be used to facilitate affect similar to the affect present during the storage of the memory material. Helping the subject get in touch with that affect could play a significant role in the retrieval process. There are many other factors that influence the role of hypnosis in memory retrieval, such as whether the material is meaningful or nonmeaningful, remote or recent, whether mood state dependency (Bower, 1981) exists, or whether the recall is forced (Orne et al., 1988). There is experimental evidence that the trance state facilitates the introduction of false material into a recovered memory (Laurence &

Perry, 1983). The controversy about the accuracy of "hypnotically refreshed" memories has led to extreme restraint in the use of hypnosis to recover material that will be used in courtroom testimony. Orne and his colleagues state good reasons for this. The first is the "fundamental unreliability" of hypnotically elicited memories. Secondly, these memories may persist in the waking state and be impossible for the witness to distinguish from what she recalled before she was hypnotized. Finally, the increased confidence that hypnosis bestows may give witnesses the appearance of unwarranted credibility to a jury.

Clinical Context of Hypnosis and Memory

Our primary interest in the relationship between hypnosis and memory lies within the area of clinical work. Hypnotic phenomena offer the clinician unique opportunities to access the patient's inner mind and its memory material in order to locate and work with the conflicts and the resources that can be found there. Brown and Fromm (1986) remind us that the hypnotic process is highly cognitive when compared with other altered states of consciousness such as mindfulness meditation. In self-hypnosis, for example, the subject is able to utilize both primary process thinking to devise and produce the hypnotic experience and secondary process thinking for such things as self-suggestion for entering trance as well as for deepening (Brown, Forte, Rich, & Epstein, 1982–83). In heterohypnosis the patient's primary process cognition may produce unique imagery that does not spring directly from the suggestions of the hypnotist, even while the patient continues to use secondary process cognition for such things as planning how to respond to the hypnotist (Sheehan & McConkey, 1982; Spanos, 1982). Secondary process cognition continues throughout the hypnotic experience; however, there is a preponderance of primary process thinking (Brown & Fromm, 1986; Fromm, 1970).

Age regression is a hypnotic phenomenon that may be induced or occur spontaneously in trance and which may be accompanied by hypermnesia. Material that has been long repressed may become available in the trance state (Brown & Fromm, 1986; Fromm, 1970; Sheehan & McConkey, 1982). This reclaimed memory material may contain a richness of imagery not usually associated with the waking state (Fromm, 1979b).

Age regression is not characteristic of other altered states of consciousness (Brown et al., 1982–83). Its appearance during hypnosis is often accompanied by a greater than usual range of affect (Brown & Fromm, 1986). Thus, the uniqueness and richness of the hypnotic experience offer therapeutic opportunities not found within the waking state. "Hypnotized people have access to bodily sensations, emotions, memories, and fantasies that are usually beyond their grasp in waking consciousness. They also tend to think about such experiences in new ways while hypnotized. These factors contribute to the efficacy of hypnosis as an uncovering and an integrative method of therapy" (Brown & Fromm, 1986, p. 15).

Like psychoanalysis, hypnoanalysis works to uncover repressed and dissociated material. It differs from psychoanalysis in its ability to incorporate trance phenomena such as intensified imagery, age regression, and hypermnesia. In both psychoanalytic and hypnoanalytic work, memory material is worked through within the context of the transference and the defenses. Although memory material is produced with either method, hypnoanalysis has the advantage of more rapid access because of the unique phenomena associated with hypnosis. Even within the hypnoanalytic situation, however, memory material may appear slowly at times, and only incomplete or partial material may be available until the patient is strong enough to tolerate more information (Brown & Fromm, 1986).

The hypnotherapist is obligated to be cautious during the uncovering process and to refrain from suggestion about what should be recalled. Patients need to be informed that memory material may not be at all precise, and that the decisions about its "truthfulness" or "not-truthfulness" belong to the patient.

It is also essential for the hypnotherapist to remember that legal issues about memory material are genuine. In many jurisdictions, material obtained during hypnosis, as well as before and after hypnosis is used, cannot be admitted into trial situations. It is recommended that informed consents about this issue be obtained from any patient before hypnosis is employed as a treatment modality.

The "False Memory Syndrome"

The term "False Memory Syndrome (FMS)" was coined by the False Memory Syndrome Foundation (FMSF). The FMSF is located in Philadelphia and is composed of academics, scientific investigators, and others with special interests in memory, as well as family members who have been accused of abuse. They have organized to counteract the abuses and distortions resulting from the introduction of inaccurate memories retrieved during therapy into lawsuits and family relations. They are opposed to anyone who accepts the idea that the memories patients retrieve in therapy may possess validity, and have made a "straw man" of a self-help book written by two authors who are not licensed therapists, *The Courage to Heal* (Bass & Davis, 1988). One of their prestigious consultants is Elizabeth Loftus (1979, 1993), an academic researcher and a recognized expert in the field of memory. Loftus (1993) has rejected the validity not only of memories retrieved in psychotherapy but also of the concept of repression itself. In essence, the worth of all uncovering psychotherapy has come under attack, and this attack is receiving a great deal of attention in the popular press.

Gannon (1993) has viewed the FMS as a sociopolitical issue that must be confronted. Noting that the acceptance of abuse as a reality in our society is a relatively recent historical development, Gannon states that when any issue so previously repressed historically finally erupts into collective consciousness, it will undergo a process of continuous unfolding until it encounters resistances that place some limits on its further development. His concern is that with its political fervor the FMS movement could overshadow contemporary consciousness of child abuse and the status of adult survivors within the community. He cites Herman's (1992) view that, in the absence of a social movement to support its reality, knowledge that is "unpopular or disavowed" may be re-repressed by society. Herman refers to Freud's repudiation of the high frequency of sexual abuse in his female patients as an example of this. Gannon reminds us of the similar historical fate of MPD, whose acceptance as a clinical disorder has waxed and waned.

Therapeutic Abuses of Memory Material

In total fairness, it must be said that there have been serious abuses in the eliciting of traumatic memory experiences and grave abuses by therapists in the management of material they have uncovered. Some therapists have invested too much of themselves in discovering trauma. This type of countertransference bias can lead to premature access to memory material with consequent increase in distortion, as well as to access of traumatic memory experiences even when they have not occurred. Through leading questions overzealous therapists can suggest to their patients events that did not transpire; this is especially easy to do with patients who are suffering from "hysteria." We have heard of a few therapists who go beyond suggestion with their patients, actually pressure them to "face the truth," and/or inform them that their personalities are identical with those of patients who have been abused.

We must never forget that the *Malleus Malifacarum* was actually written and used as a guide for the detection and prosecution of witches and sorcerers (Ellenberger, 1970; Zilboorg & Henry, 1941). Those witch hunts really did happen, and mass hysteria always carries the potential for the injury of innocent people.

Countertransference problems can also lead therapists to foster or even insist upon confrontational stances by patients on the basis of their memories. These confrontations can take place within the family, violently disrupting it, and may end with the patient ceasing to have contact with family members on a permanent basis, bringing criminal charges, and/or instituting civil suits.

We think that confusion on the part of some therapists about what to do with uncovered memory experiences within the therapeutic situation has contributed to these abuses. As we shall subsequently discuss, the resolution of traumatic memories is an internal affair, not an external one; its management belongs within the therapeutic situation and not in a shoot-out situation in a court of law.

Child abuse is genuine and serious, and the fact that it exists has particular relevance for the kinds of patients we describe in this book. However, therapists have an obligation to remain objective in eliciting material, to avoid making suggestions or leading patients into any particular kind of memory material, to remain careful about their language, to keep open minds, and to view each case as a unique research opportunity. As Rossi (1993b) reminds us, if we do not adhere to careful standards to prevent therapeutic abuses of memory material, the therapeutic community could become the repository for the group projection of what is demonic or satanic in our society. Historically there have been trends in the treatment of mental illness that have waxed and waned over the centuries (Ellenberger, 1970; Gannon, 1993; Herman, 1992; Zilboorg & Henry, 1941). Having recovered humane and scientific approaches to dissociative disorders, the therapeutic community must act responsibly about their treatment, lest we assist in the demise of respect for our own profession as well as for the patients we treat.

The Nature of Traumatic Memory Material

Some of the signs that may indicate some objective basis for memory material in actual past experiences are connected to the unique manner in which such material may appear. Usually it is accompanied by strong affect and cognitively structured in accordance with the age at which the trauma occurred (Brown & Fromm, 1986; Goodwin, 1993). Furthermore, traumatic memories are frequently accompanied by somatic phenomena and often remembered and reexperienced in the body itself.

According to Hammond (1993), memory research is frequently in conflict and what happens in the clinical situation may not be susceptible to experimental studies of memory functions. He concludes that the extreme positions of "false memory syndrome" proponents can have a beneficial effect on the field of hypnotherapy by engendering more relevant research and prompting greater carefulness by therapists during memory retrieval. He recommends a balanced middle position for the hypnotherapist on the FMS issue.

Hammond (1993) reminds hypnotherapists that there are probably good reasons for traumatic memory material to be available for recall with a fair degree of accuracy. One is that traumatic memories may be encoded differently from ordinary memories (van der Kolk, 1987a, 1994). Another is that post-traumatic stress disorder (PTSD) is a biphasic condition. Victims of this disorder may be bombarded by intrusive memories and flashbacks during one phase, only to use their dissociative coping skills to separate themselves from these memories in the other phase (van der Kolk, 1987a, 1994).

Van der Kolk's (1994) studies of memories associated with PTSD have led him to a neurological, biochemical, and developmental approach. According to van der Kolk, the limbic system within the brain stores traumatic memories. Within this system, a structure, the amygdyla, assigns and stores the meaning of traumatic events as semantic or procedural memory by allowing the nervous system to encode the emotional quality of the experience, while another structure, the septo-hippocampal system, records the spatial and temporal dimensions of experience; it also categorizes and stores material that is essential for episodic or declarative memory.

Childhood amnesia, as well as the lack of cognitive clarity for early memories, can be attributed to the developmental fact that the amygdyla matures much earlier than the hippocampus (which does not achieve full myelinization until the third or fourth year). The retrieval of traumatic memories that are processed through the amygdyla may contain many errors in details (van der Kolk, 1994).

The evidence for the dissociation or repression of childhood memory is compelling in the light of current clinical studies as well as the experiences of many therapists. Herman and Schatzow (1987) explored the problem from the standpoint of whether memories of sexual abuse retrieved in therapy could be objectively confirmed. In their sample, 74% of female victims were able to obtain objective confirmation many years later that the abuse had occurred, and 9% discovered strongly suggestive evidence for it. Interestingly enough, 11% of the patients in this sample made no attempt whatsoever to seek objective evidence of their abuse memories.

Williams (1992) conducted interviews with 100 adult females 17 years after they had received evaluations and treatment for suspected child sexual abuse. Within their charts could be found medical and forensic documentation suggesting that abuse had occurred. Using a protocol about childhood sexual experience in her interviews, Williams discovered that 38% of these women did not remember their abuse or had made a decision not to report it. Since a number of these women had revealed other highly personal material, it was concluded that amnesia for the abuse had probably occurred.

Like Spence (1982), Ganaway (1989) has distinguished narrative truth and historical truth. Narrative truth in psychotherapy, unlike historical truth, may be a mixture of "fact and fantasy." He cites Kluft's description of various kinds of memory material appearing in therapy: "photographic recall, confabulation, screen phenomena, confusion between dreams or fantasies and real-

ity, irregular recollection, and willful misrepresentation. One awaits a goodness of fit among several forms of data and often must be satisfied to remain
uncertain" (Kluft, 1984b, p. 14).

There will objections to this approach to material uncovered in therapy.
For some it may suggest that we are imitating Freud and denying that abuse
has occurred or that specific kinds of abuse such as mind control and other
kinds of cultic abuse exist. We wish to state emphatically that we do not
utilize the therapeutic relationship to gloss over or deny any kind of abuse.
Like Sachs and Peterson (1993), we regard ourselves as engaging in a process
that helps the patient reclaim her own life and history. We simply do not
think that the therapist should attempt to play God in the matter of assigning
meaning to memories appearing in the course of therapy. This is especially
relevant in view of the complex nature of memory.

The crucial issue for the clinician is to understand that as a therapist she
must accept what her patient is telling her and *must not* assume the role of
arbiter of the nature of reality for her patient. Although this position may
seem difficult, it is a necessary one for the therapeutic situation. The productions of the patient in therapy are gifts of self. The patient has had to overcome many feelings, such as shame, guilt, inner terror, and the fear of rejection by her therapist, to assume the vulnerable position of confiding sensitive
memory material. The patient is not writing a history book; she is, rather,
sharing with the therapist her innermost reality. In accepting this reality, the
therapist accepts the patient in a way she may never have been accepted
previously. Many of our patients were told they were liars, crazy, troublemak-
ers, and disgusting when as children they attempted to reveal certain abuse.
Accepting the patient's reality as the patient's reality is essential to the therapeutic alliance and to the work of therapy. It also means accepting the patient.

Case Example: Theodore

Theodore had entered treatment with me (CF) because of the crippling symptoms of obsessive compulsive disorder. During the early
weeks of treatment he learned self-hypnotic techniques, which he enjoyed using at home. During one self-hypnosis session in his hot tub he
began to get the impression that he had been sexually abused as a child.
Associated with this vague and troublesome impression were visual images of his favorite uncle. I encouraged him to keep an open mind
about all of this material.

Theodore was quite disturbed that his uncle might turn out to have
been his abuser and obsessed about whether he really wanted to know
if this were the case. Again, I reassured him that we didn't really know

what his vague impressions meant and that it was extremely important that we not decide ahead of time what kind of information, if any, might be found. I also made it clear to Theodore that *he* was the person who would decide if we would proceed with an exploration of the vague sense he had reported. Theodore made a decision to proceed because he felt that whatever "it" was had an important role in the production of his symptoms.

Ego-State Therapy techniques were used in Theodore's therapy. An ego state or subpart of Theodore's personality was a child state that held the memories of a painful and terrifying incident in Theodore's childhood. With the help of other personality parts this child ego state was able to recall, and the patient reexperienced in hypnotic age regression, the patient's brutal anal rape by the family handyman. His uncle had appeared on the scene shortly after the rape, but Theodore had been threatened with murder and could not turn to his uncle for assistance.

In this case the therapist's refusal to jump to conclusions and her request that the patient join her in maintaining an open mind allowed aspects of the patient's unconscious mind to bring out memory material in an organic way and to avoid a facile, premature, and erroneous indictment of his uncle. The decision to explore or not to explore did not belong to the therapist; it was the patient's to make.

Diagnosis of the Divided Self

Making the diagnosis of a dissociative disorder is extremely important. Dissociative conditions are often confused with many other disorders, such as bipolar disorder, endogenous depression, and borderline personality disorder. Fortunately, the prognosis for dissociative conditions which receive appropriate treatment is usually quite good when contrasted with that of certain disorders with which they are often confused.

The most critical element in the diagnosis of problems reflecting self-division is an awareness of the *possibility* that dissociation *could be* involved as a causative agent of the presenting complaint. The clinician must be oriented also to contemporary thought concerning the prevalence of traumata in childhood and their sequelae in adult life. The Dissociative Experiences Scale (DES) (Bernstein & Putnam, 1986) and the Dissociative Disorders Interview Schedule (DDIS) (Ross, Heber, Norton, & Anderson, 1989) are valuable clinical tools for helping to make the diagnosis. The diagnosis of dissociative disorders is best done by clinicians who have received intensive training in this area. Membership in the International Society for the Study of Dissociation

(ISSD) and subscription to the journal *Dissociation* are strongly recommended. We also strongly recommend specialized reading about the specifics of diagnosis for multiple personality disorder (Putnam, 1989; Ross, 1989), as well as training in its diagnosis and treatment. This can be obtained through the American Society of Clinical Hypnosis (ASCH), the Society for Clinical and Experimental Hypnosis (SCEH), the ISSD, and many local component societies of ASCH.

CLUES TO THE PRESENCE OF DISSOCIATIVE DISORDERS

Many conversion disorders, fugue states, and other conspicuous amnestic disorders present few or no problems in diagnosis. However, making the diagnosis in less clear-cut situations can be challenging (Abse, 1966). Clues to the presence of dissociative disorders and ego-state problems include amnesia for significant portions of childhood, childhood recollections of trauma or information from family members that such trauma occurred, and a history of marked changes in behavior during childhood. Patients who are highly responsive to hypnosis should always be screened for dissociative symptoms. The presence of symptoms that are ego-dystonic is an important clue. So also is the presence of the "language of parts" within the interview situation. The patient who says, "a part of me wants to do this, and another part wants to do that," is expressing a divided self and may be a candidate for ego-state exploration, as is the patient who says, "I found myself doing thus-and-so, and it just wasn't like me at all."

Sometimes using the language of poetry and metaphor to describe symptoms (Frederick, 1993)—for example, using terms such as "pools of sadness" or "wellings" to describe depressive symptoms—is suggestive of dissociative problems. Intrusive behaviors such as muscular jerking or trembling, tics, spasms, tightness, a loss of motor power, or minimal voice changes should alert the therapist to the possibility of a dissociative disorder.

Within the sensory realm such phenomena as transient pain, parasthesias, itching, "weird" feelings of heaviness or lightness can suggest such problems. Other behaviors that raise an index of suspicion are certain psychophysiologic reactions indicative of post-traumatic stress, such as nausea, headache, diarrhea, or vasomotor changes. Marked changes of affect or affects out of proportion to the individual's current situation are also suspect. Finally, refractoriness or unresponsiveness to treatment should always lead the clinician to suspect an undetected dissociative condition meriting hypnotic exploration.

Healing the Divided Self

We recognize that there are many ways that the "divided self" can be healed. Such healing took place before the advent of formal psychotherapy through the work of shamans, priests, and other nonprofessional healers (Ellenberger, 1970). Within the psychotherapeutic realm many approaches have been utilized, ranging from persuasion (Dubois, 1904) to psychoanalysis and psychoanalytic psychotherapy (Abse, 1966) and cognitive approaches (Jehu, Klassen, & Gazan, 1985). Within the Ericksonian realm emphasis has been placed on indirect hypnosis, metaphor, and internal resources (Dolan, 1991; Gilligan, 1987; Grove & Panzer, 1989). Hypnobehavioral imagery (Kroger & Fezler, 1976) and hypnoanalytic work (Brown & Fromm, 1986; Crasilneck & Hall, 1975) have also been valuable in dealing with these disorders.

We use both traditional and Ericksonian hypnotherapeutic approaches. Once the treatment parameters are established with the patient, the treatment process involves uncovering the traumata that are presumed to have caused the dissociative symptoms and strengthening the personality sufficiently to establish mastery over and integrate the uncovered material. Hypnosis is of unparalleled assistance in this process because it enables the patient to enter the psychological and biochemical state in which state-dependent learning originally occurred and permits activation of individual ego states for therapeutic work. We endeavor to help personality parts tolerate uncovering and abreaction without retraumatization, to master, renegotiate, and integrate the recollected experiences, to become strengthened, and to mature to such an extent that inner harmony can be restored. The balance between ego-strengthening in the present and uncovering of experiences from the past is critical.

We emphasize utilizing the patient's own internal resources and assist the patient in learning to direct those resources into mind/body discovery, correction, reorganization, and integration. In addition, we encourage interaction with the community, so that the patient learns to reach out beyond herself in appropriate ways and to form strengthening ties with others.

2

GETTING STARTED: PREPARING THE PATIENT FOR HYPNOTHERAPY

When two strangers meet to discuss the possibility of their making a difficult journey together into unknown lands, it is important that they make a clear agreement about how the tasks of the journey will be shared, being sure that compass and map are readily at hand. Thus, the initial phase of treatment involves the preparation of both therapist and patient for an agreed-upon experience that will include various uses of formal and informal hypnotic states.

There are three main goals in this initial stage of hypnotherapeutic treatment:

1. *To assess the appropriateness of hypnosis* and other modalities of treatment and determine the types of hypnotic approaches that will be most effective.

2. *To build the therapeutic alliance and the hypnotic relationship.* During this beginning stage of therapy, the therapist works to build rapport and a positive working alliance and explores the various possibilities of hypnotic treatment with the patient. We inform our patients that hypnosis is a valuable tool that can amplify and deepen psychotherapy and will only be used within that context. Direct hypnotic approaches are deferred with patients who are fearful of them; the therapist may elect to use indirect approaches with subsequent re-evaluation of readiness for formal trance experiences.

3. *To create a viable treatment plan.* This may include a contract for

change, agreements about such issues as frequency of appointments
and fees, and clarification of therapist policies about emergencies.

Efforts toward these three goals are made simultaneously. They will be presented in this chapter as separate but interconnected processes.

Assessment

The therapist begins to determine whether formal hypnosis is an appropriate
therapeutic modality for a given individual during the first interviews and
even during preliminary telephone screening. Caution must be exercised with
patients who exhibit active suicidal symptoms, psychotic conditions, impairment with alcohol and other drugs, borderline personality disorder, and other
conditions that present with extreme dependency and emotional liability
(Crasilneck & Hall, 1975; Wester, 1984). Though many such patients can
benefit from the use of direct and indirect hypnosis, the therapist must decide
how hypnosis can best be introduced in these cases.

An important contraindication for using hypnosis exists when the patient
is currently involved in, or plans to be involved in, legal proceedings related
to difficulties for which he seeks therapy. The patient must be informed that
in many states memory material obtained or explored with the use of hypnosis is inadmissible in courts of law. Using hypnosis in such situations may
contaminate even unrelated information, including memories held before the
initiation of therapy or hypnosis, so that the patient's testimony becomes
disallowed. To avoid these damaging consequences, we recommend the use
of an informed consent form, which includes this information as well as other
data related to the therapist's policies, provisions for privacy and confidentiality, fee structure, and other pertinent details related to the conduct of psychotherapy. Written consent indicating understanding of the above should follow extensive discussion of the issues involved as they relate to each individual
patient.

If presenting symptoms are seen to impair the individual's full involvement
in establishing a positive hypnotherapeutic context, the therapist may decide
to postpone formal hypnosis until daily functioning is more stable and a solid
therapeutic alliance has been established. Brenda, a 36-year-old patient who
had a compulsive overeating problem, was referred to me (MP) for hypnotherapy to help control her weight and manage her eating difficulties. In
taking a careful history, I discovered that I was the tenth therapist she had
seen in a period of five years, that she was depressed and had intermittent
suicidal feelings, that she had few memories of her childhood before the age
of 10, and that she used marijuana and alcohol to medicate panic attacks

and other anxiety symptoms, including episodes of depersonalization and derealization. In addition, she reported severe financial problems with her freelance computer business, which was on the verge of folding. I told Brenda that our contract would consist of several parts, with our first efforts focused on helping her stabilize her daily life, with special attention to suicidal feelings and thoughts. This might include evaluation for medication. When she was stable, we would evaluate together whether and when to begin the use of hypnosis for her eating disorder and other symptoms.

Two real dangers are the use of hypnosis by an inadequately trained hypnotherapist and its use for inappropriate purposes (Carich, 1986; Rosen & Bartemeier, 1961). Risks in the first category are posed by hypnotists who do not have adequate training in psychodynamics and therefore do not anticipate or work effectively with the powerful reactions that subjects may have to the hypnotherapist (Kleinhauz & Beran, 1981) or to powerful hypnotic techniques such as regression (Carich, 1986; Hammond, 1990b).

One important inappropriate use of hypnosis is its employment to determine whether or not a particular traumatic event, such as physical or sexual abuse, actually occurred. Hypnosis is *not* a lie detector test or a truth serum. We *do not* accept such referrals and suggest that our readers avoid such unethical situations. Other improper uses of hypnosis include inappropriate suggestions and the creation of excessive dependency. Inappropriate suggestions might include focus on pain relief without proper evaluation of the psychophysiological condition; such an approach risks reliving superficial symptoms without regard for underlying organicity. An example might be suggestions to relieve back pain that result in increased activity and further damage to undiagnosed disc problems. Hypnotherapists who imply that their role is one of "expert" risk making their subjects dependent on hypnotic interventions rather than on mutual, cooperative experience.

ASSESSMENT INTERVIEW

The hypnotherapist will want to interview the patient in terms of presenting symptoms and difficulties, family background, health and medical history, employment and educational situation, current lifestyle and personal interests, and previous experiences and beliefs about therapy and hypnosis. Several other factors (Crasilneck & Hall, 1975; Wester, 1984) may need to be considered and evaluated during the interview process:

- Why is this individual seeking therapy at this time?
- Who referred the patient? How did the patient decide on treatment?

- What are the motivations for this individual to seek help for current symptoms?
- Are current symptoms/difficulties being used to get needs met by others?

Hypnotic Communication Style

During the assessment interview process, the hypnotherapist may want to use a slightly different style of communication oriented to eliciting unconscious responses. For example, in talking with a 37-year-old woman with the post-traumatic symptoms of disorientation and inability to concentrate, which she believed were related to early childhood sexual abuse, I (MP) suggested: "Just go back in your mind to a recent time when you felt unable to concentrate. That's right; just explore that for a moment. What else comes to mind now about that? Does this remind you of similar experiences? What are they?" In another assessment interview, I (CF) suggested to a 15-year-old boy whose severe memory problems had begun at age four, "Just close your eyes for a moment, if that's okay with you, and go back to the time before you were in kindergarten, when memory was no problem, to see if you can recall what things were like for you then." This simple age regression provided a basic assessment of hypnotic responsiveness, while introducing him informally to an ego-strengthening hypnotic experience of "good memory."

These types of inner explorations, which can occur even in the first interview, set the stage for more extensive inner-directed work throughout the course of therapy. For the dissociative patient, this approach introduces the importance of accessing information outside of consciousness in a naturalistic and comfortable way.

If the patient is uncomfortable with this type of approach, quickly moves into a more regressed state with disoriented responses, or loses contact with the therapy situation, the therapist has received important diagnostic information. The therapist may hypothesize that the individual has a lack of internal boundaries for containment, so that hypnotherapy will need to proceed cautiously, and only after careful preparation.

For example, during an assessment interview, Mary, a 23-year-old woman who believed that she had been sexually abused by her grandfather, began to dissociate dramatically while attempting to respond to inner-directed questions about her difficulties. Her breathing intensified, her legs began to shake violently, and she began to lose contact. I (MP) immediately began to describe my observations of Mary's reactions and helped Mary to reorient again to the outside room, the feeling of her body in the chair, and the sound of my voice, which she was able to do with a great deal of effort.

As soon as the patient is reoriented to current time and place, it is important to discuss the implications of temporary loss of here-and-now focus. Usually the individual has experienced this kind of dissociated state in other situations. In Mary's case, she recalled similar reactions while attending seminars or watching TV programs on child abuse, when awaking from nightmares, or when listening to others describe abuse experiences. Noting the intensity of her responses, Mary and I agreed on a therapy plan that emphasized externally focused changes, such as strengthening her coping skills at work and in her communication with significant others, before reassessing her readiness for hypnotic work.

In another instance, I (CF) discovered during the first few interviews that the patient greatly feared hypnosis and wanted nothing to do with it. I responded, "That's fine. I would not want you to do something you objected to that strongly. Who knows, maybe someday we'll find out more about what it is exactly about hypnosis that is so frightening for you."

When individuals are generally uncomfortable with a more "hypnotic" approach to interviewing (e.g., "Why are you asking me these kinds of questions?" "This doesn't make sense"), their reactions must also be explored and the information utilized in treatment planning.

Assessment of Beliefs about Hypnosis

Another important aspect of the assessment process is the examination of the potential hypnotic subject's beliefs and misconceptions about hypnosis. Any previous experiences with formal hypnosis, whether with an individual practitioner, in a group setting, or with autohypnosis training, should be thoroughly explored. Several myths should also be examined at this time, whether or not the individual expresses specific concerns about them. They include the beliefs that hypnosis is the same as sleep (Wester, 1984), that the hypnotherapist has complete control over the subject (Gilligan, 1987), that hypnosis is an unusual and abnormal experience and therefore may be harmful to subjects (Udolf, 1981), that the patient may begin talking spontaneously and divulge information against his will (Wester, 1984), and that the subject will lose all conscious awareness of surroundings and have no memory of the hypnotic experience (Kroger, 1977).

These issues are especially important to explore with dissociative patients, since many of them have intense fears of going to sleep, because of the disturbing nightmares that occur, or about placing themselves in any situation where their conscious decision-making processes and vigilant defenses may be overcome. These patients need to be told directly that hypnosis is quite different from sleep, with more ego involvement and control over the process, and that hypnotic states are more like different forms of communication within the self and with the therapist than like sleep. We further differentiate hypnosis from sleep by pointing out that eye closure is not essential (Mann, 1986). It is important to emphasize that the subject and the hypnotherapist are in a cooperative endeavor and that control of the trance state is in the hands of the subject, who may accept, reject, or modify any suggestions from the therapist.

We also explain that hypnosis is simply a focused use of naturally occurring states of relaxation and inner attention and that the individual always has a choice about whether and when to talk with the therapist during hypnotic sessions. The therapist can point out that it is common for individuals to have some amount of dissociation during formal hypnosis and that some also experience complete or partial amnesia for hypnotic experiences. If a given patient wants to stay consciously aware of the hypnotic process, however, he should be reassured that this need will be addressed and worked with until comfort is achieved.

Spiegel (1986, 1993) has suggested that the experience of involuntariness may be the common denominator among hypnosis, dissociation, and trauma. He and others (Kluft, 1985a; Putnam, 1985) have pointed out that the kinds of traumatic events that mobilize dissociation as a defense seem to be those in which the individual's voluntary will is physically overridden. Thus, the natural involuntary responses of hypnosis may be viewed by dissociative patients as a repetition of a traumatic experience, where involuntariness was imposed upon them. This is why it is so important for the hypnotherapist to emphasize the patient's control during initial experiences with hypnosis.

Cooperative Approach during Interviewing

We endorse a cooperative approach to hypnosis (Gilligan, 1987), rather than an authoritarian one. This means that in addition to *obtaining* information from the patient during the assessment interview, the hypnotherapist must be open to *sharing* important information. For example, the therapist can discuss various aspects of the hypnotherapeutic process, including what the patient can expect from sessions and in between sessions, his own particular beliefs about the value of hypnosis, and the therapist's training background and professional orientation to the field of hypnosis.

This step is particularly important for dissociative patients, who are often reassured by explicit information about the therapist's beliefs about pacing and control of hypnotherapy. What we often tell patients is, "Your responses to hypnosis will help us to create an approach that is safe for you. All we have to do is to pay careful attention to what your conscious and unconscious reactions tell us." We reassure them that they will have input into decisions made at every step of treatment, but also that we fully expect that they will be empowered by the therapy process and experience more effective control over relevant areas of their outside lives. If this is not happening, we explain that the direction of therapy will be adjusted immediately.

EVALUATING HYPNOTIC RESPONSIVENESS

Another important aspect of assessment is the evaluation of the individual's responses to hypnosis. Experimental hypnotherapists have developed a number of assessment instruments, including the Hypnotic Induction Profile developed by Herbert Spiegel (1972), the Stanford Hypnotic Susceptibility Scale (Weitzenhoffer & Hilgard, 1959), and the Barber Suggestibility Scale (Barber & Wilson, 1978/79). Uses of standardized scales of hypnotizability may provide information about an individual's likely responses to certain types of hypnotic tasks. In addition, psychological tests, if indicated, can be useful in diagnosing mania, attention deficit disorder, and other psychological and organic conditions that may accompany, mimic, or appear as part of the dissociative patient's clinical profile. As Cohen (1982) points out, however, there is no study indicating that the use of these tests is superior to the clinician's evaluation obtained through more subjective and informal assessment procedures.

Experts agree that not all subjects are equally hypnotizable, since some respond immediately and significantly to direct hypnotic techniques, while others do not respond, even after extensive specialized training. The important clinical issue here is whether an individual who does not respond well to standardized hypnotic assessment may be responsive to more flexible hypnotic approaches used within the interpersonal context of a developing therapeutic alliance. From an Ericksonian perspective (Erickson, 1952; Gilligan, 1987), each individual is considered to have the capacity to respond experientially within the hypnotic relationship; the task of the hypnotherapist, then, becomes one of identifying and creating a context favorable for hypnotic development.

Clinical Assessment of Hypnotic Responsiveness

Many experienced hypnotherapists develop their own approaches to hypnotic assessment, which feature the flexible use of a variety of hypnotic approaches to determine the types of suggestions most likely to elicit positive responses.

We often schedule several sessions for the introduction of hypnosis and include progressive body relaxation, the use of imagery for creation of safety and further relaxation, and suggestions that include opportunities for visual, kinesthetic, and auditory responses. If the patient has already developed useful, positive approaches to inner focusing through previous experiences in hypnosis or meditation, those are carefully utilized and enhanced in order to develop an atmosphere of mastery and self-control. As part of hypnotic assessment, we may also introduce ideomotor signals (Cheek & LeCron, 1968); these enable the patient to indicate when inner experiences are satisfying and to signal readiness to make the transition from one strategy to the next. Such signals can be used throughout treatment as an effective way of communicating nonverbally with the therapist (Putnam, 1989).

Regardless of the types of hypnotic approaches included in this early assessment phase, it is important that the trance state be formally concluded by the therapist before the session ends and that time be reserved for reorientation and processing of the experience. This is important *whenever* hypnosis is used, but is particularly crucial for dissociative patients, since this structure helps them with the process of boundaries and can prevent "hangover" effects (Braun, 1984), which occur when formal trance states become associated or blurred with the patient's own naturally occurring states of anxiety and disorientation.

CAUTIONS IN USING HYPNOSIS WITH DISSOCIATIVE CONDITIONS

Even with careful preparation, some dissociative patients tend to respond to the introduction of hypnosis by rapidly dissociating more intensively. In this case, we reorient the individual to current time and place, explain that there are many kinds of "trance" states, and observe that he seems to be entering a trance that will not easily permit interaction and communication with the therapist. We then describe the possibility of a more "interactive" trance that involves staying in greater contact with the therapist and having a greater sense of control over inner experiences. Here the hypnotic principle of fractionation (Haberman, 1990) can be utilized to help the patient learn to move into and out of internally focused states at will, responding to suggestions first with eyes open, and then carefully comparing that experience with responses to similar suggestions with eyes closed. Such an approach promotes mastery and deepening of the hypnotic experience, rather than precipitating decompensation and further internal chaos.

Premature Exploration of Traumatic Material

A common mistake made by many inexperienced hypnotherapists, particularly ones with little formal training in the treatment of dissociative spectrum patients, is to begin exploration of traumatic material in hypnosis before adequate assessment and preparation of the patient have been conducted. This is particularly likely to occur with patients who appear "driven" by anxiety and who are already flooded with memory material and flashbacks when they begin therapy.

There is clear consensus among experts that exploratory work, such as attempting to access traumatic memories or contact alter personalities, should *not* be initiated during this initial phase of treatment (Braun, 1980; Herzog, 1984; Horevitz, 1983; Kluft, 1982, 1994; Putnam, 1989). Therapists who fail to heed this proviso may find themselves in the position of unintentionally retraumatizing their patients and jeopardizing the therapeutic alliance.

The Hypnotherapeutic Relationship

From our point of view, the most powerful hypnotic tool in the treatment of *any* individual is the hypnotherapeutic relationship. Because hypnosis is a *cooperative* experience (Gilligan, 1987; Hammond, 1990a) rather than something done *to* an individual, it is crucial to devote time and effort to developing a positive relationship rather than concentrating solely on developing technical expertise with hypnosis. According to Erickson (1952), "hypnosis should primarily be the outcome of a situation in which interpersonal and intrapersonal relationships are developed constructively to serve the purpose of both the hypnotist and subject" (p. 166).

Although building a good hypnotherapeutic relationship is basically no different from building a therapeutic alliance when any other clinical approach is to be used, there are some additional considerations. These include creation of positive expectancies toward the hypnotic process, attention to certain boundary issues between therapist and client, and focus on important transference and countertransference phenomena which can be intensified and complicated by the use of hypnosis.

CREATION OF POSITIVE EXPECTANCY

During the preparatory phase of developing the hypnotherapeutic relationship—in fact, throughout treatment—one of the therapist's major tasks is to help patients create an optimal attitude to maximize therapeutic effectiveness, particularly one of expecting that change is possible (Erickson & Rossi, 1980). A key issue with dissociative patients in developing positive expectancy involves establishing an atmosphere of trust and safety (Braun, 1986; Kluft, 1984a; Putnam, 1989; Ross, 1989). With MPD patients and severely dissociated patients, issues of trust and safety must be worked through with each alter or ego state as it appears in the therapy process.

Trust and Safety

Methods for creating trust and safety within the hypnotherapeutic relationship are numerous and include: communication skills that convey warmth, unconditional positive regard, and empathy for the patient's current experiences and beliefs; information and education about hypnosis that corrects misconceptions and addresses fears; reassurance and permission to both keep one's current level of functioning and also to change when ready; reframing, which helps to utilize attitudes and beliefs in positive ways that can be immediately accepted by the patient; and a permissive style that does not attempt to control or manipulate the patient's responses to hypnosis and minimizes resistance (Levitan & Jevne, 1987).

"Yes" set

Many experts in the field of hypnosis (Erickson & Rossi, 1980; Gilligan, 1987; Hammond, 1990a) have also emphasized the importance of creating an attitude of acceptance, or a "yes-set." As Erickson and Rossi (1980) describe it, a yes-set involves the simple association of a "certain and obviously good notion with the suggestion of a desirable possibility" (p. 32). Gilligan (1987) has discussed pacing and leading as one of the main strategies for creating a cooperative frame or yes-set. This involves making statements that acknowledge and accept both external and internal experiences of the subject (i.e., pacing) and linking them to "desirable possibilities" (i.e., leading). For example, in talking with a dissociative patient during the first assessment interview, I (MP) commented: "I don't know and you don't know just how you will respond to hypnosis when we begin that process; you've told me that you are curious about it, and you seem willing to learn more about it (*pacing statements*), but I wonder just how the part of you that is most concerned about your safety and well-being will help you respond to any suggestions that I might give so that you feel very comfortable and deeply relaxed from the very beginning" (*leading statement*).

The therapist's attitude toward the patient has also been cited as an important variable in developing positive expectancy. Hammond (1990a) has addressed the importance of a confident attitude on the part of the hypnotherapist in inspiring confidence in hypnotized individuals through a permissive yet authorita*tive* style, rather than through an authoritarian, controlling, or overly permissive one. Gilligan (1987) has stressed the value of the therapist's integrity in the hypnotic relationship, which involves setting aside various personal biases and needs and creating a context that fully accepts and utilizes, while not necessarily agreeing with, the client's experience.

BOUNDARY ISSUES

Treatment of dissociative spectrum patients must be based on good general principles of psychotherapy, including carefully defining, protecting, and maintaining the boundaries that form the parameters of the therapy context. Among those parameters are frequency of sessions, length of sessions, fees, therapeutic tasks, roles of patient and therapist, and the therapeutic contract, which will be discussed in a separate section below. Consistent management of these boundaries is particularly important for dissociative patients, who often suffer from blurred intrapersonal and interpersonal boundaries and the chaos this engenders (Beahrs, 1990).

Therapy Sessions

There is no uniform prescription for the frequency and length of therapy sessions that will best address the needs of dissociative patients (Putnam, 1989). We have found that sometimes even severely ritually abused MPD/DID patients respond well to weekly or even biweekly sessions, while certain less severely dissociated patients seem to require two or three sessions per week. Thus, decisions about length and timing of sessions should not be made on the basis of diagnosis but on optimal patient response. Sometimes fees will determine session frequency. As general policy, we see patients often enough so that therapeutic progress is continuous, yet not so frequently (e.g., more than two or three times per week) that therapy becomes enmeshed and chaotic. Putnam (1989) points out that certain aspects of treatment, such as the "development of trust and metabolism of trauma, have intrinsic rates of their own that cannot be significantly increased by more frequent sessions" (pp. 167–168).

Since treatment of this type of patient may take several years to reach positive resolution (Kluft, 1985b; Putnam, 1989; Ross, 1989), sessions should be paced according to need, with more frequent sessions, only if indicated, during times of crisis or intense uncovering and abreactive work.

Generally, we schedule sessions as 50-minute hours. Although there are some circumstances that require longer sessions, for example, patients who drive from long distances or who work more productively during 75-minute or double sessions, others cannot easily tolerate more than the standard therapy hour. Whatever the arrangement, once made, appointment length and frequency should be consistently maintained (Langs, 1988), since unplanned deviations, including running over the time allotted, can evoke boundary confusion, encourage abuse of the therapist's time schedule, and derail the therapy.

Because MPD and dissociative patients tend to overstay time boundaries (Putnam, 1989), we operate by Kluft's (1990b) "rule of thirds," and train our patients to take responsibility for beginning any hypnotic work during the first 10–15 minutes of the session. This allows time for intensive inner work, including trauma retrieval and abreaction, and for reorientation, processing of the material, and closure.

Failure to insist on adequate time (roughly 5–10 minutes) for restabilization after hypnotic experiences can result in post-session dissociation, which can disrupt future therapy experiences (Putnam, 1989). When a patient says near the end of the hour, "Oh, I think a new part wants to talk with you" or expresses the imminent emergence of a new "memory," we say firmly, "Since our time is almost up, I'll be very glad to talk with him or to explore that experience at the next session."

Fees

As with other therapeutic parameters, fees for dissociative patients should be set at the beginning of therapy and consistently maintained. In general, these patients should be treated the same as other patients in the therapist's practice. Unfortunately, with many severely impaired patients, the therapist may be tempted to suspend the regular fee structure and agree to a lower fee. We have supervised numerous cases where therapeutic progress was obstructed because the therapy fee was lower than the therapist was comfortable with.

Only in cases of extreme hardship, and with the therapist's full understanding of future implications, should fees be lowered. Otherwise, holding the patient to standards set for other patients may be part of the therapy work. With Stella, a ritually abused MPD patient on SSI income, for example, I (MP) refused to lower her fee during several initial phone requests. After several months Stella was able to mobilize resources to meet this standard, initiated therapy on this basis, and has since made excellent progress. In other cases, the therapist can give out a list of lower-fee referrals or encourage the prospective patient to pursue other community resources, such as programs for victims of violent crimes.

Therapy Tasks and Roles

As we have discussed above, the tasks of the therapist during the initial preparatory phase of hypnotherapy are to establish rapport, assess abilities to be utilized, facilitate therapeutic frames of reference, and create expectancy (Erickson & Rossi, 1980).

Therapy work with dissociative patients always involves a mixture of present-day focus (support, ego-strengthening, and life management) and past-oriented work (access of memories, abreaction, renegotiation, and integration of trauma material) (Calof, 1991). The therapist must be especially responsible in making sure that the patient can manage the demands and stresses of current everyday life before engaging in hypnotherapy aimed at exploring the depths of the past.

Another important task of the therapist at this stage, then, is to educate the patient about the various uses of hypnosis and the necessary pacing of different activities throughout treatment. For example, we often tell dissociative patients at this stage that if their lives seem unmanageable now, this quality may even intensify during work that is oriented toward reassociating past experiences. Therefore, our role as therapists will be to balance treatment, using hypnosis to help strengthen internal processes to manage the interpersonal field of daily life as well as the intrapersonal field of experiences from early childhood (Calof, 1991).

The Treatment Plan

The creation of a viable treatment plan for a dissociative patient should include:

1. Agreements about the parameters of therapy, including frequency of appointments and length of appointments.
2. Clarification about the therapist's policies for canceled or missed appointments, emergency phone calls and sessions, confidentiality, medication, and hospitalization.
3. A therapy contract with specific goals for change and the maintenance of safety.

CLARIFYING THERAPIST POLICIES

It is quite helpful during the first sessions of therapy to discuss and clarify various policies that help to set the boundaries of therapy. We often tell patients during the first session that we charge for appointments not canceled 24 hours and 48 hours in advance, respectively, for *any* reason – no exceptions. The first author explains that she charges for phone calls in between sessions beyond 5–10 minutes, while the second author holds open telephone hours each morning before 9:00 a.m. We state clear expectations that they will develop and make use of a good outside support system so that emergency phone and office visits are rare. Since we also travel frequently, we make it a point to tell dissociative patients of travel plans for the next four-to-six months and ask them what their plans will be to support themselves in our absences.

Additionally, we spell out the provisions of confidentiality, stating explicitly that we will not give or receive information about them to anyone without a written release. Since some dissociative patients are concerned about medication and hospitalization, we also explain that we rarely hospitalize patients, and will only do so if they are at risk of hurting themselves or someone else, or if we come to a mutual decision that the hospital will provide the best form of treatment during a particular stage of therapy. We also state our belief that medications can be quite helpful with dissociative conditions, particularly if there is a secondary diagnosis indicating this type of intervention, such as severe depression or bipolar disorder, but that the decision to use medication will be made only with careful consideration of patients' concerns and in such a way that every part of them can cooperate.

THERAPY CONTRACTS

As in any therapeutic situation, we do not believe that it is possible to provide good hypnotherapeutic treatment without an adequate treatment contract. After assessing the appropriateness of hypnosis as a treatment modality, obtaining relevant historical and current information in the assessment interview, and securing the therapeutic framework by clarifying ground rules, boundaries, and policies, the therapist can begin the process of constructing a contract that will contain the goals of the treatment process. Often, when complex situations present themselves, it is helpful to outline all relevant treatment possibilities, with and without the use of formal hypnosis, and to identify the possible benefits, risks, and side effects of each (Ross, 1989).

For example, after the first two interviews, I (MP) began constructing a treatment plan with Nick, a dissociative disorder patient with a history of severe sexual and physical abuse, limited financial resources, and active suicidal feelings in response to disturbing flashbacks. Identifying suicidal feelings as a priority, I suggested an evaluation for medication, more effective use of Nick's existing support system, and therapy focused on daily coping and maintenance of safety. Nick was told that he could learn to use self-hypnosis and relaxation techniques to help center himself and contain the flashbacks. He was further informed that recovering traumatic memories related to the flashbacks was a long-term project, that the work would likely uncover painful experiences difficult to come to terms with, and that such a process might affect his functioning at work and in his marriage. Based on this information, Nick agreed to a two-part contract consisting of immediate medical, social, and self-hypnotic interventions for his suicidality. Once we agreed that his condition was stabilized, we would evaluate the possibility of focusing on the underlying traumatic experiences that might be contributing to his symptomatology in the second part of the contract.

When individuals present in a crisis state, have a past history of abuse, or are diagnosed on the dissociative continuum, it is often important to assess the incidence and likelihood of self-harm and other acting-out behaviors. Therapist assessment should include underlying motivation for self-injurious behaviors such as cutting or mutilation. If these dangerous behaviors are suicidal, contracts for their control must be not only very specific and concrete but also agreed to by all parts of the personality: "I will not hurt myself or kill myself or anyone else, external or internal, accidentally or on purpose, at any time" (Braun, 1984, p. 36). If not suicidal, self-injurious behavior may be approached by obtaining further data about motivation and working toward mastery or symptom substitution. Attempting to control or stop self-injury that is not related to suicide may result in ineffective power struggles (Gil, personal communication, 1994).

Contracts can be initiated at any time during the therapy process and put in written form to prevent confusion. Ideally, these agreements should also specify consequences, such as hospitalization or increased frequency in therapy sessions for extreme self-abusive behavior. As Thames (1984) suggests, in addition to providing consistent attention to contract violations, the therapist must also acknowledge and affirm the honoring of contracts.

Language of Cooperation

In making the therapy contract, we adhere to the principle of creating a context of cooperation where "the therapist aligns with client, thereby enabling both parties to become increasingly receptive to each other" (Gilligan, 1987, p. 11). A related concept is that of utilization, which implies that every part of the client's behavior, personality, beliefs, and current situation is potentially a valuable and useful resource in attaining desirable change (Dolan, 1985).

Therefore, we attempt to use the language of cooperation (Phillips, 1993a) when composing the therapy contract. This involves the creation of a mutual "yes-set" (Erickson, Rossi, & Rossi, 1976), in which both therapist and client agree to work together toward desired changes. Thus, the therapist can identify and utilize the patient's own words and frames of reference to facilitate the transformation of seemingly uncooperative reactions into cooperation, "a feeling of being understood, and an attitude of hopeful expectancy of successfully achieving the goals being sought" (Erickson, Rossi, & Rossi, 1976, p. 59). Language patterns useful in creating cooperation and yes-set responses include the use of truisms, implication, therapeutic binds, open-ended suggestions, and suggestions that cover all possibilities (Dolan, 1985; Erickson, Rossi, & Rossi, 1976; Gilligan, 1987).

Goals for Change

We agree with Erickson's conceptualization of therapeutic trance as a means of helping patients learn to use inner potentials to achieve their own therapeutic goals by providing a "special psychological state in which [they] can reassociate and reorganize their inner experience" (Erickson & Rossi, 1980, p. 15).

Some patients, however, need help in formulating goals that are realistically attainable. In certain cases, presenting difficulties are viewed as insurmountable. When this occurs, it is often necessary to change the context or meaning of the presenting problem so that it can be viewed as a possible resource instead of a liability. This model of reframing (Watzlawick, Weakland, & Fisch, 1974) is employed in many different therapy approaches and can often be central to the contracting process in hypnotherapy.

For example, in a goal-setting session with a PTSD patient who complained about intrusive images of self-mutilation, I (MP) pointed out to him that, although I understood his complete distaste for these images and his unwavering desire to eliminate them forever, I could not help but be curious about what these images could teach us about the inner workings of his personality. When he seemed intrigued by what I meant, I further suggested that there must be a part of him that was involved in formulating these images. If he insisted on just finding a way to eliminate them, instead of attempting to locate the "image maker," he might lose an opportunity to learn some ways of cooperating with this part of him to create images that were more to his liking. Since he was interested in discovering ways of generating relaxing, enjoyable imagery, he agreed to change his initial goal to one of self-discovery.

The importance of adequate preparation for hypnotherapy cannot be overemphasized. For most dissociative patients, control is a central issue. The more effective the therapist's efforts at assessing the individual's clinical situation, in establishing a solid hypnotherapeutic relationship, and in creating a practical and comprehensive treatment plan, the more easily the "divided" patient can feel in charge of clear choices in the treatment process. Such an atmosphere of cooperation and teamwork can set the stage for healing the divided self.

3

STAGES OF TREATMENT
AND BEGINNING WORK
WITH HYPNOSIS

Once the therapist has prepared the patient for hypnotherapy by assessing the viability of hypnosis for the individual's situation, begun to establish a positive hypnotherapeutic relationship within clear boundaries, and created an initial treatment plan, therapist and patient are ready to begin using hypnosis.

The Four Stages of Treatment: The SARI Model

We initiate hypnotherapy with the dissociative patient by discussing our four stages of treatment for dissociative issues: *safety* and *stabilization*; *accessing* the trauma and related resources; *resolving* traumatic experiences and *restabilization*; and personality *integration* and the creation of new *identity* (Figure 3). We call this the SARI model. Therapist and patient must understand the necessity of completing the tasks of first establishing safety and stabilization before moving on to the subsequent tasks of working with and resolving traumatic material in the later stages. From our perspective, it is *essential* that the patient be helped to achieve a sense of internal and external safety and to have a reasonably stable daily life before attempting other therapeutic endeavors. Failure to follow this sequence often disrupts the therapy, as the patient is overwhelmed by traumatic material she is ill equipped to handle and frequently unable to recover from a retraumatizing regression.

Experts have proposed many models of treatment for dissociative conditions; however, as Herman (1992) points out, the basic concepts and sequence of recovery have emerged repeatedly, from Janet's classic work on hysteria to more recent work with combat trauma, incest and sexual abuse

36

Figure 3. The SARI Model

Hypnosis: Ego-Strengthening	Hypnosis: Accessing and Mastery of Emerging Traumatic Material	Hypnosis for Reassociation	Hypnosis for Integration and New Identity
			Ericksonian approaches to future identity; Development of new identity: internal maturation; Ego-State Therapy: personality reintegration; Integration of dissociated material
		Renegotiation (SIBAM); Working-through & processing; Connecting sensory, visual, behavioral, motoric, affective, & cognitive aspects of trauma to mainstream awareness	Renegotiation (SIBAM) of any emerging traumatic events; Ongoing processing & working-through of traumatic material
	Reconstruction of trauma material in empowering ways; "Safe remembering" approaches with and without hypnosis	Ongoing reconstruction of trauma for empowerment; Continued "safe remembering"	Continued focus on reconstructed history for empowerment & perspective; Focus on integrating what has been safely remembered & reassociated
Work & family: interpersonal issues; Emotional self-regulation; Somatic & health: post-traumatic symptoms; Therapeutic relationship alliance; Substance abuse & addiction problems; Suicidal, homicidal, & self-destructive issues	Alternate uncovering sessions with ego-strengthening; If patient destabilizes, return to Stage I	Restabilization through ego-strengthening; If patient destabilizes, return to Stage I	Restabilization of entire inner system: ego-strengthening for whole personality; Destabilization likely only from external challenges; refocus on stage I tasks at deeper levels
STAGE I Safety and Stabilization	STAGE II Accessing Trauma Material	STAGE III Resolving Traumatic Experiences	STAGE IV Integration and New Identity

(Courtois, 1991; Gil, 1988), dissociative disorder, and multiple personality (Kluft, 1993b), with a gradual progression from "unpredictable danger to reliable safety, from dissociated trauma to acknowledged memory, and from stigmatized isolation to restored social connection" (p. 155). Of course, no individual course of treatment proceeds in a stepwise linear sequence through these four stages. In fact, it can often be discouraging when issues that appear to have been resolved stubbornly reappear again and again in the process. It may be helpful to consider this process as a spiral, with earlier issues revisited throughout treatment at more advanced levels of integration (Sgroi, 1989). Therapist and patient must anticipate together the likelihood of recycling periodically through stage I issues of safety and stabilization as deeper layers of trauma are triggered by various therapy and life events.

Once all the stages of treatment have been discussed and various hypnotic strategies considered to facilitate completion of relevant tasks, the therapist can begin to determine readiness and initial needs of the patient in introducing hypnosis, conduct training in formal hypnosis, and present initial hypnotic tasks. After this process has taken place successfully, therapist and patient are ready to explore the effective use of various hypnotic approaches focused on ego-strengthening that are appropriate for the safety and stabilization stage of treatment, including positive age regression.

SAFETY AND STABILIZATION: STAGE I

This stage takes precedence over all others. We believe, along with others (Brown & Fromm, 1986; Courtois, 1988; Herman, 1992; Kluft, 1982, 1993b; Putnam, 1989; Ross, 1989), that no other therapeutic work should be attempted until a reasonable degree of safety and stabilization has been established within the therapy situation as well as in the patient's everyday functioning. Beginning strategies of therapy must address the patient's safety needs in a variety of areas, including somatic and health issues, emotional and interpersonal difficulties, the management of post-traumatic symptoms, and issues in the workplace. The use of hypnosis during the first stage is focused on ego-strengthening, mastery, and empowerment, rather than on exploring the origins of post-traumatic symptoms or dissociative responses.

Dissociative patients' functioning is likely to be disrupted in most or all of the areas under consideration. Often they present in acute crisis states and must be evaluated in terms of suicide risk and referred immediately for hospitalization, if appropriate, or for medication to reduce hyperarousal, anxiety, intrusive symptoms, sleep disturbance, and suicidal preoccupation. Some respond favorably to behavioral directives, structured "homework" assignments, and the development of concrete safety contracts to manage self-destructive behavior and improve exercise, eating, leisure, work performance, and interpersonal activities.

Another variable to be addressed at this stage is the misuse of alcohol and other drugs. Substance abuse is frequently diagnosed in multiple personality disorder (Coons, 1980; Putnam, Guroff, Silberman, Barban, & Post, 1986; Ross, 1989) and in cases of post-traumatic stress and dissociative conditions (Courtois, 1988; Goodwin, 1980; McCann & Pearlman, 1990). Courtois (1988) points out that there are two main patterns of substance abuse. First, there are patients who have a family history of alcohol or drug addiction and who were chemically dependent before as well as after the precipitating traumatic events. These individuals often require intensive stabilization in chemical dependency treatment and/or 12-step programs to achieve sobriety before proceeding with later stages of therapy. The second group consists of patients who have used alcohol and drugs to self-medicate dissociative symptoms but who do not demonstrate long-term chronic abuse or family history. This group can generally proceed more directly with the stages of dissociative treatment, although alcohol and drug use should be monitored carefully to determine whether it remains manageable and decreases as treatment continues. If it begins to escalate, more primary treatment and a return to the tasks of safety and stabilization may be required.

Other types of self-destructive behaviors must also be addressed, including self-mutilation, eating disorders, impulsive risk-taking, and continued involvement in exploitive or dangerous relationships (Herman, 1992). Many of these can be understood as reenactments of dissociated abuse or trauma. They must be brought under control during this first stage of therapy through the use of contracts (see Chapter 2), limit-setting, and symptom substitution. With more complex dissociative disorders, this can be a formidable task and often results in power struggles, discouragement, and frustration. It is extremely important that the patient be helped to achieve stabilization of self-destructive behaviors and to assume responsibility for her own body and decisions. Often the therapist's use of cooperative language and the yes-set can be helpful in this regard (see Chapter 2). More is written about this issue in Chapter 13.

As Herman (1992) points out, generally the sequence of safety is to proceed from control of the body and basic self-care toward more general attitudes of self-protection and the creation of a safe environment. Sometimes the use of adjunct services such as couples and family therapy is useful to elicit appropriate family support and to stop current spouse and child abuse and neglect. Occasionally, the therapist must insist on hospitalization to contain suicidality and self-harm behaviors or to control an eating disorder or substance abuse problem.

Although we do not often hospitalize patients, we do believe that under certain circumstances the hospital provides the best setting for achieving or maintaining safety and stabilization. We present the option of hospitalization to our patients as a positive way of ensuring continuous progress in their treatment through more extensive support as needed in times of intense stress. We point out that hospitalization may provide the controls their internal system needs at a given time, even though certain parts of them may not require this type of environment.

Other interventions include reporting children at risk to child protective services, helping to obtain information about restraining orders, or encouraging patients to seek sanctuary in a shelter. Whenever possible, we believe that the therapist should encourage the patient to demonstrate through behavioral contracts that she is capable of ensuring her own safety and preventing harm to those in her care; it is much better, however, to err on the side of safety than to minimize or ignore danger to the patient or those around her.

Hypnotic strategies useful in helping patients achieve these tasks range from formal trance experiences achieved with ideomotor signaling and positive age regression to the more indirect Ericksonian techniques of metaphor, seeding, calibration, and utilization of individual resources. In all cases, the focus during this stage is on ego-strengthening and on promoting feelings of mastery, self-control, and empowerment. The use of these and other techniques, which will be described in greater detail later in this chapter, is illustrated briefly in the following case example.

Case Example: Jennifer

Jennifer had been diagnosed as MPD by a psychiatrist at a local clinic and referred to me (MP) for hypnotherapy after both clinician and patient had determined that their therapy had reached an impasse and was no longer effective. During the first two sessions, she gave a history characterized by early and extreme physical, emotional, and sexual abuse. Her interest in hypnosis was carefully explored; therapist policies and boundary issues were explained and clarified. In discussing a therapy contract, Jennifer noted that she wanted to get to the "root" of her problems. She explained that she had been unable to do this in her work with the referring psychiatrist because inner exploration of various alters, or ego states, resulted in internal chaos, confusion, and the escalation of self-destructive behaviors, including binge-eating and cutting.

I presented the SARI model of treatment to Jennifer and clarified that we would start with stage I. In assessing her needs for safety and stabilization, we determined that she had little control over self-destructive behaviors, particularly cutting, which happened once or twice per week, and that she periodically felt suicidal even though she was taking antidepressant medications. Jennifer complained of intrusive thoughts, visual flashbacks, and body "memories"; she wanted, understandably, to focus on these for immediate relief. She was told that we would certainly address these in our treatment plan but that our first priority had to be helping her achieve a sense of mastery over her inner mind and body experiences during therapy as well as safety in her everyday life. Several sessions were spent on assessing her current health care, on the need to reassess her medications, and on directives designed to stabilize work and interpersonal issues. Specific contracts for safety were made with the alters involved with cutting; this was done by "talking through" to them without the use of formal hypnosis (see Chapter 4) and negotiating a contract that benefited each alter as well as the total personality. Periodically, Jennifer would attempt to steer sessions toward the exploration of a particularly disturbing nightmare or flashback. Each time, she was told that the pacing of that type of work was up to her, that when the contracts to control cutting had been more fully honored, we could begin to explore traumatic material. Within four weeks, cutting had ceased and other self-destructive behavior had diminished. She was then ready to begin training in formal hypnosis and to explore the use of hypnosis for ego-strengthening and further promotion of internal mastery and self-control. Her experiences in this area are described later in this chapter.

In Jennifer's case, the use of communications designed to seed confidence in her ability to establish safety and the utilization of her inner resources of self-control were particularly effective and set the stage for the use of more formal hypnosis. In other cases, the management of self-injury behaviors can be far more complex and may require extensive internal exploration to identify and resolve underlying motivations. (See the "Ego-State Therapy" section later in this chapter.)

For a number of patients, a large part of their therapy will be devoted to stage I concerns. Unfortunately, there are also some patients for whom the outpatient therapist's best efforts at helping to establish safety and stability are unsuccessful. As hard as it may be to make this assessment, it is important for the therapist to determine when a patient is not able to benefit from outpatient treatment. Such a decision may be humbling and frustrating to the therapist and disappointing to the patient, but must be viewed as acknowledgment of limitations inherent in outpatient settings for particular dissociative patients.

ACCESSING THE TRAUMA: STAGE II

Once the tasks of safety and stabilization have been reasonably achieved, therapist and patient may go on to the work of uncovering the trauma and related resources that are currently dissociated from full experience and presumably connected to the presenting dissociative symptoms. Sometimes the patient is consciously aware of the precipitating traumatic experience, such as incest, rape, or combat trauma, and can make use of indirect methods such as "safe remembering" (Dolan, 1991) while describing damaging and terrifying events. In other cases, the traumatic events have been walled off from consciousness by amnestic barriers of state-dependent memory (Rossi, 1993a) and may require deeper and more formal hypnotic exploration. Regardless of approach, we have found that the most effective pacing of reconstructing or uncovering traumatic material occurs when initiated by the patient herself; that is, even when a history of abuse or trauma is clearly indicated or presented by the patient, it is best for the patient to express a desire to find out what a particular current symptom or flashback means. If the work in this stage is therapist-initiated, the stage may be set for the patient to be passive or "resistant" rather than an active partner in therapy or even to relive symbolically the traumatic experience of being coerced into doing something she is not ready or willing to do.

During this stage of treatment, the therapist's role is to help the patient reconstruct enough of the traumatic experience so that it can be renegotiated and reassociated within the whole personality but not so much that the patient is overwhelmed and debilitated by the information. If formal hypnosis is to be used, that should happen *only after* hypnosis has been introduced to the patient in appropriate, ego-strengthening ways, and the patient has successfully completed such initial hypnotic tasks as creating a sense of inner safety and accessing internal resources designed to strengthen her for the journey back to unknown, perhaps deeply disturbing or terrifying events. Details of the hypnotic process of accessing and reconstructing the origins of dissociative conditions are presented in Chapter 6.

Therapist and patient must remember that the patient can easily destabilize during this stage of therapy. Often this can be prevented or minimized by reestablishing safety and stabilization. In this regard, we regularly alternate sessions of traumatic uncovering and reconstruction with sessions devoted to ego-strengthening and reinforcement of coping skills in everyday functioning. More is said about this in Chapter 6.

RESOLVING TRAUMATIC EXPERIENCES: STAGE III

The third stage of therapy involves reassociating the traumatic material so that the somatic, visual, behavioral, affective, and cognitive aspects of a particular experience or sequence of traumatic events can be reconnected with the mainstream of consciousness. Many dissociative patients who have experienced severe trauma and who are fueled by trauma-driven behavior and anxiety (Beahrs, 1990) are desperate to discover the meaning of post-traumatic symptoms. As Herman (1992) points out, many of these patients "insist on plunging into graphic descriptions of their traumatic experiences, in the belief . . . [that] a violent cathartic cure . . . will get rid of the trauma once and for all" (p. 172). The therapist must persistently educate the patient about the very real possibility of retraumatization if too much material is processed at a given time, of the dangers of leaping too soon to unsubstantiated conclusions, and about the benefits of careful, patient tracking of even the smallest units of material, gradually building into a more complete experience which then naturally generates meaning of its own.

Most experts in the field of dissociative disorders concur that reliving of traumatic experiences through abreaction is not sufficient, since this approach by itself offers little more than cathartic discharge and gradual desensitization (Brown & Fromm, 1986; Horowitz, 1973; Peterson, Prout, & Schwarz, 1991; van der Hart & Brown, 1992). Others (Gil, 1991; Terr, 1990) have suggested that unmanaged abreaction can instill feelings of revictimization and helplessness and contribute to characterological problems. Putnam (1989) points out that abreacted material must be carefully processed and worked through to provide lasting results; he notes that the patient must be helped systematically to identify and experience various split-off affects, sensations, and other sensory aspects of the abreacted material. If this is not done, dissociation will persist after the abreaction.

Current thinking seems to be that the primary focus of uncovering traumatic material should be on integration and regulating affects to enhance self-control rather than on emotional release and expression (Horowitz, 1973; Parson, 1984; van der Hart & Brown, 1992). Recent reports of hypnotherapy used with post-traumatic patients have focused on the importance of progressive uncovering, working-through, and integration of traumatic material so that the individual becomes increasingly capable of maintaining control over the recollections and achieves ego integration (Brende & Benedict, 1980; Brown & Fromm, 1986; Silver & Kelly, 1985; Spiegel, 1981, 1988; van der Hart & Brown, 1992).

Levine (1991) suggests that cognitive, behavioral, and even hypnotic approaches to resolution of dissociated trauma do not consider the pivotal role played by the body. In his view, rather than focus on reliving and releasing dissociated affect and ideation, the patient must be helped to *renegotiate* the trauma by identifying the patterning of traumatic responses in the body and perceptual structures and by restructuring these into flexible, integrative somatic resources.

It is also important to acknowledge the necessity of *restabilization* during this time. As a patient begins to reassociate emotional responses of rage, terror, sadness, helplessness, and confusion, to struggle with cognitive reactions of worthlessness, degradation, shame, and denial, and to recover an often bewildering array of somatic responses that have been numbed or "split off," there may be a return to more regressive ways of coping. Suicidal feelings and behaviors may be of concern, and out-of-control functioning in various areas of daily life may return. Here again, therapist and patient must anticipate together these kinds of reactions and return to the safety and stabilization tasks of stage I. The use of hypnotic age progression (see Chapters 5 and 6), which provides "views of the future," is particularly helpful in restabilizing the patient and beginning to develop a future orientation of life after traumatic experiences have been integrated. We present a comprehensive model for the use of hypnosis during this stage of treatment in Chapter 7.

PERSONALITY INTEGRATION AND NEW IDENTITY: STAGE IV

During this stage, the individual is helped to develop a new identity beyond that of surviving a traumatic ordeal or coping with difficult symptoms whose source is unknown. She must be helped to move beyond focus on the past toward the task of creating a hopeful future. As Herman (1992) points out, often the issues of the first stage of treatment are revisited here, as the patient learns to care for her body, immediate environment, and interpersonal relationships—not to secure a defensive position of basic safety but from a generative, empowering, pro-active stance. Often the individual whose decision-making has long been governed by a "divided self" can reclaim aspirations from before the time of the internal divisions or discover ambitions and desires for the first time.

Our hypnotic approach during this stage is based on the model of Ego-State Therapy developed by John and Helen Watkins (1979, 1991) which is described in Chapters 4 and 8. We have found that this model offers the most comprehensive way of helping a divided self to reintegrate. Within this framework, we have added the use of Ericksonian and other indirect approaches to support and expand the development of a "new self" and the possibilities of reeducation and new learning. The use of age progression is particularly helpful in expanding the patient's future orientation begun in stage III.

Beginning with Hypnosis during the Safety and Stability Stage

Once therapist and patient have explored the SARI model described above and have a road map of where they will be traveling together, they are ready to begin exploring specific uses of hypnosis during this journey.

Introducing Hypnosis to the Dissociative Patient

In introducing formal hypnosis to the patient, the therapist should build on the information obtained from "hypnotic" interviewing and discussions of the patient's beliefs about hypnosis outlined in Chapter 2.

From our point of view, it is important to present experiential hypnosis as a "smorgasbord" of possibilities, where the subject will have opportunities to "sample" different types of suggestions and experiences to determine likes and dislikes, what is particularly appealing, and what is less so. With each hypnotic experience, we are involved in observing our patients' overt responses as well as obtaining verbal feedback in order to adjust our approaches, while at the same time assessing individual hypnotic responsiveness (see Chapter 2). With dissociative patients, as well as with all individuals who express significant fears about hypnosis, it is a good idea to identify a "stop" signal, which can be used at any time, such as raising a hand, which can indicate any discomfort or difficulty during the hypnotic experience. When this signal appears, the therapist immediately stops the process, brings the person out of trance comfortably, and then explores the experience. This is done to demonstrate to the patient that she has complete control over her involvement in the hypnotic process, and models respect for the patient's boundaries.

Beginning Training in Formal Hypnosis

Often we present the patient's first experience with formal hypnosis as a training exercise to find out how much is already known about relaxation. Here, regardless of the task, our focus is always on establishing ego-strengthening and mastery. We explain that for five to twenty minutes, depending on the level of initial anxiety, we will be finding out how she naturally goes about relaxing her body. If this is too threatening at first, we have her just focus on her breathing for a minute or two, to see whether she can be comfortable with deep, diaphragmatic breathing (Alman & Lambrou, 1992). The therapist can enhance responsiveness by suggesting a deepening of relaxation and comfort with each exhalation (Jencks, 1984).

Once this is successful, we might introduce the concept of progressive relaxation (Jacobson, 1964), stating that we are interested in how each part of her body likes to relax along with her breathing, and that she might also be curious about this. Some dissociative patients state emphatically that they can't relax at all or express fear that they "won't be able to do it right." This type of performance anxiety can be challenging to deal with; reminders of the naturalistic aspects of relaxation, such as experiences of sitting in the warm sun or watching a movie, where the individual is automatically relaxed without making any effort, often are helpful.

As the patient is encouraged to explore the relaxation abilities of various body parts, including face and neck, arms and shoulders, legs and feet, the therapist might need to provide ongoing validation and reassurance ("That's right"; "very good") and also to keep the focus on areas of the body least likely to have been traumatized. For example, with patients where sexual abuse is known or suspected, genital and related areas (e.g., the abdomen, thighs) are to be avoided. Progressive relaxation suggestions during this phase can be mostly permissive (Yapko, 1990) (for example: "We might want to find out how well your right leg can let go of tension now, and whether you are able to feel some pleasant light feelings there, some loose, limp feelings, or some other positive sensations that are interesting to you") and carefully paced. Pacing can be facilitated by asking the subject to indicate either verbally or nonverbally whether a particular response is "happening in a good way for you right now."

A more "active" (Alman & Lambrou, 1992) form of progressive relaxation can be used with those who have significant amounts of body tension and/or control issues. Here the therapist can suggest that the patient intentionally tense up a particular part of the body and then decide when and how to relax it, noticing the amount of tension that is automatically released when she exhales. Always, the emphasis is on helping the individual have an experience of inner safety and stability.

INITIAL HYPNOTIC TASKS

In addition to the tasks of diaphragmatic breathing and progressive relaxation, there are several other hypnotic tasks to be explored in initial "training" sessions, including:

- Comfortable eye closure
- Developing an internal focus
- Ability to deepen a light trance state in a safe and comfortable way
- Comfortable responses to suggestions of imagery
- Comfortable responses to other sensory suggestions, especially kinesthetic and auditory
- Ability to initiate and stop internal experiences at will
- Reorientation to the outside room at the end of a formal induction

There are numerous excellent references (Alman & Lambrou, 1992; Wester & Smith, 1984; Wright & Wright, 1987; Yapko, 1990) for helping to achieve the above responses, and more detailed suggestions will be given in the *Exploring* section below. It is particularly important for dissociative patients to exercise the ability to start and stop their internal experiences whenever they choose. If this is an issue, the therapist can provide training experiences outside of a formal trance state. This can be done by suggesting, for example, that the patient think of a fruit, like a lemon. Next the individual can be helped to develop the focus by imagining the color, smell, shape, feeling, and taste; when ready, she can allow the lemon to disappear. This procedure can then be repeated with additional "neutral" stimuli, such as flowers, objects, and places.

The prevailing guideline for this period of exploration is *mastery*; that is, it is very important for the subject to experience mastery over each task and self-control over somatic and mental processes. This will prove to be ego-strengthening and will serve the purposes of safety and stability. We frequently tape relaxation sessions so that patients can achieve further mastery between sessions. The clinical example below illustrates this principle.

Case Example: Jennifer (Part II)

Jennifer began formal hypnosis training with several concerns. Although she had achieved positive hypnotic experiences with her previous psychiatrist, she had never felt really comfortable in her body. I (MP) reassured her that it was simply a matter of taking all the time that was needed to find out how she automatically relaxed her body without learning anything new. This was an intriguing concept to her. During the first brief training session, she signaled difficulty with body relaxation: "I can't 'get' that kind of heavy feeling you're talking about," she said. When asked, "What are you experiencing instead?" Jennifer replied that it was as if her body wasn't there at all, that she had floated away from it.

I congratulated her on the kind of hypnotic experience many people would enjoy having and suggested that she experiment with enjoying that "floating, far away" feeling and then finding out whether she could come back into her body for just a few seconds to feel what that would be like. After a pause, she responded that it was interesting, at first difficult, and then easier and easier. I invited her to practice going back and forth between the dissociated state and the experience of reconnecting with her body.

Within several training sessions, she achieved mastery over this process and it was no longer distracting to her. Subsequently, she has been able to experience greater degrees of self-control and to choose to connect for longer and longer periods of time with various body sensations.

Exploring the Use of Appropriate Hypnotic Techniques in Stage I

Once the patient has achieved these kinds of mastery experiences with each of the hypnotic tasks listed above, she is ready to move on to the more advanced hypnotic approaches to be used throughout the hypnotherapeutic process. It is helpful to introduce these techniques early in treatment, when the focus is on ego-strengthening and mastery, in order to build confidence and familiarity. Then later they can be used with more challenging material.

SENSORY AWARENESS AND IMAGERY TRAINING

Many "divided self" patients experience difficulty focusing on their sensory experiences. Often, like Jennifer in the case example above, they are dissociated from their bodies, or they may express fears of being overwhelmed, since most of their sensory experiences seem so negative due to flashbacks, night terrors, somatic "memories," and other post-traumatic symptoms. Such patients may benefit from several sessions devoted to training in sensory awareness (see also "Developing Body Awareness" in Chapter 14) and imagery. This skill is initially useful in developing deeper trust and mastery over less conscious processes; in later stages it allows patients to connect with difficult aspects of their internal experiences for sustained periods of time.

Individuals who have incomplete responses to imagery may find it useful to practice focusing on objects or pictures in the therapist's office, then closing their eyes and attempting to form an internal image. Since this approach uses the principle of fractionation (Hammond, 1992), these steps can be repeated several times for a deepening effect and the beginnings of a formal trance induction. Another helpful exercise is to suggest that the patient simply recall and describe images that are very familiar (Alman & Lambrou, 1992), such as:

- The face of a close friend
- An apple
- A pet
- Home or apartment (practice moving from room to room in the imagination)
- A well-known and enjoyable place, such as the neighborhood park, a favorite hiking trail, pleasant lake, local cafe

As therapist and patient explore responses to these suggestions, more information is obtained about the individual's "style" of visualizing, that is, whether the image resembles more closely a "felt sense," a vivid mental picture, or an inner listening to a description or connected sound. These images can then later be utilized in therapeutic trance inductions.

Kinesthetic experiences can be developed through progressive relaxation suggestions described above, and also by asking individuals to recall comfortable somatic experiences from everyday life, such as taking a bath or shower, stroking the fur of a pet, or feeling a gentle sea breeze. They are encouraged to fully vivify these events somatically as they are being described, and then to explore their internal responses.

Auditory experiences can be similarly trained by asking patients to recall a recent phone conversation they enjoyed, hearing their own and the other talker's voices, and reporting what they recalled. Other familiar auditory occurrences can also be used, such as listening to favorite music, recalling the sounds of a waterfall or the ocean, and exploring the sounds of bird calls. Training such responses might involve listening to an enjoyable recording of music, ocean sounds, or relaxation suggestions. After turning off the recording, the person can practice recalling the sounds internally. This type of approach can also be used with tastes and smells.

Another approach is to introduce structured sensory awareness exercises, such as the "Betty Erickson technique" (Dolan, 1991; S. Gilligan, personal communication, 1980), which requires the subject with eyes open to first become aware of four aspects of her external visual environment, followed by four aspects of external kinesthetic experience, and four qualities of external auditory input. This sequence is then repeated by three aspects of external visual, kinesthetic, and auditory experience, then two, and finally one. At this point, the subject is invited to close her eyes and repeat the process with internal sensory awarenesses, which might include internal visual stimuli (e.g., images, memories, colors, shapes, light patterns, symbols), kinesthetic awarenesses (sensations related to internal organs, pulse, heartbeat, responses in different parts of the body), and auditory input (previous conversations, breathing rhythms, inner sounds) (M. Lehrer, personal communication, 1988).

This exercise can be done in the therapist's office, with the subject reporting verbally the various types of awareness encountered, or as a self-hypnosis exercise using a tape of the session. With practice, the individual can usually experience deeper comfort with internal experience, greater ability to achieve a current time focus, and broader awareness of various types of sensory input.

As the patient develops more confidence and appreciation of sensory abilities using positive, familiar stimuli, the resulting internal experiences can be expanded to develop a sense of internal safety. We usually spend at least one session asking patients to experience themselves in a special, comfortable place where they are able to feel relaxed and good about themselves. Our suggestions usually include the possibility of evoking a place where the patient currently spends time or has had some real-life positive experiences.

An alternative for those who claim they have never felt "safe" or even "comfortable" is to create such a place internally, using the sensory abilities trained earlier to fully vivify the client's conscious or less conscious choice. As Yapko (1990) points out, the therapist must help the subject generate enough detail through the use of suggestion that the "special place" feels real and the individual feels accompanied on the journey, yet not so much as to intrude into what is a highly personal experience. In general, it is better to provide some structure through general, contentless suggestions, such as, "When you have found your special place, let me know. . . . Good. Now look around. What do you see?" etc. Once such a place is accessed and explored, posthypnotic suggestions are given that the patient can return to this place whenever she would like, including any time during a session or between sessions, just by thinking about or imagining this place. It is important to remember that patients have a wide range of responses, including private beaches, walled gardens, meditation rooms, spaceships, and locked towers, and that whatever is reported deserves full validation by the therapist.

As with all stage I activities, the focus is on helping the patient achieve comfort and control, stopping and starting inner experiences at will, and achieving a sense of internal safety and stability. If an individual becomes uncomfortable or frustrated with any task, the therapist needs to be flexible in calibrating (Grinder & Bandler, 1981) or in breaking down the goal into smaller, more easily achieved steps.

IDEOMOTOR/IDEOSENSORY SIGNALING

Ideomotor signaling has its roots in ancient and medieval approaches to healing and divination that resulted in various automatisms, such as automatic writing and somnambulism. It was systematically studied by Chevreul in his use of the pendulum in the 1850s (Erickson & Rossi, 1981). Milton Erickson (1961/1980) used head and hand signaling both experimentally and clinically, and Cheek and LeCron (1968) later investigated ideomotor finger signaling in a variety of clinical situations, including the exploration of psychosomatic symptoms and the uncovering of psychological trauma.

From our point of view, ideomotor signaling is an excellent approach to introduce early in the treatment process because it literally puts the "control" in the hands of the patient. With this technique, developed by Cheek and LeCron (1968) and further refined by Rossi and Cheek (1988), the patient is asked to identify finger responses for "yes," "no," and "I don't know or don't want to say." Although many (Braun, 1984; Putnam, 1989) have advocated that the therapist "put" the signals all on the same hand and identify them for the patient, we believe in a more permissive approach. We simply ask the patient, after a brief induction, to clear her mind and focus on the word *"yes,"* feeling yes in her body as well as thinking and imagining yes in her mind. We then suggest that the unconscious mind transmit an impulse to one of her fingers or thumbs; when she can identify which is the *"yes"* finger, she is asked to allow or even "help" that finger to move in some way so the therapist can also be aware of its identity. The therapist can guide the patient in identifying the nature of responses that may be occurring. For example, the therapist might say, "You don't need to do anything except observe what's happening to one of your fingers. You'll probably notice that one of your fingers is developing a different kind of feeling . . . maybe a tingling, or a warmth, or even a twitch . . . or it may be that one of your fingers just 'seems' different from the rest in some way you can't even explain. And when you're aware of your yes finger, just lift it so that I can know too." This process is then repeated with *"no"* and *"I don't know or don't want to say."*

Ideosensory signaling involves suggesting that the unconscious intensify a particular sensory experience (e.g., vivify an image; brighten a color; intensify a tension, warmth, or coolness; or make a sound or voice louder) as a *"yes"* response, or begin to dissipate the experience as a *"no"* signal. By its very nature, this type of signaling does not readily communicate itself to the therapist and requires the subject's cooperation in sharing the information verbally. Erickson and Rossi (1981) point out that ideosensory responses may be the "first, primitive somatic signals coming from an unconscious level" (p. 125). For the dissociative patient, such responses may provide needed protection from unconscious traumatic material and may present as mystifying signals that do not easily lend themselves to meaningful translation (Phillips & Frederick, 1993). Even if they are not immediately understood by therapist and subject, ideosensory signals can help individuals recognize that important communications are being sent from the unconscious, much like blushing often signals a meaningful response before the subject registers emotion at a conscious level. More will be said about the use of ideosensory signaling in accessing important ego states in Chapter 4 and in resolving dissociated material in Chapter 6.

Ideomotor and ideosensory signaling can be utilized in several ways during the first stage of treatment. First, simply introducing ideomotor or ideosensory experience requires the subject to focus her attention in a way that is trance-inducing (Erickson & Rossi, 1981). Often, no other induction to trance is needed. For those with whom formal hypnotic inductions are used first, ideomotor/ideosensory signaling is an excellent way of further deepening hypnotic trance experience in such a way that the subject feels safe and in control. Third, it can be incorporated into other approaches to hypnotic induction, such as Weitzenhoffer's (1957) "moving hands" technique as well as various forms of indirect suggestion (Erickson & Rossi, 1981). Last, the information accessed through ideomotor signaling can be considered one source of unconscious experience, and can be used to support other sources of unconscious material, such as dreams, automatic writing, and fantasies. Thus, we remind patients that ideomotor signals are no more valid than other hypnotic responses, but do provide a means of understanding other hypnotic and unconscious responses.

When introducing ideomotor and ideosensory signaling during the first stage of treatment, our goal is always to achieve safety and stability. Therefore, we may ask the subject to respond using these signals as ways of accessing an internal "safe place" or to indicate activation of feelings of comfort, relaxation, and confidence. Since this means of unconscious communication is usually interesting and productive, once the patient has achieved mastery with these signals in accessing positive inner experiences, they may be easily used later in treatment to uncover and explore traumatic or other more challenging material.

AFFECT/SOMATIC BRIDGING

This is another hypnotic technique that can be introduced early in therapy as a type of regressive technique to focus on positive experiences, and then used later with more challenging tasks involving dissociated material. Developed by John Watkins (1971), affect bridging is usually used when a patient is experiencing an emotional feeling or physical sensation of unknown origin. At this stage of therapy, however, it should be used only to explore positive feelings.

First, the subject is asked to recall a recent time when she felt a desirable feeling, such as confidence, relaxation, or relative comfort in her body. This can be done in a light trance state with eyes closed or simply in an atmosphere of exploration with eyes open. Second, the individual is invited to review thoroughly the images, sounds, body sensations, and emotional responses associated with the identified positive emotion. In the third step, the individual is asked to intensify this experience even further; this can be done through a simple direct suggestion or more extensively through the deepening of a hypnotic trance state.

Next the person is asked to "bridge" back in time to an earlier time and place when she was experiencing the same or similar positive feelings. This type of structured age regression is focused on identifying related internal experiences that are positive. The subject is asked to explore the earlier experience(s) as in step two above, and then to bring the experiences forward in time into the present moment. If desirable, the therapist can also suggest that the bridge be extended into the future, as in a hypnotic age progression (see Chapter 6).

ERICKSONIAN AND INDIRECT TECHNIQUES

Indirect approaches to the development of safety and stability are often effective with dissociative patients, and are particularly useful when more direct techniques are not productive or are resisted by the patient.

Utilization

One of the cornerstones of this method is the principle of *utilization,* or the acceptance of all the behaviors, symptoms, attitudes, and emotional responses of the patient, no matter how negative or obstructive they may appear, as assets and resources in the therapy process (Erickson, 1959). Erickson pointed out that these indirect approaches to hypnosis were particularly useful with a group of patients who, "because of their physical conditions, states of tension or anxiety, . . . concern or absorption in their own behaviors, . . . are unable to give either actively or passively" their cooperation to permit therapeutic alterations in their behavior (Erickson, 1959, p. 4). Erickson (1965) was clear that the utilization of neurotic, obstructive, and irrational qualities of the individual was just as important as the utilization of strengths, if not more so, since these negative characteristics were viewed as an essential part of the presenting problem and therefore could provide a possible foundation for therapeutic intervention.

Patients who have post-traumatic symptoms and dissociative issues may fall into this category since they are usually significantly impaired on several levels of functioning (Beahrs, 1990). They fear being controlled by the therapist in formal trance states, often have amnesia for traumatic experiences that limits their understanding of present and past fears, and are characterized by internal splitting and fragmentation that make the formation of a therapeutic alliance problematic (Phillips, 1993b). Because the utilization approach does not require this type of patient to abandon an often negative self-image as an "incapacitated victim of abuse and neglect" (Alon, 1985, p. 311), it may be viewed as a significant means of establishing a positive alliance and creating feelings of security and safety (Phillips, 1993b). As Dolan (1985) points out, by accepting and symbolically joining her in her perceptions of herself and the world around her, the therapist enables the client to feel safe enough to make contact.

Case Example: Edith

Edith (Phillips, 1993b) was a young woman in her mid-twenties whose chief complaint was of intrusive visual flashbacks. Other symptoms included increased arousal, insomnia, hypervigilance, and exaggerated startle reactions, particularly when the images were present. Her description of these flashbacks was that they had started during a terrifying LSD experience when she was 15 years old and had been present intermittently since then, especially during times of stress. The nature of the flashbacks was always the same – the image of a man's hollow face staring at her with empty eye sockets.

I (MP) asked Edith to describe previous treatment methods that had been tried and failed with her, since she had said that she had been to several other therapists, psychologists, and psychiatrists. Edith explained that she had been asked to draw, to describe in detail, and to focus in other ways on "the face," and that these efforts only left her more anxious. Other suggestions of "forgetting about" or "blocking out" the image or of viewing it as an unconscious statement about her relationship with her father had also failed. I asked her about her interest and experience with hypnosis and Edith replied that she would give it a try "only as a last resort," but that she felt very frightened about losing even more control over her mind.

My directive to Edith involved finding a way to make "the face" her best friend and truest ally. Rather than ridding herself of this image, she was to discover how "the face" could help her learn some things about herself she could learn no other way. During the next few sessions, Edith's discoveries related to the face were effectively utilized, until its appearance became a distress signal that she was becoming emotionally overloaded and a positive reminder to nurture and "de-stress" herself. By the end of two weeks, Edith reported a 50% reduction in the appearance of the symptom and a dramatic increase in her inner comfort level.

This utilization strategy required no formal hypnosis and allowed Edith to view her symptom as an asset instead of a liability. She became curious about the uses of formal hypnosis to explore inner experiences. Eventually, hypnoanalytic techniques were used to uncover and work through images of a sexual molestation by a neighbor that seemed related to "the face" image. This work resulted in improved sexual responsiveness with her fiancé and cessation of her other anxiety-related symptoms.

Reframing

A related indirect approach is the use of the patient's positive associational cues to change the context and meaning in order to *reframe* (Watzlawick, Weakland, & Fisch, 1974) problem symptoms or complaints. The reframing model developed by Watzlawick and his colleagues, which has become a central part of many different therapy approaches, is used to change the function of a problem in such a way that it can be employed as a positive resource. After the therapist has built a strong rapport with the patient, she then utilizes the undeniable "facts" of the current problem to lead to more functional, less constricting behavior (Dolan, 1985).

Case Example: Sarah

Sarah, a 15-year-old girl, was cutting classes at school, experimenting with drugs, and climbing out her bedroom window at night to be with her boyfriend. Her parents, both serious musicians, were appalled by her behavior. I (MP) explained to the family that I believed that Sarah's behavior might represent rather creative attempts at self-expression and wondered whether they had given any serious thought to her artistic abilities. Sarah immediately responded that she had always wanted to take photography, but that her parents did not view this as "true art." As we explored possibilities further, the parents agreed to enroll Sarah in the photography class of her choice, provided that she would attend other classes regularly.

In individual sessions, Sarah began to explore her own associational cues for self-expression, including imagining herself as a successful fashion design photographer and reviewing the positive memories she had about taking photographs on a trip to France with her parents. She learned that whenever she had the urge to "express herself" in inappropriate ways, it was much more satisfying to focus energy on her chosen art. Late at night, she began to read photography books and to write in her journal about all of her dreams for herself, instead of sneaking out to parties with her friends. School attendance improved along with her grades. After several months, Sarah disclosed that much of her recent acting-out behavior had been triggered by nightmares, insomnia, and startle responses. Because she was terrified of falling asleep at night due to frightening nightmares, she would medicate herself with drugs and alcohol and be too tired to attend school the next day. Within the therapeutic context of trust and mastery established through reframing, we began hypnotic explorations of the origins of these anxiety symptoms, which resulted in the retrieval of a dissociated rape experience during one of Sarah's early drug episodes.

Metaphors

Metaphors are often quite useful with the dissociated patient. One of the main advantages of metaphor and storytelling is that they can be offered to the patient in a nonthreatening manner that facilitates rapport, deepens internal communication, and allows the individual to respond comfortably, privately, and at her own pace (Dolan, 1985). As Hammond (1990a) points out, metaphor can be used to gradually "seed" an idea that may be threatening or challenging, followed by an associational "bridge" that is more directly related to the patient's problem and offers the possibility of resolution, and then reinforced with more direct communications. Key elements in the story can be indirectly accented for the patient through embedded suggestions that are emphasized by shifts in the therapist's voice, speech rhythm, breathing rate, or eye gaze (Dolan, 1985).

For example, in the first stage of therapy, metaphors can be constructed to "seed" the concept of safety, such as developing the image of a tree with deep, strong roots. Although invisible to the naked eye, those roots hold that tree securely no matter how hard the winds shake its branches or storms threaten its balance. An associational bridge might suggest that even though a particular patient does not now feel a sense of safety and security, her creative inner mind can be like the roots of the tree, providing invisible possibilities of security to support her through times when the winds of the past or the storms of the present shake her sense of stability and threaten her feelings of well-being. If the patient responds positively to these metaphorical suggestions, the therapist may then talk more directly about developing ways of feeling safe.

Pacing and Leading

Many other types of Ericksonian suggestions and language patterns can be used to build rapport and establish safety and stability in the therapy situation. The use of verbal and nonverbal *pacing and leading* is one such communication strategy that can be used without formal hypnosis. Here the therapist begins with pacing communications that are based on verifiable aspects of the individual's behavior or expressions (Grinder & Bandler, 1981). As Dolan (1985) suggests, verbal and nonverbal pacing tends to occur naturalistically between two people in deep rapport as a form of "mirroring." Such statements therefore tend to reduce differences between patient and therapist, allowing the patient to feel more trustful and the therapist to be more understanding (Gilligan, 1987).

These communications can be followed by leading statements, which suggest a new possibility that is different from, but consistent with, the patient's current behavioral and belief system. Resistance to leading suggestions is viewed as evidence that the therapist needs to pace some further aspects of the patient's experience. Effective use of this kind of therapeutic language results in creation of a yes-set (see Chapter 2) and sets the stage for more formal ways of accessing and utilizing unconscious resources through hypnosis.

There are many other indirect techniques can be useful here *with the exception of confusion techniques*. Because dissociative patients may already be experiencing internal chaos and confusion, communications that encourage confusion, such as paradox, dissociative binds, non sequiturs, interruption, overloading, and time distortion, are NOT recommended.

EGO-STATE THERAPY

Still another hypnotic approach that can be introduced during this beginning stage of therapy is ego-state work. The focus of ego-state exploration during this time is primarily on identifying, accessing, and working with positive ego states, such as those responsible for, or related to, protection, safety, comfort, relaxation, confidence, inner strength, and other positive functions and qualities.

Sometimes ego-state work can be effective during stage I in helping the patient to manage persistent post-traumatic symptoms and self-destructive behaviors. In one of the MPD cases that I (MP) supervised, the patient had been hospitalized numerous times and cycled in and out of crisis periods, usually accompanied by intense cutting episodes. Various approaches presented in this chapter were attempted with only temporary results. The patient became increasingly hopeless and the therapist increasingly frustrated. Finally, Ego-State Therapy was initiated with the alter named "Dragon," who claimed responsibility for the latest round of acting-out behavior. Instead of making a behavioral contract with Dragon, the therapist was encouraged to strengthen the therapeutic alliance by exploring further Dragon's motivation for destructive behaviors and offering an alternative that would better meet its needs. During several sessions, the therapist established that Dragon lived in total darkness with other malevolent alters separated from the rest of the inner system. After finally acknowledging its loneliness, Dragon was encouraged to explore the outer parameters of its inner dwelling place, and decided to drill a tiny peephole to connect with the light enjoyed by the rest of the personality. Gradually, Dragon found more constructive and satisfying ways of meeting its needs, and the patient experienced greater internal and external stability. This was accomplished without focusing on the traumatic material that Dragon was attempting to share with the rest of the system, an approach that might have further destabilized the patient's functioning, and without the power struggles which had resulted from contract attempts with other destructive ego states.

Ego-state work should generally not be attempted until initial hypnotic tasks have been completed successfully and the patient has achieved a good working therapy alliance and trust in her own internal process. More will be said about the mechanics of this process in Chapter 4.

Age Regression

Although the techniques and uses of age regression are fully presented in Chapter 5, several points are important to make about the use of regression in the first stage of therapy.

First, age regression during the first stage of treatment should only be used for ego-strengthening. Because this technique can involve an intense utilization of memory processes, there is a risk that the dissociative patient can "leak" into disturbing material unless the use of regression is carefully structured; even then, this can sometimes occur. If the patient cannot experience positive age regression, as described below, this procedure should be postponed until the individual demonstrates more ego strength and has had more experiences of mastery during the other types of hypnotic experiences described in this chapter.

THE IMPORTANCE OF POSITIVE REGRESSION

Positive age regression is achieved by suggesting that the patient go back in time to review her own past personal experience in order to discover abilities and resources that have been forgotten or are not currently in use. As Yapko (1990) points out, often the individual has abilities and resources that she doesn't realize she has because she does not have conscious awareness of and access to them. For example, if a patient is complaining of feeling frustrated because therapy is moving so slowly, the therapist can take the patient back in time to a variety of previous experiences where she was frustrated in learning something, and show how each frustration eventually led to mastery of the situation and feelings of confidence. A review of past experiences can also be conducted to help her recall times of feeling relaxed and comfortable, courageous and risk-taking, or strong and confident.

Typically, we ask patients during this stage of therapy which personal qualities they would like to have "at their fingertips" before making more challenging journeys into the unknown or traumatic past. When these qualities are identified based on individual patients' needs, we then construct age regressions to evoke those resources from personal histories. This technique is discussed further in Chapter 5.

PACING AND TIMING ISSUES

If an individual expresses fear about exploring her past even in a positive way, more indirect techniques can be used to help the patient approach the concept of a positive past experience. For example, the therapist can interview the patient about experiences during the previous week and help her determine which ones were positive. Often the experiences of dissociative patients are so contaminated by fear that they view all experiences as negative and need to "borrow" the therapist's neutral observational abilities until they develop ones of their own. The therapist can explore recent times with friends, leisure activities such as hikes or movies, and even quiet times at home in order to identify positive resources. This method can then be used to work backward through the recent past until the patient seems ready to respond to more formal regression approaches. Metaphor and storytelling can be used to explore past positive experiences at an even more indirect level.

Dealing with Spontaneous Regression and Abreaction

Spontaneous regression refers to unplanned access of some unpleasant or disturbing past experience. This often happens with more dissociated individuals without the use of formal hypnotic techniques. With intense spontaneous regressive experience, the patient can temporarily lose contact with the immediate surroundings along with the ability to communicate verbally. This may be because she has entered a state of *revivification* (Kroger, 1977), full regression where she is actually reliving an early, perhaps even preverbal, experience.

Because the goal of stage I is to achieve mastery and internal stability through ego-strengthening, our policy is not to explore and develop spontaneous regressions during this time. Instead, we generally communicate in the following way:

> Wherever you are right now and whatever you are experiencing, it's important to know that there is an adult part of you who can hear my voice and respond to what I'm saying. I would like that part of you to give me some kind of signal that it is present. . . . Good. Now your unconscious mind has given you a powerful experience and we certainly want to explore it in a way and at a time that will be fully useful to you. Since our goal today is to access positive experiences, I'm going to ask your unconscious mind to use its creative resources to create a safe place or container that can store all of this experience until a time that we both decide we're ready to open it up. I'd like the adult part of you to make sure this is happening and, when the process is complete, let me know by moving a finger (or nodding your head).

Once the signal is received, or if no signal is given in response to our communications, we begin reorienting the individual to the outside world by focusing attention on naturally occurring experiences, such as the feeling of her body against the chair, her feet on the floor, the sounds around her, and the furniture in the room. This helps to center or "ground" the individual. Once she is in an alert waking state, we process the experience in detail. Until safety and stability are reestablished, it may be important to calibrate hypnotic experiences by having her approach positive regression through more natural-istic, "eyes open" ways without the use of formal trance. This way of acknowl-edging without encouraging spontaneous regression seems to help patients develop a sense of mastery over their own internal process, rather than being vulnerable to its whims, and a sense of internal boundary formation, which is especially valuable for extremely fragmented individuals.

As part of a spontaneous regression, the patient may experience intense *abreaction*. Although traditional meanings of abreaction focus on intense emo-tional relivings, we use this term to indicate the reassociation and release of affective, somatic, cognitive, visual, and sensory aspects of a past experience. This may be manifest in a variety of ways, including "crying, hyperventilation, trembling of the body (or specific body parts), hysterical conversions, prema-ture disengagement from trance, hallucinations, delusions, and autistic-like rocking motions" (Yapko, 1990, p. 423). Ways of orchestrating a truly thera-peutic abreaction, renegotiation, and resolution of a post-traumatic experi-ence will be thoroughly reviewed in Chapter 6.

4

WORKING WITH THE DIVIDED SELF: THE USE OF EGO-STATE THERAPY

Therapeutic Assumptions

All theories are created in order to help us sort our data in a meaningful way. There is an unfortunate tendency to reify the constructs theoreticians utilize in their attempts to explain how things work. No one, for example, has ever seen an "id" or a "superego," because they are simply constructs. In this chapter we introduce the ego-state model as a theoretical metaphor for understanding human behavior. This energy model would be incomprehensible without the use of certain terms such as "child part," "malevolent states," or "internal self-helper." We use them with the hope that our readers will not falsely assume that we have reified these energized aspects of human personality function.

Ego-State Therapy is a "parts" model of personality. The parts discussed in this and subsequent chapters about Ego-State Therapy differs from those that are found in other "parts" models such as Transactional Analysis and gestalt therapy. The ego states we discuss are aspects of human personality that are totally unique within each person and cannot be arbitrarily divided up into, or limited to, preconceived categories such as Parent, Adult, or Child. They do not fall into archetypal categories any more than they do into those of Transactional Analysis. Moreover, they have persistent and consistent histories, cognitions, and affects and do not usually vanish after therapy sessions. For these reasons, we feel they manifest what is going on within the individual more than what is going on within the therapist's expectations.

61

What Is an Ego State?

Inconsistency in behavior is not limited to patients with dissociative disorders. Most human beings display a range of behaviors that frequently appear to be at variance with one another. For example, a quiet, conservative accountant might be scarcely recognizable as the bedecked Saturday night cowboy who shouts and sings as he vigorously performs the two-step. What is consistent about this inconsistent behavior is that it tends to appear in the same way within the same set of circumstances. Were the accountant to appear at work in his cowboy finery, displaying his Saturday night behavior, he would be considered inconsistent in a way that far exceeded the norm.

Janet (1907, 1926) recognized that there was some kind of compartmentalization in the normal human personality as well as in his patients with dissociative disorders, and Jung (1969) offered the theory of the complex in an attempt to explain how a patterned collection of thoughts and feelings, somehow bound together, could activate the personality and produce certain behaviors and feeling states. It was Freud's psychoanalytic colleague, Paul Federn (1952), however, who proposed an energy model involving ego states within the ego.

Ego-State Therapy as an Energy Model of Personality

During most of his psychoanalytic career, Freud (1933) theorized that there was a single psychic energy, which he called *libido*. He believed this life energy to be sexual in nature. Although Federn considered himself a Freudian, his way of viewing intrapsychic energy was quite different from Freud's. According to Federn, the ego is composed of ego states formed in early childhood. Each ego state has its own origin, history, thoughts, and feelings. Ego states are separated from one another by something that can be thought of as a more or less semipermeable membrane.

Federn's model is an energy model. The ego state carrying *ego cathexis* (libidinal energy attached to the ego or self) is experienced by the individual as the "I" or self. From the vantage point of this ego state the other ego states are viewed as objects or "its." They are said to be carrying object cathexis. The arrangement and balance of the ego states and the self and object cathexes are in a state of dynamic flux (Federn, 1952). In the case of the retiring accountant, the accountant ego state would have ego cathexis while he was at work. The Saturday night cowboy ego state would be viewed objectively as "not-me." On Saturday nights, the ego cathexis would shift to the cowboy, and the accountant ego state would acquire the object cathexis. The cowboy might even proclaim to his companions, "This is the real me!" as though the ego state that carried on most of the week were insignificant.

Eric Berne (1961) credited Federn when he incorporated a limited view of ego-state interaction into Transactional Analysis. Only three states were considered to exist, Child, Adult, and Parent, and all clinical data were dealt with as though they belonged to one of these states. Federn, on the other hand, thought that there were many ego states. When different ego states were present, the boundaries of the ego were perceived and experienced as different. Federn placed considerable emphasis on "ego feeling." Federn's contribution replaced Freud's structural ego with something infinitely more complex, vital, and up to date. His concept of a dynamic ego consisting of many states offered a fertile field for a new therapeutic method.

Following Federn, John and Helen Watkins (1979–1993) presented a comprehensive theoretical basis for a form of therapy that involves working with ego states directly. Their theory is an extension and an elaboration of Federn's concept of ego states and offers many clarifications about the nature of ego states and their relationships with one another. According to the Watkins, ego states can be formed in three ways. One way is as an adaptive response to the ordinary requirements of the culture. Different kinds of ego states would be necessary for survival in an agrarian society as opposed to a hunter/gatherer society, for life as a U.S. citizen in rural America in 1777 versus a San Franciscan in 1994. A child develops different ego states for play activities in constrast with those generated for dealing with school work or sitting quietly in church. Another way ego states are formed is through introjection of parental or other significant transferential figures or of important early life events. Finally, ego states may be formed adaptively to deal with overwhelming trauma. The Watkins hypothesize that an individual in the presence of unendurable trauma has an extremely limited repertoire of available responses. One is to become *psychotic*. Another is to commit *suicide*. The third available response is to *dissociate*. The dissociative formation of ego states is a creative human response to trauma (Watkins & Watkins, 1991).

Within the human personality the ego states form a family of selves. Whichever ego state is carrying the most energy at the time is said to be "executive" and is experienced by the individual as "I" or the self.

Ego states are energies within the greater personality. They are not real people who are simply smaller or younger than the greater personality but rather aspects or energies of the individual. Ego states are adaptational. They always come to help.

Ego-State Pathology

Ego states can be thought of as existing on a spectrum from the least to the most differentiated (Figure 4). People with little ego-state distinction appear to be much the same in all situations and may lack color or complexity in their personalities. Another normal situation is one in which the personality

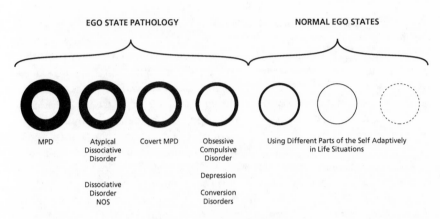

Figure 4. Ego State Spectrum

is rich with an integrated complexity of ego states that are in communication with one another and which act cooperatively. In the middle of the spectrum are ego-state problems associated with many clinical syndromes, such as depression, post-traumatic stress disorder, obsessive compulsive disorder, eating disorders, and panic attacks. When differentiation is at the other extreme of the spectrum, and ego-state boundaries are inordinately thick so that the ego states do not communicate with one another at all, multiple personality disorder is said to exist. Multiple personality disorder (dissociative identity disorder), which differs from other kinds of ego-state problems in degree, is characterized by the spontaneous emergence of walled-off ego states or alters, and the presence of some degree of amnesia. The severely separated ego states that characterize multiple personality disorder are called *alters,* although the general term ego state can also be used for them. Were the Saturday night cowboy to appear spontaneously at the accountant's workplace without the accountant's having anything to say about it, ego-state pathology would be at work and he would be suspected of having a dissociative disorder, probably MPD (DID).

Ego-state pathology occurs when one or more parts are not in harmony with the others, act on their own, and produce symptoms. Such ego states can be thought of as being walled off from the others, having thicker membranes, or simply not being in cooperative communication with other ego states. The thicker walls are viewed as protective and are frequently associated with trauma. Had these ego states not been so separated from the others, they would have been able to have experiences with them that would have contributed to their maturation and healing. Perhaps one of the therapist's biggest challenges is to recognize ego states when they present themselves in less obvious, even cryptic ways through the manifestation of strange symptoms, sensory messages, or unidentifiable visual symbols. This will be discussed in more detail later.

Ego-State Therapy

Ego-State Therapy is an interesting combination of individual, group, and family therapy techniques. Sometimes ego-state work follows an individual psychotherapy model; sometimes, a group therapy model. It can even be thought of as family therapy within an individual. *Any psychotherapeutic or hypnotherapeutic technique that can be used with an individual can be used with an ego state.* Thus, an ego state can undergo ego-strengthening, hypnotic age regression and abreaction, renegotiating of the past, hypnotic age progression, desensitization, etc., and it can participate in internal group or family therapy as well. Ego states can also be susceptible to developmentally based maturational techniques. In Ego-State Therapy the realization that all ego states are adaptive, in some way or another, is crucial. It is from this perspective that all therapy proceeds. The ego-state therapist works with a system of fluctuating energies. The goal is integration of the parts or subselves, not fusion or elimination. As Ego-State Therapy proceeds, the parts may develop more co-consciousness, that is, the sharing of mental content and feelings with one another. This advancement is one of many harbingers of integration. Integration occurs when the parts are in communication with one another and are working together harmoniously and co-operatively. Sometimes individual therapeutic work has to be done with a symptomatic part before any cooperation with other parts is possible. The ego-state therapist comes to view each ego state, as well as the internal family system, as his patient. Consequently, one of the fundamental goals of Ego-State Therapy is the development of the therapeutic alliance with each ego state. Each ego state is considered to be as important as every other ego state. The therapist who fails to make alliances, to respect each part or ego state (even the most hostile and malevolent) as valuable, and to keep in mind the adaptive nature of the states will probably find this form of hypnotherapy problematic and somewhat ineffective.

THERAPEUTIC ALLIANCES WITH EGO STATES

Forming therapeutic alliances with ego states is an essential maneuver for the beginning ego state therapist, as well as for the most advanced. The therapeutic alliance has long been held to be essential to individual psychodynamic psychotherapy. Although ego states are not real people, they are sensitive, feeling, and judging aspects of the personality, and like individual patients they need respect and empathy if they are to be cooperative in therapeutic work. Ego-state therapists find them capable of forming therapeutic alliances. The therapeutic alliance was defined by the psychoanalyst Richard Sterba (1934) as occurring when the patient was able to identify with some of the analyst's goals for treatment.

Although at times the therapeutic alliance may seem to develop almost automatically, at other times its development may have to be the main focus of treatment. Respect for the ego state is an unvarying ingredient in this process. This respect includes asking ego states for permission to explore certain sensitive areas or to engage in certain procedures such as hypnotic age regression or formal ego-strengthening. The Watkins (1991) recommend taking a case history with the ego state as one might with an individual patient. The therapist finds out how old it is, what it came to help with, and what the ego state perceives its internal function to be. He also discovers what the ego state would like to be called and what it needs for itself. In the process of becoming acquainted with the ego states the therapist resonates with their feelings in order to form the therapeutic alliance. The therapist does not take sides or favor any of these personality parts over others. Genuine interest in and honest empathy for each part are vital. Constant reminders to the part that the therapist knows it is trying to help the greater personality, the patient, just as the therapist is, are invaluable. The development of the therapeutic alliance is often helped by the language of cooperation and the use of yes-sets (see Chapter 5 for more about the therapeutic alliance).

Accessing Ego States

Ego states tend to be present even when they carry object cathexes. That means that the "executive" ego state may think of the other states as "its," but these states continue to think of themselves as "I's" and of the "executive" ego state as an object. For example, the accountant's "work" ego state would experience itself as the "I" of the personality and would view the Saturday night cowboy as an object that could be described as a past memory. Meanwhile the dormant, decathected Saturday night cowboy ego state, while not possessing as much energy as the accountant ego state, would retain enough energy to observe him and even to make plans for the upcoming Saturday night. To this ego state, the accountant would be an "it" or object who should be put on the shelf on Saturday nights. It is well to assume that, although there are exceptions, any time the therapist speaks with a specific ego state, all the other states are listening. There are many ways to activate ego states; every therapeutic method will decrease the isolation of ego states from the internal family of selves.

"TALKING THROUGH" TO THE EGO STATE

Talking through means speaking to ego states even though they may not appear to have been activated. The patient may be in formal trance, but this is not necessary. On the surface, the therapist is speaking with the presenting patient; however, the therapist is also talking *through* that person to ego states that are presumed to be present. This work can be done directly or indirectly and usually includes both approaches.

Indirect Talking Through

Indirect "talking through" is an excellent way to begin an ego-state approach. Patients need preparation for ego-state work, and it can be assumed that the parts are listening to every bit of it. An educational or informational discussion provides an opportunity for the therapist to commence work on the therapeutic alliance with any and all ego states. Below is a sample script of how to introduce the topic of Ego-State Therapy.

> You know, Jake, every human personality is composed of many parts. I mean that yours is, mine is, and so is Dr. Brown's [the referring therapist]. And the *wonderful thing* about these parts is that every one of them just wants to help us. That's what they're all about. Now some of these parts came *to help us* with very difficult things when we were children, and sometimes the way they helped us then might not be too *useful now*. It's even possible that some of the problems you're experiencing now have something to do with a part that is still trying to *help you* but needs some *help* itself to find a way for it to help you that is *better for your life now.* . . . And sometimes the parts just need some *help learning* to *understand* one another, and *learning to improve* their communication with one another, so that they *can work together* better. . . . But however we may work with these parts of you, Jake, we have to remember that every single one of them is very *important*.

Jake may object that he'd like to get rid of the part causing his symptom. This is not an uncommon response, and the ego states are waiting to hear what the therapist has to say about it. The therapist can respond somewhat like this:

> I can understand how you might feel that way, but that isn't what we need to do at all. Try to remember that the part is trying to *help you*. We need to *get to know* that part or those parts if more than one is involved, to *get to know the part* and to *understand it* . . . perhaps to *find out more about what was going on with you* when the part produced the symptom that bothers you now . . . and when we *know the part better* . . . and when the part is able to *work with us*, then it is very possible that we'll all be able to *find a new and better way* for the part to *help you*.

This simple educational exchange is filled with both direct and indirect suggestions. The italicized positive words and phrases are embedded sugges-

tions in and of themselves. There is a clear message to the ego states that the
therapist wants to guide the patient in the direction of cooperating with the
states rather than struggling against them.

Storytelling, metaphor, and other indirect suggestions can also be used to
talk through to the patient's ego states:

> I once had a patient who was very angry that he couldn't control every bit of his
> behavior. Can you imagine that? He really didn't understand how wonderfully
> complex he was . . . or that there were aspects of him that were really focused
> on his problem, but in a different way, their own way. One day he came to me
> and said that his little nephew had an imaginary playmate named George, and
> that George had told him he could see right through walls and that he could
> know what was going on in the next room. Well, my patient became very
> interested in George because his nephew seemed so relaxed when he talked
> about him. One day he told him that George had promised never to leave him.
> My patient began to wish that he might have a "George" to guide him, even
> though that seemed quite childish. I wondered if *he* didn't *already* have someone
> like that inside, you know, . . . since we retain so much of the magic of our
> childhood and so many of its wonderful helpful aspects.

Direct Talking Through

Direct talking through is a useful technique when preparing for more direct
hypnotic work. It can also play an important role with ego states that are
resisting the therapeutic process. This approach may or may not be accompanied by ideomotor signals, depending upon the clinical framework.

> I know that there is a part of Tom, some aspect of his personality, that really
> understands why he isn't succeeding with his examinations. And I also know
> that part is really trying to help him and I find that extremely interesting. I
> would certainly like to understand more about you, Part. Who knows? . . . We
> might be able to help him more if we worked together.

With this kind of "talking through" the therapist is activating the listening,
thinking, feeling, and at times behavioral aspects of the subself, and maintaining focus on that cooperative venture, the therapeutic alliance. With certain
severely dissociated patients such as multiples, the part or ego state may find
this approach so reassuring that it begins to respond with direct speech. More
frequently, less dramatic responses occur. The patient may become aware
of the part mentally, see images, exhibit sensorimotor phenomena such as
temperature or other sensation changes, jerks or twitches. At times the patient may neither report nor exhibit additional information in response to this
approach, and the therapist must be content with it as a seeding maneuver.

"Calling Out" the Ego State

Calling the ego state out may be done outside of formal hypnosis or as a direct formal hypnoanalytic technique.

"Calling Out" when Formal Trance Has Not Been Induced

Calling out the alter (the name for an ego state in MPD) is often done in clinical sessions with MPD patients without the assistance of formal trance induction (Braun, 1986; Putnam, 1989; Ross, 1989). Indeed, it can be a judicious maneuver with such patients, in that it provides the clinician with valuable information about the severity of the dissociation, the accessibility of the ego state, the ease with which it comes out, and its level of anxiety about the treatment situation. If the ego state responds to this approach, formal hypnosis can be postponed until it is specifically needed. After the patient has made it clear, directly or indirectly, that another personality state is present, the therapist asks the patient permission to make contact with it.

> Would it be all right with you if I attempted to get in touch with the part of you that goes off to the bars at night? . . . It would? Thank you. Then I would like to ask that part of Jane to come forward now and speak with me directly.

If the part comes out, the therapist can work with it; if not, nothing has been lost, and other methods of activating the ego state can be employed.

"Calling Out" in Formal Trance

Formal trance can be utilized for direct access to ego states in subjects who are hypnotizable in this way. The use of ideomotor signals provides safety for the patient and therapist. Before making any attempt to access the state verbally, the therapist can ascertain through ideomotor signals if a particular state is present and whether it would be willing to communicate verbally. If the ideomotor signal is "No," the therapist should not try to "force" the state to come out. Instead, he can begin to inquire about what some of the state's fears are, what other things need to be done first, etc.:

> I would like to ask that part of Mary that knows something about why she is taking objects out of stores without paying for them to come forth now and speak to me right through Mary's lips. You can let me know when you're here by just saying, "I'm here," or in some other way that feels comfortable to you.

Imagery Methods of Activation

Calling out methods are often preferred by therapists with patients who seem to be auditory in the way they access information, while visualization techniques may be more helpful with patients who tend to be visual. Only the imagination of the therapist limits the ways this can be set up. These techniques can be used with either formal or informal trance situations. This staircase technique is a modification of one often used by Helen Watkins (J. G. Watkins, 1992):

> Just imagine you are going to walk up or down a staircase as I count. The staircase can be entirely of your design, or, if you prefer, you can use something else, like an elevator or an escalator. . . . (The therapist then counts from 10 to 1 to help deepen the trance.) Now you can open a door and find yourself in a corridor with many rooms. Perhaps you would like to open one of the doors and meet a part of you that knows something about the panic feelings you have been experiencing.

IDEOMOTOR/IDEOSENSORY ACCESS

With more kinesthetically oriented patients ego states may be able to converse initially with the therapist through the use of finger and other ideomotor signals; the parts may also communicate with shifting sensory phenomena. Frightened ego states may prefer this manner of communicating initially as they try to get more of a sense of who the therapist is and what he wants of them. Eventually, imagery concerning the ego state may enter the mental content of the patient, the patient may have different kinds of somato-sensory experiences, or the ego state may begin to speak directly (Phillips & Frederick, 1993; Phillips, 1993a).

> I wonder if that part of Sally, the one that has been signaling to me by causing Sally's fingers to move, would consider letting me know in some other way how it is helping Sally.

Or:

> I notice that every time we mention Jake's grandfather, he feels a warm flush in his face. Is this a sign from a part of Jake's personality that knows something about *all* that?

ACTIVATING NONVERBAL, PREVERBAL, AND SYMBOLIC EGO STATES

Silence in an individual patient can represent resistance to treatment (Greenson, 1967), a communication, or a reenactment of some event from the past in which silence had been a prominent feature (Greenson, 1961; Khan, 1963; Rosenfeld, 1966). In psychoanalytically oriented psychotherapy all silences, even the "blank mind," are assumed to have meaning (Ferenczi, 1950; Freud, 1913). With victims of trauma and abuse, silence may take on yet another meaning, since the abuser may have told the victim that there would be dire consequences if he ever revealed what happened (Lister, 1982; Peterson, Prout, & Schwarz, 1991).

Certain silences are not resistances; rather, they are essential parts of the therapeutic process in which the patient and the therapist experience a loosening of ego boundaries, thus permitting a "therapeutic symbiosis" to exist (Searles, 1965). During such silences psychological intimacy can be developed and the patient can borrow the therapist ego strength until he can incorporate it.

Within the realm of hypnotherapy the meaning of silence may be more difficult to interpret, as the patient may be less verbal in general. It becomes extremely important for the hypnoanalyst to observe nonverbal cues (Brown & Fromm, 1986). Only through constant observation of these cues can the hypnoanalyst become *attuned* (Brown & Fromm, 1986) to the patient. When empathy is added to these observations, *resonance* with the patient exists (J. G. Watkins, 1978). Through the use of minimal cues the hypnotherapist may be able to help the patient utilize his inner resources (Gilligan, 1987). As the therapist moves to a larger perspective, he accepts the patient's reality and utilizes it as well (Erickson, 1959; Erickson & Rossi, 1979; Gilligan, 1987). Hypnosis can be nurturing (J. G. Watkins, 1987), offer containment, (Baker, 1983b), and facilitate therapeutically valuable *narcissistic* or *fusional* alliances. Within the hypnotherapeutic relationship the patient may be able to utilize the hypnotherapist as a transitional object (Baker, 1994) .

Some silent ego states communicate symbolically (Phillips & Frederick, 1993) and somatically (Phillips & Frederick, 1993; Phillips, in press). Symbols, as well as perceptions and activities related to the neural and muscular systems, are reported by many victims of post-traumatic stress disorder. They may present as flashbacks, which can occur as full memories, fragments which are difficult to understand, intrusive thoughts with or without affect, and overwhelming affect (Frederick, 1990, 1993a; Phillips & Frederick, 1993; Phillips, in press). Other verbal ego states may or may not be activated at the time. The therapist may begin to identify these silent, symbolic, and somatic ego states in several ways:

- Through information given by other, verbal, ego states (e.g., "I sense another part of me, but I can't describe it")

- Through persistent body sensations, movements, or other physiological reactions such as blushing, sweating, chills, or shaking

- Through visual experiences during periods of inner focusing in the form of symbols (e.g., statues, sun, moon) and abstract patterns (colors, lines, dots)

- Through nocturnal dreams and hypnotic dreams
- Through repeated patterns of behavior that do not respond to therapeutic intervention.
- Through ideomotor signals to certain questions: "Is there an unconscious part of Joe that does not want this information to be revealed?"
- Through physiologic and symbolic flashbacks related to traumatic experiences that may come in the form of fragmented tastes, sounds, smells, sights, and sensations

There are several reasons why some critically important ego states may not present directly in accessible form (Frederick, 1994d), such as an inner voice or the image of a person in response to therapeutic exploration:

- The ego states may fear the consequences of therapist intervention, such as retraumatization by the therapist, having to face painful memories behind amnestic barriers, reexperiencing traumatic material that is contained in the individual ego state, or retaliation by the abuser for disregarding threats of programming.
- The ego state may be preverbal and incapable of more than primitive, indirect expression.
- The ego state may be personality energy that is encoded in "somatic memory material."
- The ego state may fear betrayal by the therapist, such as absorption, abandonment, or destruction through fusion or other elimination, because the therapist doesn't approve of it, favors other states, or is repulsed by or frightened of the ego state.

Working with Nonverbal and Preverbal Ego States

With these silent and symbolic states the therapist must proceed with the inner conviction that *all* aspects of the personality are equally important. This orientation leads the therapist naturally, openly, and repeatedly to emphasize this message to every energy within the patient. The therapist reaches out for therapeutic alliances with these states, capitalizing on the ambivalence that has permitted some communication, no matter how little, to occur. It is vital that the therapist express interest, a wish to get to know and understand the state. Often the therapist will employ the yes-set to help the state understand that they share common goals for the patient and that the ego state can become an important co-therapist in the patient's treatment.

To the extent that it is possible, the therapist seeks to obtain and enlarge upon an *interactive* relationship with each ego state. This may be based on ideomotor or ideosensory feedback as well as feedback through visual imagery, affect, or free association. For instance, with a patient experiencing facial flushing and tingling in the right side of the body that impedes her attention and responsiveness, we might suggest:

> If these sensations are connected with a part of the personality that is important for us to know about or is related to some of the problems Annette has just been talking about, then Annette's unconscious mind can verify this by intensifying the flush and the tingling, just slightly for a yes signal, and if these sensations are not connected with such a personality part, the sensations can begin to dissipate for a no signal.

After this kind of communication has been established, it can be utilized to develop the alliance and encourage verbalization and other more complex forms of communication. Whenever possible, the therapist activates and/or utilizes the patient's own internal resources for coping with and mastering these roadblocks. The therapist may ask for help from other personality aspects, use somatic experiencing, access healing states to renegotiate memory experiences, and encourage mastery within certain recollected experiences. He should never hesitate to educate the ego state by providing direct information about the kinds of lies abusers often tell little children who lack the information and experience to distinguish them from the truth.

The therapist may encourage other external nonverbal communications such as drawing, automatic writing, keeping a journal, kinesthetic movement, or soft sculpture. This will be discussed further in the section below on externalization techniques. Consistent work with elusive symbolic or mysterious ego states provides crucial information about the patient's deepest struggles and advances maturation and integration. Symbols representing ego states are not traumatizing, as flashbacks often are (Parson, 1984). Unlike flashbacks, they do not appear to stimulate disturbing or fearful affect in patients, and in most cases they do not seem directly related to traumatic material. In addition, they can usually be verified through ideomotor finger signals related to particular parts of the personality or ego states germane to the patient's symptomatology. It is valuable to foster the involvement of the patient in understanding and communicating with the wisdom and helpfulness of these states, as well as with their frightening aspects.

We hypothesize that mysterious presentation of the patient's ego states may provide additional protection from premature disclosure of frightening traumatic material, though more data are needed to substantiate this notion. Patient, systematic attempts to link these symbolic expressions with significant parts of the personality can often unlock the mysteries of the patient's most puzzling and profound symptomatology.

EXTERNALIZATION TECHNIQUES

Some ego states are best accessed through kinesthetically expressive techniques that are projective and evocative in nature. The therapist may ask patients to express their ego states concretely in drawings or paintings, sketches, or soft sculpture. Sensory hypnoanalysis (Kline, 1968), hypnography (Meares, 1957), and sensory hypnoplasty (Raginsky, 1967) are techniques based on work with the externalized symbolic productions as manifested in hypnotic art productions. Another example is Helen Watkins' use of "Doodle Therapy" (J. G. Watkins, 1992). At times patients may achieve problem resolution on an unconscious level through the therapeutic manipulation and rearrangement of symbolic material (Watkins, 1992); this can occur at significant points in therapy. Ego states can make themselves known in a variety of ways: art productions, automatic writing, writing with the non-dominant hand, messages placed within a journal the patient keeps, sand tray work (Sachs & Braun, 1986), play therapy with children, and hypnoplay therapy with adults (Shapiro, 1988).

Externalization techniques derived from Gestalt therapy are the two-chair technique (Beahrs, 1982) and Helen Watkins' chair technique (J. G. Watkins, 1992). The utilization of any of these methods of expression is usually a function of the interest of the therapist and the communication style of the patient. They can and do yield important information about and contact with ego states and are often extremely therapeutic.

The Tasks of Ego-State Therapy Using the SARI Model

MORE ABOUT BUILDING ALLIANCES WITH EMERGING EGO STATES

The ego-state model provides a way of working with dissociated material that permits the patient to do truly therapeutic work with the least disruption to his life and ability to function. For many patients who begin treatment in a state of chaos and uproar, consistent work with ego states is important in moving through stage I of the SARI model, safety and stabilization.

Initial attempts at forming the therapeutic alliance may appear to be directed to the presenting executive ego state; however, it would be naive to view Ego-State Therapy as dealing only with one ego state at a time. The therapist's goal is to form a therapeutic alliance with the entire patient. This means that the essential wholeness of the personality is never forgotten and that it is always assumed that many, if not all, of the other ego states or personality energies are listening to what is being said. Kluft (1993a) wisely reminds therapists that the therapeutic alliance must be distinguished from transference and refers his readers to Greenson (1967) on the topic.

Just allowing ego states to form positive transferences toward the therapist is not enough to stabilize the internal system, let alone permit any therapeutic work. A certain amount of cognitive work needs to be done so that available ego states can understand *what their responsibilities are in the therapeutic process.* The therapeutic or working alliance is a partnership that occurs only when the individual comes to understand and identify with some of the important therapeutic goals held by the therapist (Sterba, 1934). For example, I (CF) explained to an ego state who wanted to bask in my benevolent therapeutic aura that we both had work to do for the greater personality. Indeed, it was a plus that we were comfortable with one another at this time, but even that could change as the work progressed and difficult tasks had to be met. The ego state wondered why we had to face difficult tasks, and I explained that the greater personality was in a great deal of pain, and that it was up to us and other members of the internal family to work as hard as we could to improve the situation within. I reminded the ego state that he would eventually have to get to know and understand another ego state that now he would have nothing to do with. Eventually, the ego state agreed that what I was proposing as "our work" was necessary, and the beginning of a therapeutic alliance was formed.

As they emerge, ego states may have many transferential attitudes toward the therapist (Watkins, 1992). These transferences should be dealt with initially as possibly helping or hindering each state's understanding of the primary importance of the therapeutic work. This helps secure the therapeutic situation by placing it in a special category of non-transferential endeavor that promises understanding, mastery, and freedom. Constant and repeated attention to why the therapist and the ego state are communicating and the nature of the therapeutic purpose also provides a "seeding of hope" (Dolan, 1991). This can be used to emphasize and strengthen the cooperation principle (Gilligan, 1987) and is ego-strengthening in and of itself. The ego state that is simply needy, in pain, and struggling is different from one which is needy, in pain, struggling, and working on solving its and the system's problems. The ego-strengthening that comes out of the formation of true therapeutic alliances is *stabilizing* and opens the door for further ego-strengthening maneuvers; these further stabilize and strengthen the entire energy system and make the therapeutic situation a *safe* one for the patient.

Promoting Cooperation and Internal Harmony

Sometimes we help our patients think about the kind of family they always wanted to have so that they can create it within. We ask them to specify the qualities they would like to develop internally, such as good listening skills, politeness, and fairness. Like members of a dysfunctional family, the personality aspects of our patients are often isolated and alienated from one another. They may engage in control and power struggles, wars, plots, secrets, and the reliving of old traumata. Maintaining such disharmony or disunity requires tremendous energy. Patients who experience it may literally feel as if they are going crazy or are being torn to pieces. Their ability to work and otherwise function in society may be seriously compromised. Formerly, many dissociative patients were hospitalized as schizophrenics because of the disruption of these post-traumatic internecine struggles (Kluft, 1983; Ross, 1989).

In working with ego states, tension exists between, on one hand, valuing and respecting the components of the human personality, being aware of their needs, capacities, and abilities to help the work, and, on the other, valuing the overriding importance of the entire system with its need for internal cooperation and harmony. The ultimate goal of Ego-State Therapy is integration; however, preparation for integration begins with the beginning of treatment. The initial treatment contract must have something to say about bringing together disharmonious aspects of the personality, and the therapeutic or working alliance with ego states must always contain the reinstitution of harmony within the family of parts as the fundamental goal of therapy. As new ego states emerge, they have to be educated about the need for this. This does not mean that words like integration, fusion, and personality unification should be used in any routine way in the early stages of treatment. Such terms can be extremely frightening to ego states, who may view the treatment goal as being structured upon their demise. It is crucial that the therapist himself not lose track of the fact that ego states are not real people; they are personality energies, and as such they cannot exist on their own; there is only one person sitting in the chair.

The therapist frequently reminds ego states of their existence within an internal family that shares a single body. They can never escape this family; they need one another. At times delusional ego states think they exist outside the body, and often narcissistic ego states believe that only they are worthy of consideration or attention or that they can take over the body exclusively. *Safety and stabilization in the patient's clinical situation are always advanced by improvements in internal relationships.* The therapist may find it valuable to think of promoting internal cooperation through a series of steps:

1. Help ego states become aware of the presence of other ego states.

2. Encourage communication between states. If it is already present, encourage its amplification.

3. Help ego states develop empathy for one another. This is often sadly missing within the internal family and is an important part of maturation as well as a significant prelude to cooperation.

4. Suggest to ego states how they might learn from one another, work together, help one another, or comfort one another.

5. Remember, never favor or take sides with one ego state; each one is important, each one has come to help, and each one can learn to participate in the recovery process.

6. Acknowledge co-consciousness and appropriate co-presence as positive signs of increased harmony.

7. Present integration as what it is: a situation in which ego states have regained much of the energy that was bound up in the suppression of dissociated material, have learned to share consciousness and to cooperate with one another, and have acquired enough growth and maturity to redirect their now ample energy toward placing the needs of the internal family system before their own.

ACCESSING TRAUMA EXPERIENCES WITH INDIVIDUAL EGO STATES

We always begin with stage I work. However, some ego states may achieve safety and stability and begin to access their memories, while others may require continued work to become safe and stable. The stages of treatment exist for every individual ego state, just as they do for the greater personality. It is possible to conduct stage III work with several ego states, while simultaneously doing intensive stage I work with another. No attempts to enter stage II of the SARI model, reconstructing and uncovering the trauma, should be attempted with any ego state until the goals of stage I have been accomplished, until therapeutic alliances are in place, and until whatever cooperation between ego states deemed necessary for the uncovering work has been established. How the reconstruction proceeds is developed collaboratively with the patient and the ego states. Together they decide what may need exploration, what ego state needs to be understood better at any given time, and what symptoms should be explored.

Uncovering and abreaction should only be done with ego states with whom communication and working alliances have been formed. The therapist should engage the ego state with the utmost respect, e.g., "Would it be all right with you if we learned today more about what was going on in Sally's life at the time you came to help her?" or "Is this as far as you would like to go today?" When the material is particularly difficult for the ego state to handle, other ego states can be brought in to assist and/or ego-strengthening procedures can be used. Emerging memories should never be allowed to overwhelm the ego state; consequently, these personality energies may have to be taught at times how to leave a situation that is becoming overwhelming. Communication between the patient and the ego state during the uncovering process is essential for proper management and pacing. Often ego states speak and communicate ideomotorically simultaneously at this stage.

Abreactive work (which will be dealt with more extensively in Chapter 6) may need to be followed by a return to stage I, safety and stabilization. The pain and fear engendered within the internal family by the remembering or reexperiencing of the trauma may call for strengthening of the therapeutic alliance, resolution of transference issues (Loewenstein, 1993), and ego-strengthening before more uncovering can occur or before the patient can move to stage III, reassociation, renegotiation, and restabilization. The patient may enter stage III slowly, as the ego states take yet another look at the experience or series of events and identify the somatic, visual, behavioral, affective, and cognitive components. All of these elements are brought into the mainstream of consciousness by sharing them with other ego states. A significant amount of time must be spent with the patient, as well as with the internal family of selves, processing reconstructed or abreacted material, reconnecting it with other recalled material, current symptoms and feelings, and allowing the patient and the ego states to master it by investing it with meaning and perspective.

Other Clinical Issues with Ego Stages

Many trauma victims lack certain natural abilities to protect themselves (Herman, 1992; Schetky, 1990; van der Kolk, 1989) because of cognitive and emotional developmental arrests. A great deal of recently published ego-state work focuses on the utilization of the therapeutic alliance and other ego-strengthening techniques, as well as the employment of cooperation among ego states, to facilitate maturation of ego states. More mature ego states are better able to deal with dissociated material and to move in the direction of integration. This topic is discussed in Chapter 8.

Some ego states are malevolent or destructive; work with them always involves the primary considerations of safety, stability, and protection. This topic will be discussed in Chapter 13.

Integration of the personality from the standpoint of Ego-State Therapy is a situation in which there is communication, empathy, harmony, and cooperation among the ego states. We will discuss personality integration and the formation of a new personal identity in Chapter 8. Essential to the integration of the personality—and to all therapeutic work with ego states as well—is ego-strengthening, which will be discussed in Chapter 5.

"Silent Partners": Work with Nonverbal Ego States

Many therapists will dispute the axiom that silence is golden. Silence may be a resistance (Greenson, 1967), a communication (Greenson, 1961, 1967;

Khan, 1963), or a reenactment (Greenson, 1961, 1967; Khan, 1963). It may give messages of acceptance, love, understanding, warmth, and contempt, indifference, coldness, and fear.

With victims of certain kinds of trauma and abuse, silence may have another meaning. The perpetrator may have threatened the victim with dire consequences if he revealed what happened. Even as an adult in therapy he may be afraid to disclose vital information and may be a silent patient (Lister, 1982; Peterson, Prout, & Schwarz, 1991).

During comfortable silences the patient can borrow the therapist's ego strength until he can incorporate it. During prolonged silences affective communication may be quite intense, and the therapist may be susceptible to countertransference reactions. Eventually, new and healthier individual identities may be experienced by both the therapist and the patient in the context of the therapy work (Searles, 1965; Whitaker & Malone, 1981).

In hypnotherapy silence may take on a different perspective (Brown & Fromm, 1986). The hypnotic situation is nurturing (Watkins, 1987), and in trance the patient may find containment by the therapist (Baker, 1983b). Narcissistic or fusional alliances of therapeutic value can be facilitated by hypnosis (Diamond, 1983, 1984); in addition, the patient may be able to utilize the hypnotherapist as a transitional object (Baker, 1994).

Case Example: Sylvia

Sylvia was 37 years old and twice divorced. She entered therapy for help with depression and alcohol abuse. She also wished to resolve lifelong patterns of involvement with men who were married and/or extremely powerful and domineering. Her counselors at an alcohol rehabilitation program had suggested that Sylvia may have been molested as a child. Initially, therapeutic efforts were focused upon helping Sylvia work through her many resistances to maintaining full involvement with Alcoholics Anonymous and to relinquish her fantasy that she was not alcoholic. As Sylvia's drinking came under control, she began to have many vivid dreams. In quite a few of them she was in a shower.

One evening while Sylvia was entertaining a boyfriend, she entered a state of panic, cried, clung to him, and expressed tremendous fear about what would ultimately be recalled in her therapy. Although sober at the time, she later had no memory of this episode. In the subsequent session an attempt was made to communicate with an ego state through ideomotor signals. The ego state indicated that she was present and that she was willing to communicate with me. I (CF) focused on the fear the state experienced when she thought of facing traumatic material from the past. I made it clear to this part of Sylvia that I would never try to force her to remember anything and that I would do everything I could to help her become stronger. I also told her that as she became stronger, I believed she would be able to tolerate an emergence of memories, possibly a little at a time. I also told her that the remembering could be an important step in her not having to be afraid so much of the time. I suggested that her being less frightened could lead to greater cooperation with other parts of Sylvia and that this in turn could help her get her needs met more effectively. She could take it at her own pace.

The ego state decided to allow Sylvia to have some information about the frightening material. Sylvia then experienced an age regression in which she was a little girl in a shower. She complained of a slimy substance that covered her. It was totally disgusting, and she could not seem to get it off her. She hugged herself and said she just wanted to curl up in a ball. When the ego state was asked if she could give more information, she signaled "Yes," and the patient saw a photograph of the entire family. The ego state was unwilling to amplify on this. She did allow her name to float into the patient's mind: "In . . . in . . . iniquity." She had clearly become my silent partner and cotherapist in Sylvia's treatment. With subsequent developments in therapy, she became verbal and changed her name to "Hope."

There are always reasons for the silence. Nonverbal ego states that are quite capable of speech or other direct forms of communication may be silent because they fear the consequences of verbal interaction, such as transference fears of punishment or betrayal by the therapist. This was the case with "Iniquity."

A productive hypnotherapeutic relationship with silent ego states may advance therapeutic situations that have reached impasse. The relationship must begin with the realization that the silent ego states are ambivalent. Any minimal communication can be regarded as the state's reaching out in some hopeful way for recognition and understanding. The hypnotherapeutic relationship with silent ego states can be achieved *when the therapist has respectful but tenacious dedication to communicating with the ego state*. The therapist can capitalize on the ego state's ambivalence and reach out for communication through the use of ideomotor signals. The therapist's utilization of his own internal resources to produce *resonance* (Watkins, 1978) or *attunement* (Brown & Fromm, 1986) is thought to be necessary for the initiation of communication. As with the silent patient, particular attention must be paid to minimal cues from the silent ego state.

The establishment of the therapeutic alliance then becomes the primary goal of the hypnotherapeutic relationship. Once any kind of communication between the ego state and the hypnotherapist has begun, the therapist's sensitivity to the style and needs of the ego state can be utilized to assist it in identifying with some of the therapist's goals for treatment. The use of the cooperation principle (Gilligan, 1987) and yes-sets and the seeding of hope (Dolan, 1991) are extremely helpful at this stage.

It is important for the therapist to seek an interactive relationship with the silent ego state. This can be based initially on ideomotor or ideosensory feedback. Communication through drawing, automatic writing, doodles, etc., may also be encouraged. The therapist encourages the ego state to enter into full verbal communication; however, it is only through an interactive relationship that the alliance can be initiated and maintained.

Transference issues must be addressed. This may be difficult initially in the face of complete silence. However, the therapist can begin to do this by stressing the importance of every ego state and asking questions about some of the more common transference problems, e.g., "Are you frightened that I may want to hurt you in some way?"

The mobilization of internal resources through the use of direct and indirect ego-strengthening techniques is particularly valuable in working with these states. Projective/evocative ego-strengthening techniques such as hypnotic age progressions (Phillips & Frederick, 1992) and accessing inner strength (Frederick & McNeal, 1993; McNeal & Frederick, 1993), as well as the activation of helpful ego states and other maturational techniques utilizing inner resources (Frederick, 1992, 1993a), can contribute greatly to the strengthening of the therapeutic alliance and the progress of therapy.

5

MOBILIZING INNER RESOURCES
DURING STAGES I AND II

Because patients with dissociative disorders have been traumatized, they show the secondary effects of trauma (Fine, 1993; Fish-Murray, Koby, & van der Kolk, 1987; Herman, 1992; Terr, 1991). Often they have not developed adequate psychological defenses, and they may be crippled by "learned helplessness" (Dolan, 1991; Herman, 1992; Seligman, 1975). With such poor defensive mechanisms, they may be incapable of protecting themselves from revictimization (Schetky, 1990), and the compulsion to repeat the trauma may further drive them in that direction. They also suffer from active symptoms that threaten to overcome them, while childlike parts of their personalities live in states of fear. Experiences of calmness, clarity, and mastery need to occur early in treatment. The patient, somehow, needs to find strength and motivate herself to take up the difficult task of solving her problems.

Ego-Strengthening and Stabilization

The patient can be thought of as having an ego that in some sense needs strengthening, both initially, in the first stages of treatment, and from time to time during the course of therapy thereafter. Strengthening is required for most patients to make and stand by a serious commitment to therapy, to hold onto hope, and to experience the reassociation of the trauma and abuse that will emerge from behind amnestic barriers. When ego-strengthening occurs, there may be enhanced self-esteem, greater capacity for self-soothing, increased clarity of thinking, better exercise of problem-solving abilities, and even the presence of increased insight. Ego-strengthening occurs with the establishment of the therapeutic alliance, which in itself begins to activate the strength the patient needs to do the therapeutic work as a partner with the therapist.

In a formal sense, ego-strengthening has been considered a valuable thera-peutic modality since Hartland (1965, 1971) recognized that most patients in therapy are "unwilling to give up their symptoms until they feel strong enough to do without them." Both Stanton (1979) and Calnan (1977) were able to demonstrate that ego-strengthening increased internal control.

Many theoretical frameworks embrace ego-strengthening. While cognitive behavioral explanations (Hammond, 1990b) are the most common, ego-strengthening can be explained in terms of Freudian theory as well. From a psychodynamic standpoint, resolution of early life conflicts extends the sphere and control of the ego, which is geared to mastery and survival. Hartmann (1961, 1965) postulated conflict-free spheres of the ego that em-brace adaptive functions. In terms of self psychology (Baker & Baker, 1987), ego-strengthening aids in the development and internalization of inner struc-tures.

From the standpoint of ego-state theory, ego-strengthening procedures increase the interplay between positive, healthful aspects of personality and extend their influence over more childlike, less constructive states (McNeal & Frederick, 1993). Additional ego-strengthening comes from the maturation of ego states and the activation of helpful ego states (Frederick & Kim, 1993).

Milton Erickson (Erickson & Rossi, 1976) said that the unconscious mind contained all the resources a given individual needed to resolve her problems. His utilization principle was based on the therapist's being able to help the patient activate her own natural inner resources. Erickson's followers have elaborated on his ideas for activating unconscious strengths that can later be integrated into conscious ego functioning.

There are three general approaches to strengthening the self or ego, which may be used in combination with the individual patient as well as with separate ego states: (1) direct suggestions facilitated by heterohypnosis and/or self-hypnosis, (2) projective/evocative ego-strengthening, and (3) Erick-sonian approaches.

Direct Suggestion and Self-Hypnosis

Direct suggestion as a method of ego-strengthening was introduced by Hart-land (1965, 1971), who conducted hypnotic ego-strengthening sessions with patients who were on a waiting list for hypnoanalytic work. Although he made his direct suggestions when patients were in deep trance, he thought it was possible to use lighter trance states as well. Hartland's suggestions were authoritarian, directive, and future-oriented. They were intended to strengthen such ego functions as concentration and memory, self-confidence, and energy. When many patients who had received an ego-strengthening session claimed they no longer needed treatment, he wisely recommended that hypnoanalytic techniques be preceded by ego-strengthening suggestions.

Although direct suggestion may have become unfashionable and today Hartland's direct suggestions seem quite formal, there is no evidence that indirect suggestions are more effective than direct ones. Using direct ego-strengthening suggestions can be extremely stabilizing for certain patients. What is important is to make a *proper match* (Frederick, 1993b). More direct, authoritarian suggestions are useful with individuals who have a great need for structure and thrive on instructions and directions; they may have child-like needs for the therapist to be in charge, especially at the beginning of treatment, before they have clearly identified their partnership role in the therapeutic alliance. Direction and direct suggestion may create a familiar place for such patients to begin their quest for growth and autonomy.

Direct suggestion in ego-strengthening has been modified by adding visual-ization and imagery, tempering of the authoritarian approach, and encourag-ing the patient to add imagery to the process (Stanton, 1979, 1989). The experience of mastery has also been found to have excellent ego-strengthening results. Both Gardner (1976) and Dimond (1981) reported success with imagery techniques, mastery, and the assumption of control of the process by the patient. All of these techniques and many others (Hammond, 1990b) have the ability to strengthen and stabilize the patient. Techniques aimed at eliminating or discharging worrisome or anxiety-filled thoughts and feelings, as well as those which "accentuate the positive" through accessing past mas-tery experiences and successes (Hammond, 1990b), can also be used, such as hypnotically visualizing the disposal of the day's anxieties and problems by tossing them into an imaginary rubbish chute. A review of past accomplish-ments can often be an excellent preface and preparation for future challenges.

These techniques can be combined with Ericksonian techniques during stage I to help achieve safety and stability. Many of them can be adapted for self-hypnosis. Audiotapes of ego-strengthening hypnotic sessions can be given to the patient for regular use, reinforcement, and training in the method em-ployed. The patient can be encouraged to take charge (master) her situation by utilizing the tapes to help her activate inner resources. It is often desirable to give the patient several techniques in sequence, as a frequent shortcoming of tapes is that their efficacy wears off after a while with certain patients. As the therapist and patient begin to uncover and identify hidden memories and their concomitant feelings, it is important to vary ego-strengthening techniques. Pa-tients who have an exacerbation of symptoms and feel overwhelmed even in the face of the most careful exploration can benefit from direct ego-strengthening during the session; during stage II they can benefit from audiotapes and ego-strengthening exercises to do at home as well.

Both direct and Ericksonian techniques help the patient experience increasing mastery of her situation during stages I and II. With a stronger ego at work, the patient may already experience her identity as changing from "victim" to "problem solver" or "the one who can deal with very painful and difficult things," etc. This changing self-concept is an invaluable asset during stage II, when the patient moves into frightening material. The patient may have to be "spelled" from the abreactive work periodically, not only to exercise the control and mastery that comes from being able to leave the overwhelming inner situation at will, but also to receive additional direct ego-strengthening.

Case Example: Sondra, Part 1

Sondra was in treatment for panic attacks with agoraphobia. She functioned well as a wife and mother, but she could not leave her home alone and frequently had panic attacks while at home. She felt divided about taking medication—part of her felt she couldn't survive without it while another part disapproved of her taking any medication whatsoever. Since we suspected that her panic attacks might be triggered by ego-state conflict, a plan was set up with Sondra to do uncovering work. As Sondra was on an extremely limited budget, she was seen infrequently (about once a month). I (CF) considered it crucial to the success of her treatment that she gain control and stability in her situation above and beyond anything that medication had been able to provide her.

Sondra was taught how to bring on a panic attack while she was in trance and how to use the hypnotic state to eliminate the attack. I then suggested to her that *any time she had a panic attack, she would be able to obtain complete relief through the use of self-hypnosis for relaxation and self-soothing.* Sondra's hypnoanalytic work went very well, and although she comes from a family with several members who suffer from panic attacks with agoraphobia, she is now able to leave the house, drive her car, and work. She has a panic attack once or twice a year. At those times she continues to follow the direct suggestion that she use self-hypnosis to completely relieve herself of the symptoms. This works for her every time.

Projective/Evocative Ego-Strengthening:
Utilizing Inner Resources from the Past,
the Present, and the Future

We frequently use the "newer" projective/evocative approaches in our work with dissociative patients. These ego-strengthening methods are designed to evoke unconscious material relevant to the status of the patient's ego strength, to activate strengthening inner resources, and, as much as possible, to place the patient in contact with information and experience from the unconscious mind. The patient not only experiences ego-strengthening but also learns something about the interplay of her unconscious mind with other elements involved in her current status. The feedback the patient gives the therapist from the projective/evocative ego-strengthening experiences is helpful in the ongoing process of evaluating of therapeutic progress.

HYPNOTIC AGE REGRESSION TO SIGNIFICANT NURTURING FIGURES

Traditionally age regression has been regarded as an avenue for uncovering the painful past, not as a source of strengthening. Yet, certain mastery types of provocative/evocative ego-strengthening include the patient's making trips into the past in order to recall and relive times of great achievement and success, of surmounting obstacles, or of overcoming deficiencies.

This technique emphasizes that, although a patient's past may contain unknown problems, it also holds unknown resources. The success of the exercise revolves around the use of hypnosis to help the patient concentrate and focus upon successes or achievements that she remembers but usually does not think about. However, positive events of nurturing, just like traumatic events, can be buried in the unconscious mind. Often these nurturing events have involved people other than members of the immediate, primary family. Conjecture might lead to speculation that some good experiences have been forgotten because they occurred in time periods that were shared with traumatic situations. We might speculate that remembering nurturing from individuals outside the primary family could have been seen as a sign of disloyalty to the primary family, or that those nurturing events were experienced by another ego state. Even though we do not know precisely why or how the good is repressed with the bad, hypnotic age regression is a rich source of recalled, revivified, positive, nurturing ego-strengthening experiences in childhood. In the technique described below, parents are left out as they are usually experienced ambivalently, and negative feelings toward them could interfere with positive ego-strengthening properties. Many patients are refreshed and strengthened by looking beyond the parental sphere for what has been overlooked from other sources.

SCRIPT FOR AGE REGRESSION TO SIGNIFICANT NURTURING FIGURES*

This script is usually used when the patient has been deepened in trance, although it can be used successfully with certain patients who are in informal or spontaneous trance.

*This script was reprinted with permission from McNeal and Frederick, 1993, pp. 173-174.

Life is very complex. Sometimes we have hard times, and sometimes we have better times. Some of our experiences are wonderful, . . . and as we go back into the past . . . we can remember times when we were very much alone . . . times when it seemed no one cared for us . . . times when we had conflicts with our parents . . . and nobody seemed available. . . .

In most human lives, though . . . it's really wonderful how it happens . . . when we are children, little kids, there are other people around . . . sometimes we have really forgotten about them . . . grown-ups who are there for us . . . who have done special things with us . . . maybe just a smile, or a word of encouragement . . . maybe a special appreciation or a trip . . . just a treat . . . or a good time . . . or even a look of admiration and appreciation. People in the neighborhood, people in the extended family . . . the school teachers . . . the janitor . . . maybe someone at a church . . . in a camp . . . maybe just someone you met in a store one day. Just take your time, allow those images, thoughts, and feelings to come to your mind. When you have a sense that this experience is complete, all you need to do is to let your "yes" finger lift.

(After the "yes" finger has lifted)

These people who have given these things to you from the past are with you now in the present, and will always be with you as part of your strength and confidence, as a reflection from the world to you of your uniqueness and your value. And you can remember, and you can notice now, how good it made you feel to be with the people you've recalled. Just let yourself experience how good it felt . . . and know that you can bring these feelings back with you from the past into the present.

"INNER STRENGTH," A POWERFUL RESOURCE
FROM THE PRESENT

Sometimes the most positive piece of information about our patients is that they have made it to our doors. They aren't dead, and they aren't dying slow deaths in back wards of mental hospitals. Somehow, they have coped with and endured the unendurable. It has been suggested that this enduring results, at least in part, from the deepest survival instinct of the personality (McNeal & Frederick, 1993). This aspect of the personality, which has been called *inner strength*, appears to function in the face of severe conflict and overwhelming trauma and to have its origins in conflict-free spheres of the ego (Hartmann, 1961, 1965). Inner strength can be thought of as "something like an ego state" (McNeal & Frederick, 1993, p. 177).

Clinically, we employ *inner strength* as a powerful ego-strengthening maneuver that emphasizes for the patient the power of her inner resources. The subjective experience of this conflict-free state is frequently a powerful and moving experience for the patient. Inner strength can be also used to strengthen individual ego states (Frederick & McNeal, 1993) and to aid in their maturation during all stages of treatment. Its stabilizing effects during the early stages of treatment are often dramatic.

SCRIPT FOR MEETING INNER STRENGTH*

I would like to invite you to take a journey within yourself to a place that feels like the very center of your being, that place where it is very quiet . . . and peaceful . . . and still. And when you're in that place . . . it's possible for you to have a sense of finding a part of yourself . . . a part that I will refer to as your *inner strength*.

This is a part of yourself that has always been there since the moment of birth . . . even though at times it may be difficult for you to feel . . . and it is with you now. It's that part of yourself that has allowed you to survive . . . and to overcome obstacles wherever you face them. Maybe you'd like to take a few moments of time to get in touch with that part of yourself . . . and you can notice what images . . . or feelings . . . what thoughts . . . what bodily sensations are associated with being in touch with your inner strength. And when those images or thoughts or feelings or bodily sensations or however it is coming to you are clear to you in your inner mind, and when you have a sense that the experience is completed for you . . . then your "yes" finger can rise.

In the future, when you wish to get in touch with inner strength, . . . you will find that you can do so by calling forth these images, thoughts, feelings, bodily sensations, and that by so doing you will be in touch with inner strength again.

And when you're in touch with this part of yourself, you will be able to feel more confident . . . confident with the knowledge that you have, within yourself, all the resources you really need to take steps in the direction that you wish to go . . . to be able to set goals and to be able to achieve them . . . and to have the experience that dreams can come true. When you're in touch with this part of yourself, it's possible to feel more calm, more optimistic, to look forward to the future. (*At this point, particular goals that the patient has shared with the therapist may be stated.*)

And in the next days and weeks to come, you may find yourself becoming calmer and more optimistic about your life . . . and you will find that any time during the day it will be possible for you to get in touch with your own inner strength by simply closing your eyes for a moment, bringing your hand to your forehead, evoking the image of your inner strength, and reminding yourself that you have within you . . . all the resources you really need. The more you can use these methods to be in touch with your inner strength, the more you will be able to trust your inner self, your intuition, your feelings, and the more will be able to use them as your guide.

Case Example: Maylin

Maylin had just been jilted by her significant other after a relationship of six years. He had informed her that he could no longer be associated with her as the relationship interfered with the purity of his artistic creativity. That the reason he gave was improbable only added to her

*This script is reprinted with permission from McNeal and Frederick, 1993, pp. 172-173.

confusion and panic. In her first session she was tearful and described many thoughts and quasi-plans about suicide. She was agitated and appeared to be somewhat confused. This was terrifying to her, especially as it was so different from her usual confident, achieving self; she also had some idea that her intense reaction to Theodore's breaking up with her was out of proportion (this suggested an ego-state conflict). Maylin gave a history of an earlier eating disorder as well as a bout of obsessive compulsive symptoms. She sought immediate medication for her distress.

After I (CF) had done further appropriate history-taking and discussed a proposed treatment plan with Maylin, she was invited to enter a state of natural trance relaxation and introduced to the *inner strength experience*. Maylin reported finding herself mentally in a suit of armor like Joan of Arc, but with some soft material there, too. She was riding a horse, and she had a great feeling of calm. After this experience Maylin decided that she would not like to take medication yet, as she felt quite calm and had time to see if she really needed it.

Patients report many different kinds of experiences that they identify as inner strength. For certain patients the experience is kinesthetic. They may experience feelings of strength in their muscles. One patient said, "I felt like a bull!" Other patients may have visual experiences like Maylin's, while still others may see colors, especially the color purple. Patients also report profound affect, such as a feeling of spiritual peace, confidence, etc. Many patients tell us of experiences in which visualization, affect, sensations in the body, and reflective thought are combined.

INTERNAL SELF-SOOTHING

Patients who have been victims of childhood trauma may have compromised self-soothing abilities (McNeal & Frederick, 1994). The psychophysiology of the post-traumatic response (van der Kolk, 1987c), as well as failures to internalize self-regulating psychological systems such as nurturing parental introjects (Herman, 1992; Horner, 1984; Winnicott, 1965a, 1965b; Wolf, 1988), appears to be a causal factor for this deficiency. Since such individuals usually have cognitive deficits as well, they may not know how or when to utilize whatever limited self-soothing abilities they possess; furthermore, since their basic body integrity may be compromised (Herman, 1992), they may not even possess normal points of reference for soothing and relaxation. Instead, they may turn to external agents and addictions to soothe themselves.

McNeal and Frederick (1994) have postulated that the lack of self-soothing ability found in many trauma patients is the result of their having inadequate or damaged stimulus barriers and inadequate mothering, so that they experience traumatic anxiety rather than signal anxiety (Horner, 1984). According to Horner (1984), the stimulus barrier is also inadequate in children who have been deprived of adequate mothering.

One of the difficulties with trauma patients is that they are frequently unable to distinguish between signal anxiety that tells them that danger is imminent and they must do something to avert it, and traumatic anxiety that simply overwhelms them (Horner, 1984). In the ordinary course of events, internal distress is followed by an experience of internal comfort that is supplied from internalized comforting functions. Thus, traumatic or overwhelming anxiety is avoided.

Freud (1920, p. 29) believed that traumatic neuroses were the result of the stimulus barrier's having been breached, and Kluft (1984b) has included the status of the stimulus barrier, along with the absence of restorative soothing experiences with parents, as a perpetuating factor in the formation of MPD. According to McNeal and Frederick (1994), other developmental issues are also involved. Trauma patients often experience a pathological state known as the "overburdened self" (Wolf, 1988). This state has occurred because of a developmental failure "to merge with the calmness of an omnipotent selfobject" (p. 72). Such patients look to others for their responses, are prone to dependency, and may develop extreme dependence on the therapist for experiences of comfort, calm, and soothing. Under severe stress, their internal structures may lose cohesion, and they may even develop psychotic symptoms.

The task for the hypnotherapist is to assist the patient in learning to use the hypnotic experience to obtain self-soothing and calming (McNeal & Frederick, 1994) as an important step in helping them "develop signal anxiety and a greater sense of mastery" (p. 14). Scripts and tapes for self-soothing and calming can serve as transitional objects and experiences (Baker, 1994) to advance the patient developmentally and help her assume care for herself and relinquish her dependency upon the therapist.

There are several kinds of hypnotic experiences that lend themselves to the production of internal calmness and soothing. Places inside where peacefulness and serenity can be experienced (Hammond, 1990b) are well recognized sources of ego-strengthening. McNeal and Frederick (1994) advocate the use of a "safe place" of the patient's own choosing for calming and soothing in trauma patients and for some of their troubled ego states.

From the ego-state standpoint, conflict-free ego states known as internal self-helpers are able to calm and soothe some patients internally (Comstock, 1991); also, more mature ego states may be able to calm less mature ones.

The *inner strength* (McNeal & Frederick, 1993) experience has a notably calming effect on many patients, and McNeal and Frederick have made some modifications in the script to capitalize on this effect for patients who are particularly in need of self-soothing.

MODIFICATION OF THE INNER STRENGTH SCRIPT FOR ENHANCEMENT OF SELF-SOOTHING ABILITY*

As you pay atttention to your breathing, you can notice that in between each inhalation and each exhalation there is a moment of quiet space . . . and you know that you have within you this same quiet space. . . . It's a place that feels like the very center of your being, that place where it's very quiet and peaceful and still. . . . And in this place you can just take a few moments and enjoy the sensation of breathing in and breathing out . . . how good it feels . . . and you can enjoy how good your whole body feels . . . your arms . . . your legs . . . trunk . . . how wonderful it is now just to take a breath and let it out . . . and just the way you can enjoy that comfort in your body . . . you can let yourself feel now . . . a deep peacefulness of your spirit . . . your feelings. . . . It's even possible that you may notice that certain images will float into your mind that are beautiful or especially comforting to you . . . in this peaceful . . . calm . . . special place inside of you . . .

Later in the original script, at a place where the possibility of calmness is associated with the direct experience of *inner strength*, the following sentence is added:

When you're in touch with this part of yourself, it's possible to feel more calm . . . knowing you have the capacity to calm and soothe yourself and parts of yourself that have needed this calming and soothing so much. . . .

HYPNOTIC AGE PROGRESSIONS

The ego-strengthening and integrating properties of hypnotic age progressions have received insufficient attention in the literature. Their value in crisis situations with MPD patients (Kluft, 1983; Torem, Gilbertson, & Kemp, 1990), in ideodynamic healing (Rossi & Cheek, 1988), and in helping the patient form a new identity (Dolan, 1985; Napier, 1993; Torem, 1992) have been clearly identified. However, until recently, it has not been appreciated that hypnotic age progressions can be used in a fairly routine fashion for ego-strengthening with dissociative disorder patients or that their frequent use can help the therapist know in an ongoing fashion whether the treatment is on track.

*This script is reprinted with permission from McNeal and Frederick, 1994, p. 11.

Many direct ego-strengthening suggestions contain a directed future orientation (Dimond, 1981; Gardner, 1976; Hartland, 1965, 1971; Stanton, 1989). However, the projective/evocative ego-strengthening technique of age progression has its roots in Milton Erickson's interest in experimenting with the utilization of future time perception during trance to help his subjects discover and achieve their attainable goals (Erickson, 1954). He had subjects in deep trance visualize the steps involved in achieving their goals within a series of hallucinated crystal balls. In this whimsical way he seemed to make a salute to historical connections with fortunetellers and soothsayers who believed that they could tap into superconscious forces.

The message inherent in Erickson's technique, which he called *pseudo-orientation in time*, was that the most powerful human psychological force, the unconscious mind, was occult, hidden from the scrutiny of consciousness. During trance the subject engaged in hypnotic age progression and discovered what her attainable goals truly were. Erickson concealed the nature of these goals from his patients by producing a profound amnesia, thus protecting the unconscious goals discerned in trance from contamination by the conscious mind (Erickson, 1966). Erickson also insisted that his subjects be dissociated from their surroundings during trance. He felt that the dissociation contributed to a feeling of an accomplished future reality, which in some way caused an internal reorganization crucial to the subject's successfully achieving her goals. De Shazer (1978) also used hallucinated crystal balls to achieve therapeutic goals, as did Havens (1986, p. 259) in what he called a "predetermination of therapeutic progress." Eventually this interest in future goals contributed to the development of solution-focused therapy (de Shazer, 1985, 1988).

Having become interested in Erickson's belief that age progression is "an active inner process of changing one's mental dynamics rather than passive expression of a simple hope or fantasy" (Erickson & Rossi, 1989, p. 241), we have discovered (Frederick & Phillips, 1992; Phillips & Frederick, 1992) that hypnotic age progressions are not only effective for ego-strengthening and integrating but also are prognostic. Although we frequently utilize formal trance for the production of age progressions, we also use informal trance and spontaneous trance occurring during the therapy session. Unlike Erickson, we consider neither dissociation nor amnesia as desirable or necessary with dissociative patients; we want our patients to be aware of their therapeutic experiences whenever possible. Positive age progressions often serve as anchors for patients who are in distress. We do not structure progressions for our patients, nor do we ask them to imagine achievements. We simply ask them to allow their minds to go forward in time, to a time when the problems at hand have been resolved, and to note what they experience. In some instances this is unneccessary, as the patient may experience an age progression in spontaneous trance and describe it, for example : "You know I can see myself somewhere out there working again, and I've lost a lot of weight. . . . I look good."

Age Progressions as a Counterbalance to Traumatic Memories

Hypnotic age progressions can be used after particularly painful and/or frightening abreactive experiences and with terrified and overwhelmed ego states. The integrating, ego-strengthening, and prognostic qualities of the attainable future appear to counterbalance the negative trance experiences of the past, as well as the residual terror, anguish, and hopelessness which has found its way into the present. The important move to the future here is a movement of feelings, of expectations, a dynamic shift that can bring hope into a previously bleak picture. This shift may be meaningful for a variety of reasons, not the least of which is promotion of self-soothing. We became aware, initially, of the self-soothing capacities of hypnotic age progressions in our work with acute psychosomatic disorders (Frederick & Phillips, 1992); we found that hypnotic age progressions could calm panic in our acutely distressed patients, thus allowing them to use their problem-solving and other ego faculties to better advantage.

Frequent hypnotic age progressions can bring about stabilization and safety and make possible the completion of certain abreactive work without a disruption of that safety and stability. Even before they reconstruct memories, many of our patients do not believe that they will be able to free themselves from the legacy of the past; these patients can be difficult to work with because they seem to be in the grips of their own "spontaneous trance," in which they are having continuous, future-projected, self-reinforcing, negative experiences (Frederick & Phillips, 1992).

We discovered that the prognostic value of hypnotic age progression had never been fully explored in clinical situations. Brown and Fromm (1986) cautioned about age progressions in depressed patients, as they apparently felt that negative progressions could become self-fulfilling prophecies. This has not been our experience with the routine employment of hypnotic age progressions in our patients. What the negative age progression tells us is that something is not right in the patient's current treatment situation. This calls for a reexamination of the treatment plan with an eye to what is now needed, e.g., more frequent sessions, medication, support groups, family involvement, or hospitalization. We explain the barometer-like function of age progressions to our patients, thus forestalling doom-and-gloom attitudes. When appropriate, we work with inner attitudes toward negative age progressions in trance as a way of locating further internal resources. Torem (1992) also uses hypnotic age progressions in a projective/evocative way by asking the patient to go forward into the future, to experience her future self, and to have the future self write a letter to the present self outside of the therapy session. This approach is particularly useful in forming a new identity that includes the future self; the future self who writes to the patient can be used as an anchor during difficult phases of treatment.

Management of Negative Hypnotic Age Progressions

Often negative hypnotic age progressions can aid the therapist in understanding the direction treatment must take.

Case Example: Harold

Harold, age 16, came for an initial interview. He had been hospitalized several times for suicide attempts and self-mutilation, and was on a major tranquilizer and an antidepressant. He was dressed in black from head to toe, and he told me (CF) that he was preoccupied with death. Because of concern about whether he could be managed on an outpatient basis, I asked him if he would consent to our taking a closer look at his preoccupations when he was in a more relaxed state. He readily agreed to this, and easily entered trance. When his age progression was complete, he was brought out of trance and said, "This is going to sound pretty strange coming from me, but I saw myself many years from now. . . . I had a master's degree in counseling of some kind, and I was helping troubled teenagers." This positive age progression was prognostic of his being able to maintain himself out of the hospital at the time.

Months later Harold was away from therapy during the Easter holiday, when he spent quite a bit of time visiting his father, who was alcoholic and emotionally disturbed and who refused to recognize the patient's difficulties. When sessions resumed, Harold was profoundly depressed. He said that he thought of killing himself and that he had begun to self-mutilate. A hypnotic age progression was negative. Harold saw himself as a corpse in a coffin. This age progression was prognostic in pointing out that his treatment was not on the right course. I explained this to him and asked him to consider hospitalization. He was reluctant to do this but agreed to telephone me if he felt he could not control his impulses. Within 14 hours he called, and a hospitalization was arranged. This was helpful to Harold, and when he returned to outpatient therapy, his hypnotic age progressions became positive again.

Although the prognostic signs of negative age progressions must never be overlooked, their presence can at times be an opportunity for the therapist and the patient to utilize the patient's trance experience to locate further information and resources. This kind of intervention turns the negative age progression into a waystation on the path to problem resolution.

Case Example: Bessie

Bessie's son, the joy of her life, had died after a short illness, and Bessie was plunged into an overwhelming depression, which numbed and paralyzed her and was punctuated by brief anxiety attacks. At the beginning of her treatment she was unable to produce a positive age progression. Of the experience she reported only the failure to see anything. Bessie agreed that the severity of her symptoms indicated that she could benefit from antidepressant medication as a way of helping her avoid hospitalization.

Bessie improved somewhat, returned to work, and continued in therapy although she didn't "believe in it." One evening Bessie called me (CF) at home. She cried and said that she finally realized there was something wrong with her that had nothing to do with the death of her son and that she wanted to work on it. I reassured her and said that her realization constituted real progress. Hypnoanalytic work, which she had previously avoided, began. The patient had become aware of a dark depressive part of her personality that took over at times.

At the end of one trance session a hypnotic age progression was requested. Bessie saw herself as dead. This was followed by images of gray, swirling, dead energy. I asked if Bessie's inner mind would be willing to allow Bessie to see a future after certain of her internal resources had been activated to help solve her problems. The response was an ideomotor "No." Then I asked if her inner mind was willing to bring into play resources that could help her work on the material of the negative age progression. This time the response was "Yes." The nature of the resources was unknown to both patient and therapist. Bessie's medication was adjusted and the frequency of her sessions increased. In the next session Bessie experienced her first traumatic memory experience.

Although Bessie's age progressions indicated ominous forces at play that could not be ignored, the utilization of the negative age progression in trance gave her hope that there were positive forces within her that were willing to work with the negative ones. The negative images also signaled the need for other kinds of ego-strengthening techniques. With Bessie hypnotic age progressions were eventually used to pace the rate and amount of memory recovery and reassociation and balance of those processes with the appropriate amount of ego-strengthening.

Ericksonian Approaches to Ego-Strengthening

Milton Erickson did not embrace theories; however, he reiterated a principle which he found to be inherent in genuine psychological growth and change (Erickson, Rossi, & Rossi, 1976). The principle involves the presence and the primacy of internal resources residing within each individual. The therapist's task is to evoke or activate the resources needed to deal with the problem or conflict at hand. Ericksonian approaches utilize naturalistic trances and often capitalize on natural ultradian rhythms (Erickson, 1986; Rossi & Cheek, 1988).

COOPERATION, INTERSPERSAL, EMBEDDING, AND SEEDING

The cooperation principle (Gilligan, 1987) recognizes and *validates* (Beahrs, 1982) the patient as having a right and reason to exist in the world just as she is with no apologies or excuses. This acceptance permits confidence and self-esteem to rise, and when that happens the patient becomes more relaxed and better at problem-solving. For example, when a patient complains that she has no positive resources inside of her and that she is terrified of exploring internally because of what she may find, the therapist can "cooperate" with this view. She may comment, "I am really glad you are being honest with me about your fears. Your honesty about your beliefs and what you need will make sure that we don't go too soon or too deeply into your inner experiences until you feel safer or more ready to do so."

Interspersal involves the emphasis on specific words or phrases in a general conversation that appears merely routine or casual (Erickson, 1966; Erickson & Rossi, 1979; Yapko, 1986). Words and phrases are used, sometimes repetitiously, to stimulate new, positive associations within the unconscious mind. Because they are being presented within another context, they have a greater chance of bypassing resistances. Here is an example of the interspersal technique:

> Last year after a snow storm had passed through, you could *see* how *calm* the lake had become. Up here we've *learned how natural* it is for those changes to take place. And even the snow can be an opportunity to *calmly take care of things*

that you haven't had time for, or you can just become *calmly absorbed in feeling so comfortable inside* while you watch the snow fall. There's something wonderful about being able to *see* the lake *clearly* again.

Interspersed within a casual conversation about a winter storm are messages that the therapeutic situation can be a natural place where the patient becomes calmly absorbed, feels comfortable, and sees clearly.

Embedding involves a nonverbal "marking" of suggestions (Yapko, 1986, 1990) through changes in voice tonality or emphasis, postural changes, etc., and is more easily understood when it is heard in a demonstration. The therapist will find her own way to emphasize embedded suggestions.

Seeding is the subtle introduction of ideas in a minor key before they are faced in a major way. The seeding of hope (Dolan, 1991) should be a priority in the early stages of treatment. Although seeding is done on a continuous basis, suggestively by the therapist, the patient can be helped to become an active participant in this process by focusing on a future identity in which she will resume ownership of what had been stolen from her life by the trauma. Small steps can be taken in this process when the patient imagines, bit by bit, what recovery will look like.

METAPHOR

As a form of therapeutic communication, metaphor is considered by many to be a hallmark of Ericksonian hypnotherapy (Erickson & Rossi, 1979; Gilligan, 1987; Lankton, 1980; Yapko, 1990; Zeig, 1980). When the therapist uses metaphor or storytelling, she is conveying messages and suggestions about certain matters to the patient without seeming to do so in a conscious way. The great strength of metaphor lies in its gentle way of avoiding direct confrontation with sensitive issues (Yapko, 1990). Disguised by the overt content of the story, messages bypass the critical objections of the conscious mind. Thus the therapist is communicating with the patient at several levels (Erickson & Rossi, 1976). We have found that metaphors and stories have tremendous ego-strengthening possibilities.

Metaphors that convey messages about strength, endurance, and triumph over obstacles can be introduced with other ego-strengthening techniques to create of an atmosphere of safety and stability.

While the material of metaphors can be chosen from any source, it should bear some relationship to the patient's own life and interests. For example, a patient who sails might be interested in a story about the endurance of a sailing vessel on high seas, and a patient who gardens would probably be open to the following story, used to address anxieties about whether improvements made in therapy would endure:

You know, I was so pleased that the bulbs had begun to sprout in my garden last week. They looked so fresh and *strong*, and I knew that the flowers that would appear would be beautiful. Well, you know we had that snow in the middle of the week. It blanketed my entire garden. I was *strongly* concerned that the new plants were going to be destroyed by it. Then the snow melted over the next day or two, and the new plants were *stronger* that ever. And yesterday the first flowers appeared.

Metaphors, like the one above, often contain embedded seed ideas and messages. The therapist must be careful not to engage in gratuitous self-revelation as a source of metaphoric material. A good rule of thumb is to limit personal references to gardens and lawns, pets, automobiles, etc. Many metaphors are introduced as if they happened to someone else; for example, "I once had another patient . . . "

ERICKSONIAN UTILIZATION OF PRESENT AND PAST RESOURCES

Ericksonian hypnotherapy is geared to helping the patient use resources from the past, the present, and the future (Yapko, 1990). Present resources can be of great assistance in strengthening the patient and providing a sense of mastery. According to Dolan (1991), they can be activated in a number of ways. With one approach the patient can be helped to choose deliberate actions or activities to interrupt flashbacks or other disturbing symptoms. For example, a patient may learn that taking a few deep breaths, beginning certain household chores, or taking a five-minute walk will interrupt the focus on troubling symptoms. Alternatively, she can be helped to initiate and utilize a trance state to access present resources such as abilities, close family ties, and friendships. These can be represented symbolically, and the symbol can be brought to mind when symptoms begin to dislodge equilibrium. Patients can also learn to trigger internal reexperiencing of current enjoyable mastery situations, such as hobbies, athletic activities, etc. Dolan (1991) recommends an autohypnotic exercise featuring an internal focus on objects in the present that have been seen, heard, and felt. The patient does this five times for each category, then four, three, two, and one. If the trance state is not sufficiently deep and comforting, the patient begins all over again with five sights, five sounds, and five bodily sensations.

Positive associational cues to past resources (Dolan, 1991) are often invaluable in dealing with past trauma. A variant of the "it takes a thief to catch a thief" strategy is used. Since flashbacks are usually precipitated by associational cues (Dolan, 1991), the patient can learn to capitalize on state-dependent accessing of inner resources from the past: strengthening, calming, validating experiences to which the patient can assign a mental emblem or souvenir as a trigger. "The associational cue can be used to strengthen the client during

the therapy session when facing difficult facts about her victimization . . . "
(Dolan, 1991, p. 101). Additionally, hypnotic age regressions can be used
to help the patient get in touch with past mastery experiences, nurturing
experiences, and memories of safety.

AVOIDANCE OF CONFUSION TECHNIQUES AND DOUBLE BINDS

Although we find Ericksonian techniques invaluable in our work with dissociative patients, we must issue some caveats. The first concerns confusion
techniques. Confusion techniques are communications from the therapist
that disrupt the patient's own conscious strategies for processing information.
The disruption allows the development of a trance process. These techniques
are used with patients who are usually thought of as resistant. In terms of the
cooperation principle (Gilligan, 1987), the therapist utilizes the mechanisms
of resistance to trance or other therapeutic movement as the basis for introducing confusion techniques. They are used in the interest of the patient who
may actually be highly motivated.

In general, it is unwise to introduce confusion techniques into the treatment of dissociative patients, who are already experiencing tremendous internal confusion. "The hypnotist does not have to produce confusion in such
people; it is already there" (Gilligan, 1987, p. 290). Gilligan has also advised
that confusion techniques are inappropriate when there is insecurity in the
therapeutic relationship, when instructions are being given, and when the
patient does not feel safe and protected. They should never be used in crises.
Gilligan (1987) does not believe there is any rationale for using confusion
techniques with patients who are " . . . willing and able to develop trance"
(p. 291). In our experience dissociative patients usually enter trance readily;
when there are problems, they can usually be resolved by more careful pacing
and the selection of a method better suited to the patient.

The therapist must also be extremely cautious about creating Ericksonian
double binds with dissociative patients. Double-bind positions give the patient two alternatives, either of which leads to further progress in the therapeutic situation. For example, a therapist might say to a patient, "Do you
want to work on retrieving memories about what happened when you were
three years old and had a tonsillectomy today, or would it be better to focus
on the source of the flashback you just told me about?" The implication of
this question is that the patient has only two choices and that memory
retrieval will be done in this session and on the therapist's schedule instead of
the patient's, whether the patient is ready for it or not. We believe such
forced timing to be inadvisable.

Double binds, even those of the most benign order, may be perceived as
attempts to manipulate or control. Gilligan (1987) has noted that the issue

of manipulation in therapy cannot be sidestepped, and the therapist needs to examine her intent in utilizing therapeutic maneuvers. We share Gilligan's observations that patients find it difficult to cooperate with a therapist who is not experienced as supportive. The therapist should also be aware that certain dissociative patients will misinterpret even the most benign double-bind interventions as a repetition of what abusers did to them. This could lead to mistrust, anger, and/or panic.

6

ACCESSING THE ORIGINS OF DISSOCIATIVE SYMPTOMS AND RELATED RESOURCES

The second stage of treatment involves accessing and reconstructing the source of the patient's current dissociative symptoms. As discussed in Chapter 1, such symptoms can be quite varied and may include anxiety related to traumatic experiences from the past; conversion and psychophysiological reactions with no organic basis; marked changes in affect out of proportion to current life circumstances; intrusive imagery, thoughts, sensations, or behaviors; various difficulties reflecting the language of internal conflict; and a lack of responsiveness to previous therapies, including hypnotherapy.

The task of uncovering and processing memory material that may be related to current symptoms is an important and complex aspect of the treatment of dissociative patients. It is very important that the therapist be clear that his role is one of facilitator, witness and advocate, and not that of investigator. Both therapist and patient must clarify their expectations about this stage of therapy. We find it helpful to discuss directly some of our beliefs about the fragmentary and unpredictable qualities of memory functioning (see Chapter 1), and the importance of keeping "an open mind" about whatever we discover together.

We begin with the patient's current understandings of past events related to his difficulties, and expand on these through journaling, art work, photographs, and discussions. We explain that the ease with which patients retrieve, master, and resolve past traumatic experiences depends on a number of factors, including: the level of trust in the therapist, the level of self-trust in internal process, mastery of necessary therapeutic tasks (e.g., therapeutic alliance, maintenance of boundaries, safety and stability and other stage I abilities), mastery of essential hypnotic skills (see Chapter 3), and previous experiences in exploring past traumatic events (Sachs & Peterson, 1994). We present the SIBAM model of dissociation (Levine, 1991), and discuss how we use it to explore and reconnect different "memory" fragments of sensation, imagery and other internal sensory experiences, voluntary and involuntary behaviors and movements, and emotional responses, before beginning to approach meaning and cognitive understandings. We reiterate again and again that our goal is to achieve mastery over material and experiences related to the past (rather than retrieval of information about "what happened"), and that we will be suggesting approaches that will help to strengthen them as they move through this stage, rather than ones that might uncover the most detail. More specifics are offered later in this chapter in the section on "Accessing and Reconstructing Dissociated Traumatic Experiences: General Guidelines."

If the patient demonstrates sufficient readiness following these preparatory procedures, we may proceed to the use of the accessing techniques presented in this chapter. If the patient is hesitant or seems to need further experience in mastering current post-traumatic symptoms before proceeding, we might introduce more indirect approaches, such as ways of utilizing dissociative symptoms. If the patient begins to destabilize in his outside life or within the therapy context, however, we return to stage I for more strengthening and safety work.

Utilizing Dissociation as a Resource

Patients fearful of exploring traumatic experiences in hypnosis can benefit from utilization techniques that allow them to master troublesome trauma-related symptoms and achieve a deeper sense of internal partnership with their unconscious processes. Following the successful use of these techniques, many patients move on to the more difficult process of uncovering and reconstructing the traumatic experiences underlying their symptoms.

Milton Erickson believed that many dissociative processes can benefit human beings when properly utilized. Although many associate Erickson with metaphor and other forms of indirect suggestion, which he emphasized near the end of his life, he spent much of his career in hypnotherapy producing and utilizing hypnotic phenomena in formal trance situations (Hammond, 1990a). He used quite a bit of direct suggestion, often employed simple inductions (Lehrer, 1986), and trained many of his subjects to produce at will certain hypnotic phenomena, such as hallucination, amnesia, and dissociation.

His emphasis on self-hypnosis as an invaluable tool for self-discovery and activation of powerful unconscious healing processes is sometimes overlooked. He was impressed by the ability of the individual to employ hypnosis as a way of living a better life. From Erickson's viewpoint, one of the advantages of the hypnotic trance was its ability to produce many useful hypnotic phenomena, including: "the opportunity hypnosis gives the patient to dissociate himself from his problems, to take an objective view of himself, to make an inventory of his assets and abilities, and then, one by one to deal with his problems instead of being overwhelmed with all of them without being able to think clearly in any direction. Hypnosis offers an opportunity to control and direct thinking, to select or exclude memories and ideas, and thus to give the patient the opportunity to deal individually and adequately with any selected item of experience" (Erickson, 1945/1980, p. 34).

Dolan (1991) has also pointed out that dissociative responses can often be utilized therapeutically. Since dissociation develops in an attempt to survive overwhelming psychological or physical stress (Spiegel, 1988), individuals who have experienced trauma are often quite skilled at this process, though they may not be consciously aware of dissociating. Consequently, they are likely to dissociate when tension rises during therapy.

There are several signals that should alert the therapist to dissociative responses. These include a sudden stillness in the patient's body or cessation of movement, an abrupt numbing or flattening of emotional expression, "spacing out" where the patient forgets what he was just talking about or the question that was asked, or a lapse in verbal response time where the patient appears to be "off somewhere else" (Dolan, 1991, p. 115).

One way of utilizing dissociation is to encourage this response at times when the patient wants or needs to protect himself from unwanted traumatic associations or related symptoms such as flashbacks, intrusive thoughts, or fear reactions. This approach was used with Mark, a doctoral student in anthropology who had twice failed his comprehensive examinations.

Case Example: Mark

In discussing his reactions during previous examinations, Mark revealed that he had become terrified and that he was unable to retrieve information that was very familiar to him. He had had to leave the room and abort the examination because of these reactions. His history included severe physical abuse and neglect by his father and sexual abuse from his stepmother, most of which he recalled and had worked with in previous psychotherapy. We both believed that the examination situation had triggered some of this material because it was a circumstance in which he similarly felt "trapped"—he could not escape if he wanted to obtain his degree.

I (MP) explained the mechanism of dissociation to Mark and suggested that he could learn to choose when and how to use this as a resource. First, I asked him to pay attention to beginning sensations of anxiety while I asked a series of questions about his background. At any time he began to feel even "a little uncomfortable," he was to let his mind drift away from the question for a moment or two, and then to respond verbally, "I don't want to answer that now." As he practiced this technique, Mark reported feeling calmer and more in control of the interview situation. I then asked him to practice this approach at home in study sessions, giving himself permission to "space out" for a few moments whenever he felt the beginnings of even slight anxiety, and choosing consciously to return to study when he felt ready to concentrate. After a week of using this self-utilization approach, Mark reported that he felt his study time had become more productive.

During the next few sessions, I introduced formal hypnosis to Mark following the guidelines discussed in Chapters 2 and 3. He had several positive experiences with ego-strengthening, including the creation of an internal safe place, and was able to access positive internal resources of confidence and mental alertness through positive age regression. I then introduced the use of dissociation in hypnosis, suggesting that he could use his dissociative skills to "send away" traumatic material and related anxiety responses to a safe, secure internal container that would remain locked away outside of his awareness until he chose to open it again. During a formal induction procedure using an affect bridge, Mark retrieved his previous anxiety responses during the two comprehensive examinations he had failed, created a sturdy internal vault with a time lock set to open a month after his current exam, "sent" all of his fear reactions into the fault, and imagined closing and locking the door securely. He immediately experienced a sense of relief that his fears, along with all the past experiences connected to them, could be stored in an internal compartment in his mind where they would not interfere with his examination focus.

These experiences were followed by his use of self-hypnosis to focus inward to check the security of his inner vault before each study session at home and to create an internal library where all his knowledge was stored in well-organized volumes. Then mental rehearsal, age progression, and Ego-State Therapy techniques were employed to prepare further for the exam. After a total of eight sessions, Mark took and passed his examination successfully. As of this writing, he is still involved in hypnotherapy and Ego-State Therapy to help manage binge-eating behaviors that seem related to unresolved traumatic experiences.

Erickson's use of dissociation in terms of time and body disorientation for pain control is well-known. His concept that ideomotor signaling was an important dissociative phenomenon that could assist in deep uncovering and healing is mentioned less frequently, however, as are other similar uses of dissociation. Erickson believed dissociation to be the mechanism for hypnotic age progressions (pseudo-orientation in time), and he strongly espoused the use of a therapeutic technique he termed objective thinking. This dissociative technique allows the patient in hypnosis to dissociate himself into an observer who watches his participant self. Thus traumatic incidents could be viewed more objectively, and as we would say today, without the danger of retraumatization. He often used dissociation paradoxically, to help patients reassociate dissociated traumatic material by watching it rather than reexperiencing it.

Many patients like Mark can benefit from utilizing dissociation and containment in situations where their concentration and ability to focus are impaired. Dolan (1991) has discussed a variation of this approach, which involves teaching patients to calibrate their states of inner alertness from one to ten and to raise and lower their anxiety on this imaginary scale through self-suggestion, thereby achieving mastery over dissociative responses. She has also proposed the dissociative displacement of anxiety reactions such as flashbacks and nightmares: Patients are taught to use self-hypnosis to allow one of their cataleptic arms to have the fear experience while the rest of them remains unaware of the experience. Those who use this technique effectively indicate "slight ideomotoric tremors or rigidity, but without any accompanying images or emotions" (Dolan, 1991, p. 120).

Naturalistic Age Regression and Progression

Regression back in time to the traumatic events underlying dissociative symptoms and conditions does not always need to be formally induced with suggestions in hypnosis such as "Let your unconscious mind help you to drift back in time to the source of this symptom." However, whether the therapist is using a naturalistic or formal approach, it is important to begin with positive regression, that is, helping the patient orient to pleasant memories from the past to be used as positive resources in the recall process. When formal hypnosis is not being used, individuals can be encouraged to recall recent experiences of relaxation and enjoyment, systematically moving back in time to earlier memories. Later, during regression to traumatic experiences, the patient can use these positive memories to titrate the recall of, or provide distance from, distressing memories. More will be said about the use of formal age regression and progression later in this chapter.

Often, patients can simply be encouraged to discuss the details of their lives before or around the time of the trauma as a way of reclaiming a sense of identity and continuity with the past. Herman (1992) suggests several important aspects of this process, including encouraging the patient to talk about important relationships, ideals, and struggles prior to the time of trauma, and helping the patient to reconstruct the traumatic experiences in a narrative that gradually becomes anchored in sequential time and includes feelings, images, and somatic responses.

Dolan (1991, p. 140) recommends a "safe remembering" approach that involves first establishing associational cues for comfort and security, such as imagining a favorite "safe chair" at home (p. 125), and symbols of present-time safety, such as a wristwatch or clock in the therapist's office. She then proceeds with a combination of "eyes open" recall and a fractionated "eyes closed" approach that allows the patient to move in and out of past and present states of awareness, depending on needs for comfort and moment-to-moment readiness levels. During this process, the associational cues and symbols are focused on as needed.

Another indirect approach to age regression is suggested by Erickson's use of automatic writing (Erickson & Rossi, 1979), which in some cases can allow the emergence of traumatic material in a naturalistic way through handwriting that occurs outside of the patient's awareness. With multiple personality disorder and highly dissociated patients, this can be suggested when it is clear that one of the ego states is ready to disclose past information that the rest of the personality is not yet ready to hear. The therapist can instruct the willing ego state to write down the information as a journal entry or in letter form to the therapist, without the conscious awareness, though with the cooperation, of the main personality. The writing can then be kept by the therapist until the rest of the personality is ready to read it.

This procedure can be used either outside therapy sessions in self-hypnotic trance or during a therapeutically induced hypnotic state. After appropriate ego-strengthening suggestions, the patient is instructed to hold a pen in his non-dominant hand and, when ready, to allow his unconscious mind to guide the hand in writing all by itself on a pad of paper the information from the past that would be appropriate and helpful to him in understanding current difficulties. A variation is to suggest that the individual imagine an inner blackboard and report what is being written by a dissociated, imaginary hand (Watkins, 1992). This can be further embellished with the use of a "split-screen" technique (Spiegel & Spiegel, 1978), where the second screen allows the patient fast-forward, slow-motion, and other technical liberties.

Further instruction may be needed to enable the writing to become truly automatic (for example, "You'll find there's no effort needed on your part, and you will simply be aware of a nice pleasant urge for that left hand to write all by itself while your right hand rests comfortably in your lap," or "Your conscious mind can be quite curious about those little movements that are beginning and just what they will spell out after that hand is finished with its helpful work." Dolan (1991) adds a conscious focus on the patient's associational cues and symbols for safety by having him write a word that reminds him of these resources in the corner of the page where he can see it, if desired, throughout the process. However, many subjects require extensive training before they are able to engage satisfactorily in automatic writing (Cheek, 1994; Edelstien, 1981). For such patients, alternatives include hypnoplasty, hypnography, and the use of sculptured or drawn images.

Another naturalistic uncovering technique involves dreams (Edelstien, 1981; Erickson, 1970/1980). The therapist can suggest in or out of trance that the patient can "have a dream or series of dreams related to the source of these symptoms that the unconscious can remember to tell the conscious mind." One patient had not responded to any other kind of uncovering technique, including ideomotor/ideosensory signaling; his first clue to past traumatic material came in a dream where he as an adult was rescuing a baby "who looked like me" from being drowned in a toilet. Though he rarely remembered dreams, this one was quite vivid for him, and provided a disguised, curious bridge to the past, which was later augmented with information related to early traumatic experiences obtained through questioning with a pendulum.

Regardless of what naturalistic approach to regression for uncovering is used, *it is essential to follow regressive work with orientation to the present and future.* Sometimes, the therapist can simply remind the patient that, while one part of him has been recalling the past and some of its upsetting feelings and thoughts, another part of him has remained in present time and can receive those experiences into adult awareness. The following kinds of suggestions can then be given: "Take a few moments now while your adult self fully receives that information from the past. . . . And if your unconscious mind is aware of resources available now in the present that were not available at the time in the past that the other part of you has just recalled, those resources can be added in now. . . . Just take some time to notice what difference that makes." Though our style is generally to be permissive and let the patient respond to these open-ended suggestions for present-time integration in his own way, at times we add more structure. Commonly, we might suggest that the adult self comfort the younger self who was there during the past experience through words, touch, or any other means. More details of this renurturing approach are given below in the sections on Ego-State Therapy.

After orienting the patient naturally to the present, the therapist helps him orient toward the future. This can be done with simple future-pacing suggestions, such as, "And, of course, your unconscious mind will extend these understandings into the future in ways that will be helpful to you. Take a few moments now to consider the important differences the new understandings you have received today from the past and from the present will make in the days, weeks, and months ahead. . . . " Occasionally, it is helpful to structure a more complete age progression experience as part of naturalistic uncovering work. Ways of achieving this are discussed in the section below on direct hypnotic methods.

Ideomotor/Ideosensory Approaches

This approach to uncovering is useful when the patient has little or no recall of traumatic events from the past, has no conscious knowledge of the origins of current symptoms and difficulties, or seems to require a more systematic approach to uncovering than naturalistic approaches provide. Originating in the work of Erickson (1961/1980) and further developed by Cheek and LeCron (1968), Rossi and Cheek (1988), and Cheek (1994), these approaches have the advantage of allowing careful monitoring of the uncovering process and seem to promote the development of internal boundaries by placing tangible responsibility for past discoveries within the patient rather than within techniques or suggestions used by the therapist.

As we noted in Chapter 3, our approach to ideomotor signals is permissive in allowing the subject to establish his own finger signals during each therapy session, either through awareness of minimal finger movements or through more idiosyncratic ideosensory responses (e.g., warmth, tingling, heaviness) that can be translated by the patient into finger movements for therapist identification. As in the method described by Cheek and Rossi (1988), we establish three separate signals for "yes," "no," and "I'm not ready to know yet."

Although no formal induction is required with ideomotor signals, we usually introduce a brief sequence of suggestions for relaxation, the development of internal focus, and ego-strengthening. Next, once finger signals are established, we begin ideomotor questioning. If desirable, these signals can be tested by asking responses to neutral questions, such as, "Is today Wednesday?" This can develop further confidence in the signaling process. We remind the patient that he may have conscious associations to the questions asked, but that we are interested in the unconscious responses that will be transmitted through the finger signals. We also emphasize that the unconscious activity is the transmission of some sort of signal to one of the fingers and not necessarily the movement that follows; this instruction helps to allay performance anxiety.

Typically, the first question asked is whether the patient's unconscious mind is willing to help in the uncovering process. If a "yes" response is obtained, we ask whether the subject's unconscious mind is willing to take him back in time to the source of the patient's current symptoms or difficulties. If a "no" response is obtained to either of these questions, we ask, "Is there anything that is needed *before* this can be done?" If no significant information emerges in response to this question and a "yes" response is still not forthcoming, we ask, "Is Jack's unconscious mind willing to review all the information related to the answer to this question at an unconscious level, outside of his conscious awareness?" Almost always, we get permission for this internal review. We then suggest that when the review is complete, the unconscious will give a "yes" signal. When we return to the original question, we invariably obtain a "yes" response. Apparently, there is something about giving more explicit control over the recall process that measurably increases cooperation. Another way of strengthening cooperation and perhaps avoiding spontaneous abreaction is to ask, "Would it be all right to review any experiences from the past related to your current difficulty from today's perspective, here in my office?" (Cheek, 1994).

Once unconscious responses have indicated permission to release information from the past related to current symptomatology, we instruct the patient to drift back in time and allow his unconscious mind to identify the source of current difficulties, suggesting that his "yes" finger can lift when he is oriented in some way to this past experience. When the "yes" signal appears, we ask the individual to notice whatever comes into consciousness, including images, sounds of an internal voice, memories, body sensations, symbols, colors, or any combination of these possibilities. We allow time for thorough exploration, emotional release, and reframing (Cheek, 1994; Rossi & Cheek, 1988) of this material. Occasionally, a patient will comment, "Nothing is happening." This response may require a more directive approach, gently inviting him to "drift a little deeper into trance, where no effort is needed just to let another part of his experience float up to the surface" or perhaps further questioning, such as "What can you see internally now?" or, "How does your upper body feel right now?"

If at any time during the exploration of past experiences a "no" signal appears (e.g., in response to the question, "Is it all right for Jack to know more about that at a conscious level at this time?"), we immediately honor this protective response of the unconscious and validate it for the patient as a way that his unconscious mind is taking care of him. We then shift to a future orientation and ask whether the unconscious would be willing to share this information with the conscious mind at a time and place in the future and in a way that would be fully comfortable and helpful to the patient. Almost always, there is a clear "yes" response. We validate this as indicating an appropriate need for privacy and autonomy.

As with other types of regression, *it is important to shift from the past orientation into the present and future*. We ask whether there are resources or understandings Jack has as an adult that were not available during the past that would be helpful. This step is very important for therapeutic reframing and full reassociation of the past experience. When this is complete, we move into the future: "Would it be okay for Jack's unconscious to take him forward in time now to some time in the future when he has fully integrated this experience in a way that is useful for him (or has resolved his current symptoms and completed therapy)?" This age progression is fully explored and its use as a resource is validated for the patient, providing further ego-strengthening.

Rossi and Cheek (1988) point out the numerous advantages of the ideomotor approach. Ideomotor questioning is easy to learn and use, allowing patient and therapist access to a wide range of state-bound information that may not be available at more conscious levels of verbal functioning. Approaching significant, dissociated life experiences through a controlled progression of self-paced steps can often facilitate rapid desensitization, reframing, and sometimes even complete resolution of current symptoms and difficulties (Dolan, 1991). Since no formal induction is required, this method of age regression to traumatic experiences can be used safely and effectively by beginners in hypnotherapy. When there are "resistances" or obstacles to the investigation, these become immediately obvious and can be respected and resolved by the patient's own creative unconscious processes, further strengthening his level of unconscious cooperation. Finally, this approach allows the subject to retrieve important information related to past traumatic experiences in a gentle, respectful way without necessarily revivifying or reliving the original experience. Ideomotor signals can be used to verify that the exploration has been complete for healing purposes and can be a "gauge" throughout therapy to determine progress made with other hypnotic techniques (Dolan, 1991). And, since verbal communication is not essential to this type of regression, the subject retains complete control over the level and timing of disclosures to the therapist.

Some patients do not respond to ideomotor signals. Occasionally, this is because of psychodynamic issues such as performance anxiety or a tendency to "try too hard," which blocks unconscious processes, necessitating a shift to other types of therapeutic regression. For some patients, the issue may be difficulty in responding clearly either "yes" or "no" (Rossi & Cheek, 1988). Other difficulties may be due to transference issues between therapist and patient; these may need to be resolved through verbal interaction before this approach can be effective. Another important subgroup of patients may not respond to such signals consistently because they are not yet ready to explore (and perhaps find) past experiences that may be disturbing to them. For example, one patient, Sean, had clear ideomotor responses during ego-strengthening sessions, but produced unclear signals after we shifted to the exploration of past experiences that might be connected with his current dissociative difficulties. After acknowledging his fears, we returned to further stage I work, and were later able to use imagery, which Sean found less threatening, to access past traumatic material.

Increasingly in our practices, we are seeing patients who respond more readily to *ideosensory* than to ideomotor signaling. This seems to be true for those individuals who experience dissociated traumatic experiences primarily through body sensations, rather than through modalities such as images, thoughts, or internal voices or sounds. Ideosensory responses can be utilized by the therapist just as effectively as ideomotor responses, though more patience and careful tracking of responses are required. A clinical example is offered below.

Case Example: Janet

Janet (Phillips, 1993c), a 34-year-old, divorced administrative assistant, was referred for adjunctive hypnotherapy by her primary psychotherapist. Both Janet and her therapist suspected early childhood sexual abuse but had not been able to retrieve any recollections of such an experience. During the first several sessions, after obtaining a thorough history and discussing important clinical issues, I (MP) introduced formal hypnosis to Janet using the guidelines in Chapter 3. In response to progressive relaxation suggestions, Janet reported feeling a "cold wave" washing over her body. She further acknowledged that she was frequently aware of this sensation when she woke from nightmares in the middle of the night and during times when she had practiced meditation or other forms of relaxation. Since Janet was willing to explore this sensation further, I suggested that we view this as a possible signal from her unconscious that might help us understand her internal experience. Janet was asked to focus intensely on this sensation, which was located primarily in her chest. Ideosensory signaling was then used as follows:

MP: Now, Janet, I'd like you to pay attention to this cold wave in your chest. I'm going to suggest to your unconscious mind that if this sensation is related to an important early experience, your unconscious can intensify this cold sensation as a "yes" signal. If the "cold wave" is not important to the understanding of an earlier experience, you'll notice this sensation beginning to disappear as a "no" signal. . . . Just take a few moments and let me know what happens.

J: (*Pause*) The cold wave is definitely getting stronger.

MP: Good. Then we have verification from your unconscious that this may be somehow related to an important past experience. Let's go a little further. I'm going to suggest to your unconscious that, if it would be appropriate right now for us to know more about this earlier experience at a conscious level, the cold wave can intensify a little more for "yes," or begin to dissipate for "no."

J: (*Pause*) It seems to be getting a little stronger now.

MP: Okay, just drift a little deeper, Janet, and let your unconscious share whatever information is appropriate and helpful for you to have now about this at a conscious level.

With more ideosensory questioning, what came into her awareness was the image of Janet as a small child being sexually molested by a worker on her father's delivery route as she lay naked on a cold, metallic table. In this case, the ideosensory signal seemed connected to a dissociated traumatic experience, allowing access to it and providing an opportunity to reassociate and renegotiate other aspects of related early experiences.

In some instances, individuals who respond through ideosensory signals seem to manifest extraneous signals that distract both therapist and patient. We believe that such responses, which usually appear after initial ideosensory signals have already been established, may protect the dissociative patient from traumatic material and therapeutic intervention (Phillips & Frederick, 1993). We encourage the patient's unconscious to determine their importance. If Janet had suddenly reported a warm, tingling sensation in the right hand, I might have said, "Since your unconscious has already verified the cold wave as your important signal for today, I'm going to ask your unconscious for clarification. If the warm, tingling sensation in your hand is connected to our investigation of the past experience identified with the cold wave, it can intensify; if this warm tingling is not connected in any significant way, it will begin to disappear." Almost always, these extraneous signals vanish fairly quickly. Though they may be acknowledged for their protective function in slowing down the therapeutic process, the therapist should not allow them to "derail" or confuse inner exploration.

Since ideosensory signals can be viewed as primitive precursors to more developed forms of unconscious communication such as ideomotor signals and manifestations of ego states, they should not be overlooked. However, if decoding these signals proves difficult, an alternative is to suggest that the patient's unconscious translate the ideosensory response into a more recognizable signal, such as an unconscious head movement (Dolan, 1991; Rossi & Cheek, 1988).

Direct Hypnotic Methods

For patients who find ideodynamic signals "artificial" or otherwise unappealing or unproductive, the same kinds of state-bound information can be elicited and safely reconstructed through direct hypnotic suggestion.

AGE REGRESSION

Many types of structured suggestions can be given to help the subject go back in time. Hypnotic suggestions that make use of a patient's visual imagination include various "special vehicle" approaches: trains, planes, time machines, magic carpets, space ships, elevators, and escalators that transport the individual back in time to the source of current symptoms or difficulties. The following example of an age regression approach, initiated after a hypnotic induction and deepening, features a "special train" (Yapko, 1990, pp. 258–259):

> . . . And now . . . you can let yourself have the experience in your mind . . . of going to a special train station . . . a train station unlike any you've ever experienced . . . where the trains that run are so unusual in their ability to take you back in time . . . and you can go back in time . . . to experiences that you haven't thought about in a long, long time . . . and you can see yourself getting onto the most interesting-looking train . . . and you can find your way to a seat that is so comfortable to sit in . . . and then as you feel the train begin to move in a gentle and pleasant way . . . you can experience the movement of going backwards in time . . . slowly at first . . . then faster . . . building a powerful momentum . . . and as you look out the window . . . and see the events of your life moving past you like so many telephone poles you pass on the way . . . and then the train begins to slow down . . . and then it comes to a stop . . . and now you can step off the train to find yourself in that situation that was so important to you . . . and being in that situation now, you can see the sights, hear the sounds, and feel the feelings of that time and place . . . this time and place . . .

Another visually oriented regression technique involves the imaginary viewing of a movie, TV program, or videotape related to the patient's life. Here suggestions can be highly structured, for example: "Imagine yourself viewing a special movie of the events related to the fears and nightmares you have been having recently. You will notice that you have a remote control so that you can speed up, slow down, freeze, rewind, or turn off the movie at any time. The movie can be watched from a comfortable distance, as if it were happening to someone else . . . with the sound off, the color dimmed or changed, as needed, to ensure that you can watch without feeling any more of the feelings of the characters on the screen than are needed for your healing process."

A variation of this is the split-screen technique (Spiegel & Spiegel, 1978) where the patient is invited to imagine an internal viewing screen. On one side of the screen, he is invited to project internal resources that evoke feelings of calm and safety; on the other side, he projects a traumatic experience or scene. At any time that the patient feels overwhelmed in reviewing the traumatic scene, he is instructed to change his focus to the positive resource side of the screen, a procedure which provides titration for trauma-related affects and reactions. The TV, movie, and split-screen techniques are more depersonalized variations of age regression and can provide detachment and distance from past trauma, particularly for dissociative patients who fear the emergence of intense affect. Additionally, patients can be encouraged during viewing of traumatic scenes during age regression to "just watch the picture" without the sound or the feelings, followed by further recall experiences which might feature only the important feelings and thoughts, without the images. Such dissociation of visual details from affects (Hammond, 1990b) can provide protection from emotional flooding and retraumatization.

Alternative visual techniques involve viewing traumatic material through special binoculars, or the distant end of a telescope, or even through a camera lens. Some individuals prefer to look through a book of time, library of time, or special photograph album where the unconscious can turn to a page where the events related to current symptoms or difficulties are recorded.

Another structured uncovering approach that provides protection for the patient who is particularly fearful of recalling an unknown event believed to be traumatic in nature is the "emanated image dissociation" technique developed by Steve Lankton (1992). After formal induction and deepening, the patient is asked to create an image of himself, usually a younger self. This fantasized image then watches the traumatic event from some dissociated perspective, such as on a movie or TV screen. When the fantasized image has completed this viewing, and the patient indicates readiness, the image may communicate the trauma to the patient. If more protection is needed, additional interim self-images can be added, so that, for example, image 1 watches image 2 watching image 3 watching the trauma. When the subject is sufficiently desensitized, interim images can be removed and the patient can watch the traumatic event directly.

For subjects who are more somatically and emotionally oriented, the use of an *affect* or *somatic bridge* is a powerful and highly productive regression technique. This approach (Watkins, 1971, 1990) allows the patient to bridge from a current emotional feeling or body sensation of unknown origin back to the source of this reaction. Several steps are involved. First, the patient is instructed to focus on the target feeling or body sensation while in a hypnotic state. The therapist helps to intensify this response by asking for detailed descriptions and associations. Then the subject can be told that the feeling or sensation will be used as a kind of bridge to the past, for example:

> Just allow your unconscious to use this feeling or sensation as a bridge back in time. You can find yourself traveling across this bridge to a time and place in the past when you first experienced this feeling (or sensation). As I count backwards from 10 to 1, you'll find yourself drifting back, to an earlier time, an earlier place. You'll begin to feel smaller and younger, until, by the count of 1, you will be reexperiencing the situation that originally produced that feeling (or body sensation).

The therapist then asks the subject what he is experiencing and begins to explore whatever is taking place.

In some instances, the patient does not return to the original source but regresses to an in-between or even a fairly recent situation where the target feeling or body sensation has been evoked. This kind of response suggests that protection may be needed from the original experience. It is important for the therapist to fully accept and explore the patient's unconscious selection. Clinical judgment must be used to determine whether additional bridging suggestions should be given to achieve an earlier regression during the same or subsequent sessions.

AGE PROGRESSION

As with naturalistic regression, *direct age regression should be followed by orientation of the subject back to the present and into the future.* Many structured suggestions, such as Erickson's crystal ball technique (Erickson, 1952, 1954), can be used to provide a future orientation in time and further integration of dissociated material from the past. For example, the following suggestions can be given after exploration through age regression:

> And now, when you're ready and with the help of your unconscious mind, you can imagine a special crystal ball. In this crystal ball, your unconscious mind can project your future self, as you will be when you have fully integrated the experience from the past that you have discovered today, when it is an asset to you, free of the distressing feelings and reactions you experienced just a few moments ago, when it truly is a *help* to you. Just take a few moments now to allow this to occur. . . . When you have something in mind, just let your head nod "yes" to let me know.

The subject's responses to such suggestions should be fully accepted and explored.

A variation of this technique (Napier, 1993) is to suggest a journey into the future where the individual meets his future self while walking down a pleasant pathway. The patient is given an opportunity to observe the appearance and location of this future self, to engage in an inner dialogue, and even to step into the body of the future self to experience the physical sensations and body posture of the more integrated self.

Because we have discovered (Frederick & Phillips, 1992; Phillips & Frederick, 1992) that age progressions provide ego-strengthening and integrative experiences, as well as prognostic indicators, we routinely introduce age progression into every uncovering experience. More information is provided about the formal uses of age progression in Chapter 5.

Ego-State Therapy Approaches

As discussed in Chapter 4, any hypnotic technique that can be used with an individual patient can be used with an ego state. When working with patients who want to, or are willing to, investigate the origins of current symptoms and difficulties that appear to be post-traumatic, we frequently introduce Ego-State Therapy. Specific indications for this have already been presented; they include an awareness of internal conflicts or fragmented reactions to presenting therapy issues and symptoms (e.g., "Part of me wants to find out what happened and another part is very frightened of knowing"), unproductive responses to other hypnotic approaches, and multiple personality disorder or similar dissociated personality structure.

During the uncovering process, ego states can be activated in any of the ways discussed in Chapter 4. Therapeutic communication can then be established in order to obtain information relevant to current distressing difficulties. The reconstruction of early traumatic experiences can be greatly enhanced by developing a strong therapeutic alliance and negotiating appropriate contracts with ego states who are related to such experiences. Below is a case example that illustrates this approach.

Case Example: Amy

Amy (Phillips, 1993c), a 36-year-old single woman, stated that previous therapy had not gotten to the "root" of her problems, which included hypnagogic sleep disturbances and nightmares, numbing of feelings and difficulty with intimate relationships, intense anxiety and panic feelings at work and when dating men, and frequent episodes of "spacing out" and inability to concentrate. Amy also complained of several psychosomatic problems, including severe, intermittent leg pain that had been diagnosed as phlebitis.

After several introductory sessions following the guidelines described in Chapters 2 and 3, autohypnosis was introduced. This helped Amy to reduce anxiety and panic episodes and dramatically relieved her leg pain. As everyday stress decreased and stabilization increased, Amy reported several disturbing dreams in which her father appeared to be sexually seductive with her. I (MP) suggested Ego-State Therapy as a way of getting in touch with the part of her that might have special knowledge or information that could explain this dream material.

At the beginning of the session where we had planned to initiate Ego-State Therapy, Amy reported the reappearance of her leg pain. I suggested that this pain might somehow be connected to the dream material with her father. Amy was willing to explore this possibility. After a basic hypnotic induction, I introduced the somatic bridge technique, asking Amy to explore thoroughly the pain shooting down her right leg and to follow that body sensation as a bridge back in time to an earlier time and place where she had experienced a similar body sensation. Through ideomotor finger signals, Amy indicated a rapid regression to a scene in the backseat of her father's car, where she saw herself as a little girl about six or seven years old "looking very frightened."

I asked Amy to find out whether she could communicate with the little girl ego state; she reported that she had gotten her attention but that she seemed reluctant to speak to Amy. I then asked Amy's permission to "talk through" (Ross, 1989), to the young ego state and subsequently for her to talk with me through Amy's voice. After establishing verbal communication, I interviewed the "little girl" about the nature of her fear:

MP: Would it be okay to tell me what's happening right now to scare you?

A: *Shakes head no.*

MP: Why can't you tell me? What would happen if you did? Do you know?

A: (*Very soft child's voice*) He'd do something bad to me.

MP: Can you tell me who would do something bad?

A: He told me not to tell. Daddy told me not to tell anyone.

MP: You're afraid of Daddy?

A: *Hesitant head nod yes.*

MP: Can you tell me about the pain in Amy's leg?

A: Yes . . . Daddy mashed it when he was on top of me doing those bad things . . .

During the rest of the session, we retrieved information about a sexual assault by Amy's inebriated father. With the cooperation of the "little girl" ego state, the traumatic experience and several related events were reconstructed and renegotiated in an empowering way (see Chapter 7).

In Amy's case, a slowly built alliance with the "little girl" allowed this important part of Amy to be a full participant in the therapy process. From her verbal and nonverbal communications, it became clear that this ego state contained most of the physical and emotional reactions related to the trauma, as well as most of the cognitive information about what had happened. Failure to identify and involve this dissociated part of Amy's personality most likely would have resulted in a therapy that continued the trend of not getting to the "root" of her problems. With the cooperation of this key ego state, full reassociation of the traumatic experiences with her father became possible, along with eventual resolution of traumatic sequelae.

Accessing and Reconstructing Dissociated Traumatic Experiences: General Guidelines

The therapist's attitude is critically important during the process of retrieving and working through traumatic material from the past. As Herman (1992) points out, it is not enough for the therapist to be neutral or nonjudgmental. The therapist must systematically accept each of the patient's perceptions and recalled internal experiences as a compassionate witness, without making assumptions about either the facts or the meaning of the trauma material to the patient. The therapist must also develop a tolerance for uncertainty and help his patients to do the same, since the details of past experiences may continually change as they are reconstructed through numerous unconscious explorations, particularly if they cannot be sorted with the help of consciously remembered historical information.

WORKING WITH TRAUMATIC MEMORY MATERIAL

Therapists must have a clear understanding of their role. Therapists who wish to approach uncovering work with a focus on social or political activism must be willing to accept appropriate therapy and supervision to project a more balanced, neutral attitude. Responsible hypnotherapists know that child abuse *does* occur, that memory experiences of it frequently appear when hypnoanalytic techniques are used, and that not all memory material produced is subject to verification (see Chapter 1).

When resonating actively and empathically (Watkins, 1978) with the material the patient is sharing, the therapist may simultaneously have various reactions. He may believe that the patient is having a "true memory" of something that happened in the past; he may believe that he is hearing a distorted memory that contains a nucleus of truth but has been distorted by perception or cognition and reworked with other remembered and fantasy material over the years; he may find that he cannot accept the story the patient is telling, as it conflicts with his own beliefs about what is possible.

We believe that the therapist's role is to help the patient discover and deal with the thoughts, feelings, mental images, bodily sensations, and meanings associated with various types of "memory material" or "memory experiences." The assignment of truth and meaning to this material belongs to the patient and not to the therapist. For example, a therapist may believe that a patient was a victim of cultic abuse while the patient believes this is impossible, or vice versa. As difficult as it may be, the therapist must accept that the meaning of the experience belongs solely to the patient. Whenever the therapist undertakes the task of telling the patient what "really" happened instead of helping him discover his *own* truth, the therapist is countertransferentially infantilizing and controlling the patient.

When hypnosis is involved in uncovering work, there are additional considerations. Yapko (1992) warns that experiences recalled through the use of hypnosis are not made more *true*, even though they may become more vivid, more detailed, and therefore seem more convincing. Like lie detector tests, hypnosis can only access certain inner experiences believed to be related to unconsciously dissociated memories. Hypnosis is not refined enough to distinguish between fact and fantasy. For this reason, we do not accept referrals on the basis of using hypnosis to find out whether events such as sexual abuse "really happened." We educate referral sources, potential patients, and the patients within our clinical practices that there is no such thing as "true memory." We point out that an individual's perceptions of events are almost immediately distorted by many factors such as mood, past history, and degree of novelty for the current stimulus (Yapko, 1992). Often, we suggest that the patient recall the last time he attended a party or dinner where several people were in attendance. We ask him to imagine what would happen if we interviewed each person as to his or her memories of the event just an hour following; most patients respond that each person would have a different story to tell even though they all experienced the same basic events. The patient is then asked to apply this principle to events that took place in his own life, sometimes over twenty years earlier.

One reason we use the Ego-State Therapy model with so many of our patients is that it provides a framework for understanding the mechanism of dissociation. Most patients can accept the current understanding about dissociation as a naturally occurring protective mechanism that operates when an individual's normal defenses are overwhelmed (Spiegel, 1986) and also serves as a creative resource to protect personality functioning. Depending on the patient's level of sophistication and need for information, we might further explain that, instead of being the splitting of an already existing whole personality into various parts, dissociation is thought to involve the assigning of traumatic experiences, as they occur, to specific ego centers or states in the personality (Crabtree, 1992; Janet, 1887). In the kind of dissociation that involves the formation of multiple ego states, there is no real amnesia or forgetting. Simply put, the traumatic experiences of a secondary ego state were never available to the primary ego state or ordinary consciousness. In these cases, the therapeutic task is simply one of eliciting the cooperation of all the ego states related to earlier significant traumas so that their knowledge and experiences can be shared.

EXPLAINING THE UNCOVERING PROCESS TO THE PATIENT

To explain the uncovering process, we often use the metaphor of assembling a giant jigsaw puzzle without the picture on the box (Putnam, 1989). Our task is to patiently gather puzzle pieces offered by the unconscious through dreams, hypnotic experiences, current and past symptoms, and responses to various "triggers." As more and more pieces are available, they will begin to fit together naturally until eventually the patient begins to "see" the "whole picture." Often, wanting to resolve intense doubts and conflicting feelings about traumatic material uncovered in hypnosis, the patient will insist that the therapist validate a partial version of events without further exploration, or push for more aggressive retrieval of further "memory" material before dealing with the emotional impact of the details already recovered (Herman, 1992). When this happens, the therapist must gently but firmly remind the patient that the whole story is not yet known and more puzzle pieces need to be collected in an open-minded manner with respectful curiosity. Sometimes we may comment to a patient who persists in these demands, "It is hardly surprising that you seem to want to get this process over with. These feelings may, in fact, be another clue about the kind of traumatic experience you had. Most people who are undergoing an overwhelming stress or are being abused understandably want to 'get it over with.'" This provides further information and reassurance to the patient that his pushing reactions are normal within the context of trauma.

SPECIFIC GUIDELINES FOR MEMORY MATERIAL RETRIEVAL

There are several guidelines that are important to follow in the process of accessing and reconstructing past experiences that may be related to the sources of present symptoms:

1. The therapist's role is one of data collector, not criminal investigator. His task is not to prove any particular hypothesis but to keep collecting information from the patient's conscious and less conscious experiences and to support the patient during an intensive sorting-out process.

2. The patient needs to access only what is helpful in resolving his current symptoms and difficulties; he does not need to recall and work through *every* major trauma. We respect the desires of some patients "not to know" the details of these earlier experiences and support their receiving only that information from the unconscious that will help them make inner adjustments and improve the quality of their lives now.

3. We do not "know" what happened in the past or what was really "true." In fact, we support the patient in accepting the fact that "absolute truth" is never possible to attain, though personal truth can be expanded through the hypnotherapeutic process and will go on being expanded throughout life as part of many different growth experiences.

Abreaction

Traditionally, abreaction is defined as:

> An emotional release or discharge after recalling a painful experience that has been repressed because it was consciously intolerable. A therapeutic effect sometimes occurs through partial discharge or desensitization of the painful emotions and increased insight. (American Psychiatric Association, 1980, p. 1)

Many clinicians believe that abreaction enables therapy to progress more rapidly (Hammond, 1990). Others view abreaction as a way of providing relief to the patient and of resolving hysterical and other psychogenic symptoms related to a traumatic event (Watkins, 1992). Although some dissociative patients may need to experience abreaction as part of working through traumatic experiences, abreaction is no longer considered a primary goal of therapy with these patients, as an end to itself. Instead, emphasis in the trauma literature has shifted recently to mastery of traumatic material, reeducation and cognitive restructuring, continuity of experience, and facilitation of corrective experiences and ego-integration (van der Hart & Brown, 1992).

Specific guidelines for the hypnotic initiation of an abreactive experience include a thorough discussion of the abreactive process with the patient, including indications and contraindications for its use in his particular case. Fears and concerns should be explored thoroughly and the patient reassured that he will be consulted at every juncture and that the therapist will not proceed without his permission. The patient should also be informed that the traumatic experience does not need to be completely explored and resolved in one session. There are ways of pacing the experience so that he can stay in charge and experience mastery over the material.

Next, a general hypnotic induction can be used to guide the subject into a relaxed internal state of readiness. It is helpful to utilize ego-strengthening experiences introduced during stage I, such as recall of a personal "safe place" inside, activation of internal resources such as confidence and strength, and review of previous challenging situations where the patient has achieved mastery. Following this, it is important to ask permission of the subject's unconscious mind to "go back and explore, understand, and *resolve*" (Hammond, 1990, p. 524) whatever happened in the past that is related to the specific symptom the patient is experiencing in the present. Once permission is obtained through ideomotor, ideosensory, or some other signal, any age regression technique can be applied to take the subject back to the time just *before* the traumatic episode; in this way, resources that may have been lost through subsequent amnesia or dissociation can be recovered. This strategy may allow the therapist to assess the patient's pre-traumatic functioning (Watkins, 1992). Additionally, such a technique may help to prevent "blocking" or other resistances that can occur with a more direct, retrospective approach to traumatic experiences (Rossi & Cheek, 1988).

Once the pre-traumatic time has been explored and utilized, the subject can be brought forward in time to the beginning of the relevant traumatic event. Appropriate suggestions can include, "You will find yourself thinking and feeling just as you did then, and everything that you're thinking and feeling, just say out loud" (Hammond, 1990b, p. 524). The therapist continues to encourage the subject to describe his surroundings, as well as what he is thinking, feeling, seeing, hearing, and smelling, throughout the process. The goal is to revivify the experience as much as possible, intensifying relevant affect to the extent that it is useful to the patient. Only after the affect has naturally subsided does the therapist offer reassurance, interpretations, or cognitive structuring.

ABREACTION DO'S AND DON'TS

1. *Proceed cautiously with patients who may have insufficient ego strength.* Make sure there is a strong therapeutic alliance. Use ego-strengthening to prepare the patient or individual ego states for abreactive work. "Test out the waters" with positive age regression experiences that may include abreaction.

2. *Decide on abreaction based on evidence of need from the patient.* The therapist should help to identify evidence of spontaneous abreactions which might include vivid nightmares that seem related to a traumatic event, vivid hypnogogic experiences, conscious flashbacks, and reactions which the individual cannot connect to the past but seem disproportionately related to current circumstances. *Do not initiate* abreactive work based on your own curiosity, or because you think it would be "good" for the patient.

3. *Decide on the abreactive approach that will be used in consultation with the patient.* Discuss and anticipate reactions and outcomes and alternative plans of action that can be activated if the chosen approach is unproductive or overwhelming.

4. *Help to manage the abreaction.* Always set up a "stop signal" that allows for the immediate cessation of the process if the patient feels out of control or flooded. If the patient becomes overwhelmed, be ready to suggest a distancing approach, such as the use of an imaginary "remote control" device that can freeze the action if necessary. Fractionation and titration approaches can allow the patient to "dip into" an inner experience briefly and then "dip out" again to process whatever was activated. If resolution cannot be accomplished in one session, use some type of containing approach to allow the patient to store the material safely (e.g., in a special vault in your office) until the next appointment. *Do not* interrupt an abreactive session because of your own discomfort. This is damaging to the patient; it is better not to begin an abreaction until you are sure you can see it through to completion.

5. *Always formally terminate an abreaction process.* If hypnosis is used, a reverse of the initial induction can be used, like walking back up the stairs. This structure promotes integration of the material and reinforces the importance of internal boundaries. Make sure that the patient is fully oriented to the present situation and that there is at least some time to process immediate reactions. Acknowledge that further integration and processing will be necessary.

6. *Help to set the pace for abreactive work.* It is important not to allow the patient's trauma-driven anxiety to "get it over with" to dictate the movement of therapy.

<h3 style="text-align:center">CAUTIONS WITH ABREACTION</h3>

Most experts currently working in the area of dissociative disorders agree that revivification of a traumatic event and the reliving and cathartic release of emotions are *not* sufficient to provide a successful experience and, if used without appropriate cautions, may result in a malignant or retraumatizing experience (van der Hart & Brown, 1992; Watkins, 1992). Many emphasize the need for a more cognitive approach focused on integration (Brende & Benedict, 1980; Brown & Fromm, 1986; Erickson & Rossi, 1979; Miller, 1986; Peebles, 1989; van der Hart, Steele, Boon, & Brown, 1993). Kluft (1986) has distinguished between abreaction, working-through, and grief work. Braun (1986) and Ross (1989) have stressed the importance of using abreaction within a meaningful and appropriate cognitive framework, which allows the expression of traumatic emotions in a planned, controlled manner followed by debriefing. Others (Hammond, 1990b; Kluft, 1982; Watkins, 1992) have emphasized the necessity of repeating abreactions so that the traumatic event can become neutralized and so that relevant alters and ego states can share what may be separate abreactive experiences of the same event. Van der Hart and his colleagues (1993) have viewed the realization (formulation of cognitive and symbolic meaning) and integration of traumatic experience as an ongoing and crucial part of the therapy process.

Many hypnotic methods are used to protect subjects who become overwhelmed or flooded with affect. These techniques encourage at least partial dissociation or distancing from the event, so that the patient becomes more of an observer, as well as increasing a subjective sense of control, choice, and security in the experience. Kluft (1990a) has suggested the use of an inner library where traumatic events can be stored in specific volumes that can be opened or closed at the patient's initiation; a "slow leak" technique, involving the use of a metaphorical story, which gives the subject permission to recover and release traumatic affects in a slow, intermittent manner; and a fractionated approach, which encourages the subject to "freeze" different aspects of traumatic responses (e.g., experiencing the scene without the feelings but allowing the feelings to surface later during therapeutic discussions and at appropriate times outside of therapy sessions).

Other techniques involve having the patient view the traumatic event on a visualized movie or television screen, through a camera from different angles and through different lenses (Hammond, 1990b), as discussed earlier in this chapter, or even projecting another person who "looks like" the patient and can be a "stand-in" for the patient who participates in the traumatic event while the individual observes and describes the experience (Erickson & Rossi, 1979). Another useful approach, particularly with affect involving anger and rage, is the silent abreaction technique developed by Helen Watkins (1980). Here the hypnotized subject imagines smashing a boulder, which represents the traumatic event (or perpetrator) and all of the related feelings, using a hallucinated sledge hammer in a secluded, safe place. The abreaction takes place internally, providing safety and control for the patient in an office setting that may be less than soundproof. As with other techniques, ego-strengthening and post-traumatic reframing suggestions then follow. More is written about suggestions following abreactive procedures in Chapter 7.

Time distortion can provide further protection for the subject. For example, suggestions can be given to allow certain alters or ego states who are terrified to "sleep through" or otherwise bypass the abreaction (Kluft, 1989), to extend periods of relaxation or "sleep" between periods of abreaction so that minutes of rest seem like hours (Hammond, 1990b), to calibrate completion of the emotional release (e.g., " . . . allow all of the pain that needs to come out to do so during the next X minutes") (Kluft, 1990a), or to move back and forth between past, present, and future time orientations within an abreaction experience.

Regardless of which kinds of abreaction techniques are used, the therapist MUST BE TRAINED IN THESE PROCEDURES. It is unethical to "practice" such approaches on dissociative patients without adequate training and supervised practice. In addition, particularly for less experienced clinicians and hypnotherapists, ongoing supervision and consultation are crucial to ensure that these powerful approaches are used in ways that are truly therapeutic. Abreaction can evoke powerful expressions of feeling that can be frightening for even the most seasoned therapist; we recommend that a therapist not attempt an abreaction experience until he is certain that he can see it through to completion. To interrupt or withdraw from such a procedure, or to try to tone down its intensity to satisfy the therapist's needs, may be more traumatizing for the patient than the original trauma itself. For more on this topic, see Chapter 10.

ALTERNATIVES TO ABREACTION

We advocate and use several alternatives to abreaction. First, with patients where there is significant risk of destabilization or risk of flooding during hypnotic or inner-focused exploration, we often use more structured, indirect approaches to retrieval and processing of past traumatic experiences. This may include having the patient begin by telling a cognitive summary of a memory that is known to him, that is relatively comfortable to talk about, and that has some relevance to current symptoms or difficulties. We encourage patients to tell their narratives first *without* accompanying somatic, affective, or sensory reactions, while we listen without interruption or interpretation (Sachs & Peterson, 1994). Together, we explore the cognitive summary, this time to emphasize resources that were contained in the basic outline of the event. For example, in exploring a remembered incident of sexual or physical abuse, such resources might include the patient's attempts at defense or protection ("spacing out" or dissociating during the experience, numbing of physical pain, decisions not to make noise while being abused for fear of escalating the abuse, etc.), attempts at self-care after the incident, or subsequent decisions about ways of avoiding or minimizing recurrent abuse. These resources are emphasized and expanded to help the patient achieve a further sense of mastery over the event.

If this can be done comfortably with evidence of containment and without spontaneous abreaction, we may encourage the patient to retell the experience, this time pausing to explore when there is expression or indication of sensory and affective components of the "memory." For example, we might ask, "Yes, and when that happened, how did you begin to feel? Do you feel any of that now?" or "What thoughts went through your mind then?" or "As you tell me about this, can you see the place where it happened? Tell me a little now about what you see." If this step can be completed successfully, we may then have the patient make a list of other known experiences, ranked from least to most distressing. We then might proceed, beginning with those least disturbing, to explore further events in this fashion so that the patient begins to develop skill and confidence in exploring fairly familiar traumatic experiences and beginning to connect sensory responses. Such a structured procedure, designed to ensure mastery experiences and strengthen coping skills (Sachs & Peterson, 1994), can lead the way for use of more internal focusing (perhaps using hypnosis), and exploration of lesser known and more threatening traumatic experiences. It also can provide opportunities for cognitive restructuring by the therapist of such beliefs as, "It was my fault somehow," "I could have made sure it didn't happen again," "There's no way I'm ever going to be able to put this behind me." This process can also be augmented by the use of journaling, creative arts, and sandtray work to expand understandings of the experience.

Van der Hart and his colleagues (1993) have described a structured approach, based on the previous work of several experts, called "parallel synthesis." This procedure, designed for MPD patients, involves compiling a written account of a traumatic event which has been divided into 10 segments, based on the stories of various alters. During hypnosis, those alters who are to synthesize their versions of the traumatic experience are brought forward, and those who have been designated by prior agreement to withdraw from the experience are instructed to go to previously established safe places for protection from the information. The therapist then counts from 1 to 10, beginning with 1 at the beginning of the trauma, and ending with 10, when the event has ended. Each segment mentioned by the therapist is preceded by its designated number. During the synthesis experience, which is marked by the various numbers, all involved alters are invited to share their versions of the experience with each other, so that the account becomes unified and relieves the dissociative barriers. This process can be repeated several times, interspersed with hypnotic experiences of resting and ego-strengthening, until the patient indicates that an adequate percentage of the experience has been synthesized successfully.

A second alternative to formal abreaction is the somatic experiencing approach developed by Peter Levine (1991). Here, patients are encouraged to begin with any component of the SIBAM model of experience that is currently known to them (sensation, image or internal sensory representation, behavior or movement, affective feeling). The therapist carefully tracks the reported internal experience of each component; no formal trance induction is used and patients may have their eyes open or closed. As the tracking proceeds, spontaneous associational bridges (cognitive, sensory, physiological, and affective) move the patient through other elements of the SIBAM model. We have found that patients may be less likely to "flood" during this procedure than during hypnosis, and find it especially useful with patients with somatic symptoms and heightened body sensitivity. More information about this approach is included in Chapter 7. A short case example is given below.

Case Example: Monica

Monica is a 52-year-old woman with a history of known incest experiences with her brother, and a strong but vague sense of sexual abuse with her father. Recently diagnosed with breast cancer, she had a lumpectomy to remove a tumor on her left breast. She had always felt "squeamish" about lovers touching her breasts. Now she was in a state of panic because her doctors had recommended monthly self-examinations and professional examinations every six months. Thoughts of explorations of her breasts by herself or others made her "nauseous." Monica sought hypnotherapy with me (MP) to help her with this difficulty.

After careful preparation and introductory experiences with hypnosis following the guidelines in Chapters 2 and 3, we began hypnotic exploration of her reactions to her breasts using ideomotor finger signaling. Despite provisions of internal safety and containment, Monica became

overwhelmed by fear and unable to focus. We ended hypnotic exploration and discussed other alternatives.

After explaining the SIBAM model to her, I asked her to simply sit
quietly for a moment, begin to think about her breasts, and report to
me her internal reactions. The following exchange took place:

> M: I notice that my stomach is very tight and a little queasy.
>
> MP: What else are you aware of?
>
> M: I'm thinking of my brother. I remember him as a little boy,
> about five years old. He was so trusting of me. It makes me
> want to cry . . . (*sobs*).
>
> MP: And as you think of him and feel that sadness, . . . is there
> anything else that you notice now?
>
> M: I notice that I'm feeling calmer. My stomach is a little more
> relaxed . . . now I see a picture of him and me on the bath-
> room floor. I think we're playing sexually. I feel worried be-
> cause I know we're doing something my parents wouldn't like,
> and they might come home at any minute, but it feels good to
> touch this way and I want to keep on doing it.

This was followed by retrieval of other details of sexual and nonsexual
experiences with her brother and related somatic, sensory, affective, and
postural movement responses. At no time did she feel overwhelmed,
and at the end of the experience, Monica stated that she had never been
able to focus on those experiences in such a helpful way.

After several more such sessions, accompanied by outside activities of journaling and painting a watercolor of her breast as she wanted to be able to view
it, Monica began to initiate self-exploration of her breasts during bubble
baths. Eventually, she was able to experience breast examinations with significantly more emotional and physical comfort and to enjoy having her breasts
touched during sex. She is beginning now in therapy to discuss the possibility
of exploring early experiences unknown to her that may be related to other
anxiety symptoms.

Once abreaction or other means of accessing traumatic experience has been
initiated and completed, the therapist must use approaches to reassociate,
renegotiate, and resolve the original traumatic event. These procedures are
described in the next chapter.

7

RESOLVING DISSOCIATED EXPERIENCES

Clinical experts in the field of dissociative conditions agree that the uncovering of traumatic or other dissociated material must be followed by extensive and ongoing processing and working-through of related feelings, cognitions, imagery, and body sensations (Brende & Benedict, 1980; Grinker & Spiegel, 1945; Putnam, 1989; Spiegel, 1981). Systematic methods of using hypnosis to reassociate dissociated experiences at a conscious level of awareness, renegotiate the original traumatic experience utilizing present-day adult resources, and restabilize the patient's ego functioning will be reviewed in this chapter.

Reassociating Dissociated Experiences

Putnam (1989) points out that, if traumatic material that has been recovered through hypnosis and/or relived through abreaction is not brought into conscious awareness within a short time after the original retrieval, "much of it may be redissociated, re-repressed, or otherwise blocked from conscious recall" (p. 247). Thus, helping the patient reassociate, or reconnect with, traumatic experiences after her initial recall is a therapeutic task as essential as the uncovering process itself.

ORGANIZING TRAUMATIC MATERIAL

The first and perhaps most basic intervention following the emergence of dissociated material during hypnosis is to help the patient recall and organize the material in some type of coherent form in a conscious waking state. Herman (1992) suggests that "patient and therapist slowly reassemble an organized, detailed, verbal account, oriented in time and historical context" derived from the fragmented components of imagery, body sensations, emotional responses, and fantasy or symbolic material that may have surfaced during hypnotic regression, abreaction experiences, or other types of explorations.

Therapy sessions that are focused on dissociated traumatic experiences should be followed by sessions focused on acknowledging feelings, associations, and responses to the emerging material. Patients must be asked directly what they remember from uncovering experiences and about their subsequent reactions to them. Although the therapist must be respectful of patients' tendencies to avoid processing traumatic material by discussing other topics, and even by introducing crisis situations, she must redirect the focus of the session back to the traumatic material in the following manner:

> I'm noticing that you have not brought up what we explored here during the last session. What you're talking about today is also very important, but I'm interested in knowing what you remember from our last session and how you've been thinking and feeling about all that you experienced. If you're not ready to talk about it, or are feeling uncomfortable about doing so, I'd like to explore those feelings as well.

McCann and Pearlman (1990) point out that many resistances can emerge in the course of exploring dissociated memory material, including the fear of not being believed, the concern that the recovered traumatic experiences are not "real," the belief that the therapist may be repulsed or disgusted by the details of the trauma, the fear of confronting the patient's own reactions to the trauma, including overpowering feelings of shame, rage, and helplessness, and the concern that talking about the uncovered material will only make the patient feel worse. These apprehensions need to be identified and explored in detail.

The therapist must offer specific reassurances to such fears and include explicit information about her own approach to working with traumatic material. We tell our patients that these kinds of fears are a normal part of uncovering and working with dissociated experiences and that we fully expect that they will appear often during this stage of therapy. We remind them that we will attempt to find a pace that is effective for them; if they begin to feel worse or to deteriorate in some way, this will be a signal that the pacing needs to be adjusted until they feel in control and stabilized again. We discuss ways of titrating the discussion of memory material, such as fractionated recall; the importance of utilizing inner resources that begin to transform the material into a healing experience; and the necessity of taking as much time as needed to complete the processing of one dissociated experience before moving on to others. We reassure patients that they will not be pushed or encouraged to talk about more than they are ready for and that we can offer immediate assistance to decrease distress that might arise when discussing or recalling the uncovered material, including help in closing down the process completely.

Severely dissociated and MPD patients may have little or no recall of an abreactive or hypnotic regression experience. One way of handling this difficulty is to use audiotaping or videotaping to provide direct feedback following uncovering sessions (Caul, 1984; Hall, Le Cann, & Schoolar, 1978). The therapist may also choose to summarize the traumatic details for the patient, after thorough exploration of whatever details the patient does remember related to the session. We prefer to help highly dissociated patients develop ways of staying as present as they wish during abreactive and hypnotic uncovering sessions. The "host" or executive ego state can be taught to create a safe listening or viewing room, for example, from which she can hear and watch another ego state's account of a traumatic event at a safe distance. Such an internal room can be created with the use of hypnotic imagery and "tested" for safety and adequate functioning during practice sessions.

Another important issue with these kinds of patients is the recognition, acceptance, and resolution of contradictory versions of traumatic events that may occur during therapy. In some cases the patient may have told the therapist one version of the events and yet have revealed a very different version during an abreaction or hypnotic uncovering session (Putnam, 1989). In other cases, a single event, when explored by several ego states or alters, will be experienced in very different and sometimes conflicting ways. The therapist must help the patient accept each version and work toward a resolution of contradictory details.

Sometimes it is helpful to go through the sequence of a traumatic event several times during one session. The patient can be encouraged to view each repetition from a different perspective, in "fast motion" or "freeze frame," or through a different camera lens. With each reexperiencing of the dissociated event, therapist and patient gather more details and conflicting perceptions become clearer. The therapist must be alert for breaks in the continuity of a recalled experience. Many (Kluft, 1982; Putnam, 1989; Rosen & Myers, 1947) have observed that repeated abreaction with interspersed sessions focused on the recovered material may be necessary for full uncovering of traumatic events.

One way of promoting the resolution of contradictory perceptions and emotional reactions is to structure opportunities for ego states to share their different perceptions with each other, much as family members would discuss their memories of a commonly experienced event. This kind of reassociation requires well-developed lines of internal communication; the absence of such links is an important reason why premature attempts to uncover and abreact traumatic material frequently fail (Putnam, 1989). The "parallel synthesis" procedure (van der Hart et al., 1993), described in Chapter 6, offers a structured way of involving alters with different versions of a traumatic event to share and synthesize their experiences. Helen Watkins (Watkins & Watkins, 1991) has introduced an internal therapy room where all of the ego states involved in a particular experience, for example, can sit together (with or without the therapist introject) to discuss particular memory material. Caul (1984) has reported the use of similar techniques. Such approaches help to facilitate co-consciousness among various ego states in the personality and to promote a sense of continuity of various time sequences.

Once sufficiently consistent information has been obtained related to a specific traumatic experience, the therapist can help the patient further organize this material through the construction of a visual time line. This records the basic details about traumatic events along with other positive milestones that give a more complete, accurate view of the development of the patient's life (Dolan, 1991). Many patients find this concrete approach to be very calming and integrative following uncovering work. Other types of artwork such as photography, painting, and sculpture can supplement this process (Greenberg & van der Kolk, 1987).

Similarly, patients can be encouraged to keep a daily journal in which they write reactions to emerging traumatic material. Highly dissociated and MPD patients can use this approach to work toward co-consciousness, with various ego states taking turns writing and commenting on others' accounts (Ross, 1989). Other patients can benefit from writing exercises that allow ego states who are in conflict about the occurrence or form of traumatic events to converse, write letters to each other, and otherwise begin to integrate the patient's complex reactions to uncovered traumatic material (Torem, 1993b, 1994). Many individuals can also be encouraged to pursue creative writing activities as an additional way to reassociate experiences.

COGNITIVE RESTRUCTURING

An important aspect of reassociating and resolving dissociated traumatic experiences from the past is the identification and transformation of erroneous and distorted cognitive beliefs. Fine (1990) points out that for many of those who endure traumatic experiences, such as incest, reality has been shattered. These individuals then reconstruct a world view based on "distorted beliefs and misguided assumptions that will determine their causal attributions, set up their strategies for predicting outcomes, and dictate their life views" (p. 163). She has listed ten cognitive distortions that are common among victims of childhood sexual abuse, which are also applicable to those who have experienced other types of dissociated traumas: dichotomous (e.g., black/white, all/nothing, good/bad) thinking, selective abstraction, arbitrary inference, overgeneralization, catastrophizing, time distortion, distortions of self-perceptions, excessive responsibility, circular thinking, and misassuming causality.

Others have discussed various cognitive schemas that can be disrupted by early experiences of abuse and trauma. These include frame of reference (e.g., causality, hope for the future, and locus of control), safety, trust/dependency, independence, power, esteem, and intimacy (McCann & Pearlman, 1990). Ross (1989) has presented erroneous core beliefs that are often present in MPD patients. These assumptions are: different parts of the self are separate selves; the victim is responsible for the abuse; it is wrong (or dangerous) to show feelings; the past is present; the primary personality can't handle the memories; I love my parents but she (i.e., the main personality) hates them; the primary personality must be punished.

Although the degree of cognitive impairment is affected by such factors as age of onset of the traumatic or abusive experience, the intensity of traumatic stimuli, and the duration of early traumata, there is no doubt that cognitive inflexibility will impair the individual in her adjustment to a nontraumatic environment (Fine, 1990). The task of the therapist is to assess the nature of cognitive disruption and begin to confront, challenge, and change flawed thinking and beliefs.

One approach for cognitive intervention is to use the BASK (Braun, 1988) model of dissociation (*b*ehavior, *a*ffect, *s*ensation, or *k*nowledge) to monitor the various aspects of the patient's experience that have been disrupted by trauma. The therapist can use a Socratic method of questioning to identify the cognitive errors related to knowledge and then to facilitate dissonance followed by cognitive reframing (Fine, 1990).

Ross (1989) outlines a similar approach involving revealing inconsistencies in the individual's logic structure when dealing with such faulty beliefs as, "The victim is responsible for the abuse." He advocates first attempting to help the patient or individual alter examine her beliefs about children in general, such as the premise that children are not responsible for traumatic things that happen to them, e.g., having to move to a new city or losing their parents in a car accident. He inquires more specifically about whether the patient believes that children who are being sexually abused currently in the same city are at fault for what is done to them. Next he asks, if this is true for all other children, why isn't it true for the patient herself? What makes her so "special and different that she's the only child in the world who is responsible for her abuse?" (Ross, 1989, p. 264).

Jehu, Klassen, and Gazan (1985) identify several cognitive techniques that can be used to interrupt or restructure belief systems related to early abuse experiences. These include:

- Providing information
- Analyzing logic to determine whether evidence supports the conclusion drawn

- Decatastrophizing
- Distancing (i.e., helping the patient shift from a subjective to an objective perspective on her beliefs)
- Reattributing or reassigning responsibility
- Assigning activities designed to disconfirm distorted beliefs and confirm more accurate ones.

Stress inoculation training has been useful in helping rape victims with fear, anxiety, and phobic reactions (Veronen & Kilpatrick, 1983). Such an approach emphasizes an analysis of cognitions and internal dialogue and images, followed by muscle relaxation, breath control, imaginal role-playing, thought stoppage, and guided self-dialogue to interrupt negative cognitions. Courtois (1988) points out that behavioral techniques used to change target behaviors, such as stress management training, desensitization, relaxation, assertiveness training, anger management, problem-solving, goal-setting, decision-making, and sex therapy, may lead to subsequent changes in cognition and affect. She also suggests that guided imagery and metaphor, used separately or in conjunction with hypnosis and relaxation, can help the patient break through stereotypical thinking and imagine alternatives.

Ego-State Therapy Approaches

Dealing only with affective responses to emerging traumatic material without examining and correcting related cognitive schema can be retraumatizing to patients and leave them at risk for further victimization (Fine, 1990). We usually approach this task through the use of Ego-State Therapy.

Case Example: Amy (Part II) (See Chapter 6 for Part I)

Amy (Phillips, 1993c) had uncovered the possibility of sexual abuse by her father through hypnotic ego-state work. As "adult" Amy began to feel and express anger toward her father for molesting her, the "little girl" ego state became fearful of punishment by her father. This conflict reflects the disruption of several cognitive beliefs and schema: The past is present, or time distortion (*the abuse is still happening and I am in danger*); disturbed safety schema (*I am not safe anywhere*); it is wrong to show anger (*if I never show anger, I will not be abused*); and the victim is responsible for the abuse (*I deserve to be punished for being angry*) (Fine, 1990; McCann & Pearlman, 1990; Ross, 1989).

Even though the "adult" ego state understood that her father was not present and could no longer hurt her, the "child" was frightened and unmoved by attempts to point out discrepancies in her thinking. What worked in this case was helping the "little girl" Amy learn about constancy as it related to safety by creating through imagery a safe place in the form of a high tower. During several sessions, she had numerous experiences which convinced her that no one from within or without could find or invade her tower without her full knowledge and permission.

Conflicting needs were negotiated. Agreements were made with "adult" Amy about expressing her anger only during therapy sessions when "little Amy" felt safe in her tower and could receive reassurance afterwards. Eventually, more complete expression of all trauma-related affect was possible with full cooperation of both ego states.

Another ego-state therapy approach to cognitive restructuring is to identify ego states that hold more highly developed beliefs. The therapist can then create an appropriate situation where those with more functional and flexible cognitions can educate the more affected or impaired ego states, as in the case of Barbara.

Case Example: Barbara

Barbara, a dissociative disorder patient with a binge-eating disorder who had experienced ritualized sexual abuse by her father and uncle, had uncovered, abreacted, and begun to reassociate many of the traumatic events from her childhood and adolescence. As she became aware at a conscious level of the many layers of fear related to these experiences, she also began to realize how various terrified ego states used food to provide additional protection from men who might be attracted to a slender body and want to touch her. As we explored the fears of these ego states, one, "The Shamer," who admitted initiating much of the overeating behavior, stated her belief that Barbara was responsible for the sexual abuse because she found it partly pleasurable; therefore, she should be punished by the guilt she felt when overeating.

I (MP) "called out" several other ego states who believed that adults were responsible for physical, emotional, and sexual abuse to children, regardless of the child's behavior. They confronted "The Shamer," explaining that the fact that her body responded was a biological reaction and did not indicate cooperation or consent. I reinforced these ego states and added an example: If, while ironing, an individual accidentally touched her finger to the hot iron and raised a blister, that did not prove that she "enjoyed" burning her finger—only that the finger had a biological blister response to the hot stimulus (Ross, 1989). This only temporarily satisfied "The Shamer," who remarked, "Well, that might explain her response the first time it happened, but once she realized what would happen when she was touched that way, she should have put a stop to it. What would you say about someone who kept on burning her finger over and over again?"

The helper ego states agreed that more education was needed and a "master teacher" ego state came forward who had taken some courses in child development and knew about Piaget. The "master teacher" met with "The Shamer" during private internal sessions and took her through a series of deductive and inductive reasoning exercises to expand her cognitive schema.

In addition, the "Internal Dad" ego state, who held the belief that sex was all that mattered and love was "too much trouble," became willing to be educated about different types of love by "spiritual guide" ego states in order to end his inner isolation and gain more acceptance by other parts of Barbara's personality. He began to learn about touch that was comforting rather than sexual and about the benefits of loving someone else and being loved in an unselfish way.

As these cognitive learnings took place, and several child ego states who were afraid and needed the protection of food began to create other forms of internal protection and safety, Barbara's binge-eating episodes decreased. Gradually, over several months, she began to change her patterns of eating and lose weight as she integrated more functional cognitive beliefs.

EPISODES OF DEPERSONALIZATION AND DEREALIZATION

Some dissociative patients report experiences of feeling "unreal" sensations of being detached from or outside of their bodies, or feeling like they are in a dream world and have lost their identities. These episodes may occur before beginning work on traumatic experiences, or they may appear during the course of the work as traumatic material is reassociated.

Generally, the therapist must accept and understand these experiences as very disturbing dissociative responses, and reassure the patient that she is not "going crazy." Often, such symptoms are very difficult to work with, since the patient is unable to connect with herself or the world around her in the usual, familiar ways.

We often utilize these symptoms as we would other types of dissociative phenomena (see Chapter 6): as clues to past reactions to the original trauma experience, as possible signals for the need for protection from retraumatization during the therapy process, or as indicators that slower pacing and additional attention to the integration of traumatic material into personality functioning may be needed.

We also use Ego-State Therapy, if indicated, for further exploration of these types of symptoms. One patient who was experiencing these types of episodes discovered that, during times when he felt "unlike himself" or experienced the world as "unreal," an ego state was present who claimed that he did not need to be in the body or in the outside world. Though not malevolent, this ego state, who called himself "Mr. Wonderful," clung tenaciously to the narcissistic delusion that he was "a figment of his own imagination" and needed nothing more. Several sessions were needed to form an adequate therapeutic alliance. Finally "Mr. Wonderful" trusted the therapist (MP) enough to explore what it would be like to be inside the patient's body for a minute or two. This was a powerful experience for him, and after several more such guided experiences, he acknowledged that he had never had a "place to belong," and ultimately decided that being fully "inside" the patient's body brought him more satisfying options. Subsequently, the patient reported greater personality integration and the incidents of depersonalization and derealization ceased.

Other approaches to these types of dissociative symptoms are reported in Chapter 14.

MANAGING INTRUSIVE TRAUMATIC MATERIAL

Sometimes during the course of reassociating and resolving traumatic material, fragments of "memory," including images, emotional feelings, and body sensations, become intrusive and overwhelming. Often, affects and sensory experiences that relate to the traumatic material can stimulate intense emotional states that the patient experiences as crisis; additionally, the anniversary of a traumatic event or details related to that event can evoke strong reactions (McCann & Pearlman, 1990), as can other events that resemble or symbolize the original trauma (Peterson, Prout, & Schwarz, 1991).

The literature on therapy for dissociative and post-traumatic experiences suggests several ways for managing this kind of overwhelming and intrusive material. Guidelines for managing fluctuating states of intrusion and denial include supporting the patient in reducing external demands, making plans for rest, relaxation, and exercise, temporary use of anti-anxiety medications, systematic desensitization, and encouraging the "dosing" or titration of traumatic material by helping the patient shift focus away from traumatic stimuli and then move slowly and safely back into it again (Horowitz, 1976).

A variety of cognitive-behavioral approaches have been used to manage intrusive symptoms with reported success, e.g., behavioral rehearsal to resolve startle and anxiety responses (Fairbank, De Good, & Jenkins, 1981), and stress inoculation training to manage trauma-related anxiety and rage through the use of relaxation techniques and cognitive coping skills, including positive self-dialogue (Ayalon, 1983; Novaco, 1977; Veronen & Kilpatrick, 1983).

Others have advocated the use of flooding or implosive techniques, a variation of systematic desensitization. This involves direct exposure to traumatic stimuli, such as intrusive images, coupled with relaxation training. There is some evidence that this approach may be associated with reduced anxiety and incidence of intrusive symptoms (Keane & Kaloupek, 1982; McCaffrey & Fairbank, 1985; Veronen & Kilpatrick, 1983). However, most of the outcome studies have been conducted only with Vietnam veterans or with very small samples without control groups. Since this technique involves recreating trauma conditions, which can evoke lack of control or intense helplessness, we prefer to use approaches that give more control and initiative to the patient. These are discussed below.

Self-hypnotic Approaches

In addition to self-management approaches advocated by Horowitz (1974, 1976) and cognitive-behavioral strategies, self-hypnosis is helpful during this stage of therapy in mobilizing the ego strength of the patient to cope with intrusive trauma material.

In some cases, it may be important to explore the patient's metacommunications, or self-suggestions, during intrusive experiences. For example, patients who are fearful when trauma-related images or intense body sensations sometimes appear following uncovering sessions, discover the following kinds of negative self-suggestions in their reactions: "Oh, no. Now I really am going crazy. I'm out of control. It feels like I might die. . . . Death must be better than this. I just can't take this anymore. . . . I'm so screwed up—I'll never get any better and this proves it." In exploring such anxiety-provoking reactions, the therapist points out that such suggestions provoke more fear, self-devaluation, and a very negative "trance" state. As patients learn to identify these kinds of thoughts through writing assignments or just by focusing on their internal self-dialogue during intrusive experiences, they become able to substitute more positive self-suggestions such as: "I know this is related to the work I'm doing in therapy. It's another piece of the puzzle from my unconscious. From past experience, I know it will pass in a few minutes and then I can do some writing about it. I'm going to get comfortable now and begin to relax my body so that I can begin to experience a positive state of self-hypnosis." With practice, this kind of self-intervention not only helps to modulate intense affect, but can also create a sense of mastery over the traumatic material and increase the patient's capacity for self-soothing (McCann & Pearlman, 1990; McNeal & Frederick, 1994).

Another self-hypnotic approach involves the use of imagery to attach positive associational cues and anchors (Gilligan, 1987) to anxiety-provoking stimuli. For example, a patient who is bothered by intrusive thoughts of self-loathing following uncovering sessions may imagine that these thoughts are like leaves floating on the stream of her conscious awareness. She can watch as they drift toward her until she sees them more clearly, and then float down the stream and disappear out of her sight. A related image during more overwhelming times is that of a waterfall; the patient can imagine standing under this waterfall, allowing the thoughts and feelings to pass over her and continue moving with great speed down the stream, where they tumble over and between rocks, splitting and breaking apart, until they completely disappear. At some point, the patient may notice that her experience is changing and that the waterfall seems more real, that she can actually feel the spray, hear the sounds more clearly, and smell the damp, clean smells around the falls. Other techniques include the use of real-life anchors, such as listening to music that reminds the patient of a happy, carefree time in her life; holding the car keys, which remind her of here-and-now autonomy and freedom; or using other current symbols of comfort and safety (Dolan, 1991). For example, Zoe, who experienced intense panic episodes, learned to evoke calming responses connected with playing the piano, using a piano charm that she first carried in her hand, then wore as a necklace, and eventually replaced with imagery.

A third self-hypnotic strategy involves the development of a special inner sanctuary or safe place where the patient can retreat internally. Here the patient can spend time exploring a private beach, beautiful garden, or other natural setting, or engage in absorbing activities such as painting or listening to a favorite selection of music in an inner study or studio. This strategy is particularly useful with patients who do not have a strong external support system or access to the types of private settings that can be easily imagined. With those who are highly dissociated, it is important to suggest that *each* ego state or alter imagine the safe place in its own way (Kluft, 1989).

Another approach involves creating symbolic containers to hold the intruding traumatic material. For example, Kluft (1989) describes the "time-lock technique," where the patient imagines a strong vault into which the intrusive feelings, images, and thoughts are placed. The vault or other secure container can be stored in the therapist's office or some other safe location. (One patient imagined his vault, which contained intrusive feelings related to sexual abuse by his older cousin, in a special submarine on the ocean floor off the coast of an obscure group of islands.) The patient then sets the timer to open at the beginning of the next therapy session or some other appropriate time. Other patients choose actual objects, such as boxes with lids or other containers, where they can symbolically place traumatic material until they are ready to deal with it (Napier, 1993).

Directives and Self-Utilization Approaches

Another approach to the management of intrusive traumatic experiences involves therapeutic tasks and directives. Derived from a utilization perspective, these tasks elicit each individual's unaccessed potentials or resources, while creating new learning related to the therapeutic goal (Zeig, 1986).

For example, a patient may become aware that feelings of rage surface after uncovering traumatic material related to an early experience of incest. The feelings may continue to be dissociated at first; that is, the anger may surface in life situations where the patient becomes disproportionately outraged. The therapeutic goal is to provide a way to reassociate the feelings to the trauma in such a way that the patient can experience mastery and control over the experience. The case example below illustrates one indirect way of reassociating post-traumatic feelings of anxiety, so that the patient stayed in complete control of the process. Similar approaches (e.g., using journaling or letter-writing activities) can be used for preliminary reassociation of other powerful post-traumatic emotions, including anger and rage, and may be more likely to promote self-paced mastery than techniques that require more direct emotional expression.

Case Example: Meredith

In the case of Meredith (Phillips, 1993b), intense feelings of terror and helplessness related to experiences of sexual abuse by her psychiatrist as an adolescent had become displaced onto tasks involving paperwork and responding to daily mail. I (MP) told Meredith that I believed that her feelings of fear and victimization really fit more closely with her recently uncovered experiences with Dr. F. I wondered whether the word "mail" might have a special meaning for her unconscious mind. She immediately commented that it was as if "mail" had become "male" in her mind, and that her fear reactions seemed to reflect that shift.

Since she had only partially uncovered the sexual abuse experiences in hypnosis, indicating through ideomotor signals that she was not ready to know more about them, I utilized her rather obsessive personality style to suggest that she thoroughly explore her reactions to paperwork by writing down her feelings and thoughts in great detail in a daily journal. I told her that I believed this might be a productive way of accessing her feelings about Dr. F. without the pain of confronting them more directly.

For several weeks, Meredith faithfully recorded all of her reactions to the paperwork dilemma, including her intense feelings of shame, anger, helplessness, and fear; we spent each session reading and discussing her entries together. Whenever she expressed interest in talking about other topics in our therapy sessions, I gently but firmly steered her back to the paperwork issue, explaining that we must be very diligent in processing the symbolic expressions of her unconscious emotions. Eventually, she told me that she was tired of talking about the paperwork, that she was ready to focus again on her experiences with Dr. F., that she wanted to find out more of the details of what had happened through hypnosis, and that she believed the paperwork difficulties would resolve themselves. Hypnotic exploration was then resumed, and Meredith was now able to reassociate her internal images and sensory experiences with full affect.

Whenever the anxiety symptoms related to answering and sorting the "mail" resurface, she is learning to work with them on her own, using them as a symbolic avenue back to the deeper feelings about the sexual trauma, which she is able to express in her journal. Using this approach, Meredith is developing a sense of mastery over her trauma responses and achieving greater reassociation and integration of feelings.

Other patients may respond to more straightforward directives. Some benefit from such rituals as writing down the trauma responses, reading them, and then burning them (de Shazer, 1985). Individuals who don't respond to writing tasks may be able to express feelings of anger, fear, or sadness on an audiotape, gradually adding to it until they believe they have fully expressed their reactions (Dolan, 1991). Another possibility is to calibrate responses to intruding traumatic material (Napier, 1993), such as looking at traumatic images for one to five seconds before initiating a positive, here-and-now activity, or focusing on emotional or sensory reactions for up to a full minute, choosing not to act on them while searching for possible triggers from past experiences, and then shifting to more positive body-based experiences such as taking a walk or soaking in a hot bath. These kinds of therapeutic tasks teach patients that they have many choices about coping with intrusive traumatic reactions and seed the possibility of eventual control over these experiences.

Renegotiating and Transforming Traumatic Experiences

The primary treatment focus during this phase should be on ego-integration of the dissociated material (Brende, 1985; Brende & Benedict, 1980; Brown & Fromm, 1986; Horowitz, 1986; Spiegel, 1981, 1986, 1990; van der Hart

& Brown, 1992; van der Hart, Brown, & van der Kolk, 1989; Watkins, 1992). In addition to helping the patient uncover and reexperience traumatic events that have been dissociated, the therapist must focus on helping patients transform their experience of the trauma in some way. Simply assisting the patient in reliving the trauma is not sufficient for healing and may, in fact, prove retraumatizing. The therapeutic difference is helping the patient to make new meaning out of the old experience (Peterson, Prout, & Schwarz, 1991) and to have an emotionally "corrective" experience (Watkins, 1992). This section presents several methods that can help in the transformation and renegotiating process.

IDEODYNAMIC HEALING APPROACHES

The ideodynamic approach is based on state-dependent theory, which holds that dissociated or state-dependent memories remain active at unconscious levels and precipitate psychological and psychosomatic conditions (Ellenberger, 1970; Rossi, 1993a; Rossi & Cheek, 1988). The inner search for and accessing of unconscious potentials are initiated through a series of suggestions that ratify the use of unconscious processes for problem resolution. Then unconscious potentials can be used to reframe the original negative experience as a positive challenge. Reframing can be encouraged in several ways, such as suggesting that the subject review the past experience or memory related to the current difficulty as an objective bystander while wondering how the unconscious can help to resolve this in a creative way, or by accessing inner resources that were not available at the time of the original traumatic event and reviewing the original experiences in light of these current strengths.

As part of the therapeutic reframing, suggestions and opportunities are given for creative transformation of the initial problem. This is facilitated by such questions as: "Is there anything else we need to know so that you can resolve this situation?" or "Is there anything else that would help you begin to heal from this experience?" Once essential healing resources are elicited and applied to the relevant past experience underlying current difficulties, the therapist establishes a future orientation to promote continued healing and coping through suggestions such as, "Would it be okay to go forward in time now to a moment when you have fully resolved this situation?" and "When your inner mind knows that it can continue with this healing process of resolution all by itself, letting your conscious mind have whatever information it needs to participate, your yes finger will lift." At each step of the process, if a "yes" response is not obtained to ratify therapeutic progress, questioning cycles are repeated until satisfactory responses are obtained.

Case Example: John

John was referred for hypnotherapy to address severe insomnia. In his primary therapy, he had worked through many of his reactions to incest that occurred during adolescence and had resolved some of the symptoms typical of many PTSD patients, such as panic attacks, hypnagogic experiences, and difficulties with concentration and focus. His insomnia persisted, however, and seemed to be triggered by early morning trucks that passed his house.

John was agreeable to hypnosis, which he had used successfully to stop smoking several years before. The first few sessions were spent introducing John to hypnosis using the guidelines in Chapters 2 and 3. The next three sessions were spent using a variety of direct and indirect suggestions related to sleep continuity and reframing of the truck noises. When John had little or no response to this approach, I (MP) suggested ideodynamic exploration. John was amenable to this but expressed some reservations about opening up "too much" from the past, wanting only to resolve the sleep problem so he could continue on with other therapy. He had been told that his birth was quite difficult and specifically did not want to get into a "birth trauma" experience. He was reassured that this approach would give him maximum control and choice about exploring any past experiences.

Once "yes," "no," and "I'm not ready to say" finger signals were established, the following interaction took place (ideomotor responses are in boldface):

MP: Does John's unconscious mind understand the source of his current sleep difficulty?

J: **Yes.**

MP: Would it be okay to explore the source of the sleep problem at a conscious level now?

J: **Yes.**

MP: Was the source of the problem before the age of 20?

J: **Yes.**

MP: Was the source of the problem before the age of 15?

J: **Yes.**

MP: Was it before the age of 10? . . . Before the age of 5? . . . Before the age of 2?

J: **Yes . . . yes . . . no.**

MP: Just to verify . . . Was the source of the sleep problem between the ages of 2 and 5?

J: **Yes.**

MP: Is there anything John needs to know about this time in his life in order to resolve his insomnia?

J: **Yes.**

MP: John, just drift a little deeper and allow this information to come into your awareness. It may be in the form of a thought, feeling, image, or body sensation, . . . or perhaps as a voice that you hear. . . .When you're ready, just tell me what you're becoming aware of.

J: I'm thinking of the birth of my little brother. I was about two-and-a-half years old and it was a hard time for me. . . . Now I have an image of my parents fighting with each other. It was very disturbing.

MP: Does John's unconscious believe that this inner disturbance he felt in the past as a little boy is similar to the disturbance John feels when he hears the trucks in the present?

J: **Yes.**

MP: Does John's unconscious believe that his life is very different now, that he is safe and secure in his life now even though the feelings may be similar to the ones back then?

J: **Yes.**

MP: Does John's unconscious believe that there are adult resources that were not available back then that can be added to resolve his past fears as well as the ones that now disturb his sleep?

J: **Yes.**

MP: Is John now free to sleep through the night without being disturbed by the trucks?

J: **Yes.**

MP: Is John's unconscious mind willing to continue to work with his conscious mind so that full resolution of this problem is achieved and to share additional information about the source of this problem at a time and in a way that will be completely helpful and healing to him?

J: **Yes.**

MP: And now I'd like to suggest that you drift on into the future to a moment when your insomnia has been completely resolved and you are enjoying full nights of sleep without any reactions to the trucks. . . . That's right, and when you have completed this experience, your "yes" finger will lift.

Four days later John called to report that he was sleeping well, no longer having significant startle responses to the trucks. He did not feel in need of further sessions for this problem. At six-month follow-up, he was still doing well.

This case provides a clear example of how ideodynamic exploring can provide a systematic, safe way to explore and transform past experiences. In this instance, resolution of a trauma-based symptom was completed with little awareness of related traumatic events themselves. This type of approach may be particularly useful in working with a dissociative patient who has completed the uncovering stage of treatment and wants to resolve persisting symptoms in an integrative fashion without reopening traumatic wounds. Traumatic incidents can be restructured, using available adult resources to reexperience the trauma from a different perspective while developing a general sense of mastery over the past.

EGO-STATE THERAPY APPROACHES

From an Ego-State Therapy viewpoint, this stage of treatment involves providing corrective behavioral and emotional experiences related to past traumatic events so that the patient can achieve a favorable outcome in her present life. The Watkins, developers of the ego-state model, believe that "there must be a re-doing, a corrective action, either in fantasy or in reality, which must be more than a cognitive understanding. The patient in the regressed state must make a specific behavioral move to change the situation and leave it with a favorable memory, not a failure one" (Watkins, 1992, p. 65).

One of the primary ways of creating corrective experiences is by strengthening relevant ego states and increasing the degree of cooperation within the internal system. Often, this can be accomplished simply by asking for an ego state who can come in and "help" another ego state (Watkins, 1992, p. 177).

Case Example: Kim

Kim is a 38-year-old dissociative patient who had been involved in uncovering work that suggested that she had been sexually molested by her next-door neighbor, whom she called "Gramps," when she was about five years old. During several hypnotic sessions, information about these experiences had been elicited, using regression procedures described in Chapter 6. We processed her various reactions and helped her reassociate certain details of the sexual abuse experiences that were relevant to current sexual difficulties in her marriage.

At the beginning of a subsequent session, Kim stated that she needed somehow to "get past the sexual abuse" and learn to have a more full and satisfying sexual response with her husband. In discussing possible ways of addressing these needs, Kim decided that the "little girl" part of her who had been traumatized needed help in resolving the abuse experiences. She agreed to review hypnotically some of the traumatic events in order to resolve them more completely.

After a brief formal induction during which Kim achieved progressive body relaxation and accessed her "safe place," we spent a few minutes reviewing some of her internal resources, such as "inner strength," which for her was a pink light and a sensation of warmth in her chest, and feelings of confidence, which we had accessed early in our work through positive regression experiences. Kim then signaled that she was ready to connect with the "little girl" ego state who had been traumatized.

I (MP) simply asked that Kim's unconscious mind locate the "little girl" part of Kim who had been badly hurt by what had happened with Gramps. Kim reported that she saw the "little girl" sitting on Gramps's knee in his basement room looking very scared and frozen. Starting to weep, Kim said, "She looks so little and afraid; she can't move. She can't get away." When I asked whether there might be another part of her who might come and help this "little girl," Kim described the entrance of a "young adult" who looked like her. After a pause, Kim continued her description: "She's storming down the basement steps, takes one look and picks the little girl up and holds her securely. She says to Gramps, "How dare you! You ought to be ashamed of yourself, using a little girl who has trusted and loved you in such an awful way. I will never leave her alone with you again, and if you ever try to touch her inappropriately, you will be sorry you were ever born.""

Kim further described Gramps's shrinking back in his chair dejected and ashamed and the relieved reactions of the "little girl" as she was taken out of the scene by the "young adult." I then asked for Kim's permission to speak directly to the grown-up in the scene. Our interaction continued as follows:

MP: I'm very glad you were willing to come in and help the "little girl" like that. You did a terrific job.

K: Thanks. I'm glad too. I couldn't stand to see her treated that way. What a bastard! And Kim just didn't seem to know what to do. . . .

MP: Kim's very lucky to have you to call on. You're very decisive and strong. By the way, what shall I call you?

K: Just call me Micki; I've always liked that name.

MP: Okay, Micki. . . . You know, the "little girl" will need more support now that she's out of that situation with Gramps. She's bound to be pretty traumatized by what happened. Can you help? She'll need to learn about how to feel safe again and when she can trust men and when she can't. And when she gets older, she'll need to learn about what kinds of touching are healthy and what kinds aren't. Can you help with any of that?

K: Well, I can help with some of it. I can certainly keep her safe and help her to be strong and confident in intimate situations. I'm not sure about helping her learn about touching and intimacy and stuff like that. I'm not very good at it.

MP: That's fine, Micki. Kim and the "little girl" can count on you for many important things. Is it okay with you if we find someone else inside who might be able to teach her about touching and sexuality?

K: Sure.

At that point, I asked Kim's unconscious for another part of her that might be able to provide additional support. An ego state named "Helper" arrived who had experience working with children and could teach sex education to a wide range of ages. "Helper" agreed to work with "Micki" to provide different types of care to "the little girl" as she needed it, including helping her find more age-appropriate activities when Kim wanted to be intimate with her husband.

Two weeks later, Kim reported that her sex life was much more satisfying, that she was now initiating and actively experimenting with sex. Two months later, Kim began having intermittent orgasms with her husband after being anorgasmic for most of her 15 years of marriage.

Kim's experience illustrates that ego-state work can be initiated at any point in the treatment process. In this case, her own desire to help the "little girl" whom she had viewed in her imagery of past trauma events created a natural opening. The accessing of "Micki" and "the Helper" provided strength to the main adult personality as well as corrective experiences for the damaged part of her personality. In addition, such a strategy promotes personality integration by encouraging cooperation between two ego states and the sharing of strengths and resources, as well as knowledge of the traumatic events. Over time, "Micki" and "Helper" seemed to blend together to appear more like the "adult Kim," and then eventually they disappeared altogether, as the main personality became more capable of continuing the corrective process.

With some individuals, it may be necessary to be directive when staging corrective experiences related to early trauma. The therapist may need to educate various alters or ego states about the nature and purpose of the others and to promote empathy for their feelings and needs (Watkins, 1992). For example, in working with Amy (see pp. 116, 134), as more of the traumatic experiences with her father became reassociated into the mainstream of her awareness, the main adult personality became very resentful of the "little girl." At one point, Amy complained, "All she does is cry and feel scared. I wish she weren't a part of me at all."

During this part of treatment, it became necessary to utilize two ego states, "the Princess" and "Borg," a friendly giant, who could provide soothing and reassurance to "the little girl" and orchestrate appropriate internal corrective experiences, while at the same time educating adult "Amy" about the importance of "the little girl" part of her. On multiple occasions, "the Princess" and "Borg" were directed to spend time with the "little girl," teaching her various coping skills and engaging in specific activities aimed at correcting trauma-related deficits. Eventually, these two helper ego states became more fully integrated into the main personality, so that adult "Amy" herself could empathize with and respond to the "little girl's" needs, further repairing past feelings of betrayal and mistrust.

The kind of internal conflict Amy experienced between her main personality and the "little girl" who was traumatized by her father becomes more complex when working with highly dissociated patients, including those with MPD (DID). The Watkins (1991, 1993) report special circumstances that occur when an ego state that contains a dissociated trauma along with related trauma responses is "split off" or dissociated from the main personality. In their case of Rhonda, a dissociated alter named "Mary" contained the rage related to early childhood abuse experiences; she was vindictive and inflicted her anger against the main personality. Satisfactory resolution of traumatic experiences was not possible until "Mary" was directed to "give back" the anger to "Rhonda," who then could express the rage outwardly. After this intervention, "Mary" became a covert, benevolent ego state who was supportive of "Rhonda" and insisted that she remain responsible for her own feelings about the abuse.

Some patients have too little ego strength to achieve positive renegotiation of trauma experiences. Helen Watkins (Watkins, 1992) reports an attempt to strengthen a child ego state by suggesting that it could age progress in order to confront the abuser. The "child" state responded, "No, I'm just a tiny little kid" (p. 67). The therapist then volunteered to intervene in the scene by offering to restrain the abuser so the child state would feel safe enough to express his feelings. The scene was completed successfully; the patient expressed his rage, physically and emotionally, and trauma-related symptoms were resolved.

Although we concur with the Watkins that it is important to intervene with such individuals rather than abandoning them to the retraumatizing reliving of traumatic events, we prefer other interventions to strengthen child ego states. For example, we have used a variation of James's (1989) technique, which involves having the child ego state imagine that she was visited by the "Princess of Power" during the night and woke up as the most powerful person in the world. She is then asked to revisit the traumatic episode to find out what happens, as she is now able to say and do whatever she wants. We also encourage the development of necessary ego strength through future orientation and age progression experiences and through having more mature ego states provide empowering experiences for less developed ones.

HYPNOTIC RENURTURING

Hypnosis can be used to provide renurturing experiences to the traumatized patient. This approach has its origins in methodology ranging from hypnoanalysis and object relations (Murray-Jobsis, 1984, 1985, 1990a) to the work of Milton Erickson (Erickson & Rossi, 1989). In both variations, the hypnotherapist actively stimulates change through unconscious responses to direct and indirect suggestions. This is in contrast to the ego-state approach, which orchestrates change by using the patient's ego state resources to provide the nurturing experiences. Hypnotic renurturing will be discussed in Chapter 8.

SOMATIC EXPERIENCING

Another model effective in renegotiating and transforming dissociated traumatic experiences is the somatic experiencing approach developed by Peter Levine (1991, 1994). Levine has emphasized the importance of helping the patient renegotiate the trauma response by evoking psychophysiological resources in somatic and perceptual systems. Most clinicians recognize that post-traumatic conditions result from a complex interplay of mind and body responses and appreciate that dealing with somatic experience may be essential to full resolution of traumatic experiences (Bentzen, Jarinaes, & Levine, 1993; Herman, 1992; Levine, 1991; van der Kolk & Greenberg, 1987). However, many hypnotic approaches to treating dissociated traumatic experiences often fail to emphasize the somatic aspects of experience, both in accessing traumatic responses and in renegotiating them.

Levine's model (Bernhardt, 1992; Levine, 1991, 1994) is based on an ethological understanding of how animals and humans respond psychophysiologically to overwhelming threat of danger and the shock that can ensue.

From this perspective, humans are programmed biophysiologically to go through natural defense mechanisms of orienting to the threat, fight/flight responses, and shock reflexes. When any of these are blocked or thwarted, Levine activates appropriate biological responses to the traumatic situation, exchanging active defenses for passive ones, which allows the nervous system to resolve an unfinished pattern and reassociate dissociated traumatic experiences (Bernhardt, 1992).

For clinicians unfamiliar with this model or untrained in somatic approaches to psychotherapy, several hypnotic techniques can provide a somatic focus when exploring traumatic material and attempting resolution or renegotiation of traumatic events. These include sensory exploring (Alman & Lambrou, 1992), the somatic bridge (J. G. Watkins, 1990), and ideosensory signaling (Erickson & Rossi, 1979). Sensory exploring involves simple tracking of the somatic aspects of inner experience in order to reassociate them with conscious awareness, while the somatic bridge is a form of age regression that allows the subject to bridge from a current body sensation back to its origins (see Chapter 6). Ideosensory signaling has been discussed previously (see Chapter 6) as a way of accessing and exploring past, dissociated experiences that may be connected to current somatic symptoms and signals. These techniques are discussed further in Chapter 9.

IMAGERY

Imagery, with and without hypnosis, can be used to help the patient transform and resolve traumatic experiences from the past. Imagery has long been considered to be effective in helping to create physiological as well as psychodynamic and behavioral changes (Kroger & Fezler, 1976; Singer, 1974), ranging from Jung's "active imagination" approach (Jung, 1964) to guided affective imagery (Leuner, 1977), psychosynthesis (Assagioli, 1965), and emergent uncovering (Reyher, 1977).

Harry Stanton (1990), who has made many contributions in the field of ego-strengthening, recommends a process that he calls "dumping the rubbish." This involves having the patient imagine herself filling a laundry sink with water, dumping all her unwanted fears, anxieties, and guilts from the past in the water, which becomes darker and darker, and then pulling the plug and watching the dark, inky water disappear down the sink. An alternative is to imagine taking an elevator down to deeper levels of the mind, where there is a beautiful room with a crackling fire in the fireplace. The subject is asked to imagine all the unwanted fears, doubts, and resentments related to past traumas in the form of accounts that have all been paid. These are lying on a table in front of the fire and can be picked up and burned, one at a time, so that the subject feels a sense of relief. Beverly James (1989) has used a similar approach with traumatized children, which can be modified for child ego states. This technique involves imagining a garbage bag and then filling it with current difficulties as well as fears and bad feelings related to past traumatic experiences; the bag is held as an internal container to be opened when therapeutically useful or discarded and destroyed.

Helen Watkins (1990) has suggested an imagery procedure called "The Door of Forgiveness" to help in the reduction of guilt about the past. The individual imagines a hallway at the end of which is a door marked "The Door of Forgiveness." If she sees doors on the side of the hallway, those can be entered first, and the rooms explored in order to resolve experiences from the past that involve guilt. When the patient is ready, she opens the "Forgiveness" door and enters a room where she has an experience of self-forgiveness. This technique can be repeated or extended as needed.

A frequently used and often effective imagery technique (Bresler, 1990; Rossman, 1987; Zilbergeld & Hammond, 1988) is to invite the subject to meet an inner "advisor" or "guide." Bresler (1990) suggests a rather elaborate journey where the subject enters a favorite or special place and is approached by an "advisor" who knows everything about the individual's past, present, and future. Inner dialogue is encouraged so that the subject can receive assistance from the advisor on any problem of concern, including ways of resolving past experiences related to trauma and abuse. The patient can be encouraged to utilize this as a self-hypnotic approach whenever needed.

Another strategy particularly helpful for MPD (DID) and ritual abuse patients is the image of an internal "control room" or "circuit room." As Hammond (1990b) points out, this imagery can be used to reprogram destructive brainwashing administered by cults or to defuse messages given by abusers such as, "I'll kill you if you ever tell anyone what happened." The subject is asked to imagine a circuit room in the brain where all beliefs, attitudes, and behaviors are stored. She is asked to locate the particular circuit board (or plug, etc.) that is connected with the problem belief or message, to disconnect it from its wiring in some way, and to reconnect it with a positive belief or message. A variation is to use a computer room (Price, 1990) where an old, dysfunctional "program" can be identified, erased, and replaced with a new program that supports therapeutic goals.

Yet another use of imagery involves hypnotic review. One approach is to suggest that the individual imagine, while reviewing the traumatic experience, what was needed then, and to notice the impact that it would have if that need were met. A second approach is to suggest that, while the patient is reviewing the traumatic experience, she add something important and helpful to the experience that she never noticed before. This suggestion can stimulate an unconscious search, resulting in some type of creative adjustment (Dolan, 1991). As Dolan (1991) points out, there are important advantages to using imagery to introduce new information while the patient is already in the original trauma state: "It appears that the lingering symptoms associated with a past trauma may be most effectively mitigated when the client is in a state that to some degree elicits the actual feelings associated with the original event" (p. 154).

METAPHOR AND OTHER ERICKSONIAN TECHNIQUES

The use of stories and metaphors can also be helpful during this stage of treatment. Mills and Crowley (1986) have suggested that metaphor works toward therapeutic change by "indirectly activating unconscious resources and potentials to resolve [the] problem/symptom" and enhancing total personality functioning (p. 122). One important use of metaphors is the "seeding" of various healing possibilities. This can be done throughout the third stage of therapy, using various language patterns, stories, parables, and analogies to "seed" hope for traumatized individuals, who often feel helpless about resolving current difficulties and hopeless about moving into the future.

Yapko (1990) emphasizes the use of metaphors for seeding the ability to set limits with others, achieve goals in the future, learn flexibility, and manage stress—all behaviors that imply resolution of trauma-based experiences. The Lanktons (Lankton & Lankton, 1983, 1987) have discussed the construction of therapeutic metaphors to achieve such affective goals as power, mastery, relief, and a sense of belonging, and to achieve redecision goals, such as deciding to say goodbye to a disappointing parent or to find a part of the self who decided not to have feelings and help that part make a new decision. Wallas (1985) has told stories that involve the seeding of new learning and growth experiences for those who have been abused, abandoned, or otherwise traumatized. Dolan (1991) uses metaphors to elicit unconsciously defined, but not yet developed, responses, such as learning to put each traumatic memory in perspective by sorting out related information.

An important function of metaphor is to match indirectly the patient's experience. In fact, many who specialize in the use of metaphors suggest that the analogical resemblance of the story to the unconsciously elicited definition of the problem and solution may be essential to its effectiveness (Dolan, 1991; Lankton & Lankton, 1987). Stories that reflect hopefulness about healing and result in positive resolution of struggles similar to the patient's can stimulate a more optimistic view. Metaphors related to the ordeal of setting a broken bone (Hammond, 1990b; Phillips, 1989) or surviving a natural disaster such as a hurricane, earthquake, or fire, for example, can often be beneficial to those who are engaged in the challenging process of resolving traumatic experiences. More about the use of metaphor can be found in Chapter 5.

LIVING METAPHOR AND RITUALS

A related technique is the use of "living metaphor" (Mills & Crowley, 1986) or ritual. These can be incorporated into the patient's daily life and are designed to create experiences that help to further resolve traumatic experiences. Dolan (1991) describes rituals involving making taped or visual messages to the "traumatized child" part of the personality and those which help to provide nurturing experiences that were missed in childhood, such as bedtime stories, visiting the zoo, playing games, having a pet, or indulging regularly in such treats as ice cream, meals in restaurants, and bubble baths. With certain patients, however, including MPD patients (Kluft, 1991), such approaches may result in a dysfunctional reification of child ego states (Gilligan, 1993), which may promote further splitting instead of personality integration. Engaging in such activities may send a message that "a child alter is indeed a child instead of a dissociated group of childhood memories, which have consolidated in a fragmentary identity" (Spiegel, 1991, p. 19), and can also become a distraction from the important task of dealing with traumatic memory material. The therapist must exercise clinical judgment here and stop the use of this kind of intervention if the patient becomes confused or overly fixated on child ego states.

Sometimes rituals can be helpful in resolving traumatic residue. Combs and Freedman (1990), for example, describe "cleansing" ceremonies, which involve selecting a stone to symbolize the "weight" of past hurts or debris from childhood abuse and, after meditating on its meaning, hurling it into the ocean or some other body of water. They also have helped patients design funeral ceremonies where they acknowledge and bury past losses; these can include rituals to "bury" the abusive perpetrator as well as funerals for the protective mother or father who never existed. It is important to allow the patient to "co-create" such activities and to have as much input as possible (Gilligan, 1993). In fact, an ambiguous structure seems to work best in allowing individuals to discover their own learnings (Combs & Freedman, 1990).

SPECIAL ISSUES

Occasionally, there are patients who are so badly damaged that they report having *no* inner resources available for renegotiating traumatic experiences. When asked during hypnosis for resources that might be available now that were not available then, the patient might signal ideomotorically "No" or "I don't know," or may report verbally, "This is too hard. There's just nothing there." When this occurs, we have found several strategies to be helpful.

First, it is important for the therapist to "seed" the future possibility that such resources can be made available at a later time. In ideomotor work, often when the patient has responded negatively to inquiries about available resources, this can be followed by a "yes" signal to the question, "Is Mary's unconscious mind willing to make appropriate resources available at a future time that is right for her?" The therapist can also "seed" future discovery of inner resources by embedding suggestions in conversations with the patient (e.g., Have you ever felt hopeless about something ever coming through and just when you were about to give up, somehow it happened?), through metaphorical examples, or through posthypnotic, future-oriented sugges- tions. With one ritually abused patient who had only latency-age ego states for renurturing activities, I (MP) continued to seed the future discovery of more adult resources. Finally, during one session when the "helper" ego states were particularly overwhelmed and discouraged, I took them on a guided journey that resulted in the discovery of "Aunt Josephine," an aunt with whom the patient had spent a wonderful month one summer in her teens. The patient had completely forgotten this resource, and it had not appeared during earlier searches of the same kind. The utilization of "Aunt Josephine" added several important missing links in her internal system and helped to move the patient successfully toward integration and eventually successful termination. Matura- tional work with immature ego states is discussed further in Chapter 8.

During the therapeutic process, the patient "takes in" various positive aspects of the therapist in an ongoing fashion. This can be accelerated and intensified when the therapist helps the patient learn to utilize hypnosis audiotapes as a transitional experience (Baker, 1994) and as an opportunity to introject certain calming and self-soothing activities (McNeal & Frederick, 1994). Audiotapes of hypnotic sessions can help the patient learn self-care and can themselves become transitional objects; their use by certain patients may symbolize the beginning of the end to internal emptiness.

Another approach is to give directives to patients for the current explora- tion of outer resources that can subsequently be internalized. Many patients have not had enough positive social experiences for their internal models and introjects of others to be fully useful to them. Suggestions might include participation in appropriate 12-step programs, support or therapy groups, spiritual or church organizations, classes and educational experiences, or sports and recreational activities.

Restabilization during the Third Stage of Therapy

Individuals who have been subjected to intense trauma may have been pre- vented from developing normal sleep, eating, or endocrine cycles and may con- tinue to suffer physiological disturbances even after the dissociated trauma has been fully reconstructed (Herman, 1992). In such patients, the delicate balance achieved during the earlier stages of therapy may be upset during the working-through of feelings related to reassociated traumatic experiences. These patients may require medication (or a reevaluation of current medications), and careful pacing of therapy experiences. Special attention may need to be devoted to somatic issues and adjunct therapy may be indicated (see Chapter 14).

During this stage, as the patient attempts to reassociate dissociated experiences, and then to renegotiate and transform the trauma in corrective ways, other difficulties may arise that may necessitate restabilization procedures. Herman (1992) notes that many traumatized patients have difficulty mourning loss, fearing that the task is insurmountable or that doing so would give victory to the perpetrator. From her point of view, resistance to grieving traumatic loss can take on many disguises, such as fantasies of magical resolution through revenge, forgiveness, or compensation. As these resistances are confronted and worked through, the patient must come to terms with the impossibility of "getting even," achieving true forgiveness toward a usually unacknowledging and unrepentant perpetrator, or receiving special compensation from the therapist which will make it possible for her to heal (Herman, 1992). This can be a particularly vulnerable time; as magical hopes are destroyed, the patient may be plunged into deep despair and grief.

We recommend carefully monitoring patients during this stage of therapy. When patients indicate a downward spiral in affect or in the management of their outside lives, we change the direction of therapy. Instead of a focus on past traumatic experiences, we shift to a here-and-now emphasis on stage I tasks. Therapeutic activities involve helping the patient not only to feel safe with new affects and perspectives gained during the course of therapy but also to use these to solve current challenges. Self-hypnosis can be an important tool in restabilization, as can many forms of ego-strengthening. Age progressions are particularly useful in providing prognostic indicators of the effectiveness of current therapy directions (see Chapter 5).

Often, patients lose sight of gains they have made and are making. For example, Faye, an MPD patient, described a return to intensified binge-eating during this stage and reported a disturbing awareness of negative inner voices who were engaged in delivering self-demeaning and shaming messages. I (MP) pointed out that, although this kind of experience must be uncomfortable for her, we needed to acknowledge the progress she was making. At the beginning of therapy, she had no awareness of her internal organization, which left her helpless and confused. Now she was hearing distinct inner voices belonging to various parts of herself, many of whom she could identify, who had helped her retrieve many past experiences that had once been lost to her. Faye remarked, "Yes, that's true. And now that you mention it, I'm even starting to hear positive voices. That's really exciting to me." It was further suggested that she might begin to view the inner negative voices differently in the future, since they would likely be accompanied by the emergence of positive ones.

Other patients need reassurance that this phase of therapy, which often has a timeless quality, will not last forever. As Herman (1992) suggests, "the moment comes when . . . the trauma story no longer arouses quite such intense feeling" (p. 195). The patient's interest in remembering and mourning the past eventually begins to lose its central place in her life, and she begins to put her traumatic experiences in context with other chapters in her life. As she finds her attention naturally returning to current concerns, she will need reassurance that she is not being disloyal to the self who was traumatized, but is ready to move on to the tasks of stage IV, further integration of dissociated experiences and building new identity.

8

INTEGRATION AND NEW IDENTITY DURING LATER STAGES OF TREATMENT

Spiegel (1993) has pointed out that dissociative disorders are, in essence, disorders of self-integration. With individuals who have used dissociation extensively to cope creatively with trauma, the development of a unified sense of personal identity may be compromised because of the inability of the subunits of consciousness to communicate and interact with one another (Spiegel, 1993).

Integration of Dissociated Experiences

BASK/BATS MODEL

Braun (1988a) has proposed the BASK model of dissociation to describe the disruption in experience during dissociated states. According to Braun, individuals in non-dissociated states experience events almost simultaneously across four dimensions: *b*ehaviors, *a*ffects, *s*ensations, and *k*nowledge. In states of dissociation any one or all of these elements may be disconnected from the mainstream of conscious awareness. This model has been helpful to many therapists who treat dissociative disorders because it provides a blueprint for the restoration of continuity of experience (Braun, 1988b; Fine, 1990) and it facilitates the description and conceptualization of a wide range of clinical phenomena (Braun, 1988b).

Braun (1988b) has since proposed a shift from BASK to BATS with *t*hought, a more dynamic process, substituting for *k*nowledge. He has suggested that congruence of all BATS elements would yield a "healthy individual" (p. 19) or an integrated personality. The BASK/BATS model has been used to link dissociated information, retrieved primarily from hypnosis, to gain congruence across all four dimensions of experience among various parts of the personality.

SIBAM MODEL

Although we have found the BASK/BATS approach useful in providing therapeutic grounding as dissociated individuals are integrating their traumatic experiences, we prefer SIBAM, an alternative model of dissociation proposed by Peter Levine (1991, 1994), who approaches trauma issues from both neurophysiologic and behavioral viewpoints. This model emphasizes somatic aspects of the trauma response across the dimension of *s*ensations (proprioceptive, kinesthetic responses), *i*magery (internal representations of external stimuli, including visual, auditory, tactile, gustatory, and olfactory), *b*ehaviors (voluntary and involuntary, including gestural, emotional, postural, autonomic, and archetypal), *a*ffects (includes but is broader than emotion: "the felt sense"), and *m*eaning (includes but is more comprehensive than cognition, thought, and knowledge).

In Levine's model dissociation or fragmentation of different dimensions of experience is considered along with "over-association" or overcoupling, where experiences are joined together in ways that cannot be integrated (Bernhardt, 1992). The concept of overcoupling explains the response of the Vietnam veteran who hears a car backfire and dives under a table for protection, or of an individual who begins to remember a positive experience from the past and then quickly associates to a negative element and ultimately becomes flooded with terrifying aspects of that association.

In these examples, traumatic responses have become over-associated with non-traumatic responses so that the individual cannot separate the two. The therapeutic task is to track the patient's shifts from body sensations, to image fragment, to involuntary movements of autonomic system activation (e.g., shaking, changes in skin color, temperature, or pupil dilation) and affective responses (emotional feelings and "felt sense" of the experience), and then to discern whether these elements are dissociated or overcoupled. If they are dissociated or separated, they require association and connection; if overcoupled, they need to be separated and compartmentalized. For example, if a patient begins to "flood" or indicate sensate experiences of overcoupling, the therapist can interrupt this process by asking him to focus on another component of SIBAM. "And as you feel those sensations that are so fearful, are you aware of any mental pictures or images right now?" This kind of intervention helps to create needed separation or containment. If a patient becomes disconnected or dissociated during tracking, as indicated by comments that, "Nothing is happening now," or, "I'm not aware of myself at all right now," the therapist can suggest that the patient return to a previous SIBAM awareness and "bridge" back and forth between that and his present sense of disconnection in order to build a sense of connection again. Tracking SIBAM elements in this manner leads naturally to meaning once the patient has connected fragments into a more complete trauma-related experience. According to Levine (Levine, 1991,1993; Bernhardt, 1992), this process and other applications of the SIBAM model can facilitate a higher level of integration and organization within the nervous system as well as within the psychodynamic self. The case example below demonstrates the use of SIBAM to help in the integration of dissociated experiences.

Case Example: Marion

Marion is a 46-year-old medical doctor who has been in treatment for two years. She was initially referred for hypnotherapy for the retrieval of traumatic material as an adjunct to her psychotherapy. With the support of her referring psychotherapist, she has since chosen to continue with hypnotherapy as a primary modality for working with memory material indicating incest experiences with her father.

During this particular session, which followed several months of work focused on uncovering and renegotiating a series of traumatic sexual abuse experiences with her father, with an uncle, and with a high school acquaintance, Marion is reporting anxiety symptoms and intense body tension related to unspecified pressures she has been feeling. When I (MP) suggest the possibility of exploring these using the SIBAM model, she agrees and enters a light self-induced trance state, which has become our procedure for inner exploration.

Marion almost immediately reports a sad feeling on the right side of her face. When asked what else she was experiencing, she describes something pressing on her chest like a knee or hand. Since these sensations seemed to be disconnected or dissociated from one another, I ask her to explore them further, bridging back and forth between the two. Subsequently, she describes a "sick feeling" in her stomach and a feeling of constriction in her chest, like "I can't breathe." Marion realizes that she wants to move the pressure off her chest but cannot because it's too heavy and she is little and helpless, lying flat on her back; then she connects with the sad feeling and sobs quietly.

She then moves spontaneously into a state of heightened activation; deciding to scream, she describes her blood as "rushing." Her fists clench, and her left leg tightens. She reports that she is now screaming and crying loudly. Noting that these responses might be overcoupled, and that Marion is trembling and shaking, I ask what else she is aware of at that moment in an attempt to engage her observing self in separating momentarily from the over-associated responses. Marion reports that she sees someone coming to pick her up; she begins to feel safe in these arms, believing they are those of her nanny. She describes somatic and emotional feelings of relief and comfort; she feels ready for sleep. There is less difference now between the right and left sides of her body, except for tension in the right side of her face, neck, and jaw. After several more cycles of tracking SIBAM dimensions, she feels complete.

As we discuss the session, Marion observes that she has connected resources of comfort to experiences that had been terrifying to her, where she had felt completely helpless. Her body is now relaxed, and she expresses the belief that she can learn to do this for herself whenever she is feeling overwhelmed by things outside herself.

The SIBAM model is an excellent map for helping patients integrate traumatic experiences and their sequelae in a self-paced fashion. It allows individuals such as Marion to arrive at new meaning by forming complex, naturally occurring associations in the mind and the body. The therapist becomes an observer and "tracker" who simply requests additional information as needed and directs the patient to engage in activities of connection or separation, depending on the extent of dissociation or over-association manifest at any time.

Integration of the Personality

In the best of all possible worlds, integration of the personality would be the outcome of psychotherapy with all dissociative conditions. Although it is a goal commonly agreed upon as desirable with MPD patients (Kluft, 1993a; Putnam, 1989; Ross, 1989; Watkins, 1992), its precise definition and nature remain a topic of disagreement among workers in the field (Kluft, 1993a), as well as among developmental psychologists such as Piaget (Erikson, 1964) who speaks of "unity."

From our viewpoint integration is the alternative to the chaos and "fear and trembling" that prevail when reassociation has not been accomplished. It is the natural situation that prevails when ego states are not sitting on volcanoes of dissociated, terrifying, painful material, have achieved sufficient maturity, are communicating with one another and working together empathically and cooperatively, and are experiencing the consciousnesses of one another. The ego-state model does not provide for the elimination of covert ego states detectable with hypnosis, nor does it consider this to be an achievable goal. In normal subjects and in integrated patients covert ego states may be activated hypnotically from time to time. What does change with integration is the experience of "I-ness" and the individual's ability to function in a unified and consistent way.

Our discussion of the integration of ego states is based on our belief that the ego-state model is an excellent theoretical metaphor that allows us to understand and work therapeutically with aspects of the human personality. Ego states are energies, metaphors, and personality aspects – not homunculi. Because of the apparently seamless and harmonious functioning of the ego states and the pervading phenomenon of co-consciousness, the self is no longer experienced as divided. As this sense of division no longer prevails, the subjective feeling of "we-ness" or of a sense of alienation from a mysterious part or parts of the self fades. The self is experienced as an "I," although at first it may be a new and different "I" from what the individual has known. The feeling of differentness of the "I" exists for several reasons: co-consciousness is pervasive, the ego states involved in integration have undergone growth and maturation, and the resulting identity or subjective sense of self is truly that of a new identity or self. As a patient told one of the authors, "I am one person now. . . . I feel like a . . . like a crab that got rid of its hard shell, like I have to toughen up a little, but I've grown much larger."

The Integrative Spectrum

As we observe patients in the process of moving toward integration or moving away from it, we think of the phenomena we see as being located somewhere in what we call the *Integrative Spectrum* (see Figure 5), which spans the entire continuum of possibilities for relationships among ego states – from the most completely separated to the state of personality merging. The utilization of such a model can help the therapist understand what some of the obstacles to

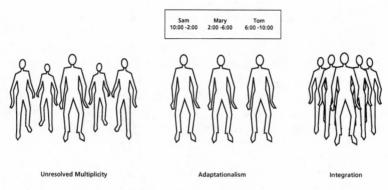

Figure 5. Spectrum of Integration

integration might be, what needs to be done to further integration, and what factors may help and which could hamper the stability of the integrative process. This spectrum can be understood more clearly if the concept of co-consciousness is formulated in greater detail.

CONTINUED PERSONALITY DIVISION

We can follow our patients' progress toward integration by identifying where they are on the integrative spectrum. Some patients may choose to remain divided. For example, a patient with MPD may choose to have the alters retain their separateness and separate identities and activities, or a patient with a dissociative condition such as panic disorder or PTSD may choose to "live" with the symptoms rather than resolve them with further work toward integration. As we and others (Kluft, 1993a) have noted, some unintegrated MPDs are making claims that this is a good and chosen way for them to live. Although some patients will continue with this kind of choice, it is not unusual for them to return to treatment because it has not been a satisfactory one for them. One of us (CF) saw a patient who went to live with her MPD lover, choosing to remain divided since her ego states were getting along to some extent with one another as well as with her lover's. Subsequently, the patient discovered that she could not tolerate either her lover's lack of integration or her own and chose to reenter treatment and face difficult and painful material.

We understand that the retention of separateness may be chosen by patients, but we do not generally endorse it, since we believe it represents a failure to recognize that different personalities exist in order to manage ongoing pain and that a continued arrangement of separateness is a way of continuing to live in pain (Ross, 1989). Fear about exploration of necessary material, continued fear of abusers in the external and/or internal environment, unresolved narcissistic/delusional material about power among several ego states, and fear of death by ego states (Beahrs, 1982; Watkins, 1992) are factors that contribute to this kind of choice. For some patients, however, especially very complex MPDs, living in less pain than before may be as far as they choose to go or practically are able to move on the integrative spectrum. As therapists we can only do our work; we cannot make the difficult choices for our patients. Financial constraints are important considerations, as many individuals with dissociative conditions cannot work and the public sector seldom affords anything other than supportive care for these patients (Frederick, Scopelli, Van Auken, & Sorum, 1994).

ADAPTATIONALISM

Farther along the integrative spectrum is the situation in which ego states maintain their separateness but have developed some working level of communication and cooperation. Patients at this stage often continue to speak of themselves as "we." Milton Erickson (Erickson & Kubie, 1939) doubted that any closer relationship among parts was possible and felt that a working relationship among them was quite satisfactory. Kluft has called this arrangement (in which function receives priority over integration) *adaptationalism* (1993a, p. 104). Our work indicates that parts that are having a hard time developing co-consciousness need to do further uncovering/reassociation work and may need further help with maturation. We are impressed with the transformation of ego states as patients move toward integration, and we are suspect of arrangements in which unchanged parts have worked out agreements to maintain open separateness and alternating function. In the latter case, ego states divide the management of memories, feelings, and tasks among them. For example, an arrangement could be made that ego state A would assume all the problems and mechanics of meeting new people, thus sparing ego states B, D, and D from the anxiety associated with this kind of social maneuver. Once a newly met person became the object of possible intimacy, ego state A would turn the "intimacy business" over to ego state B – an ego state that "did" intimacy. Similarly, another ego state might specifically manage sexual intimacy. Such an internal situation is not one that allows the patient to have a continuous sense of self or to be able to develop true intimacy.

In his significant follow-up of MPD patients, Kluft (1985b) found that most patients treated to integration were able to report " . . . enhanced quality of life and continuing gains" (Kluft, 1993a, p. 104). Those who failed to proceed toward integration continued to have difficulties and to relapse under stress. These patients had not completed their work and many of them returned for further work toward integration. We are in complete agreement with Kluft about this and about his criteria for integration, with one exception. That concerns the ability to activate ego states in the integrated patient with hypnosis. Kluft believes that the hypnotic activation of alters is a sign that integration is not complete, while we consider the hypnotic activation of ego states/alters a normal phenomenon. We do not think that it is, in the absence of other evidences of failure of integration, pathological.

SIGNS OF INTEGRATION

Early signs of reaching integration on the integrative spectrum can be seen in the following:

- the patient's feelings, behaviors and reveries
- the transference
- psychophysiologic reactions

- the patient's dream life
- trance material

The patient, previously concentrating on the therapy process as the most important part of his life, may begin to shift the focus of his energy to the outside world, into relationships, projects, or quests. Sometimes patients will say "It's all done" about their internal work. We know it's never "all done" for any of us, and we realize that some patients who display such behavior could be in denial or flight into health; nonetheless, when the therapist evaluates such material within the context of what is happening in the therapeutic situation, the possibility of its having meaning in terms of the integrative process must be considered. The other side of the coin from "It's all been done" is represented by the patient who says, "There's something I have to do before I leave here." This task may be spelled out by the patient or it may, for a while, remain nebulous or even frankly unknown. Another early sign of integration is a fluctuation of energies or of affects. In some patients there may be serious regression and a severe exacerbation of symptoms, as though it all has to be played out one more time and more so before it changes. Sometimes we note a "farewell event" represented by some symptom or acting-out behavior. An open initiation of discussion about termination on the part of the patient can, at times, be exactly what it appears to be, although the possibility of avoidance, flight, and resistance always exists.

For many patients integration is heralded by otherwise unexplained feelings of sadness and grief, as they unwittingly mourn the old, unsatisfactory, but quite familiar state of affairs, which is already in the process of passing away. Within the framework of the transference, changes may occur as integration proceeds. Lukewarm transferences may suddenly become intensely positive or negative, and transference fantasies and dreams may increase in frequency, while transference reactions that had been quite strong may attenuate.

Within the patient's dream life other signs of integration may be visible. There may be repetitive dreams and review dreams (Glover, 1955), or the dream picture may illustrate energy shifts within the system. For example, it is not uncommon for patients to report that their dreams have become populated with dead or dying bodies, which represent the spontaneous flight of energies from certain ego states to more vital and developed parts of the system. Other patients may dream archetypically about new senses of self: One patient told me (CF) that she dreamt she was crouched on all fours in a circle with a pack of wolves. "We were all howling. . . . I can remember shouting, 'It's my time to howl tonight!!!' And you know, it is my time to howl." The healing part of the patient, who had been quite inhibited in her social behavior and had thought herself to be an introvert, was finally able to join more natural and expressive aspects of herself.

The loss of investment of energy in certain ego states and the wish of the greater psyche to expel toxic material often show up in the integrative process psychophysiologically. The patient may experience vomiting and/or diarrhea, vasomotor, or other phenomena. Trance material may change. Suddenly, an ego state frequently activated by the trance state may no longer be there: "He's not there. . . . No one seems to know what happened to him." Confusion may develop among ego states about who other states are or even about who they themselves might be: "It's Frankie . . . at least, I think that's who I am." The roles of ego states may change rapidly; for example, hostile ego states may undergo swift transformations into loving helper states. The therapist may readily share some of the confusion of the ego states during certain stages of rapid changes and shifts as the integrative process forges a new identity. From time to time, patients will develop their own highly idiosyncratic ways of dealing with this process. For example, a patient may announce to the therapist that he has developed an Internal Parent who can care for him properly, or may say, "I don't really feel a need to do ego-state work anymore. The different parts just aren't there the way they used to be."

As therapy and the integrative process proceed, increased cooperation occurs. Although the patient may be aware of separate ego states, he may sound somewhat uncertain or less concerned about who is communicating and whether some states may have vanished. There are signs of co-consciousness and co-presence within the system. When integration and co-consciousness become more advanced, the patient speaks of himself as "I" and makes statements such as, "I'm a whole person now." Some ego states may still be capable of hypnotic activation after integration. Resolution of the patient's problems will ideally take him along the integrative spectrum to this state and beyond.

The successful completion of integration depends upon sufficient reassociation and working-through of traumatic material and sufficient maturation of ego states. Although certain very immature ego states may fairly easily merge when traumatic material is resolved, integration cannot be completed until powerful ego states possess enough maturity to allow themselves to experience co-consciousness and to place the needs of the greater personality first.

MERGING OF EGO STATES

At the extreme other end of the spectrum from the total separation of personality parts from one another is merging of personality parts. Although some merging may occur spontaneously during the integration process, and at times personality parts may ask the therapist to help them merge, we do not consider merging of parts to be essential for integration. Our model is one in which changes in the permeability of boundaries among ego states occur. Integration becomes a manifestation of the results of those changes and of the deepening of the harmonious relationships among the states:

> Integration means making the boundaries between various alters permeable, increasing communication and cooperation, then returning the various sub-personalities to the status of "covert" ego states which cannot be contacted except under hypnosis. We feel it is unnecessary to attempt to "fuse" them into a unity, since this is not the state of the "normal" personality. (Watkins, 1992, p. 176)

In the shifts of energy that occur during the integrative process, the actual number of ego states may diminish because merging may be elected or occur naturally among personality parts that no longer have any internal reasons to remain separate. When this occurs, the parts may not be detectable under hypnosis. The therapist may discover that two parts have merged while retaining the name of one of them, or that merged parts may acquire new names indicative of their transformation.

We prefer to use the term *merging*, instead of the more commonly used term fusion. There are several definitions of fusion in the literature. It is sometimes used synonymously with unification and integration (Kluft, 1993a), but is thought more precisely to indicate the moment at which subpersonalities merge with one another (Kluft, 1993a; Putnam, 1989; Ross, 1989) as a necessary step in the process of integration. Within the Ego-State Therapy framework fusion has referred to a merging of personalities (Watkins, 1992), which may occur during the integration process but which is not a prerequisite for it.

Co-consciousness

In the ego-state continuum (see Figure 4, p. 64), ego states are normally separated from one another by something that can be thought of like a semipermeable membrane. At one end of the continuum is the situation of extreme *separateness*; at the other, certain variations of the normal human personality. The key word in understanding ego-state pathology is *separateness*. Total separation of any ego state from the other members of the internal family is always accompanied by lack of understanding and harmony. It is also a sign of clinical or subclinical pathology, as well as susceptibility to dysfunction under stress.

Members of families or of other functioning groups depend on one another for clear communication and cooperative activity. This analogy can be applied to the internal family. Internal communication and cooperation increase as treatment proceeds. Ego states begin to recognize that other ego states exist; then they begin to talk with one another or to communicate in other ways. One of the therapist's goals is to help ego states grow up enough to develop empathy for other ego states. Eventually, cooperative ventures toward commonly held goals occur, and co-presence can be observed; ego states eventually begin to share thoughts, feelings, fantasies, experiences, and goals with other ego states. They become like close siblings. At some point many ego states begin to share their conscious contents with other ego states. They are no longer just siblings; they are special siblings, twins, monozygotic triplets. This sharing of consciousness is called co-consciousness.

Co-consciousness, a goal toward which we consciously strive, plays a major role in the stages of integration discussed below. Although the therapist will utilize additional approaches to integration, it is necessary that continued exploration, uncovering of remaining dissociated material, and reassociation accompany them. The biggest obstacle to integration is the failure to uncover and reassociate sufficiently.

The Stages of Personality Integration

Personality integration can be conceptualized as proceeding through certain stages. Not every stage will be necessarily visible; moreover, individuals may, at times, appear to "leapfrog" over certain stages. The usefulness of conceptualizing stages is that it gives the therapist an opportunity to identify what needs to be done during the integrative process to move ego states along in the process.

- *The stage of recognition* involves the achievement of overt recognition that other ego states exist. The relationship among ego states may be like that of strangers, neighbors who never see one another or never speak with one another, or even enemies. The therapist may have to point out to ego states that other parts are there and that they are important, indeed, that every part is as important as every other part. The therapist actively encourages ego states to make themselves known, and welcomes the appearance of difficult or hostile parts as a manifestation of an increase in trust. For some patients who deny their dissociative difficulties this first step can be revealing: "I wasn't able to get in touch with my parts until I became more integrated. I just denied they were there before that." The therapist becomes the "translator" and mediator, for example, explaining hostile ego states' adaptive qualities, protective inclinations, and great fear of other ego states to the rest of the doubting internal family.

- *The stage of development of communication* among ego states follows recognition. An ego state may say of another, "I don't want to talk with that brat, Sally, she's a wuss, stupid, too." The therapist must deal with this resistance, and urge, encourage, and give parts reasons to initiate communication with other parts. For example, the therapist might say, "I understand that Sally may not be as strong as you, and that you may not understand her, but she needs some of your strength, and it is just possible that she may have something to offer you . . . you know, Sally really knows how to show her tender feelings." Reminding parts of their joint membership in the internal family and pointing out to them how their failure to communicate is causing the greater personality difficulties are helpful.

- *The stage of development of empathy* for other ego states is a crucial step in the integrative process because it frequently exposes parts to the pain of other parts, enlarges their affective range, and moves them maturationally. With many ego states it can be pursued directly. "How would you feel, I wonder, Joe, if someone did that to you?" At times metaphor and other indirect interventions are indicated.

- *The stage of cooperative ventures* toward commonly held experiences, goals. These ventures include maturational maneuvers that permit the ego states to move closer and closer to one another, as well as group activities that enhance the closeness and cohesiveness of the group. These are the activities of siblings. The therapist has an opportunity here to encourage these internal activities and to assign tasks that will further the maturational process. For example, adolescent ego states might get together to build a playhouse for child ego states or organize a school where they can learn age-appropriate skills. The technique of the "blending of consciousnesses" (Fine & Comstock, 1989) can be useful when parts appear to be stuck at this level and need different input to move on. In this technique, the parts are asked to share consciousness with one another on a temporary basis. This can be excellent for previewing the next stage, dealing with fears about it, and meeting specific problems successfully.

- *The stage of sharing of interiority* involves thoughts, feelings, fantasies, experiences, and goals among other ego states. At this point the ego states are like very close siblings or best friends. The therapist may ratify this activity, but it usually appears spontaneously. At this point the therapist may capitalize on the situation by introducing age progression for views of the post-integration future while working on fears of and resistances to integration.

- *The stage of co-consciousness* is signaled by a sharing of consciousness, perceptions, intentionality, and goals by ego states. If the therapist has done the uncovering/reassociation work and any necessary maturational work, co-consciousness, which may be intermittent and partial at first, will become more and more pronounced.

- *The stage of continuing co-consciousness* is something like "twinship." Parts may begin to have difficulty perceiving their separateness. On occasion some parts request "fusion" in this stage and are able to utilize fusion rituals. The therapist must watch for a flight into health due to resistances to the state of continuing co-consciousness or resistances caused by the influences of as yet unrevealed ego states or unresolved traumatic memories.

When co-consciousness has become a continuing process, some ego states may spontaneously merge with one another, while others may display separate identities that are as effective in their separateness as the line drawn across the floor of a house that is situated in two states. As John Watkins would say, both states are members of the federal union. Their internal disagreements would be no greater than those observed by any reflective person. What truly characterizes this stage is the deepening of intimacy through a sharing of thought and feelings. Ego states in the previous stage may have agreed to carry out a project together; in this stage they communicate such things as their most terrifying fears of the past, their most deeply held enthusiasms and trepidations for the present, and their closely held dreams of the future.

The therapeutic work toward integration must begin during the first session and must be a conscious goal for the therapist throughout the course of treatment. We discuss integration with our patients early in treatment in terms of an ego-state model, with emphasis on harmony and cooperation among aspects of the personality. We are careful to emphasize the importance of every personality part at that time. Like Ross (1989), we do not believe that it is useful to speak constantly about integration during the course of treatment, as such overemphasis could stimulate anxiety about the process and in our opinion be a manifestation of countertransference problems.

The Development of a New Identity

The development of a new identity is a complex process. Many therapeutic strategies may influence it in a positive way, especially those that assist development of immature states along several epigenetic maturational lines and those that utilize present and future resources to foster the development of a new identity.

Maturation of Ego States

Ego states may fail to proceed to integration because they lack the maturity to take on the tasks of integration. An ego state that is incapable of cooperation, for example, or empathy, is not a candidate for the development of co-consciousness any more than a two-year-old child is a candidate for running a marathon. A certain amount of development is essential before adult tasks can be taken on. A great deal of the maturational work that needs to be done with personality parts is often done rather automatically by skilled therapists. Tactical integrationalist approaches (Fine, 1993), which employ psychoeducation among other maneuvers, introduce maturational tasks such as identifying with internal role models or learning that certain behaviors bring certain results.

Since maturation usually proceeds along several lines, the therapist may have to consider cognitive and psychosexual issues as well as object-relations problems and psychosocial development. A wide range of maturational techniques may be employed because trauma produces multiple developmental deficits.

The Issue of Repairing Cognitive and Developmental Deficits

Victims of childhood abuse and trauma display evidence of cognitive (Fine, 1990; Fish-Murray, Koby, & van der Kolk, 1987), affective (Fine, 1990; Herman, 1992), and behavioral (Fish-Murray et al., 1987; Herman, 1992; Terr, 1991) abnormalities. The use of the BASK model or the SIBAM model (Levine 1991, 1994) can assist in revealing the presence of lagging faculties or disparities in development. The difficulty is that there may be incredible inconsistency of developmental damage among ego states: Several ego states may think well, be appropriate about boundaries, and initiate and execute mature behavior, while others may be grossly immature, lack object permanence in Piaget's sense, and be stuck in developmental issues of nurturing, object constancy, and separation-individuation. Some ego states may be so immature that they are incapable of joining in the work of memory retrieval because they are unable to understand the nature of the memories of other ego states or don't know who the therapist is (Loewenstein, 1993). For instance, during a hypnotic session with a patient, one of us (CF) heard a new voice say: "Who are you?" An immature ego state had finally gotten enough courage to emerge but simply didn't understand much of the game or the players. While a gradual release of internal memory is useful in situations where these immature ego states are found, their maturational defects retard the progress of integration and may at times need to be dealt with in other ways. Although the process of therapy itself is presumably a maturational tool in which the patient identifies with the goals of the therapist, who offers constancy, rationality, and safety, such approaches alone may move maturational development at a snail's pace, if at all.

The theme of utilizing the hypnotic experience to deal with developmental defects can be found in several places. Let us say emphatically that we do not endorse the idea that patients can be "loved into health" (Fine, 1993; Kluft, 1993a). We believe that kind of approach is generally rooted in lack of appropriate training and/or severe countertransference difficulty. We do maintain that some developmental work may be necessary with certain personality parts if they are going to meet the tasks of participating in the uncovering work and move into more cooperative relationships with other aspects of the personality. Various approaches to this have been proposed: Some are overt, such as hypnoplay therapy (Shapiro, 1988); some are less obvious, such as psychoeducation (Fine, 1993). Between the two extremes of developmental work can be found several other approaches within the hypnotic tradition whose examination will be useful in understanding how internal maturational work leading to integration can be accomplished.

Hypnosis may permit the patient to tap inner resources for self renurturing in ways that will not be invasive.

The February Man

Milton Erickson (Erickson & Rossi, 1980) was quite interested in how certain hypnotic experiences might help patients overcome certain developmental failures. In one of his February Man cases, Erickson (Erickson & Rossi, 1980) worked with a woman who was expecting a baby and feared that her own upbringing with a cold mother might have left her unprepared to deal with her child in a nurturing and empathic way. Erickson introduced himself into several hypnotic age regressions with this woman as a friend of the family, a kindly, nurturing man who visited every February. During these hypnotically experienced visits he was warm and encouraging to the little girl. Erickson's work with this patient was quite successful, as she began to be a better mother to herself and was able to mother her child quite well. Erickson felt that he had given the patient a "corrective emotional experience" through this trance work, that is, that he had supplied something essential for her further development.

For Erickson the "corrective emotional experience" was not necessarily a nurturing one as in the February Man case. It could be something quite different; the common denominators were that it changed internal belief systems and self-perceptions and that hypnosis was an effective way of providing it (Erickson & Rossi, 1980).

Creative re-mothering

Ways of repairing defects and filling unmet early needs for nurturing have been sought persistently in psychotherapy. In the 1940s and 1950s certain therapists attempted to repair bad mothering or to make up for insufficient mothering by actually giving nurturing physical attention to some of their more regressed schizophrenic patients or by attempting to do this symbolically (Boyer & Giovacchini, 1967).

Sechehaye captured the attention of many therapists when she wrote of a young schizophrenic woman who was able to make significant improvements after she accepted an apple offered to her by her therapist, who said: "It is time to drink the good milk of Mummy's apples" (1947, p. 51). Schwing (1940), Azima and Wittkower (1956), and Rosen (1962) followed the same tradition. These methods are of interest because we still encounter their variants in our workshops and supervision work with practicing therapists. This happens most obviously when child ego states appear and the therapist is tempted to play with them, help them to explore the world, and assist them with socialization. We do not endorse these approaches. They appear to be engendered by significant countertransference problems and/or a lack of knowledge about how to deal with dissociative disorders. In our opinion they represent serious acting-out on the part of the therapist. We have yet to see real gain come of such attempts to deal with maturational issues. At best they appear to put the therapeutic process on hold. Finally, we are concerned about any method that fosters dependency in patients rather than helping them to discover their own internal sources of healing and growth.

Nevertheless, there is, within hypnosis, a creative approach to re-mothering that deserves serious attention. It involves the idea that, somehow, the trance state can be utilized for the construction of the subjective experience of a different childhood and a different kind of mothering experience with a therapist who could be incorporated as a transitional, positive parent figure. Erickson (Erickson & Rossi, 1980, 1989) opened the door for this kind of approach with the February Man and his "corrective emotional experience."

Joan Murray-Jobsis has used hypnosis successfully with borderline and psychotic patients for many years (Scagnelli, 1976; Scagnelli-Jobsis, 1982). Her interest in using hypnotic suggestions to effect permanent changes in the patient's internal sense of not having been nurtured adequately led her to develop the techniques of renurturing and creative self-mothering (Murray-Jobsis 1990a, 1990b). These techniques involve guiding the patient through early developmental stages in hypnotic age regressions into which fantasies of having the renurturing done correctly by an idealized mother are introduced. Murray-Jobsis utilizes these techniques to help patients develop a sense of having been adequately mothered, as well as to establish bonding, boundaries, and normal sense of separation-individuation. McMahon (1986) has also done work with creative re-mothering, with emphasis on the patient's being in control of the way it is done and how fast it proceeds.

These hypnotic approaches can yield excellent results without creating dependency or causing the patient to look to the therapist for all the solutions. We modify the techniques greatly, in that we ask other ego states within the patient to take over the mothering (Frederick, 1992, 1993a; Phillips & Frederick, 1991). We request that more mature ego states help less mature ones deal with specific issues. Sometimes an immature ego state may need to be nurtured or to develop bonding; at other times separation-individuation or other developmental goals may be achieved with the help of the more mature states. Often we do not know all the details about how the tasks were accomplished, although on occasion some patients report this material in great detail. What we share with Murray-Jobsis and McMahon is the conviction that hypnosis can be used to assist with the correction of developmental issues where mothering has been inadequate or negative.

When no nurturing ego states are present, we use ego-strengthening techniques, reinforce the introjection of positive current models as ego states, or help the patient transform past experiences into new and helpful ego states (Frederick & Kim, 1993) to develop this self-nurturing ability.

Therapist and Ego States as Transitional Objects and Containers

The hypnotic process and the interaction with the hypnotherapist may foster maturation of objects relations. Baker (1994), working with seriously disturbed psychotic patients, has shown how the therapist can use the hypnotic experience to serve as a container for the patient until his growth and defenses have sufficiently developed. Baker (1994) has also used the hypnotic experience to facilitate the therapist's acting as a transitional object for the patient, a bridge to permit subsequent growth and development. In his observations on transitional objects and transitional phenomena in MPD patients, Fink (1993) cited Marmer's work (1980). According to Marmer, certain alters can represent transitional objects, which are important to the patient because traumatic experiences did not permit them to use external transitional objects. Fink feels that alters based on self-representation can be stabilizing for the patient. They may play an important role in the homeostasis of the system. His observations of such alter activity involve one case in which transitional alters were frantically clung to as protection against what seemed like the state of being alone that would result from integration; in another case such alters were able to work with the therapist.

The issues raised by Marmer and Fink are not to be ignored. Like therapists, ego states can serve as transitional objects that may work for or against integration. How does the therapist assist in the transfer of the internal transitional object's nurturing to other, frightened parts? This situation calls upon the creativity of the therapist, a belief in the adaptive nature of every ego state, and knowledge of group dynamics. Within the system there are inherent sources of strength that can be activated at such junctures through projective/evocative ego-strengthening (see Chapter 5).

The internal world of the patient is rich with ego states that can help less mature states achieve object permanence and object constancy, as well as a host of more advanced maturational tasks. They are able to do this naturally with guidance from the therapist, who can select those ego states whose phase-specific tasks (Erikson, 1980) involve generativity and integrity. In this sense ego states do internal parenting (Beahrs, 1982). More mature ego states can become involved in nourishment and in the setting of limits and boundaries (Beahrs, 1982). The therapist is in a unique position to identify developmental issues in the cognitive, psychosexual, object relations, and psychosocial realms and to guide more mature ego states' work with less mature ego states (Frederick, 1992).

Climbing Erik Erikson's Ladder

Many of our contemporary insights about human development within the social context come from the work of Erik Erikson (1950–1980). Erikson thought that the growth of every individual ego was inextricably linked with identity as member of the social group. He (1980) saw psychosocial development as parallel to psychosexual development but going beyond it to encompass the entire life cycle. Erikson's life cycle consists of phases. Specific to each phase is a developmental task, some major aspects of which must be completed before the individual can successfully confront the tasks of the next phase. Erikson's phases are usually described in terms of the possible successful outcomes versus the possible failures. The phase tasks are:

1. Basic trust vs. mistrust

2. Autonomy vs. shame and doubt

3. Initiative vs. guilt

4. Industry vs. inferiority

5. Identity vs. identity diffusion

6. Intimacy vs. isolation
7. Generativity vs. stagnation
8. Integrity vs. despair

According to Erikson, the individual progresses through these stages by virtue of mutuality with his/her social environment. Development occurs because life cycles are "cogwheeled," meaning that, " . . . caretaking persons as representatives of their society. . . ensure that the developing individual will be viable" (Rappaport, 1959). Personality parts must go through these epigenetic stages as the whole person develops and matures. The achievement of these developmental goals in dissociative disorder patients may be uneven and, at times, quite delayed. The therapist stimulates activities among ego states relevant to the emerging appropriate phase-specific tasks. During the early stages of treatment more mature ego states orchestrate activities dedicated to promoting trust, autonomy, and initiative. Engaging in cooperative projects, learning to increase frustration tolerance, establishing role identity within the internal family (e.g., a malevolent part being able to establish itself as a particular kind of helper), and developing intimacy (e.g., the parts growing closer together) are important tasks during the middle stages of treatment.

The major "life cycle tasks" of the final stage involve generativity and integrity. These maturational tasks tend to move the internal system in the direction of integration. As the therapist works toward integration, he must sometimes deal with these issues directly, pointing out what needs to be done and actively working with ego states; at other times the parts can be observed to proceed almost autonomously and majestically into these areas. The process of reassociation, the stability of the therapeutic situation, and the accomplishment of stage-appropriate tasks provide the groundwork for the growth process. As parts deal with generativity and integrity, they often transmute themselves. A once raging hostile ego state is now a sweet, loving, caring internal force.

Case Example: Steven

During several hypnotic sessions with Steven, a three-year-old child ego state that hid in the darkness and refused to communicate verbally was encountered. He refused to allow any light into his environment. Through ideomotor signals this ego state eventually revealed that he thought I (CF) would soon kill him off.

I worked with several older ego states and asked them to spend time with him and to talk with him, even if he didn't answer them. I ex-

plained to them that he was frightened and needed both their understanding and their help. The parts spent time talking with this isolated
child part, and he was able to understand that neither the therapist nor
an older, angry alter who approached him constituted a danger to him.

Within two months he began to engage in verbal communication.
His name was Stevey. Eventually, Stevey confessed to me his wish that
he could grow older like another ego state, Steve, who had aged ten
years within a four-month period in real time. He was able to reveal his
fear of recalling a "bad situation" that he was still too frightened to
think about.

Stevey, in a poignant moment, revealed a longing for an ice cream
cone, and in a display of trust he accepted a symbolic ice cream cone
from another ego state between therapy sessions. After this his environment became flooded with light, he began to "hang out" with more
mature ego states, and was able to face frightening memory material.
Over a six-month period he matured considerably and had developed
an interest in games and computers.

FOCUSING ON THE PRESENT AND FUTURE TO TRANSFORM PAST IDENTITY

The patient may have significant difficulty with integration if the therapist
does not help him focus on the present and the future. The paradox of this
phase of therapy is that ego states that are frozen in past experiences and must
reassociate them must also pay attention to present-day interests, activities,
feelings, etc., and develop future aspirations and goals to assist in the formation of the patient's new identity. Patient and therapist may find themselves doing a balancing act at times. Often the failure to integrate appears to
spring from the patient's having nothing in the present as interesting and
exciting as the horrors of the past. Identity in this instance becomes frozen in
multiplicity, adaptationalism, or the dubious role of "survivorship." It is
the responsibility of the therapist help the patient get out of the trap of the
past.

Focusing on present successes and emerging shifts of interests related to
freedom and flexibility can reinforce the positive forces in the patient's life:
newly emerging interests and sensitivities, new assertiveness, new trust, new
warmth, new appreciation. Patients can be encouraged in activities that seem
to resonate with these changes: take a pottery class, go on wildflower hikes,
join a computer club, or investigate the religions of the world. There will be
an inevitable shift in relationships and friendships. This aspect of the work
can be promoted hypnotically both directly and indirectly. Metaphor and
storytelling are particularly useful here (Dolan, 1991).

Case Example: Dora

Dora had been in therapy with me (CF) for a year and a half. Although the parts had had little to do with one another initially, they eventually formed a working group, uncovered some traumatic memories, matured, and uncovered more traumatic memories. On the integrative spectrum Dora was at the adaptationalist stage: Parts cooperated but more work needed to be done. At this point Dora experienced a surge of interest and energy in many activities, both old and new. She looked up old friends, confronted a friend who constantly whined and complained, and began to make new friends and to date again. She also undertook the study of wildflowers with great enthusiasm and with some new friends learned to cross-country ski. She spent very little time with her relatives, although they had been her main social contacts for years. Her life had changed dramatically. Dora knew that there were more secrets to be examined, more painful moments to confront and experience, and that the parts of her personality needed to get much closer together; she also knew experientially something about why this was all worth it and what exciting directions her emerging new self could take. For the first time she began to think about her future.

Future Orientation, Hypnotic Age Progressions

It is gratifying when our patients become increasingly comfortable with integration; it is exciting when they grow in spurts, reaching out for growth as if it were necessary to their lives. This represents a churning of energy associated with the life cycle milestone, adolescence. It is during adolescence that the individual begins to consider whether the impossible is possible. Wise caretakers are usually discerning about the potentials of their adolescent students, their need for exploration, investigation, and trying on. Many of our patients will bring forth long suppressed talents, interests, and abilities. Therapy is an opportunity to explore untapped potentials. It is not unusual for patients to embark on new careers, leave dead relationships or other structures such as dead (to them) religions, find a new aesthetic appreciation of life, or discover a spiritual self. The movement to realize the potential within is a movement into life, away from the dead past.

Frequent use of hypnotic age progressions during integration assists the patient in making ongoing contact with previously unrecognized unconscious resources for future development. Kluft (1989) employs structured hypnotic age progressions to move certain personality parts to ages when they can comfortably fuse with others.

This kind of work can be done with unstructured or structured hypnotic age progressions. Dolan (1991), Torem (1992), and Gilligan (1993) encourage patients to write letters to themselves from the future as a way of filling out the details of the future projections and giving them more reality. Dolan (1991) uses a "time line" with certain patients, allowing them to project their future activities into a written schedule. Gilligan uses rituals for a change of identity. The therapist becomes a ritual specialist who helps the patient plan the ritual over the course of weeks or even months.

"Over the Rainbow": Developing a New Identity in the Termination Phase

People who have had successful therapy for significant problems frequently report that the termination phase of treatment can be extremely unsettling. The old configurations are no longer present, and the inclination to resort to old ways of coping just doesn't feel "right." This is an organic process and varies from person to person. No single technique can address the complex needs of this process. The therapist's function in this stage of treatment is very much like that of a midwife. An assortment of techniques, including inner strength, internal self-soothing, and future orientations, can be useful. The "I" that is present is new and continues to be formed in the post-integration period. It takes a certain amount of adjustment for the patient to live an ordinary life when most of his/her life has been spent in ceaseless obsessive compulsive rituals. There is no preparation for the influx of fresh perceptions and experiences, new competencies, novel insights. The ensuing months and years afford opportunities for the identity to continue to grow and change. For some patients integration means needing ongoing therapy to work through non-dissociative personality issues (Putnam, 1989; Ross, 1989). They are now able to address such difficult tasks without confusion. It is our experience that some personality problems may resolve themselves as the dissociative material is worked through. However, this is not true with every or even most patients, and post-integration therapy may have to address these issues. For most patients integration means having to learn how to deal with sexuality, work, creativity, and spirituality in a totally new way.

Therapy post-integration may be necessary for some of these issues. The ongoing use of self-hypnosis, ideodynamic healing, and self-help groups can also be useful.

9

DISSOCIATIVE SYMPTOMS IN DISGUISE

Many patients come to us with flashbacks, lapses of memory, and somatic reexperiencing, all clearly suggestive of dissociative difficulties. Others, however, may initially complain of symptoms characteristic of other syndromes, such as eating disorders, depression, and obsessive compulsive disorders. Only later does the dissociative nature of some of these symptoms come to the fore. Here we will describe symptoms of "masked dissociation" and outline some treatment strategies in these situations. Some of the cases we present fit the stress-diathesis model. This means that there may be genetic elements that predispose and shape the specific manifestations of psychopathology, as with obsessive compulsive disorder or panic disorder, but that current life stressors, as well as dissociated early trauma, enter the fertile genetic field to create the clinical manifestation of what otherwise would only be a predisposition.

The clinician can be faced with quite a puzzle to assemble, since many patients with difficulties that are not primarily dissociative in nature may also manifest some dissociative symptoms at times. There are also disorders, such as bipolar disorder and cyclothymic disorder, that can imitate dissociation, and these can be especially misleading at times because the flaring of their clinical symptoms is often precipitated by trauma.

It is important to discover whether certain clinical syndromes are masked dissociative disorders, since many dissociative disorders can be treated successfully. The ego-state approaches we describe are hypnoanalytic techniques that are based on an energy model of personality (see Chapter 4) and a metaphoric way of using that model. We remind the reader that ego states are personality energies – not "little people" inside. The usefulness of the newer term dissociative identity disorder (American Psychiatric Press, 1994) in casting light on this matter has been stressed by Beahrs (1993).

179

Eating Disorders

There is a recognized connection between child abuse and the whole spectrum of significant eating disorders (Goodwin & Attias, 1993; Goodwin, Cheeves, & Connell, 1988; Herman, 1992; Terr, 1991; Torem, 1986). Disturbed behavior surrounding the act of eating has often been associated with "classic clinical descriptions of multiple personality disorder (MPD) and incest victimization syndromes" (Goodwin & Attias, 1993, p. 327). Goodwin and Attias (1993) have cited abusive eating practices such as starvation, the forced feeding both of food and of substances that are not food, oral rape, and fellatio in the childhood experiences of many of their eating disorder patients, as well as emotional abuse about issues of weight and appearance. Both Herman (1992) and Goodwin and Attias (1993) have noted that eating and other meal-related activities may have been part of childhood abuse situations. Goodwin, Cheeves, and Connell (1988) found a high incidence of incest in their eating disorder patients.

Many of these patients have been found to be highly hypnotizable (Bliss, 1986; Torem, 1986), and dissociative symptoms have been reported in 75% of a group of bulimics studied by Abraham and Beaumont (1982). Torem (1984, 1986) also described eating disorder cases that appeared to be dissociative in nature. He (Torem, 1987) later observed that, although the eating disorders of anorexia nervosa and bulimia have been increasing in prevalence and many studies concerning them can be found in the literature, "their etiology remains obscure and their treatment controversial and less than satisfactory" (Torem, 1987, p. 101). However, he felt it important to identify those eating disorders that have a dissociative etiology (Torem, 1984, 1986, 1987) and described the successful use of Ego-State Therapy (Torem, 1987) with this category of patients. He also reported a high incidence of eating disorders among MPD patients (Torem, 1992, 1993a), as had Putnam et al. (1986).

Torem (1987) recommends a screening process with eating disorder patients. The therapist listens carefully for statements suggestive of dissociation and ego-state conflict. His examples include patients' descriptions of what happens to them when they experience the symptoms of anorexia or bulimia: confusion, fear, a sense of self-dividedness, trance states, lack of ego-syntonicity, and the feeling that something else inside has the control.

Torem has reported various non-hypnotic and hypnotic ways of getting in touch with personality parts producing dissociative eating disorders; he uses Bandler's reframing model (Bandler, 1978) for his therapeutic communication with ego states. This model emphasizes separating pattern from intention, negotiation for new behavior, ratification of the new behavior, and an "ecological review" of the system for acceptance and commitment to change and action.

Previously, we reported on the successful treatment of eating disorders that are dissociative in nature; Phillips (in press) described the successful treatment of overeating that was a dissociative symptom of post-traumatic stress disorder. She was able to detect elusive ego states that had manifested as somato-sensory symptoms. Frederick (1994a) reported the hypnotherapeutic treatment of ego-state-driven eating disorders in dissociative post-traumatic stress disorder patients. Their eating disorders alternated with other symptoms whose function is also to suppress post-traumatic symptoms, memories, and reexperiences of the original trauma (Goodwin & Attias, 1993).

We recommend that the therapist take a careful history with eating disorder patients and carefully screen them for dissociative signs and symptoms. Ideomotor exploration is invaluable. These patients need a great deal of ego-strengthening in their therapy. Although the eating disorder may symbolically reenact the original trauma, as well as suppress post-traumatic symptoms, in many cases it is also a self-soothing activity (McNeal & Frederick, 1994). The patient may find it difficult to surrender her symptoms until she is equipped to care for and soothe herself in other, non-destructive ways (Frederick, 1994a; McNeal & Frederick, 1994).

We cannot overemphasize the need for careful, ongoing medical check-ups and treatment in conjunction with psychotherapy and hypnotherapy for our serious eating disorder patients. These disorders are frequently life-threatening and can lead to death from such symptoms as electrolyte imbalance and cardiac arrhythmias. Insisting on medical treatment is one of the most valuable stabilizing moves the therapist can make. Patients at times attempt to resist this in the early stages of treatment. It is not negotiable.

Case Example: Nancy

Nancy (Frederick & McNeal, 1993) was a 38-year-old, twice-married woman who had consulted a psychotherapist because in the course of quitting smoking she had become addicted to nicotine polacrilex (Nicorette), a chewing gum that contains nicotine and is helpful in smoking cessation. The therapist noted that Nancy appeared depressed, and she was referred to me (CF) for evaluation and possible medication.

When seen in consultation, Nancy revealed that she suffered from long-standing bulimia with purging and induced vomiting. The bulimia had been partially controlled by her smoking (and later by the Nicorette), but it continued to erupt in the form of frequent uncontrolled eating binges. Since she had been taking Nicorette, she no longer felt impelled to induce vomiting after the binges.

Nancy had a history of precocious sexuality, promiscuity, and substance abuse (multiple drugs and alcohol), which had been in remission for five years; she also described symptoms of depression, as well as occasional suicidal thinking, nightmares, episodes of panic, and a troublesome voice inside her head telling her it was going to kill her.

Nancy was active in 12-step programs, had given up her sexual acting-out, and had been faithfully married for several years. She was extremely aware of the ticking of her biological clock, and she knew she would have to resolve her symptoms and stop using Nicorette to partially control the eating binges before she would be able to have a baby.

The patient's therapist decided to transfer the case to me, as it was felt that certain hypnotherapeutic approaches might be quite beneficial to the patient, especially if they were integrated with other aspects of her psychotherapy. She was given Prozac (fluoxetine) for partial symptomatic relief of her depression, as she had noticed some encroachment of her symptoms on her job performance.

Nancy progressed well in her treatment. With the use of ego-state approaches a communicative though nonverbal ego state called "Teeny Bouncer" appeared. Through ideomotor signals, Teeny allowed the patient to have some memories of childhood sexual abuse; further, she indicated that there had been other devastating trauma in childhood, but that it would be dangerous for the details to come out at this time. I believed that the patient and her family could not tolerate long-term working-through of early childhood trauma, which was still safely and adamantly shrouded by the amnestic barrier. However, treatment of the eating disorder was deemed essential from the standpoint of the patient's physical well-being, especially in view of her intention to become pregnant.

The ego state, Teeny Bouncer, became verbally communicative over the course of therapy. She was a protector part and produced the eating binges; she was in charge of the Nicorette addiction, and occasionally threatened to kill the patient. Work with Teeny Bouncer and other, more childlike ego states increased their communication and cooperation. This helped the patient resolve a number of conflicts in a successful way. The ego-strengthening technique, *inner strength* (see Chapter 5), was used with the greater personality to help her remain stable during the uncovering and working-through of traumatic material. Nancy's self-esteem increased, and the depression remitted. The Prozac dosage was lowered, and a plan was set up for the patient to come off this medication. The bulimic episodes virtually vanished. A compromise had been worked out with certain ego states so that the patient could have one reasonable overeating episode a week, one that was quite within the realm of normal behavior.

The patient was generally pleased with her progress, and she would have been agreeable to staying in psychotherapy as long as was required; however, her insurance money was running out, and a significant problem remained: She was continuing to use Nicorette to help control her eating binges.

Transference issues involving the patient's disappointment that she had not been able to get over her symptoms completely were explored, as were her wishes that she could continue her therapy to completion by paying for it from an unlimited source of funding. After careful consideration, I decided that Nancy was not holding onto her symptoms in order to prolong therapy and get me to treat her for no fee, nor did I think she was retaining them to frustrate me. Rather, the patient's disappointment seemed to be with herself. She had set a time limit for her therapy at its inception.

The patient's self-blaming attitude about the lack of complete resolution of her symptoms led me to ask the ego state, Teeny Bouncer, if it would be helpful for her to get to know a strong part of Nancy's personality in a direct and personal way. It was explained to Teeny that being able to share this enormous strength would probably be very helpful in dealing with Nicorette. The ego state was interested in having this experience. She had been somewhat aware of inner strength when the greater personality was introduced to this part, but her experience had been more that of an observer than of a participant. I explained to Teeny that there was a strong survival part of Nancy's personality that had always been there to help Nancy and the parts survive every terrible event in Nancy's life. By going to what seemed like the center of Nancy's being, Teeny Bouncer could directly experience this strong part.

I guided Teeny Bouncer through the inner strength experience in hypnosis (see Chapter 5). Teeny experienced religious imagery involving light and felt a sense of great calm and peace. In the next session, the patient was asked to have a hypnotic dream about the outcome of her difficulties. She reported:

> There was a man and a woman. . . . They were Indians, Native Americans. . . . I was that woman. . . . They were making a trip on horseback. . . . The woman was strong, serene. . . . I knew that no matter what happened, she could deal with it.

At the time of treatment termination, Nancy had reduced her Nicorette consumption from twenty or more pieces a day to two pieces a day, and she continued to overeat a socially acceptable amount once a week. She had a clear schedule for completing her Nicorette cessation program. Nancy and I agreed that she was following important priorities for her, and that she might experience a need to resume therapy at a later time in her life.

In a one-year follow-up phone call, she reported that she had not had any Nicorette in ten months, nor had she returned to smoking. She continued to "pig out" once a week as before, and she considered her eating disorder to be under control. She said that she was doing extremely well, was proud of her accomplishments, and was in the process of having some medical tests relevant to her plans to have a child.

In this case, bulimia with underlying dissociative pathology was a prominent feature; the ego state responsible for the symptoms was able to shift energy to other kinds of symptoms (cigarette smoking, Nicorette addiction). The projective/evocative ego-strengthening technique, inner strength, was useful in its resolution, and the therapy was adjusted to meet the patient's unique needs. Nancy's wish to fulfill her biological capacity for motherhood was seriously respected. The decision not to explore other possible childhood abuse was negotiated with the ego state, as the patient did not have the financial resources to continue therapy. The disruption caused by further exploration might have damaged her ability to conceive and care for a child. The internal family of selves agreed that they were willing to allow an amelioration of her bulimia and other addictive symptoms.

Depression

Depression is often thought to be multiply determined by biological factors, by experiences of loss, personality structures, and learned patterns of coping. Although DSM-IV (American Psychiatric Press, 1994) lists no category for dissociative depressive disorder, depression is a common symptom among patients who have been trauma victims. It is a prominent feature of MPD (DID) (Braun, 1986; Putnam, 1989; Ross, 1989) and of post-traumatic stress disorder (Terr, 1991).

Newey (1986) was the first to report the treatment of depression with Ego-State Therapy. One of the authors (Frederick, 1993a) described successful ego-state work with two patients whose intermittent depression had been refractory to previous treatment. In their treatment she emphasized regression and abreaction with ego states as well as ego-strengthening and mobilization of inner resources. Listing a number of signs and symptoms of ego-state pathology, such as the absence of ego-syntonicity, unusual affect, the language of parts, and the use of metaphoric descriptions of symptoms by the patient, Frederick advised clinicians to be alert for their appearance with depressive patients.

Case Example: Felicia

Felicia (Frederick, 1993a; Phillips & Frederick, 1991) had been successfully treated for a pervasive depression that had been accompanied by alcohol abuse and massive exploitation by her boyfriend, an amiable sociopath. She had joined Alcoholics Anonymous and moved to another city, where she was pursuing further educational and career possibilities. For some time she had been unaware of any depressive symptoms. Then she realized that she had resumed an old pattern of periodically experiencing what she called "wellings." These "wellings" would appear like a bolt out of the blue. She would be overcome by a tremendous feeling of sadness and discover that she was crying. The patient recalled that these short-lived episodes had been present in her life for as far back as she could remember. Their presence had been eclipsed by the massive depression from which she had recovered.

Felicia's mother had suffered from severe alcoholism and had literally drunk herself to death. Her father had been loving and supportive when he was present. However, he was a physician who had worked many hours when she was a child, and his wife had managed to conceal her alcoholism from him for many years, until it had become far advanced. The patient had significant gaps in her memory for her childhood. It is interesting that the patient did not bring up the "wellings" as a therapeutic issue until she and her siblings had been able to scatter the ashes of her mother, which she had been carrying around for years. Felicia was severely apprehensive about hypnotic exploration of the problem. Nonetheless, she wished to undergo it, for she wanted to be rid of the "wellings" and whatever they represented.

A decision was made by the patient and the therapist to conduct ego-state exploration. The patient was helped to enter trance, and particular attention was paid to deepening, as she was quite apprehensive. The ego state that knew something about the wellings was asked to come forth. The patient began to say that she was frightened. Her voice changed in pitch and timbre. It was evident that a child ego state was in the midst of a scene of a particular trauma, and there was visible evidence of fluctuation among ego states as they appeared to struggle for the "executive" position. The patient began to report being in a room of a house she had lived in as a child. She was aware of the floor heater.

Her mother was standing over her. The patient's hair was long. She was in a state of terror. Ideomotor signals indicated that the trauma had been repeated a number of times. At this point the patient seemed to be stuck. She was not able to proceed in memory toward resolution; nor was she able to leave the scene.

I (CF) helped her to leave the scene and to deepen her trance. The technique inner strength, in which the individual is guided into a projective/evocative experience of the strong survival part of the personality (Frederick & McNeal, 1993; McNeal & Frederick, 1993), was used. The patient was able to experience inner strength as her "business" personality: wearing suits, having short hair, and being a "hardass." It was suggested in trance that the patient could remember at her own pace (which would be guided by this strong part), when all the parts of her personality were ready for this to happen. It was also suggested that it would be valuable for her to use self-hypnosis to stay in touch with this strong part.

After the patient was brought out of trance, she reported that her feeling of terror had been extreme, although she had no inkling why. An appointment was scheduled for the following week. However, the patient called my answering service when she arrived at a nearby town some half-hour away: "Tell Dr. Frederick that I know exactly what it was!"

The following week Felicia revealed that the memory of her mother's burning her hand on the floor heater grate had just popped into her mind while she was driving. The retrieval of the memory was accompanied by a great sense of relief. She was deeply concerned about what kind of trauma might have been leveled at her younger siblings.

The "wellings" disappeared. The patient chose to put further hypnoanalytic exploration on the back burner as she focused on some imperative issues involving her living situation and work. She has since obtained an excellent job in a distant city; after some time she was able to get rid of the exploitative boyfriend who had followed her to her new environment. She understood that more of the past might well have to be worked with, and she was encouraged to pay careful attention to the messages some of her ego states might send her in the future through symptoms in her emotions and her body. She continues to do well over fours years later.

Panic Disorder and Agoraphobia

Panic disorder and agoraphobia are seldom described in terms of dissociative etiology in the literature (Frederick, 1993c), even though frankly dissociative symptoms, such as derealization, depersonalization, and dizziness, have been reported by Grunhaus (1988) as part of the clinical picture of panic disorder in approximately 90% of cases cited.

Panic attacks commonly occur in MPD (DID) patients (Bliss, 1986; Putnam, 1989; Putnam et al., 1986; Ross, 1989). Certain situations may trigger switches of alters or ignite post-traumatic flashbacks with resultant phobic or panic symptoms (Putnam, 1989). The symptoms of panic disorder and phobias have been reported as sequelae of incest (Fine, 1990); also, Herman (1992) has described "annihilation panic" in the chronically abused patient. This state, originally described by Adler (1985), is usually precipitated by a fear of abandonment and may lead to self-mutilation as it is not susceptible to self-soothing.

Case Example: Craig

Craig was a 38-year-old consulting engineer who initially denied any history of phobias or anxieties. He was an avid skier. He sought treatment because he had developed a panic attack after being stuck in a chairlift. He began to feel "strange," and developed an adrenaline rush, sweating palms, and chest pain: 'I felt stuck, really stuck!!' He thought he might be having a heart attack.

Craig was able to recall feeling similarly "stuck" in a freeway jam when he was 18. He also recalled another episode in some cave. "Part of me said, 'Run down that tunnel!!' The other part said, 'This will be embarrassing.'" He revealed that he had grown up in a turbulent and dysfunctional alcoholic family; he often feared he would lose his mind. He sometimes felt like he was drifting away.

In the second session, Craig was asked to close his eyes and simply let his mind drift forward into the future, to a time when the problems that had brought him into therapy had been completely resolved. He was asked to notice where he was and what he was doing so that we could discuss it when he had completed his experience. This was a hypnotic age progression (Phillips & Frederick, 1992). It was positive: He was able to picture himself both having a pleasant flight in an airplane and skiing happily on the mountain.

In the third session, Ego-State Therapy was begun. An ego state that called itself "Death" revealed that he had come to protect Craig. This ego state emerged very early in the patient's life. It described helping at a time when the patient had nearly drowned.

After several sessions of consistent work in and out of trance, Death was willing to undergo regression to an even earlier time when the patient's life was threatened. This was during his birth experience. The

patient had been stuck in his mother's birth canal and had to be removed with the assistance of forceps. Death said that this experience
was also connected with the patient's chairlift experience of being stuck.
Death's menacing symptoms had been attempts to help the patient
survive. Death agreed that it would be acceptable now to "clear the
circuits" for this experience, as he realized that Craig was not really
in life-or-death danger anymore. In the following session the patient
reported: "In the past couple of days I feel like I've dumped a bunch of
stuff. . . . I've lightened up. . . . I'm having fun. . . . I'm grateful for
my family."

    After a period of integration, the patient was discharged free of symp-
toms; he felt the quality of his life had greatly improved. He had been
seen for 12 sessions. No medication was used with this patient at any
time; he has been symptom-free for two years.

Obsessive Compulsive Disorder

Until recently obsessive compulsive disorder (OCD) has been thought to be
"a relatively rare extremely debilitating condition which is highly refractory to
treatment" (Turner, Bidel, & Nathan, 1985). New epidemologic data suggest that obsessive compulsive disorders and related disorders are much more
widespread than previously believed (Turner et al., 1985). A persistent feature of this disorder is its ego dystonia (Salzman & Thaler, 1981). Although
the purpose of the symptoms appears to be the relief of anxiety, the ego-
dystonic nature of the obsessions produces anxiety in and of itself, an anxiety
that is a consistent characteristic of the disorder. Other characteristics include
a belief on the part of the sufferer that she lacks voluntary control over the
symptoms and awareness that the thoughts she entertains and the acts she
must perform are not reasonable and may even be preposterous (Salzman &
Thaler, 1981).

    As the pendulum has swung far from psychodynamic approaches in the
treatment of OCD, serotonin reuptake inhibitors such as fluoxetine and ser-
traline have been used with success (Goodman, McDougle, & Price, 1992).
Combinations of medication and behavior therapy are now in vogue.

    Within the hypnosis literature, hypnoimagery (Kroger & Fezler, 1976)
and hypnoanalytic approaches (Crasilneck & Hall, 1975) have been used
with these disorders. Erickson and Kubie (1939) reported a case of permanent resolution of symptoms of obsessions and compulsions in a young
woman through the use of hypnosis with emphasis upon automatic writing
and crystal gazing. They discovered her to have a "dual personality." The
personality activated with hypnosis knew about the trauma that had precipitated the symptoms. When the therapist was able to get the two aspects of

the patient's personality to communicate with one another, the traumatic material was brought to consciousness and symptoms were resolved. Ross and Anderson (1988) have described patients with OCD who were also subsequently diagnosed as having multiple personality.

One of the authors (Frederick, 1990) reported the use of Ego-State Therapy to effect rapid treatment of a patient with obsessive compulsive disorder who did not have MPD. Since then she has seen two additional patients with whom Ego-State Therapy and some medication were used in combination for an extremely rapid resolution of severe, crippling OCD symptoms. In these cases the link between the obsessional and compulsive symptoms and childhood trauma was marked, and many clues to the dissociative nature of the difficulty were present.

Case Example: Priscilla

Priscilla came to therapy with me (CF) after her children's pediatrician expressed grave concern about the effect of her OCD symptomatology on her children. Priscilla spent most of her day scrubbing and washing: her hands, clothes, the groceries, etc. At times she stayed up into the early hours of the morning making certain everything was clean. Her hands were abraded from the constant washing. She so feared not being able to get things clean enough that she had the entire family remove all of their "outside clothes" in the hallway and change to "inside clothes" before they entered the house. She had become house-bound, and her symptoms were worsening. She had had unsatisfactory experiences with two previous therapists. She felt as if she were "possessed" because the reasonable side of her knew that her activities were bizarre. Several members of her family of origin also had OCD symptoms.

Although Priscilla was unable to take large or even ordinary doses of any serotonin reuptake antagonist available because they produced cardiac arrhythmia, she was able to take a very small dose (10 mg/day) of flouxetine (Prozac) for help with her considerable depressive symptomatology. In her first hypnotic session ideomotor exploration indicated the presence of an ego state that was associated with the patient's OCD symptoms. Priscilla reported visual imagery of a dark wall and simultaneous feelings of fear, an impending sense of dread, and hopelessness.

In her therapy sessions Priscilla described how she was raised in a cult-like fundamentalist religion, which several members of her family continue to practice. Her mother was "always right about everything," and the patient was initially convinced that I would soon share her mother's knowledge about how bad she was. As her story continued to unfold two themes emerged. One was of her mother's self-justified sadism and severe need to control; the other was that her father left the family when she was a little girl and that her sister had told her he had molested them. Of this the patient said in an elevated voice: "I don't ever want to remember that if it happened to me, and at the same time I think it's what's causing me to be sick! Tell me that's not the cause." I told Priscilla that we didn't know what the causes were yet, and that she wouldn't have to remember anything until the parts of her personality were ready. I suggested that if she had been abused by her father that this would certainly be terrifying to childlike aspects of herself.

In the next session Priscilla described memory experiences of being sexually molested by her father that had unfolded over the past week. She also said that her symptoms were beginning to lose their intensity, and that she and her family had made a trip to a rural resort that featured hot geysers and bubbling mud. The family planned a picnic in their own backyard as their next project. She volunteered, "The wall has crumbled."

I was away for a month. Priscilla had the option of seeing another therapist in my absence, but she asserted herself and said she did not want to do this. Upon my return she informed me that she could scarcely wait to see me to tell me how much better she was. She attended her children's soccer games regularly and was thinking of resuming piano lessons. Her symptoms were steadily resolving, and she now had a lot of time on her hands. Her biggest news was that they had bought a puppy. Ego-State Therapy revealed a complete disappearance of the wall. The space it formerly occupied was filled with warm light, and the associated feeling was one of lightness, happiness, and hope. I asked the ego state if it would be willing to cause those feelings to grow more intense if this meant that resolution of Priscilla's difficulties was well in process. The patient's face became wreathed in smiles, and she later reported that the feelings of lightness, happiness, and hopefulness had increased dramatically.

Although she improved within three months, Priscilla continues in treatment once every two or three weeks. Nine months after the beginning of therapy she drives the car alone, browses in drugstores and shopping malls, uses public bathrooms, is planning a camping trip, has started a retail business that involves close contact with the public, and has more time on her hands than soap and water. They have bought another puppy.

Obsessive compulsive disorder is a complex clinical phenomenon. We do not know what role trauma may play in its development and which symptoms may be dissociative in nature. Is there a true spectrum from the most biologic in origin to the most psychological in origin among these patients? If so, what is the pattern of the distribution curve? These questions await investigation. We do know that Ego-State Therapy promises certain patients relief, and that it can be used at times with small amounts of medication and at others with no medication at all. Ego-state exploration should be considered with patients with obsessive compulsive symptoms when marked ego dystonia is present, when there is unexplained affect, or when other signs of dissociative symptoms are present.

Borderline and Other Personality Disorders

Borderline personality disorder is defined in DSM-IV as: "A pervasive pattern of instability of interpersonal relationships, self-image, and affects, and marked impulsivity beginning by early adulthood and present in a variety of contexts . . . " (American Psychiatric Press, 1994, p. 280). Five of nine areas of dysfunction are required for the diagnosis. They include such symptoms as a frantic effort to avoid real or imagined abandonment, alternating extremes of idealization and devaluation in relationships, identity disturbance as manifested by a persistent, marked stable self-image or sense of self, impulsivity, certain self-destructive behaviors (suicidal behavior, self-mutilation), instability of affect, chronic feelings of emptiness, anger that is inappropriate, intense, or uncontrolled, and transient paranoid ideation that is related to stress or severe dissociative symptoms.

Borderline personality disorder (BPD) is thought by many to be the result of early developmental failures (Baker, 1981; Brown & Fromm, 1986; Gunderson, 1984; Kernberg, 1984; Masterson, 1981). These failures result in a lack of appropriate integration of internal object representations which are extremely unstable, prone to fragmentation, and often split. Borderline patients cannot form stable transferences. Instead, the transference is marked by splitting, boundary diffusion, fragmentation of representations of both the self and the object, and panic states (Brown & Fromm, 1986). The hypnotherapist's task in working with BPD patients is to provide an environment that facilitates stability and permits the patient, over a period of time, to repair developmental defects and integrate object representations (Baker, 1981; Brown & Fromm, 1986).

The greatly increased frequency in the diagnosis of dissociative and post-traumatic conditions has been accompanied by a decline in BPD diagnoses. This has been perplexing to some. Kroll (1993) reminds us that five books written by experts in the field of borderline personality disorders between 1975 and 1988 make only brief and transient references to dissociative episodes or symptoms in BPD patients. Aware that dissociative phenomena are seen in increasing numbers in consultation and emergency rooms, Kroll (1993) offers an explanation for this: "The best conclusion that I can reach to explain the apparent increase in prevalence and prominence of dissociative symptoms in borderlines is that the psychiatric profession has coached patients in what symptoms they are expected to display" (p. 214). Boor (1982) also wondered whether a change in "diagnostic inclinations" (p. 302) might account for the sharply increased incidence of MPD diagnoses.

Nevertheless, DSM-IV has changed the criteria for the diagnosis of BPD to include the presence of severe dissociative symptoms. The issue is not a simple one. Clinicians in the field of dissociation have also been wondering about the connection between borderline personality disorder and the dissociative disorders, particularly multiple personality disorder. Some (Baker, personal communication, 1992; Clary, Burstin & Carpenter, 1984) believe multiple personality disorder to be a special type or class of borderline personality disorder, whereas others (Horevitz & Braun, 1984) believe them to be distinct diagnostic entities. Many believe MPD to be frequently misdiagnosed (Boor, 1982; Coons, 1984; Putnam et al., 1986) and confused with other personality or affective disorders as well as with schizophrenia.

Kemp, Gilbertson, and Torem (1988) addressed the problem in a study to identify diagnostic variables. In their comparison of two patient groups diagnosed as MPD and BPD respectively, they used psychological testing, psychosocial histories, and clinician reports, and rated the level of psychosocial stressors as well as the highest level of adaptive functioning. They found the two groups "remarkably similar" (p. 44); however, they noted certain trends. MPD patients had more stable histories, higher I.Q.'s and a higher level of education, made more reports of childhood abuse, and were less frequently involved with the law. "It is possible that a key difference between the two groups is the acknowledgment of a memory disturbance" (p. 44) by the MPD group. Kemp, Gilbertson, and Torem (1988) felt the two difficulties to be related and suggested that sophisticated research and statistical techniques would be required to explicate the nature of their relationship.

Another way of viewing borderline pathology that we find extremely useful is that proposed by Herman (1992). According to Herman many survivors of childhood abuse have a "disguised presentation" (Gelinas, 1983) and may acquire a number of diagnoses before the traumatic roots of their difficulties are recognized. These patients may transferentially relive their trauma by becoming involved with the health care system in much the same way they were involved with their abusers in childhood. There they may receive neglect, mistreatment, and revictimization, as well as pejorative diagnoses. "The most notorious is the diagnosis of borderline personality disorder" (Herman, 1992, p. 123).

Herman believes the diagnoses of borderline personality disorder, somatization disorder, and multiple personality disorder are directed at symptoms that were once included among "the hysterias" (Abse, 1966; Ellenberger, 1970). Patients within these three categories are highly hypnotizable and display high levels of dissociation. Herman (1992) finds their interpersonal relationships similarly troubled. Like borderline patients MPDs also have stormy interpersonal relationships, develop "special" relationships, engage in boundary violations, and become terrified of real or threatened abandonment. Herman believes that patients labeled as "borderline" and "MPD" suffer from "complex post-traumatic stress disorder." Borderline patients, like dissociative patients, develop traumatic transferences (Herman, 1992, pp. 136–140).

Herman's (Herman, Russell, & Troki, 1986) investigations with borderline patients were able to document severe childhood trauma histories in a majority (81%) of cases studied. "The specific relationship between symptoms of borderline personality disorder and a history of childhood trauma have now been confirmed in numerous other studies" (Herman, 1992, p. 126).

We treat patients in the borderline category with special mindfulness of traumatic transference and countertransference issues. We employ a variety of hypnotic approaches, including Ego-State Therapy, to help with safety and stability, to uncover and reprocess trauma, and to facilitate maturation at the object relations, psychosexual, psychosocial, and ego-state levels. Most of all we attempt to remain flexible, as the focus of therapy may shift rapidly from trauma to developmental issues to life-and-death crises.

Case Example: Juan

Juan is a 38-year-old patient with a primary diagnosis of borderline personality disorder. The first two years of therapy were spent in helping him achieve full sobriety as a recovering alcoholic and drug addict. When he began to focus on his childhood experiences, he started to retrieve information related to sexual abuse experiences with his father and two uncles. Ego-State Therapy was very helpful to Juan during this time in allowing him to access and integrate a series of traumatic experiences.

Two years ago, Juan began developing symptoms that resulted in neck surgery to fuse two of his cervical discs. After a "plateau period" of several months, Juan began deteriorating physically and emotionally. Hypnosis sessions, at one time helpful in achieving relaxation and mastery over pain levels, became frightening and confusing, occasionally resulting in access to psychotic material. Ego-State Therapy, once integrative for Juan, seemed to lead to further fragmentation and de-spair.

In his discouragement, Juan began to consider decreasing the fre-quency of his sessions with me (MP), and even terminating treatment. I decided to seek consultation and made several changes in our work together, based on the consultant's suggestions. First, we validated the intense feelings that had been triggered by the surgery and understood how this medical trauma had evoked more primitive traumatic re-sponses than previously identified in therapy. Next, we began to moni-tor his medication more closely, observing that his most recent cycle of deterioration had occurred at about the same time his neurologist had begun trials of several tricyclic antidepressants, including imipramine, for Juan's headache pain, believed to be related to occipital neuritis. At the consultant's recommendation, his medicating psychiatrist and I decided to try a low dosage of trifluoperazine (Stelazine), an antipsy-chotic medication.

Juan had an immediately positive response to his medication change, and we were able to restabilize our therapy relationship. When we resumed our hypnotic work, sessions were carefully structured to help him strengthen his positive "self" and "object" experiences by working with a series of images in a prescribed sequence (Baker, 1983b). First I suggested the development of images of himself in positive, relaxed circumstances followed by images of me associated with similar positive, relaxed feelings. Ultimately he was able to access images of the two of us in my office engaging in dialogue that felt nurturing and reassuring to him. These images were used to neutralize affect related to increases in pain levels, achieve a sense of mastery in approaching disturbing life problems, and to manage negative transference experiences so that he could maintain his positive feelings of connection to me. As of this writing, Juan's pain levels have dramatically and consistently reduced, and he is hopeful about his future success in coping with the long-term implications of occipital neuritis.

Juan illustrates the fact that borderline patients often require attention to structural, pre-neurotic pathology in addition to appropriate treatment of trauma experiences and dissociative issues.

Somatic Expressions of Trauma

Somatic symptoms of psychosomatic disorders have been reported with high frequency among those suffering from post-traumatic stress syndromes (Horowitz, Wilner, Kaltreider, & Alvarez, 1980; Krystal & Niederland, 1968; Niederland, 1981). Courtois (1988) has discussed the appearance of a wide variety of anxiety-based medical symptoms in those who have experienced childhood incest. James (1989) has observed that many traumatized children behave as though alienated from all or parts of their bodies, and Monane, Leichter, and Lewis (1964) have noted a wide range of neurobehavioral dysfunctions in this population. Herman (1982) has postulated a link between somatization disorder and childhood abuse. She suggests that somatization disorder may be best understood as a variant of complex PTSD and treated as a manifestation of an underlying childhood trauma experience.

Some of these somatic phenomena include flashbacks, which are often misdiagnosed as psychosomatic conditions (Herman, 1992). As Peterson, Prout, and Schwarz (1991) point out, various psychophysiological states, such as insomnia, fatigue, and elevated stress, may trigger dissociated somatic states. Thus, it may be particularly difficult to differentiate flashbacks from anxiety responses to nontrauma-related stimuli (Phillips & Frederick, 1993). Because of this complexity, it may also be difficult for the clinician who is untrained in somatic approaches to know how to approach and treat these phenomena.

The effectiveness of Ego-State Therapy in treating various aspects of the trauma response has been discussed throughout this book. We have also explored the use of Ego-State Therapy in the treatment of various somatic expressions of trauma, and incorporated hypnotic techniques such as sensory exploring (Alman & Lambrou, 1992), sensory restructuring (Erickson & Rossi, 1979), somatic experiencing (Levine, 1991, 1994), somatic bridging (Watkins, 1990), and ideosensory signaling (Erickson & Rossi, 1979) into ego-state methodology. Some of these approaches are illustrated in the following case example.

Case Example: Lois

Lois is a 40-year-old computer programmer who first consulted me (MP) for alcohol and drug addiction issues. Once she had been fully stabilized in her recovery process, dream material began to surface in which her father was being sexually seductive. Along with this, Lois reported several acute anxiety symptoms, including panic about going to sleep at night, difficulty concentrating on work tasks, headaches, and stomach pains after eating. Since Lois believed that these symptoms might be related to the dreams, we decided to explore these using hypnosis.

During the first session designed to focus on the dream material, I asked Lois to review her current anxiety symptoms and to begin focusing on body sensations that were occurring at that moment. Once she described her current somatic state, we used somatic bridging (Watkins, 1990; see Chapter 6) as an age regression technique, suggesting that her unconscious could help her travel back in time to an earlier time and place when she was experiencing similar physical sensations. After a brief pause, Lois described an image of herself as a little girl standing in her father's shadow. The "little girl" watched as her father touched himself around the fly of his pants; then the image faded. As we processed her reactions to this experience, Lois spontaneously retrieved several details that were a part of her conscious memories and helped them to make "more sense" to her.

As we continued our explorations, two child ego states were identified related to sexual abuse material: a three-year-old who appeared in the first session and had been sexually abused by her father on several occasions in the garage behind her house, and a ten-year-old who was molested frequently by her father at night in her bedroom. These ego states were activated primarily through ideosensory and somatic bridging approaches that utilized current somatic symptoms and sensations. As more material emerged, we also used sensory exploring (Alman & Lambrou, 1992) approaches, which involve simple tracking of various sensory aspects during hypnosis so that they can be reconnected with the mainstream of consciousness. During one ego-state session, as Lois explored a dream image of blood, she spontaneously accessed an image of bleeding from her vagina as her father penetrated her. She began feeling the pain in her body and described "white light coming in and beginning to move toward that light." I encouraged her to stay with her experience of the light and also to feel the sensations in her vagina at the same time, rather than dissociating. As she did, she saw an image of a little girl reaching out her hand: "She doesn't want to be left there. . . . I take her hand. Now my whole body feels different . . . like all of me is here now. I feel whole."

As we continued to access and work through these kinds of inner experiences, Lois was given an opportunity to renegotiate the sexual abuse experiences, using the somatic experiencing model (Levine, 1991). This involved activating somatic resources in her body that had been previously immobilized by fear and helplessness and was accomplished in different ways as Lois imagined smashing her father's head, running from the room, and using her legs to push him off her onto the floor. As she described these images, I suggested that she actually experience her muscles completing these movements, helping to further reassociate her body in positive ways with other aspects of her experience.

Not only do these types of somatic approaches to hypnosis and Ego-State Therapy help to access traumatic experiences that may have somatic encoding, but they can also help the patient to achieve relief from psychosomatic symptoms. Further, tracking of sensory aspects of traumatic experiences through impaired ego states, reassociating them to full consciousness, and renegotiating traumatic events so that more complete physiological functioning is restored, can help the patient to achieve more complete personality integration (Phillips, in press).

Identifying and utilizing somatic experience in the treatment process appear to be essential for full resolution of traumatic experiences (Bentzen, Jarinaes, & Levine, 1993; Levine, 1991, 1994; van der Kolk & Greenberg, 1987). Many approaches to the treatment of trauma-based disorders, including hypnosis, often overlook the vital role played by somatic responses in the potential for recovery. Somatically based hypnotic techniques of sensory exploration, ideosensory signaling, and somatic bridging can be incorporated by therapists who do not have formal training in body-based therapies, thereby providing healing for the "body self" (Bentzen, Jarinaes, & Levine, 1993) as well as for the personality.

INDIRECT EXPRESSIONS OF EGO STATES AS DISGUISED SYMPTOMS

Mystifying symbolic visualizations may also be reported by many post-traumatic patients. They may be accompanied by somatic and sensory phenomena related to the neural and muscular systems, although they may appear as flashbacks which may not be identified as such initially. These flashbacks, " . . . can occur as full memories, fragments which are difficult to understand, intrusive thoughts with or without affect, and overwhelming affect" (Phillips & Frederick, 1993). Flashbacks may come in the form of smells, tastes, sensations, sights, and sounds" (Dolan, 1991, p. 14). At times fragments of imagery that are disturbing and apparently meaningless may appear (Horowitz, 1986). These fragments may be " . . . inexplicable, foreboding, highly symbolic in nature" (McCann & Pearlman, 1990, p. 30).

Like individual patients, individual ego states communicate in many ways (Frederick, 1990, 1992; Phillips & Frederick, 1993; Phillips, in press), including symbolic, sensory, and motor signals as well as affective and physical manifestations. Ego states signaling their presence in such elusive ways are attempting, often repeatedly, to establish communication with the therapist. Because these ego states in disguise also seem to frustrate initial attempts at recognition, they may be overlooked and even avoided by both therapist and hypnotic subject. Patient, systematic attempts to link these symbolic expressions with significant parts of the personality can often unlock the mysteries of the patient's most puzzling and profound symptomatology.

Ego states associated with significant pathology can manifest in mysterious and enigmatic ways such as symbolic visualizations and somatosensory signals. The therapist can learn to recognize them and to distinguish them from flashbacks. Unlike flashbacks, the symbolic visual experiences do not stimulate fearful affect in patients, nor do they seem directly related in most cases to the traumatic material with which they are associated. Their connections with particular parts of the personality that are in some way connected with symptomatology can usually be verified ideomotorically.

Conflicts among ego states can be revealed through a physiologic manifestation, such as a warm flush, a welling of tears, or a one-sided numbness. When these conflicts threaten to derail uncovering work, they must be negotiated and resolved satisfactorily. The full complement of hypnoanalytic techniques, such as regression, abreaction, and ego-strengthening, can be used with these mysterious, highly symbolic, and sensory ego states.

10

TRANSFERENCE AND COUNTERTRANSFERENCE ISSUES

The difficulties in treating dissociative spectrum patients may evoke complex feelings and reactions in both therapist and patient (Chu, 1988; Comstock, 1991; Greaves, 1988; Kluft, 1988; Loewenstein, 1993; Putnam, 1989; Watkins & Watkins, 1984). This chapter presents an overview of traumatic transferences that can develop in the dissociative patient and considers their interaction with countertransference issues. Methods of developing positive countertransference response states are also explored.

Transference Issues with Dissociative Patients

The concept of transference offers a useful framework for understanding the dissociative patient's often complex responses to his therapist. Learning to recognize, manage, and communicate with the patient about important transference issues is an important part of any therapist's work. This section highlights information about transference in general and traumatic transference in specific, and offers suggestions for resolving traumatic transference problems in work with the dissociative patient.

DEFINITIONS OF TRANSFERENCE

Transference has been defined as "responses to a therapist that are primarily based on, and displaced from, significant childhood figures, especially parents and siblings" (Langs, 1977, p. 151). Most current views of transference involve an interpersonal "field" (Loewenstein, 1993). From this viewpoint, manifestations of transference originate from an interplay between the patient's reactions to the therapist and actual therapy events, in addition to the patient's unconscious reactions to important people from his past and present life (Gill, 1982; Langs, 1977; Peebles-Kleiger, 1989).

Historically, Freud discovered the phenomena of resistance and transference and considered them barriers to the therapy process. At the beginning of his work, he viewed the main objective of analysis as achieving cathartic abreaction and recovering traumatic memories; transference was simply an obstacle for the analyst to circumvent or help the patient overcome (Greenson, 1967).

Freud (1905) first emphasized the positive role of transference in the case of Dora, a dissociative (then termed "hysterical") patient. With Dora his failure to recognize and handle a transference reaction led to premature termination and therapeutic failure. Subsequently, he maintained that transference, which can be one of the greatest obstacles to psychoanalysis, "becomes its most powerful ally, if its presence can be detected each time and explained to the patient" (Freud, 1905, p. 117). Freud then began to view the analysis of transference and resistance as the central focus of the therapeutic process. He wrote of the twofold powers of transference in presenting the analyst with both the greatest difficulties and the "inestimable service" of making the patient's "hidden . . . erotic impulses immediate and manifest" (Freud, 1912, p. 108). He warned against the dangers of transference gratification by the analyst, emphasizing the need for therapist neutrality, "like a mirror, . . . [showing] nothing but what is shown" (Freud, 1912, p. 118). Freud also suggested that the ego could be greatly expanded and strengthened by analyzing transference experiences.

According to Freud, transference is a repetition, a new edition of an old object relationship (Freud, 1905). Basically, a person in the present is reacted to as though he were a person in the past. Transference is the experiencing of emotional responses toward a person in the present which do not fit that person but are a repetition of reactions originating in relation to significant persons of early childhood, unconsciously displaced onto figures in the present (Greenson, 1967). Transference can consist of any of the components of an object relationship, including feelings, drives, wishes, fears, fantasies, attitudes, and ideas, or defenses against these elements (Greenson, 1967). The transference repetition may be an exact duplication of the past relationship, a replica, a reliving, a new edition, or a modified version usually in the direction of wish fulfillment (Greenson, 1967).

Transference reactions are more likely to occur in later life toward those who perform a special function that was originally carried out by parents. Consequently, authority figures, physicians, teachers, lovers, therapists, and employers are particularly likely to evoke these kinds of responses. Animals and inanimate objects, as well as groups and institutions, may also elicit transference responses.

CHARACTERISTICS OF TRANSFERENCE

Transference reactions are always inappropriate in their quality, quantity, or duration in the current context. An inappropriate current reaction is an indicator that the person who originally triggered the response is probably a figure from the past. For example, a new patient who had been told in great detail the directions to my (MP) office, was late for his appointment and very angry at me because he lost his way. In exploring his reaction, he recalled that his mother would send him on errands, always withholding an important part of the directions and then blaming him for his inability to complete the task. His anger toward me was unrealistic but fit perfectly with his unexpressed past reactions to his mother's behavior.

Almost always, intensity in emotional reactions to the therapist is suggestive of transference responses. Although some emotional responses to the therapist are appropriate and realistic, these may have a transference core that can be fruitfully explored (Greenson, 1967). Absence of emotional reactions is equally suggestive of transference, since withholding intense reactions can indicate underlying fear or shame.

Another characteristic of transference is ambivalence, or the coexistence of opposite feelings. The root of ambivalent reactions to the therapist is the splitting of therapist into good object and bad object, each of which elicits intense reactions. Usually one aspect of the ambivalence is unconscious. Thus, when there are love feelings for the therapist, there are usually covert hateful ones as well. Ambivalence can be easily perceived when the feelings are mercurial and change unexpectedly. In other cases one aspect will be tenaciously held in consciousness while its opposite is defended against, or one component will be displaced onto another person, often another therapist or professional figure (Greenson, 1967).

Among the most noticeable characteristics of transference are repetition, resistance to change, and tenacity. Transference reactions are never wholly satisfying because they are only substitutes for real satisfactions (Fenichel, 1941), yet the continual search for gratification is one of the primary motivations for transference. Repetition may be also be a means of achieving mastery over a past relationship. Greenson (1967) suggests that the ego, which was passive in the original traumatic interaction, actively reproduces the event when it chooses, and thus slowly learns to cope with it as a belated attempt to master the original interpersonal anxiety. Related notions are that repeated transference acting-out may be an attempt to complete unfulfilled tasks (Lagache, 1953), master the environment, and achieve pleasure in competence (Fromm, 1984).

TRAUMATIC TRANSFERENCE

The therapist who works with dissociative patients needs a working understanding of traumatic transference, which may seem like an intense life-or-death reaction to the therapist and the therapy situation (Herman, 1992), "as if the patient's life depends on keeping the therapist under control" (Kernberg, 1984, p. 114).

Herman (1992) has described several aspects of traumatic transference, which can have a dramatic impact on the therapeutic relationship. One factor is the terror the patient feels related to the violence of the perpetrator. As Lister (1982, p. 872) put it, "The terror is as though the patient and therapist convene in the presence of yet another person. The third image is the victimizer, who . . . demanded silence and whose command is now being broken." Along with terror is the experience of helplessness and total abandonment at the moment of trauma. Herman (1992) points out that the greater the feeling of helplessness and abandonment, the more desperately the victim of trauma feels the need for an omnipotent rescuer. Often the therapist is cast in this role, and when the idealized expectations are not met, the patient is enraged, his rage toward the abuser being displaced onto the therapist as rescuer.

Trust is a major issue in the traumatic transference (Courtois, 1988; Herman, 1992; Kluft, 1984a; Putnam, 1989; Spiegel, 1986). As Spiegel (1986, p. 72) has pointed out, "The patient unconsciously expects that the therapist, despite overt helpfulness and concern, will exploit the patient for his or her own narcissistic gratification." Because of this tendency, virtually all aspects of therapy may be unconsciously perceived by the patient to indicate abusive intent. For example, accessing and working with traumatic memory material may be experienced as retraumatization by the patient, no matter how carefully conducted or explicitly agreed to by the patient. Herman (1992) suggests that traumatic mistrust creates a difficult therapeutic bind for patient and therapist. If the therapist backs away from the trauma, the traumatized patient doubts the therapist's ability to listen to the details of his story and feels abandoned; yet, if the therapist does not back away from the trauma, the patient may suspect him of exploitative or voyeuristic intentions.

Since trust is the earliest developmental task in Erik Erikson's (1950) schema and the foundation on which all others are built, the traumatized patient's failure to establish basic trust leaves him severely impaired. Identity development is disturbed, along with the ability to form healthy and mutual relationships and to experience intimacy (Courtois, 1988). Braun (1986) has stated that issues of trust arise at every major point in therapy of the dissociative patient. Since fear reactivates mistrust responses, the therapist should not take the development of trust for granted in the therapeutic relationship, but rather should expect that trust issues will resurface throughout the treatment process, particularly at times of growth and risk-taking.

The mechanism of projective identification is considered central to the traumatic transference process. In projective identification, the patient "not only sees the other as having feelings not tolerable to the self, but also exerts an intense pull on the other to identify with and temporarily embrace those very feelings, however uncharacteristic they may be for that person" (Peebles-Kleiger, 1989, p. 519). For example, if the new patient described earlier in this chapter had been utilizing projective identification, he might have been uncommunicative about his feelings in being late, while I (MP) might have felt irritated and angered by him, without understanding why. A major difference between projection and projective identification is that with the latter defense, neither therapist or patient is consciously aware of the origins of the problem feelings.

Through projective identification, the patient may induce the therapist to reenact the trauma relationship outside of consciousness. Herman (1992) has indicated that the chronically traumatized patient has often developed an exquisite attunement to his victimizer's cognitive and emotional states, which is transferred to the verbal and nonverbal communications of the therapist. Because he has no trust in the therapist's benign intentions, he pathologically scrutinizes every word and gesture in an attempt to protect himself from damaging reactions he expects to receive. Drawn into these dynamics, the therapist may inadvertently reenact some aspects of the abusive relationship (Herman, 1992).

Transference feelings related to trauma may also be projected onto the therapist, further hampering the development of a trusting relationship. Courtois (1988) pointed out that shame and self-hatred, related to the patient's belief that something inherently wrong with him caused the abuse to occur, may be projected onto the therapist along with the expectation of a reenactment of any nonprotection or blame for the abuse. Dynamics of overresponsibility can also be projected onto the therapeutic relationship, with the patient being overly considerate and conscientious or in other ways counterdependent in order to avoid rejection and betrayal. In this situation, the patient is not able to ask for caretaking directly, but may become furious if the therapist cannot "read his mind" and know his needs as the patient is able to do with others (Courtois, 1988). Other feelings in the traumatic transference may include guilt, grief and loss, and rage and anger.

Another less common aspect of traumatic transference is a "perceptual illusion" experience where the therapist is literally perceived by the patient as a specific abuser (Spiegel, 1986). Loewenstein (1993) calls this "flashback transference" (p. 57). Briere (1992) agrees that this is a perceptual distortion rather than a manifestation of projective identification. Since MPD and highly dissociated patients display altered perceptions and trance-like phenomena on a routine basis, certain alters and ego states may consistently hallucinate the therapist as an abusive figure from the past. On occasion, some alters may even provide misleading auditory and visual impressions of the therapist to other alters. As a result, these alters may relate inadequately to contemporary reality in the therapy situation. It may be useful in working with dissociative patients to assume that these kinds of phenomena are occurring in the transference field, and if they are identified, to convey that such perceptions may be functioning as a protective or compensatory measure (Loewenstein, 1993).

Severely dissociated and MPD patients are capable of generating highly complex transference reactions. As Putnam (1989) points out, the trigger for the transference response will certainly influence its form, but the primary determinant seems to be the nature of the internal personality system. For example, if a patient's internal system is composed mainly of helpless child alters, the transference reactions toward the therapist may be ones where the therapist is perceived in various ways as the sexual abuser from the past and the alters are regressed, helpless, and terrified in their therapy responses. If most of the system consists of adolescent alters who attempted to handle past sexual abuse, transference reactions may be more manipulative and seductive.

Resolving Traumatic Transference Issues

A basic tool in resolving difficult transference issues with dissociative disorder patients is the therapist's ability to help the patient establish and maintain a *strong working alliance*. As Greenson (1967) points out, the core of the working alliance is formed by the patient's motivation to overcome his pathology and his sense of helplessness, by his conscious willingness to cooperate, and by his ability to respond purposefully to the interventions of the therapist.

Loewenstein (1993) has noted that building and maintaining a good working alliance can be extremely challenging with more complex dissociative disorder and MPD patients, who find in the therapist's acceptance an "implicit endorsement of their wish to be cared for and an absolution of the need to . . . share the burdens of the work of the therapy" (p. 30). The alters or ego states in an MPD system may have somewhat independent transference reactions to the therapist, adding a level of complexity. Thus, alters may have a number of different reactions to the same therapy stimulus, which may be expressed simultaneously, sequentially, or in chaotic combinations (Putnam, 1989).

In work with MPD (DID) and some dissociative patients, it is important to note that the working alliance may be different with each of several different alters or ego states. As we stressed in Chapters 4 and 8, the therapist must work slowly and methodically to establish a solid alliance with each emerging subpersonality, including those that are nonverbal or preverbal.

Guidelines for maintaining a good working alliance with dissociative patients include:

1. Be prepared to educate and remind patients repeatedly of their duties and responsibilities in the therapy process in comparison with the therapist's role. If the patient is not working adequately in therapy, this deficiency must be confronted and underlying feelings worked through.

2. Emphasize patient choice in approaching, sustaining, or completing any therapy task. This will help the patient clarify that therapeutic work is valuable in and of itself and not as a vehicle to obtain the therapist's approval or caretaking.

3. Use the cooperation principle to involve the patient as an active partner in the therapy process. If the patient is not contributing, we often insist that he supply at least one idea, understanding, or possibility before matching with one of our own.

4. If working with an MPD or complex dissociative disorder patient who is having difficulty sustaining a good working alliance, check for readiness with various ego states, since they may have different and conflicting needs in the therapeutic relationship.

A second important tool in the management of transference issues is the use of *consistent boundaries and limit setting*. As Briere (1992) points out, survivors of childhood abuse and trauma have been taught that relationship boundaries are "negotiable" and that roles cannot be counted on consistently. Boundary issues come up repeatedly in the work with dissociative patients. Because of early abuse and neglect, these patients are often desperate to receive the kind of nurturing and love that was absent in their families. This may be expressed as a wish to be "loved into health" (Kluft, 1984a) by the therapist. The therapist must deal with various "pulls" for reparenting through interpretation rather than through boundary violations and inappropriate gratification.

The therapist may want to discuss the importance of healthy boundaries as part of the healing process early and often in the therapy, emphasizing that clarification and maintenance of consistent boundaries are central tasks of therapy. The purpose is to help the patient gain mastery through new learning rather than to experience retraumatization through reenactment (Loewenstein, 1993). It may also be useful to introduce a related focus on internal boundaries and the development of internal coping, soothing, and growth mechanisms through increased internal cooperation and communication rather than reliance on the therapist to meet these needs. While this shift is occurring, the therapist may need to be active in setting limits on abusive behaviors directed at the patient himself and toward others, including the therapist. It may be helpful to acknowledge that, since the patient has had little experience in forming non-abusive relationships, it is understandable that his primary way of operating is by anticipating abuse and responding adaptively. The therapist will need to be a vigorous advocate for non-abusive values and insist on achieving safety from self-abusive behaviors and from abusive situations and relationships.

A third tool in the resolution of transference issues is the *exploration of the origin of inappropriate reactions to the therapist*. Two general principles are important in working with the origins of transference reactions: (1) determining the person or persons in the past on whom the patient's current behavior toward the therapist is based, and (2) identifying the period from the patient's life that generated the transference reaction. The second point is important for some dissociative disorder and MPD (DID) patients in establishing the level of functioning, which may help to explain a particular subpersonality's reactions in the present (Putnam, 1989).

The purpose of exploring the origins of transference reactions is the promotion of mastery. Reenactments and transference experiences can be considered symbolic communications about past experiences that cannot be directly mentioned (Miller, 1981, 1984). The therapist can help the patient identify and confront previously repressed or otherwise split-off interpersonal experiences with strong, consistent support and focus on the underlying relationship dynamics. Engaging with the therapist in such an exploration requires that the patient identify at least partially with the therapist's observing function (Sterba, 1929, 1934), so that he can learn to separate experiencing ego from observing ego functions (Greenson, 1967). Thus, such an endeavor may help the patient expand his ego functioning while gaining mastery over past experiences that have prevented him from having satisfying intimate relationships; at the same time, the process will strengthen his healthy participation in the current therapy relationship.

Case Example: James

James, a 48-year-old man, was referred to me (MP) by his therapist from a nearby city. He had left this city three months previously to start a new job and was experiencing a difficult transition. James was floundering at work, unable to complete the required work because of panic attacks and trouble focusing; he was also finding it difficult to commute to therapy. His therapist had diagnosed him with borderline personality disorder; he also stated that James believed he might have had some history of abuse, since his younger brother had clear abuse memories related to a nanny who had lived with them for many years during childhood, though he himself had none. I agreed to see James for an evaluation period of four sessions to help assess what he needed and to determine whether a transfer was indicated.

During the first four sessions, James appeared to be bright, highly verbal, and motivated. He responded well to strategies designed to help him stabilize his anxiety and focus his attention on work tasks more successfully, although he was far behind on several important projects. With my support, he decided to talk to his boss about a less pressured path to advancement, so that he could lower his stress level and professional expectations. At the end of one month, he decided that he wanted to continue to see me, but that it was important to have some kind of continued contact with Alex, his former therapist.

After discussing the importance of clarifying roles, we decided that I would now be his primary therapist, though he would have contact with Alex once monthly. I mentioned the importance of deciding on a termination date in his other therapy, and he said that it was hard for him to even think about that. When I tried to explore his feelings about ending with Alex, James was able to give little information about his reluctance. We left it that he and Alex would talk about this and decide how to resolve it, and that I would check in with him about this issue in a few weeks. With his permission, I also talked with Alex, who agreed on the need for a formal termination in the near future, but wanted to leave the decision more open-ended, so that James could see him as long as he needed to. I disagreed with this way of proceeding, and said I thought it would be confusing for James; we agreed that they would consider a termination date within three months.

For several sessions, James continued to make progress, but then he experienced a series of "woundings" with me. First, he was locked out of the building one morning when the janitor inadvertently relocked the door, so that the office was not open at the time James arrived.

Second, James was very disappointed that I would not extend a session when he was feeling upset and "unfinished." Despite the offer of a second session later in the week, or phone contact, as is my usual policy, he perceived me as "cold" and "abrupt" with him. On the third occasion, James canceled his appointment at the last minute because he had received a call that his uncle was critically ill and he had been up late talking with family members. I offered him another session but told him that I would have to charge him for the late cancellation. He was enraged, believing that I was taking advantage of him in his vulnerable state.

As we explored these incidents, which occurred very close together, James was very angry and defensive. He would say only that he had not felt "close" to me from the beginning and should have paid attention to his feelings, that I was not right for him, and that he wanted to seek another therapist. He was unwilling to consider interpretations that these incidents must have made him feel quite rejected by me, stating that I was just being "clinical" with him, nor would he consider interpretations that these feelings might be related to other historical relationships. I asked about the status of his relationship with Alex, and James snapped, "It's none of your business." Feeling at a dead-end, I told him that I needed to talk with Alex to evaluate what was happening. He gave his permission reluctantly.

When I talked with Alex, I found that, despite our agreement, James had been seeing both of us weekly. I told Alex that I could not continue to see James under these circumstances, because he was splitting and projecting me as "bad therapist." Alex agreed to set a termination date three months later for a time after I was to return from a month-long trip, which James had known about since his first session with me. Our next session was more productive, with me saying that I was surprised to find that he was still seeing Alex weekly and that I believed the double therapy was contributing to his confusion and difficulty connecting with me. James seemed to accept this and agreed to the new limits. For the sessions preceding my trip, he worked well in our contract to focus on work and his relationship with a new girlfriend that was anxiety-producing for him. When I invited him to process his conscious feelings about my being gone and to attend to the unconscious meanings encoded in his therapy material, little surfaced. James simply stated that he felt okay about it, except for getting through his work without regular support. We discussed the options of his having more contact with Alex or seeing the professional who would be standing by during my absence. I anticipated with him that other feelings might come up, and we discussed ways he might cope with them. I also reassured him that he could reach me directly should he need to, and we reviewed the process for direct contact with me.

On my return, it was obvious that James had had serious reactions to my absence. He was quite angry, quite suicidal, and very depressed. While I was gone, he had had a serious crisis—his condom had broken during sex and his girlfriend refused to have sex with him, fearing AIDS. He felt betrayed by his girlfriend, frustrated by the confusing information he had received from various clinics and doctors, and very alone in having to deal with this emergency. In addition, his uncle, to whom he was very close, had died; he felt so unstable that he had not allowed himself to feel any of his deep grief about this loss. And finally, he had missed several deadlines at work, which resulted in a stern confrontation with his boss. The summer vacation he had looked forward to would be postponed, while he worked overtime to complete overdue projects. As we explored his feelings related to these issues, I gently asked whether he had used any of the backup support arrangements we had discussed before I left. He replied emphatically that he had not felt comfortable calling anyone—not my professional stand-in, not Alex, and not me—because he felt I had as much as left the planet and was not available to him. When I remarked that it seemed he had felt totally alone with no one to turn to, he pushed away this interpretation and spent most of the last minutes of the session in angry silence.

At the next appointment, James told me he had decided to leave therapy with me, that he had felt uncomfortable from the beginning, and that he should have paid attention to these feelings. He realized this was not a good time to terminate, since he was feeling suicidal, but he could not handle the pain of feeling unsafe with me and the isolation of having nowhere to turn. As part of our discussion, I asked whether he had terminated with Alex. He said, "We didn't really terminate; things just fizzled out. I've had no contact with him since you left." James was unwilling to explore any of his feelings with me about this, or about his relationship with me, commenting that "he just didn't feel safe." An interpretation I made about how confusing and lonely it must have been to be just connecting with me while he was attempting to disconnect with Alex and then have things "fizzle out" with both of us was again met with mostly silence. Since he remained insistent on termination, I framed the situation as an impasse and recommended that we both get separate consultation to try to resolve our stalemate.

Presenting this as an opportunity for him to learn more about the workings of psychotherapy, as well as his relationship with me, James agreed to this suggestion.

James's experience with consultation appeared rather unproductive. The consultant, with James's permission, called me to say that James was unwilling to explore most of the issues that had arisen between us and was insistent on termination. My experience with consultation was more effective. As we looked at all of the pieces of the puzzle, the consultant commented that it was as if I were the "live-in nanny" left to take care of James, since his real parent (Alex) was not available. Since his previous therapist had not been willing to let go of him in a bound-aried manner, it may have been that James's fear, confusion, and be-trayal related to unknown childhood experiences with the nanny had been projected onto me. We also discussed other aspects of the impasse, such as James's unwillingness to explore connections between any of his current difficulties with me and any of his past experiences, including family dynamics, and strategies for approaching these issues with him.

At our next session together, James began by saying he understood that his consultant had spoken with me over the phone and that I had agreed with his decision to terminate. I said, "No, that's not true. I don't want to terminate with you, nor do I believe that that is a good idea. But if you have decided that's what you want, I will help you have a good ending with me." This statement seemed to make a big impact on James. He stammered, "Well, that makes a big difference . . . I thought you really didn't want to work with me." As we continued to talk, James said he wanted to understand what had gone on between us. When he referred to the series of "wounding" incidents, I remarked that they had all been boundary issues and asked whether he had had these kinds of experiences with others. He explained, "Boundary issues? Of course! That's something my very first therapist [with whom he had had a very positive relationship] taught me about. You're right—I can see that now. If that's what's been going on, then I want to stay and work on this with you." I acknowledged that I thought that was at least part of what had been going on; we agreed to a three-month assessment period in order to focus on our relationship and determine whether we could continue working together.

After that session, James began to deepen his relationship with me. He also spontaneously accessed a few memories related to his nanny, including one flashback that was frightening to him, and we began to examine how those dynamics related to what had happened. As of this writing, James is engaged in stage I work, stabilization of his sense of safety within our relationship and in his outside life. He is committed to his work with me and feels he is mastering the process of accessing and exploring some of the deep and painful feelings related to our impasse and other relationships in his life. His job situation is now secure. His probationary status has ended; he is completing work on time and beginning to excel in his performance ratings.

Several aspects of traumatic transference are reflected in this case. First, it was clear that trust was a central issue in our impasse. James effectively pushed away any of my attempts to connect with him and to explore issues underlying his anxiety and difficulty concentrating; he was consistently defensive about my attempts to deal with issues related to his referring therapist. It seemed that I was in the classic bind described by Herman (1992): James feared exploitative or hurtful intentions whenever I tried to approach the traumatic issues; yet when I backed away he saw me as cold, uncaring, and abandoning. Second, his fear that I would hurt him, related to his underlying terror that I was a potential abuser, was masked by withdrawal, defensiveness, resistance, and anger. As Herman (1992) suggests, I may have been in the role of an omnipotent rescuer, whom James hoped would protect him from the confusion of the unboundaried ending with his referring therapist; when I failed at this task, he was enraged. Third, the elements of transference projection and projective identification seemed to be operating. Much of his fear and anger seemed to be projected onto me as representative of his referring therapist and quite probably his nanny and his parents as those who failed to protect him and participated in hurting him. Through the mechanism of projective identification, I began to take on characteristics that are quite unusual for me, including emotional withdrawal and detachment, as well as inattention to boundary issues in the transfer from his previous therapist. More will be said about my reactions as therapist in the section below on traumatic countertransference.

TRANSFERENCE IN HYPNOTHERAPY

Most hypnotherapists and hypnoanalysts believe that hypnosis tends to bring the patient's inner conflicts and repressed affects into focus more rapidly and more deeply than any other type of therapy (Fromm, 1984; Watkins, 1992). This phenomenon is attributed to the patient's closer contact with the unconscious than in the waking state. Thus, in addition to the issues discussed above, there are additional considerations that arise in the relationship between hypnotherapist and subject.

From a hypnoanalytic viewpoint (Fromm, 1984), three types of transference phenomena may be identified and utilized in the hypnotic relationship: infantile dependency transferences, oedipal transferences, and sibling transferences. Others emphasize the importance of considering the patient's capacity for object relatedness in understanding transference phenomena (Smith, 1984).

Smith (1984) has identified three elements that help to define transference phenomena in the hypnotic relationship. First, the patient often has some "curative fantasy" (Ornstein & Ornstein, 1976) about being helped by the hypnotherapist. Second, hypnotic experiences with the therapist are influenced by the patient's "bad object" system that results from cumulative trauma experiences (Smith, 1984). Third, the patient's responses to hypnosis and the hypnotherapist are affected by his capacity for adaptive regression, that is, regression in the service of the ego (Bellak, Harvich, & Gedeman, 1973), which promotes mastery and receptivity in the hypnosis process.

In another conceptualization, Diamond (1984, 1986) has identified three relational dimensions of the hypnotherapeutic relationship. The *hypnotic working alliance* consists of reality-oriented fantasies about what hypnosis can accomplish, as well as more irrational or "magical" fantasies, such as the idealized hypnotherapist implicit in Milton Erickson's "my voice will go with you" approach (Diamond, 1986). The *symbiotic or fusional alliance* involves experiencing the hypnotherapist as part of the self; this is explained by primitive incorporation processes (Baker, 1985). A third dimension is the *hypnotic real relationship*, which is a contemporary relationship separate from the transference elements related to the past or to fantasy.

Regardless of one's theoretical perspective, attempts to understand and utilize various transference issues involved in the hypnotic relationship can result in a better "fit" between patient and therapist, particularly when the transference, working alliance, contemporary, and symbiotic needs of the patient can be better met (Diamond, 1986). For example, the transference needs of a dissociative patient may require more structural hypnotic approaches to stimulate the capacities of the observing ego, such as the use of imagery to develop object constancy related to self and the therapist (Baker, 1981). Symbiotic alliance needs might necessitate the use of more nurturing, ego-strengthening suggestions at certain times in therapy. Informational direct suggestions might be used to strengthen the real and working alliance dimensions, and more indirect, Ericksonian suggestions used to enhance the irrational working alliance (Diamond, 1986).

Countertransference Issues with Dissociative Disorder Patients

Working with dissociative patients can pose some risks to the therapist's psychological health (Kluft, 1989; Watkins & Watkins, 1984), due to the powerful reactions that are evoked. Unless these reactions are understood and contained, they can lead to disruptions in the therapeutic alliance, conflicts with other professional colleagues (Herman, 1992), and personal stress reactions. This section presents information on countertransference, describes traumatic countertransference responses, and suggests guidelines for resolving traumatic countertransference issues with dissociative patients.

DEFINITIONS OF COUNTERTRANSFERENCE

Countertransference can be defined as the conscious or unconscious reactions in the self of the therapist to the person or pathology of the patient (Grellert, 1992). Freud (1910) originally considered countertransference as an unconscious reaction of the therapist to the patient's transference and a hindrance to the treatment process. Later, as with transference, Freud (1912) began to note the more positive function of countertransference.

Most analysts after Freud (e.g., Bion, 1967/1984; Searles, 1960) have come to view countertransference as a process providing positive opportunities to understand the therapeutic relationship and the patient, although some (e.g., Langs, 1980, 1988) have retained the pejorative view of countertransference as an inevitable sign of unresolved therapist pathology. Searles has written that "countertransference gives one one's most reliable approach to the understanding of patients of whatever diagnosis" (1960, p. 190). Many (Fromm-Reichmann, 1950; Racker, 1957; Winnicott, 1949) have expanded the concept of countertransference to encompass the entire emotional reaction of the therapist within the treatment setting.

TRAUMATIC COUNTERTRANSFERENCE REACTIONS

Because of the nature of traumatic transference and other factors related to trauma, dissociative patients often evoke complex and unique countertransference reactions from therapists (Kluft, 1988, 1989; Putnam, 1989). As Herman (1992) points out, the therapist may experience to a lesser degree the same kinds of trauma-induced reactions as the patient. This phenomenon is known as traumatic countertransference or "vicarious traumatization" (McCann & Pearlman, 1990, p. 131). Traumatic countertransference can include "the entire range of the therapist's emotional reactions to the survivor and to the traumatic event itself" (Herman, 1992, p. 141).

Herman (1992) identifies three major aspects of traumatic countertransference. First, the therapist may develop vicarious post-traumatic stress symptoms. These may include somatic disturbances; emotional feelings of helplessness, incompetence, and mistrust; and dissociative symptoms including panic, confusion, depersonalization, and derealization. Countertransference responses in the second category are mediated by projective identification. These include identification both with the victim's rage, grief, and hopelessness, and with the perpetrator. The third set of responses involves other traumatic feelings and defenses, including various defenses against helplessness and bystander guilt.

Post-traumatic Stress Symptoms

Therapists who work with sexually abused patients can expect to experience symptoms of contact or vicarious victimization. These can include "intrusive reactions (intense fear, startle responses, hyperalertness, nightmares and night terrors) alternating with numbing and denying responses (withdrawal, avoidance, distancing, exhaustion)" (Courtois, 1988, p. 236). These kinds of PTSD responses have also been reported by therapists of dissociative patients in general and MPD patients in particular (Herman, 1992; Kluft, 1989; Loewenstein, 1993). Usually such symptoms surface when the therapist feels overwhelmed and horrified by the details of the traumatic experience and when other professional and personal stresses coincide.

Since much of the psychological stress associated with victimization and trauma is related to the shattering of basic assumptions about the self and the world (Janoff-Bulman & Frieze, 1983; Terr, 1994), the therapist may be vulnerable to losing faith in the world as safe and meaningful. He may feel more personally vulnerable and fearful, and more distrustful even in close relationships (Herman, 1992). The shattering of basic trust and safety assumptions may also generate feelings such as detachment, callousness, and cynicism.

Dissociative symptoms can also be part of countertransferential PTSD responses. Therapists may experience altered perceptions, including intense imagery with aggressive or sexual content, negative hallucinations, depersonalization, trance-like experiences, "spacing out," and inability to think (Loewenstein, 1993). Loewenstein (1993) reports instances of countransferential trance logic, where therapists accept literally their patients' perceptions that child alters have the same needs as actual external children. In one case, a therapist decided not to send the police to a suicidal patient's house because of concern that this would be upsetting to the adolescent alter who was "out" (p. 69).

Traumatic Countertransference Related to Projective Identification

Projective identification is defined as a "resonating field" where the patient views the significant other as having feelings which are intensely intolerable to him and exerts a strong pull on the other to identify with and temporarily embrace those same feelings (Peebles-Kleiger, 1989). Through this process, the therapist can find himself identifying with the patient's intense helplessness, which he may experience by underestimating his own competence or by minimizing the patient's strengths and resources (Herman, 1992). Putnam (1989) and Kluft (1989) have described experienced therapists as feeling "deskilled" and professionally intimidated by MPD patients.

In addition to identifying with the patient's helplessness, the therapist may also identify with his rage. Extremes of anger may be experienced, from wordless rage to frustration to righteous indignation. This anger may be directed at other colleagues who fail to understand, at members of the patient's family who failed to intervene, and at society at large for denying or failing to resolve the problem of victimization (Herman, 1992). If unclaimed, the therapist's anger may disempower the patient from feeling and expressing his own anger or may trigger guilt in the patient for causing such a reaction. Additionally, if the patient projects intense anger onto the therapist, the therapist may become enraged at being identified as an authority figure and potential abuser (Courtois, 1988). To avoid distancing or rejecting the patient and possibly derailing therapy, the therapist must develop tolerance for the patient's rage and cope with his own anger.

The therapist may also identify with the patient's intense grief and loss. It is common for the therapist to experience strong feelings of sadness and grief when the traumatized patient discloses the details of his experience. Therapists working with Holocaust survivors report "sinking into despair" (Danieli, 1984); those working with Vietnam veterans describe feelings of surviving a "tour of duty" (Peterson, Prout, & Schwartz, 1991, p. 189); therapists treating MPD patients may become "engulfed" by their misery and suffering (Kluft, 1989). Failure to cope adequately with these reactions can lead to such defenses as distancing or subtly shifting the subject matter when the patient begins to explore traumatic material.

An even more disturbing type of identification occurs when the therapist identifies with the perpetrator or victimizer. This may take many forms. The therapist may find himself becoming skeptical of the patient's traumatic experiences or may try to minimize or rationalize the abuse. In some cases, he may feel disgust, contempt, or even hatred for the patient (Herman, 1992). Another form of this type of identification has been called "privileged voyeurism" (Courtois, 1988), where the therapist experiences an attraction to and excessive inquisitiveness about the trauma, or treats the patient as an object of curiosity. Kluft (1984a) describes therapist feelings of "initial excitement, fascination, and overinvestment" when working with MPD patients. Coons (1986) similarly describes therapist feelings of "vicarious enjoyment" when working with this population. Krystal (1968) has observed that working with traumatized patients forces therapists to come to terms with their own capacity for evil and sadistic tendencies.

Traumatic Countertransference Related to Other Defenses and Feelings

Many therapists report unbearable feelings of helplessness when working with traumatized patients. To defend against these feelings, they may assume the role of rescuer (Herman, 1992). Sometimes this involves overgiving and failure to maintain professional boundaries; the patient is treated as fragile, overly special, and in need of constant special arrangements, such as extra or extended sessions and daily crisis phone calls (Courtois, 1988). In the extreme, this type of defense can lead to feelings of grandiosity or omnipotence, with the therapist "playing God" or attempting to "love the patient into health" (Kluft, 1989, 1993b).

A related feeling is witness or bystander guilt. In this type of countertransference reaction, the therapist may feel so guilty for being spared what the patient had to suffer that he may have difficulty enjoying the comforts of his own life (Herman, 1992). In an attempt to protect the patient from further pain, the therapist who has not experienced similar trauma himself may discourage exploration of the trauma or engage in behavior that overprotects and disempowers (Courtois, 1988). The therapist who himself has been traumatized, on the other hand, may have more personal guilt stemming from his own unresolved or unexplored trauma experiences. Failure to resolve these kinds of feelings may result in assuming too much responsibility for the patient's experiences, which can eventually lead to burnout and boundary violations.

Case Example: James (Part 2)

In the case of James presented above (see p. 207), I (MP) demonstrated several countertransference reactions. In retrospect, my responses seem to resemble complementary projective identification, where I was treated as an internal projected object (nanny, referring therapist, and parents). As I learned more from James about his associations to our dilemma and examined them with the help of my consultant, it seemed as if I had identified with the role of nanny, being treated as a careless interim guardian and responding as one, with insufficient attention to the inappropriate boundaries of the therapy transfer. Further, I assumed the role of "bad therapist," by not establishing clear boundaries, like the referring therapist and James's mother, whose inconsistent attention James experienced as love. James "pulled for" a state of no-boundaries; yet he was deeply confused and enraged by my failure to intervene and firmly insist on structured termination with his previous therapist. I thereby assumed the role of the parents who failed to protect him from likely early abuse and took on their feelings of detachment and neglect.

On further examination, it also seems likely that I identified with James's traumatic rage, which took the form of frequent frustration and righteous indignation at his accusations that I was cold and uncaring. These feelings alternated with the sense of helplessness and detachment inherent in my ineffectual responses to his referring therapist. Some of my reactions also resembled post-traumatic symptoms of emotional numbing; my lack of connection to James was striking. I was largely unmoved until he threatened to terminate; even then, my initial attitude was one of dispassionate, mechanical attempts to move things forward. I also observed that James was one of the only patients for whom I did not keep regular notes—in fact, I had not written for several months when I first sought consultation!

Fortunately, with the help of good consultation and the use of the guidelines presented below, these countertransference reactions were fully resolved. I now feel very empathically connected to James, committed to and moved by our work together. As the complex transference and countertransference issues in this case indicate, professional consultation can be invaluable in breaking through completely failed communication between patient and therapist and understanding the complicated web of projective identification and other traumatic reactions.

Special Countertransference Issues with MPD (DID) Patients

MPD (DID) patients, in particular, elicit a wide range of feelings in the therapist because various alters evoke unique and separate reactions. For example, in working with a 45-year-old MPD patient with chronic psychophysiological complaints, I (MP) found myself in the course of one session aware of feeling angry toward an adult alter who had been careless about self-care, nurturing toward a traumatized child alter who was reporting terrifying flashbacks, and overwhelmed by the demands of an adolescent alter who was pushing against the time boundaries of our session, wanting more time and attention from me.

In addition to the multiplicity of transference reactions that occur, difficulty also arises from the nature of certain countertransference reactions that are evoked when treating patients who have been the victims of a variety of early traumatic experiences. First, there is the potential for evoking the therapist's own unconscious memories of infantile helplessness, while eliciting empathy and compassion in the adult therapist (Grellert, 1992). An additional challenge is the therapist's role as co-container of the intense emotions that arise from intense relivings of past traumas, both within therapeutic abreactions and in spontaneous regressive experiences. As Grellert (1992) points out, the therapist must accept at least partly the full emotional impact of revivifications and at the same time serve as an objective observer and eyewitness to trauma events. Kluft (l984a) notes that empathizing with patients' experiences of traumatization can be grueling: "One is tempted to withdraw, intellectualize, or defensively ruminate about whether the events are 'real'" (p. 53).

Other problematic countertransference responses can involve management of the therapy, with the therapist feeling overwhelmed by the sheer volume of information to be tracked and processed, pulled to be present and "real" with the patient rather than maintaining a neutral therapeutic distance, and frustrated in working with internal dissociative systems that are constantly changing as various alters come and go (Putnam, 1989). Still other issues for the therapist involve coping with patients' seductive and manipulative behavior, which can be a way of testing to see whether the therapist will be like previous sexual abusers; dealing with fantasies of reparenting the dissociated, traumatized patient; and managing feelings of omnipotence and grandiosity when the therapy is going well and those of anger and hurt when being attacked or degraded by the patient (Putnam, 1989). Actively suicidal and crisis states in the patient provoke additional complex reactions in the therapist (Comstock, 1991).

RESOLVING TRAUMATIC COUNTERTRANSFERENCE

In early stages of therapy with traumatized patients, the therapist needs to anticipate the kinds of reactions discussed above, to allow ample time for his own self-analysis, and to arrange for good consultation and supervision with therapists who are competent in the use of hypnosis and in the treatment of dissociative patients.

Countertransference can be useful if dealt with in an interactive manner. Many patients who experienced trauma before they could speak communicate in such primitive ways that the therapist receives information indirectly through various defensive mechanisms, such as projective identification, projection, and parallel processing (Comstock, 1991; McDougall, 1979). This valuable information needs to be introduced explicitly into the therapy experience.

For example, with one dissociative patient who was beginning to deal with intense memories of a sexual molestation by his music teacher, I (MP) found myself feeling repulsed and disgusted, in contrast to usual feelings of warmth and concern. As I studied my feelings, I began to wonder whether one of his internal ego states might be projecting similar negative feelings internally. When I asked whether there was a part of him that might be having negative feelings about his experiences, he replied that he was indeed hearing an inner voice tell him that he was "disgusting" and "repulsive." As soon as this was disclosed, my negative feelings abated immediately and the patient began to deal with his own internal conflict in revealing information about the molestation.

Since most countertransference responses begin on an unconscious level, the therapist must analyze and manage the clues manifest in his own conscious feelings, somatic reactions, dreams, and fantasies in relation to the patient in order to stay alert to possible disruptive countertransference in the therapy (Comstock, 1991). An equally important source of data is the exploration of nonvalidating responses of the patient to therapeutic interventions and the decoding of subsequent patient perceptions of the therapist (Langs, 1988).

Guidelines for identifying and resolving countertransference issues include:

1. First focus on your own responses to the patient and the therapy relationship. In addition to emotional, somatic, dream, and fantasy responses mentioned above, other signs of countertransference include: alterations in usual fee schedule, overlooking failure to comply with basic rules of therapy or medical procedures, allowing telephone abuses, neglect of history-taking, and repeated discussions about the patient with other colleagues.

2. Carefully study possible countertransference responses in terms of words, images, feelings, and associations that may relate to your own personal life or history.

3. Sometimes taking these first two steps can resolve the countertransference response. If the reaction persists, however, secure consultation for help in separating personal issues from responses to the patient's transference. As Herman (1992) points out, just as no survivor of trauma can recover alone, no therapist can work effectively with trauma alone. If you become aware that your reactions are indeed related to the patient's transferential issues, communicate about this to the patient.

4. In order to discuss transference and countertransference, create an atmosphere of free, thoughtful exchange (Hedges, 1992). For instance, "I've been thinking about our work together and have been having some thoughts and reactions that I would like to share with you. I'm curious about what they might mean in terms of our relationship and in terms of your work here. Would you be willing to look at them with me and see what we can figure out together?" This kind of joint venture is harder to present to some patients than others; exercise judgment about readiness. Sometimes it is better

to hold the information until the patient is better prepared to explore it.

5. Avoid ventilation, discharge, confession, or any sense of blame or accusation (Hedges, 1992). No matter how carefully the presentation, powerful countertransference communications are likely to feel intrusive, accusatory, hurtful, or upsetting to the patient. Therefore, it is important to process countertransference reactions until they are relatively uncharged and present them to the patient in the most neutral reframe. Maintain a position of curiosity and open reflection.

6. Anticipate the patient's likely negative reaction and include this information in the communication. For example, "I want to talk to you today about an issue that has been upsetting when we've tried to discuss it in the past. I have considered your reaction that I don't know what I'm talking about, but somehow this keeps coming into my awareness and I believe we need to find a way to consider it together so that we can find out why it keeps surfacing and why you are so angry about discussing it with me."

7. Finally, avoid investment in being certain or "right" about the connection between countertransference reactions and the patient's issues. The therapist can never be certain of separating cleanly countertransference that is personal material from reactions to the patient's material (Hedges, 1992). Both of us have had the experience, as have most experienced clinicians, of having countertransference communications that were rejected repeatedly by the patient resurface later in the therapy in a form that the patient could accept and use. Maintaining an attitude of openness and uncertainty when dealing with these issues is essential.

COUNTERTRANSFERENCE AND THE HYPNOTIC RELATIONSHIP

Many views of the hypnotherapeutic relationship have been described that involve the therapist's hypnotic responses. Guze (1956), Erickson (1964), Diamond (1980, 1984), Scagnelli (1972), and Gilligan (1987), among others, have all contributed evidence of the hypnotist's experiencing trance states during hypnotic work. Gill and Brenman (1959) wrote of subject-hypnotist reciprocity, suggesting that hypnosis requires a "dovetailing of the unconscious fantasies of the two people involved" (p. 60). They also presented data to suggest that the ability of the patient to enter hypnosis, as well as the depth of trance, varies with changes in the transference-countertransference situation. They conclude that hypnosis is a modality by which therapist and patient regulate the amount of closeness or distance between them. Watkins

(1963) has viewed the hypnotic experience as a reflection of transference and countertransference needs between the two participants. Lindner (1960) has emphasized the "shared aspects" of the relationship, with both patient and hypnotist experiencing rewards from hypnotic experiences.

Such an interactive approach requires viewing the "subject and hypnotist as a unit" (Diamond, 1986, p. 111). Thus, the capacity of the hypnotherapist to be with his own, as well as the patient's internal experience during hypnosis, and his ability to convey such qualities as "confidence, sensitivity, flexibility, persistence, empathy, and a realistically objective outlook" (Diamond, 1984, p. 10) may well be as critical as the patient's capacity for entering into the intense, intimate process of hypnotherapy.

Clinical as well as empirical evidence has been advanced to demonstrate that hypnotic relationship variables, along with various qualities of the hypnotherapist, can enhance the hypnotic subject's response. Hearn (1978) found that more positive attitudes of hypnotists were linked to increases in scores for low-hypnotizability individuals. Barber (1980) found that indirect suggestion and therapist attitude could increase hypnotizability for individuals with "0" hypnotizability scores. Banyai, Meszaros, and Csokay (1982) have presented data suggesting that hypnotic depth is partially a function of the hypnotist's active participation, as indicated by his ability to achieve a "mutual tuning in." Diamond (1984) has suggested that the effective hypnotherapist must have the capacity to feel and experience the patient's unconscious affect and images within himself, while remaining knowledgeable about and comfortable with his own internal experience, simultaneously providing sufficient comfort and direction for the patient to come to terms with his own inner life.

It is widely held that hypnosis involves regression on the part of the patient in the service of the ego (Fromm, 1979a; Gill & Brenman, 1959; Shor, 1979; Watkins, 1992). This regression places the therapist in the role of parent or authority figure (Pardell, 1950). Some hypnotherapists experience the hypnotized patient like a child and respond accordingly, for example, through alterations in the voice when speaking to an age-regressed individual (Lazar & Dempster, 1984). The therapist's response to the hypnotized patient's regression appears related to his own individual dynamics and may range from creative, "childlike," playful responses (Hilgard, 1971) to defenses against the regression, perhaps by internally denigrating the hypnotic subject as "too dependent or needy" (Lazar & Dempster, 1984). Dealing effectively with such regressive "pulls" is an important task of the hypnotherapist. From an interactional perspective (Diamond, 1984), hypnotherapeutic skill can therefore be viewed as a function of: (1) the hypnotist's attainment of matured object relating and comfort with deeper levels of relationship, (2) empathic capacity, (3) personal and therapeutic trance skill, (4) integration of healthy receptive, passive, and active cognitive and behavioral skills, and (5) the self-supervisory capacity to deal effectively with one's own internal and countertransferential reactions in response to individual patients.

Developing a Positive Countertransference "Trance" with the Dissociative Patient

Because the therapist's responses, attitudes, and countertransference reactions are such critical variables in the hypnotherapeutic relationship, and because dissociative patients evoke such strong feelings in the therapist, it is important to consider ways of developing positive "trance" states when treating these patients (Phillips, 1994).

One requirement for creating a positive countertransference trance state is the willingness of the therapist to enter into *interpersonal trance* experience. Freud first introduced the idea of "free-floating attention," encouraging the therapist to suspend conscious judgment and catch "the drift of a patient's unconscious with his own unconscious" (Freud, 1923, p. 239); we see this as a form of interpersonal trance.

Milton Erickson was a strong proponent of the interpersonal trance state in the hypnotic situation. He expressed the belief that " . . . the unconscious of one individual is better equipped to understand the unconscious of another than the conscious aspect of the personality of either" (Erickson & Kubie, 1940, p. 62). Erickson emphasized an externally oriented interpersonal trance state as valuable for hypnotherapeutic work, writing, "If I have any doubts about my capacity to see the important things I go into a trance. When there is a crucial issue with a patient and I don't want to miss any of the clues I go into trance" (Erickson & Rossi, 1977, p. 42).

Gilligan (1987), a long-time student of Erickson's work, suggests several ways for the therapist to develop an externally oriented trance state (p. 77):

1. Ensure comfortable positions for therapist and patient.
2. Go inside for a few moments; identify and relax any resource of physical or emotional tension.
3. Defocus on the content of the session and begin to focus attentionally on the patient's breathing patterns, muscular tension, body posture, emotional state, and movements.
4. Breathe comfortably and easily, and if possible, synchronize breathing with the patient.
5. Establish and maintain eye contact with soft focus, which can evoke the beginnings of an externally oriented trance state.

6. Allow effortless mental process, letting thoughts, images, and associations "drift" through consciousness.

7. Allow speaking to occur freely and easily.

This type of interpersonal trance allows the therapist to be "a-part-of-yet-apart-from" the subject (Gilligan, 1987, p. 78). The therapist is free to tune into unconscious spontaneity and creativity as well as to attain heightened observational abilities in tracking the subject. The issue with dissociative patients is frequency and pacing in the use of interpersonal trance. It is not enough to simply "trust the unconscious." The therapist will need to balance the use of interpersonal trance experience with the use of highly conscious analytic processes in order to gather important information and plan therapeutic interventions accordingly. Such pacing will vary with therapist style and patient needs. Development of such interpersonal trance states can be enhanced through the therapist's own self-hypnosis training and practice.

A second way of establishing a positive countertransference trance state is to use hypnosis to *manage interpersonal boundaries and repair object relations.* Baker (1981, 1983b) and others (Gill & Brenman, 1959; Lazar & Dempster, 1984) have noted that the hypnotic experience lends itself to shifts in intimacy and attachment between patient and hypnotist. The hypnotherapist can regulate psychological distance; for example, when he is observing, emotional distance between patient and hypnotist may increase, and when he allows himself to "experience" with the patient, intimacy is likely to increase (Lazar & Dempster, 1984). Watkins (1978, 1992) has spoken in similar terms about the use of "resonance"; through inner experience, the therapist "co-feels, co-enjoys, co-suffers, and co-understands with his patient" (p. 282). As with interpersonal trance and conscious analytic processes, it is important for the therapist to balance resonance and objectivity.

Smith (1984) has suggested that the hypnotherapist can use countertransference reactions and other observations to infer ego processes currently unavailable or undeveloped within the patient. The therapist can then intervene hypnotically as an enabler of healthier ego processes, including object-relational capacities. Baker (1981) has proposed an approach for severely disturbed patients, including borderline and psychotic individuals, which involves using hypnosis to maintain the patient's "connectedness" to the therapist so that regression can "be processed 'in the service of the ego,' or 'in the service of the therapist's ego' who lends his observing ego functions to the patient" (p. 139).

Baker's (1981) techniques include using hypnotic imagery and fantasy to develop self and object constancy in the following sequence: helping the patient create an image of self in a pleasant activity alone; opening his eyes and looking at the therapist, closing the eyes and returning to the positive image of self; developing images of the therapist associated with continued feelings of relaxation and well-being; alternating between images of therapist and images of self and then picturing the two together; developing positive fantasies involving patient and therapist in parallel activity and then in interactions; and finally, when ego functioning is stabilized through these steps, developing positive images for other significant objects and interpersonal experiences (pp. 141–142). Such a process seems to facilitate the positive introjection of therapist as "good object" and of the self as "good me," as well as the development of more integrated object relatedness. We frequently use variations of Baker's approach with post-traumatic patients who also have borderline and narcissistic spectrum issues. A brief case example appears below.

Case Example: Leah

Leah, a 35-year-old patient, has a history of severe sexual abuse with her uncle in early childhood and emotional and physical abuse experiences with her parents. She was referred to me (MP) for hypnotherapy to help her manage compulsive overeating symptoms. In talking with her previous therapist of 11 years, I learned of her borderline diagnosis and her difficulties in maintaining constancy in her relationships with herself and others.

Leah's transference issues began to emerge during the first session. She stated, "I don't know if I can trust you . . . you seem so stern. Like just then, you didn't want to answer my question completely." As we continued on, my experience of Leah seemed to parallel her struggles to form and keep a positive connection with me. I explained various uses of imagery in hypnosis to help her feel more connected with herself and with me. She was willing to try this approach, especially since she had had positive experiences with imagery in her earlier therapy.

I asked her first to form a series of images of herself in relaxing, comfortable surroundings; she was able to do this with some difficulty. At first, she could hold the image briefly, but would immediately drift into more negative visualization, such as an image of herself being lost in a dark cave. Gradually, Leah could focus on positive images of herself for longer and longer periods of time and connect them with inner relaxation and comfort. She also learned to use these self-hypnotically between sessions to manage her anxiety when she felt her eating getting out of control. After several months, she was able to form positive images of me in my office, first alone, as she saw me writing my notes about our sessions, later in an office scene with her where I was reassuring her about how well we were working together, and connecting these with similar internal feelings of relaxation.

When more difficult transference issues arose later in therapy, I was able to modulate my immediate countertransference reactions (usually anger or impatience) and to suggest to Leah: "You are struggling with some powerful feelings about me today. Let's set the stage for exploring them together by finding some of the images we've worked with before and using those as a beginning focus." After several minutes of recalling images of herself relaxing in a meadow and sitting in her kitchen with her cat on her lap followed by the positive images of the two of us in the office together, Leah was ready to explore effectively her current reactions to me.

Using this process has helped me to manage my negative countertransference responses to Leah, and has helped her to maintain a more positive, constant relationship with herself and with me so that she has been able to contain and work through some very threatening transference feelings. Leah has also used this structured imagery effectively to manage overeating behaviors and to gain greater understanding of the connection between her symptoms and relationship issues.

Achieving a positive countertransference trance state with a dissociative patient can result in an enhanced "holding" environment—attached yet individuated, separate yet connected and engaged, similar to that advocated by Winnicott (1965b) and indicative of the special state of consciousness termed "I and thou" (Buber, 1976), that may be the most potent form of a therapeutic context. Through this approach, patient and therapist may appreciate and benefit from the "shared rewards" of hypnotic trance experience and enter into a powerful context of mutual growth and discovery.

11

OBSTACLES TO TREATMENT

There are many reasons why therapy "stalls" or fails. This chapter reviews some of the issues that contribute to failed therapy with dissociative disorder patients, along with appropriate therapeutic strategies.

External Conditions

One of the common external contributors to discontinuation of therapy is failed finances. This can stem from a number of factors. Often, dissociative patients, particularly those who are severely dissociated or have an MPD (DID) diagnosis, have been chronically debilitated by their symptoms and unable to function at any but a low-paying job, if they are able to work at all. Unable to afford the type of professional treatment their condition requires, they may be forced to accept financial help from parents or relatives. As treatment progresses, donors' financial situation may change, or patients' recovery may begin to threaten those who support them financially, thereby precipitating a crisis which patients·are unable to resolve in order to continue therapy.

We have found it best in these situations to hold our boundaries constant (that is, not to offer lower fees) while exploring and interpreting the meaning of this change to the patient and then considering various possibilities. Occasionally, we may agree to postpone payment for a short period or, in rare circumstances, to continue for a brief, specified period (e.g., two months) at a lower fee, to allow the patient to reorganize her resources so that she can return to full fee. It is important to send a message that the therapist is confident that the patient will be able to do what is necessary to obtain the type of treatment that is needed. If there is no way to resolve the issue, we support a break in therapy or possible transfer to a lower-fee therapist with adequate experience and training in working hypnotically with dissociative conditions.

An increasingly important issue is the patient's health care coverage. At times, the absence of adequate insurance precludes ongoing outpatient treatment by experienced therapists. Occasionally, such patients can be referred to dissociative inpatient units that accept Medicare. Once stabilized, these patients may be seen in appropriate low-fee outpatient groups (if available). Other dissociative patients face restricted coverage by managed health care systems, which often limit treatment to ten sessions. Time-limited therapy necessarily must focus on safety, stabilization, and ego-strengthening issues with dissociative patients; additional treatment needs may not be met unless referrals can be made for ongoing work to appropriate lower-fee individual therapists and groups.

Sometimes a patient's insurance coverage may change during the course of treatment; when this occurs, we follow the general policy of holding our fees constant while exploring relevant options and helping the patient make the best choice, taking into consideration all of her needs. When a PTSD patient seen twice weekly told me her insurance coverage had been severely reduced and was pushing me to lower my fee, I (MP) commented: "You must be the one to weigh complex financial and emotional factors and decide how to obtain the best treatment for yourself at a price you can afford. My job is to consider the possible negative consequences to your therapy if I should lower my fee. I know how important it has been for me to be consistent in all my policies so that you have known what to count on with me; I also know it is important that I view you as someone who can meet her responsibilities, even when those change, and who can find creative ways of solving challenging problems such as this one." After subsequent discussion, the patient decided to reduce sessions to once per week while pursuing financial alternatives. Two months later, she had found a way to reinstitute twice weekly sessions and had strengthened her self-confidence during the process.

Other external factors that may lead to a "crash" in therapy include geographical moves or changes in scheduling. Occasionally, these patients encounter a dramatic change in scheduling that results when they become healthy enough to move into a higher-functioning job that requires a more complete commitment of time, or when job or school requirements change and make it difficult for the patient to schedule appointments during the therapist's regular schedule. Again, we find it best in these circumstances to hold our boundaries, rather than offering appointments after our usual office hours, which can compromise the therapy frame.

Both of us are willing, from time to time, to see patients who travel from considerable geographical distances because there are no appropriate therapists in their immediate areas, or because they have moved away after beginning treatment with us. In these circumstances, we may arrange longer appointments, such as double sessions. With these patients, we are careful continually to reevaluate the goals and progress of therapy, making sure that the patient has enough regular contact to make continuous progress on therapy issues. If this is not possible with the patient's current resources of time and money, we help the patient make arrangements to seek other forms of treatment. Permitting therapy to continue without the basic ingredient of sufficient contact may be colluding with the patient in avoiding work on difficult issues related to underlying trauma.

Case Example: Linda

Linda (Frederick & Phillips, 1992), a very complex dissociative disorder patient, had extreme difficulty stabilizing in therapy. Each time she began to make progress on a particular issue, another crisis would arise. Usually these were medical in nature, as Linda suffered from TMJ (temporomandibular joint difficulty), lupus, rheumatoid arthritis, severe migraine headaches, and later from several life-threatening infections. Finally, after two years of treatment, Linda had begun to achieve a period of stability in her outside life, so that we could consider exploring some of her history and the inner workings of her personality. At this point, Linda moved an hour's drive away to live with her boyfriend, with whom she had created her healthiest relationship to date. After a few months, her sessions became erratic, as she struggled with a relapse of her lupus and arthritis conditions. Despite my (MP) careful interpretations and her own insights that she was somehow avoiding deepening the work she needed to do in therapy, she continued to miss appointments. Finally, I set the limit that I would not continue to see her unless she could arrange to come at least weekly, because in my opinion we did not have the necessary framework to conduct good therapeutic work.

Linda responded to this intervention by renewing her commitment to therapy. Shortly thereafter she shared important information about dissociative experiences that she had previously withheld. I was able to make an MPD (DID) diagnosis and to discuss it with her in a way that she could accept. During that session, she commented, "If we had tried to deal with this any earlier, I would have run out the door. Now I can handle it." For the next 18 months, we did solid therapeutic work, making alliances and negotiating conflicts with her three main alters. Linda's alters began to cooperate; she reported less depression and a cessation of dissociative episodes, and she began to be successful in her housecleaning business.

Unfortunately, at this point in therapy Linda again suffered a series of setbacks due to external circumstances: Her apartment caught fire, resulting in the loss of much of her personal property, her relationship deteriorated and eventually ended, her insurance coverage of 80% of her medical costs was canceled, and she had a fall at work that exacerbated some of her other medical problems. After dealing for several weeks with Linda's erratic attendance, I again set the limit of regular weekly sessions in order to continue treatment. At this point, Linda chose to terminate. Several months later, she wrote me that she was suicidal and worried about being able to maintain her safety. I talked with her by phone, reestablishing the ground rules under which I would be willing to work with her, and offering an optional referral. Linda decided on the referral, stating that she did not have the money to see me. I made an appropriate referral to a psychiatrist at a county mental health clinic who is experienced in working with MPD (DID).

Linda has called me several times since. She decided not to see the psychiatrist, stating, "Even though he's good, he's just not for me," and telling me that she was working to get enough money so that she could resume treatment with me. Each time I have responded, indicating my willingness to see her under the established ground rules and expressing my confidence that she can do what is needed to make treatment with me possible, if that is what she wants.

Therapeutic Relationship Factors

There are a number of issues within the therapeutic relationship that can lead to the end of a therapy. Elkind (1992) has reviewed three categories of difficulties that lead to ruptures: a lack of fit between patient and therapist, impasses where therapist and patient are entrenched in a problematic way of relating, and situations where patient or therapist has been wounded in an area of "primary vulnerability" (p. 11). These categories are reviewed below as they relate to dissociative patients.

PATIENT-THERAPIST MISMATCH

Lack of fit between therapist and patient may be related to several factors. Occasionally, there is a mismatch because of the different life stages of patient and therapist. For example, it may be difficult for a young therapist to empathize with an older patient who has recently remembered early childhood sexual abuse experiences and to match her life cycle needs effectively. Or there may be personality mismatches, for example, when a holistically inclined patient sees a therapist who obviously suffers from the consequences of poor health or self-care. Sometimes there is a lack of fit in therapeutic style and orientation. For example, a dissociative patient with little sensory or emotional capacity, or even alexithymia, may find herself working with a therapist whose primary orientation requires access to sensory or somatic states of awareness. Often such patients fare better with a cognitive-behavioral approach until they have enough strength to begin learning about their internal states. If the therapist is unwilling or unable to provide this type of flexibility, however, treatment may reach a stalemate.

Other difficulties can occur from limitations in the therapist's knowledge. For example, dissociative patients may often find themselves in treatment with well-meaning professionals who do not know how to diagnose or treat dissociative conditions. I (MP) consulted on an MPD case where the well-intentioned primary therapist told the patient that she herself was responsible for "figuring out" what was going on inside her–that neither he nor anyone else could help her. Fortunately, the patient sought outside consultation and the psychiatrist was willing to admit his limitations. After a painful transition period, the patient weathered a transfer to an appropriate therapist and continued to see the psychiatrist periodically for medication needs.

Occasionally, personal issues of the therapist and patient connect in such a way to create a mismatch. For example, a dissociative patient who is preoccupied with the injustices of the world might connect with a therapist who shares such a primary political focus. The ensuing therapy might avoid deep, intrapsychic issues and fail to address the patient's underlying trauma and her defenses against it. Problems also arise when there is disharmony in personal beliefs, so that the patient feels misunderstood or devalued.

Unfortunately, in such instances, the dissociative patient may not recognize the problems in therapy as a poor match. She may consider the therapist as an "expert" and reenact her own patterns of dependency and learned helplessness, assuming the difficulty to be of her own making. The patient's familiarity with disturbed attachment, along with the other problems that brought her to therapy in the first place, may operate to maintain the patient in the relationship rather than to facilitate a change (Elkind, 1992).

IMPASSE IN THE THERAPEUTIC RELATIONSHIP

Therapy may also stall with a dissociative patient due to unrecognized and unresolved transference and countertransference issues. In addition to those situations covered in Chapter 10, several others may contribute to derailment of therapy. Freud (1937) recognized that psychotherapy could be interminable if the patient lacked sufficient ego strength or a lack of capacity for attachment and self-evaluation, if therapy goals were inappropriate or unrealistic, or if the therapist had too many unresolved psychological issues.

Winnicott (1960) viewed such impasses as analyses of the "false self." He attributed circumstances where the patient experiences little progress, or even worsens, to the therapist's failure to recognize the patient's false self adaptation and to go beneath this defense to the patient's "real self." Such an approach is particularly important with survivors of trauma, who have learned to deny their "true" selves and persist in adaptive patterns to mirror the needs of significant others, including the therapist, in order to protect themselves from further damage. The therapist who undertakes the task of helping the patient achieve a new self organization that integrates aspects of both the true self and false self must be prepared to support the patient through a long transitional time. This task may be greatly facilitated through the use of ego-state therapy, which can identify the parts of the patient's personality that are aligned with "true self" and "false self" traits, and enable the patient to use internal resources to integrate such splits.

Therapeutic impasses can also result when the patient is unable, for a variety of reasons, to use the therapist in the ways that are needed (Elkind, 1992). Sometimes this situation requires therapeutic flexibility and willingness to examine "resistances" to being used by the patient in certain ways that are necessary to the patient's development but antithetical to the therapist's style or professional needs. At other times shifts may be required in the usual ways of relating to the patient.

Case Example: Kristi

In working with a dissociative patient named Kristi, who was uncovering difficult material related to incest experiences with her cousin, I (MP) noticed that she seemed to be able to go only so far into the material without either dissociating or flooding. In discussing her dilemma, Kristi mentioned that she perceived me as being distant and uninvolved. We explored this perception for quite a while. Although she accepted the interpretation that in my silence I became like her mother who failed to protect her and silently allowed the abuse to occur, Kristi continued to suffer and to talk seriously about ending therapy.

Finally, after a particularly difficult session, when Kristi left the office withdrawn and frustrated, I encouraged her at the beginning of the next session to imagine freely what she would like me to say or do when we were engaged in uncovering work. Kristi remarked that she wanted me to become much more active and "push" her into difficult feelings and sensations. My immediate internal response was resistance, but I told her that I wanted to think about her feedback. I then went on to interpret other aspects of our interaction. Later, in private reflection, I realized that my resistance stemmed from a firm belief in non-intrusive approaches to trauma, with permission for the patient to take her own time and navigate traumatic material in her own way. To cross this boundary seemed intrusive and retraumatizing; yet we seemed to be at a complete impasse unless I was willing to offer Kristi something different.

During the next appointment, I shared this information with Kristi, noting that the kind of response she seemed to need from me went against much of my training and professional experience with trauma survivors. Nonetheless, because I cared about her and our relationship and viewed this as a possibility for me to grow as a therapist, I told her that I would be willing to try out a slightly different approach because not to do so might result in her continuing to feel abandoned by me. With great care given to monitoring Kristi's subsequent conscious and unconscious reactions to this shift, I proceeded by being a bit more active and "pushing" her at certain key points when she signaled a need for this. The impasse was resolved relatively quickly. Kristi told me that my willingness to be responsive to her had allowed her to get deeper into her experiences of the traumatic incidents from her past. As more time passed, it also appeared that this intervention allowed her to deepen her trust in me. Kristi was able to work through all the stages of therapy successfully and later had a successful termination. On follow-up she continues to do well, and is continuing to integrate the changes she made during therapy into a post-traumatic identity.

As Elkind (1992) points out, sometimes it is possible for new momentum to emerge from either patient or therapist or both, as in the work with Kristi. In other cases, consultation can provide a fresh, objective perspective.

WOUNDING IN AREAS OF PRIMARY VULNERABILITY

When patients are wounded by therapists in areas of special sensitivity, especially in ways that result in retraumatization, a particularly painful situation results that may jeopardize the integrity of the therapeutic relationship. Elkind's (1992) research has indicated that patients who remain feeling damaged by a therapeutic relationship that terminated in a painful impasse are in most cases patients who have been wounded in areas of primary vulnerability. She defines "primary vulnerability" as related to "the preservation of the cohesiveness and connectedness of the self" (p. 100). Examples within her model include Kohut's (1984) description of disintegration anxiety, Balint's (1979) concept of "basic fault," which involves a lack of basic attunement by the therapist, and Winncott's (1965a) discussion of the "unthinkable anxieties" of infancy.

As Elkind (1992) points out, attempts to understand these basic types of wounding by looking only at the adult dimension of the therapy relationship are woefully inadequate. What is required is an understanding of the depth of primitive anxieties that may originate from the relationship that "begins at birth between the mother and the actual baby and that begins at conception in the mother's psyche" (p. 118). When the patient is wounded in an area of such primary vulnerability, and the therapist is unable to empathize with or help the patient understand her wounding, Elkind speculates that this is because the therapist herself may have been thrust into an area of personal primary vulnerability. Effective intervention in this area of relationship dynamics most certainly requires understanding early object relations, the nature of attachment bonds, and other primary processes far beyond the dissociative process.

Case Example: Lillian

Lillian is a 54-year-old borderline patient whom I (MP) have seen off and on over a ten-year period. A patient with a history of abuse and neglect throughout her childhood, beginning in early infancy, Lillian had broken off and reestablished therapy with me several times, usually following an incident that she experienced as my abandonment of her. Each time, even as she was able to see the connections with early experiences of primitive fears of abandonment and betrayal of trust through my interpretations and her own insights, she left feeling she could not tolerate her disappointment and despair. After each break in therapy, lasting from months to years, Lillian got in touch with me, desperately wanting to work out her issues.

During the most recent challenge to our relationship, following a two-week vacation that had been announced to her over six months previously, Lillian again began to struggle with her feelings of abandonment. She threatened again to leave therapy, her plan being to move back in with her actively alcoholic father, whom she had spent so many years struggling to leave. At this point, feeling angry and defeated, I sought professional consultation, which I had not had for my work with her since the last "cycle." During consultation sessions, the nature of Lillian's "primary wounding" became clearer to me in light of her earlier family history as well as her history with me. I was also able to clarify the nature of my own wounding in this situation, which stemmed from depriving myself during the writing of this book of my usual support systems, a personal shift that had triggered some of my own early childhood issues. With more careful attention to needs for personal support, and more consistency in therapeutic interpretations that better supported the framework of the therapy relationship, Lillian is beginning to manage her own feelings of abandonment and to better internalize my support and caring of her. As of this writing, she remains in treatment and continues to deepen her work with me.

DIAGNOSTIC ERRORS

Another difficulty that can contribute to impasse situations with dissociative patients arises from inaccurate or incomplete diagnoses. Putnam and his colleagues (1984) found in his study that the typical MPD patient averaged 6.8 years from her first contact with the mental health system and had received an average of 3.6 different diagnoses prior to receiving an accurate diagnosis for MPD. It is not unusual for such patients to have received as many as twenty divergent psychiatric diagnoses, depending on active symptoms and orientation of the treatment provider at the time of diagnosis. Similar difficulties in determining the accurate diagnosis of other post-traumatic conditions have also been discussed (Herman, 1992). Factors related to these difficulties include professional bias against PTSD, MPD, and other dissociative categories as invalid, stigmatizing, or overused. Dissociative patients may withhold relevant data early in treatment or present trauma-related information that cannot be corroborated (Peterson, Prout, & Schwarz, 1991). In addition, diagnostic errors with MPD (DID) may be related to patients' increased awareness of secondary gains related to MPD, therapists' enhanced awareness of the dissociative disorders without adequate training in differential diagnosis, and the fact that professional "understanding of the nuances of dissociation is in its infancy" (Perry, 1994, p. 13).

Because dissociative patients exhibit such a complex array of symptoms and complaints, it is especially important to obtain a full DSM-IV diagnosis on all five axes in addition to an assessment of dissociative features using appropriate dissociative scales. Failure to do so may result in therapeutic impasse and continued failed therapy experiences. Many of these patients have numerous medical and somatic complaints that deserve proper attention as well as underlying personality disorders, addiction problems, and significant life circumstance issues; if left undiagnosed and neglected, these may compromise treatment. The non-medical therapist in particular may miss conditions that indicate the need for medical intervention and medication. Regular consultation, as well as willingness to continually reevaluate and update diagnostic impressions, will help to reduce difficulties in this area.

Patient Factors: Not Every Sailor Completes the Voyage

There is a variety of patient factors that contribute to an incomplete or failed therapy experience. First, many dissociative patients are not ready or willing to undertake the sometimes arduous tasks of achieving stabilization and safety in their external lives so that they can then begin the work of exploring early trauma. Stage I work (see Chapter 5) may involve resolving abusive relationship issues, dealing with active substance abuse, or stabilizing medical or psychological conditions that compromise daily functioning and may require medication or intensive medical intervention. Both of us have had patients who were self-medicating their symptoms through alcohol and drugs choose to drop out of treatment rather than confront and receive appropriate treatment for their chemical dependency. In several cases, these patients have eventually returned, ready to make the commitment to substance abuse recovery and gradually moving on to the later stages of the underlying trauma work.

A related issue involves patients who have achieved, either through their own efforts or in treatment, a hard-won stability and decided not to "stay the course." For many reasons, the decision to stop therapy at the end of stage I may be viable. Those who have stabilized but who are likely to experience considerable ongoing stressors that stretch their coping skills to the limit may not be good candidates for uncovering work. Those whose functioning depends on consistent alertness, such as physicians, mental health workers, teachers, and new mothers, are examples of patients who may not withstand such exploration. For example, I (MP) saw in consultation a woman in her second trimester of pregnancy with two young children who had amnesia for her childhood before the age of 14. Although her family history indicated the possibility of severe abuse, she was functioning well in the present. After careful evaluation of potential benefits and liabilities, she decided with my support to leave her amnesia intact and return to explore this only if there was a compelling need to do so after her children were older.

Such individuals may be better served by very slow-paced supportive therapy with very gradual engagement of early traumatic material (Ross, 1989) or by personal support systems with no formal therapy. It is important to recognize that not all patients who have suffered early trauma will benefit equally from intensive therapy of the type we have described in this book. Many of them are good candidates for a few well-staged sessions of brief therapy, which can help them marshall their own resources to cope with a life adjustment issue (Edelstien, 1990).

Finally, some patients may be untreatable by us. We exclude from therapy patients who will not work within a viable therapy contract and secure boundary framework. Those who insist on being seen four or five times per week are similarly excluded, because we neither offer nor believe in that model of therapy. Those with a history of severe violence, sociopathic behavior, or need for more structured inpatient environments are also excluded from our outpatient practices. It is important for each therapist to determine her own criteria for exclusion based on past experience with certain patient variables, limits of knowledge and experience, and availability of resources.

For example, although I (MP) have had extensive experience in treating adolescents, I currently exclude them from my practice because my travel schedule precludes providing the more secure, constant environment that many of them require in their therapy experiences.

The Divided Therapist

The outcome of therapy can be seriously affected by problems that arise from various degrees of self-division within the therapist. These therapist difficulties can be thought of as existing on a continuum extending from the most ordinary and healthy kinds of internal therapist conflict to situations in which significant dissociative disorders are present within the therapist (see Figure 6).

THE SPECTRUM OF THERAPIST SELF-DIVISION

At one end of the continuum are therapists who experience normal self-doubt or self-questioning. Moving along the continuum one finds situations in which the therapist has become countertransferentially symptomatic to a greater or lesser degree during the process of treatment. Further along, somewhere in the center of the continuum, are secondary post-traumatic stress disorders (PTSD) that therapists may develop while treating dissociative disorder patients. At the extreme end of the continuum are therapists who bring into the treatment situation significant ongoing dissociative disorders. These may make treatment impossible from the very beginning, or imperil it at any point.

Healthy Therapist Self-Questioning

   Dr. R. is a therapist. One morning his telephone rang at 3 a.m. It was a patient, Theresa, who carried a diagnosis of borderline personality disorder. She was complaining of feelings of emptiness and worthlessness.

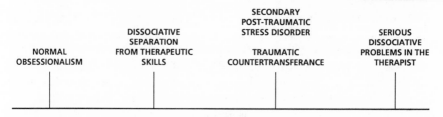

Figure 6. Spectrum of Therapist Self-Division

Dr. R. had trained with Dr. X., who told him that he must be available to his borderline patients 24 hours a day. Dr. R. stayed with this phone call for an hour and a half. Dr. X. would have been proud of him. Yet, before Dr. R. was able to get to sleep again he found himself wondering if he had really done the right thing. He began to doubt the appropriateness of the interaction, and wondered if he might be infantilizing the patient.

Dr. A., another therapist, was awakened by a borderline personality disorder patient, Joan, at 3 a.m. She had trained with Drs. Y. and Z. According to them such phone calls indicated Joan's failure to deal with issues appropriately and to set boundaries in the therapy sessions. Dr. A. dealt strongly with her patient and reasserted her own boundaries. The patient was to head for the nearest emergency room if she could not cope with the small hours of the morning. Like Dr. R., Dr. A. began to experience doubts about what she had done. Her supervisors would approve; so did she. Yet, somehow she felt she might have been more nurturing or simply . . . more human.

It is not unusual for therapists to feel divided during the treatment process or even generally with respect to their identities as psychotherapists. In the National Art Gallery in Athens there is a sculpture by Rene Magritte called *The Therapeutist*. This sculpture depicts an old and faceless therapist whose clothes are run down. He wears a disreputable pair of worn carpet slippers. At his feet is a shabby portmanteau that has begun to fall apart (no doubt his bag of tricks). However, with careful scrutiny it can be seen that the hands of the sculptured therapist are young, strong, and sensitive. It would seem that Magritte has captured the essence of the sense of dividedness experienced by all therapists. Although concepts of countertransference and counter response have been used to explain certain aspects of this sense of dividedness, they have never been adequate in the face of the universality of these phenomena in sensitive therapists. The ability of the therapist to be able to perceive self-division can be an extremely powerful force for progress in psychotherapy. If understood, it can contribute to therapeutic empathy, to the therapist's understanding the true nature of her patient's problems, and to creative reexaminations of treatment approaches. A healthy awareness of ordinary self-divisiveness by therapists can be the beginning of truer, deeper understandings of their patients.

Countertransference Dissociative Splits

We refer the reader to Chapter 10 for more detail concerning countertransference manifestations of dissociation. Therapists may experience a number of dissociative phenomena and become dissociatively separated from their clinical skills when working with dissociative patients (Dolan, 1991; Greaves, 1988; Kluft, 1989; Loewenstein, 1993). We have observed dramatic evidence of this in our workshops and supervision of other therapists. Therapists may also develop selective amnesias and perceptual distortions, space out, share some of the cognitive distortions of their patients (Dolan, 1991; Loewenstein, 1993), or overly distance themselves or "numb" out (Dolan, 1991).

The therapist's own unresolved problems may be evoked by the material of the patient. Dolan (1991) has recommended that the therapist analyze the situation by writing down her concerns in a self-dialogue, alternating right and left hands, for the purpose of resolving "old developmental issues." Psychotherapy for the therapist may be necessary for these kinds of difficulties. Dolan (1991) has also noted that there is a significant number of therapists who are themselves sexual abuse survivors. Therapists who are survivors may be more prone to the symptoms of secondary PTSD.

Secondary Post-Traumatic Stress Disorder

> Trauma is contagious. In the role of witness to disaster or atrocity, the therapist at times is emotionally overwhelmed. She experiences to a lesser degree, the same terror, rage, and despair with the patient. (Herman, 1992, p. 140)

We agree with Dolan (1991), who believes that any therapist might experience the symptoms of secondary PTSD, although therapists who are trauma victims are more susceptible to them. She has identified as a salient symptom of this situation the need to make sexual abuse an almost constant topic of conversation. While peer group support is important for the therapist, she suggests that the therapist note if this material is intruding into her social life. Therapists who experience nightmares may have to ground themselves with some of the same strategies they have taught their patients. And, when the therapist becomes aware of "numbing" with her patients, it is time to take some time off, get away from therapy, and become involved with physical activity. Dolan emphasizes the necessity for therapists with secondary PTSD symptoms to become connected with community life again, and has offered a few practical suggestions for therapists interested in preventing and reducing the symptoms of secondary PTSD. They involve the construction of rituals, including changing into "fun" clothes after work, having specific after-work rituals that demarcate the rest of the day from work (such as having a cup of tea, working out, going for a walk), and altering one's case load so that it contains fewer trauma victims. This subject is treated in greater detail in Chapter 10.

Therapists who find themselves having to rely on these kinds of strategies to maintain their balance need to reevaluate the quality and meaning of their lives. Are they relying too much on their work for fulfillment? Have they stifled their creativity in other areas? Are they alienated from nature? Do relationships with the "normal" people in their lives mean anything to them? If the therapist's life is not truly satisfying and enjoyable away from her therapy practice, this may be a signal that personal therapy is in order to help her reclaim her own life again.

The Wounded Healer: Therapists with Dissociative Disorders

> A fifth of the patients in the NIMH survey had graduate degrees (Putnam et al., 1986). I know more than 20 multiples who are actively practicing professionals. They tend to be in the health professions such as social work, psychology, and psychiatry. . . . having MPD does not preclude the ability to perform, but it is a handicap. (Putnam, 1989, p. 101)

> The treatment of one's professional colleagues is an honor and a privilege. . . . They require our compassionate attention and the full exercise of our skills. Their prognosis is good. However, some of the very traits and characteristics that have followed from and may have allowed to withstand what has befallen them may prove serious barriers to their treatment. (Kluft, 1990c, p. 121).

We see therapists in supervision, and we see others as patients. We do not blur the boundaries between the two functions. The therapist-patient may experience special needs for confidentiality (Kluft, 1990c); however, the unvarying rules of psychotherapy and the persistence of good boundaries must be maintained by the therapist if treatment is to succeed. We refer the reader to Kluft's (1989, 1990c) cogent and sensitive articles concerning issues in the rehabilitation of psychotherapists who have been overwhelmed by their work with MPD patients and those who have various dissociative disorders.

As Kluft has indicated, not every therapist in treatment will decide that she wants to treat MPD in the future. It is our experience that some may develop interests in other aspects of psychotherapy or research; others may put their work with dissociative disorders on "hold" until they have resolved most of their problems. Many are able to continue to work with dissociative disorder patients while they are in therapy if they obtain the necessary training and supervision. Like Kluft (1990c), we tend to pursue the work rather slowly with them, as we place a high value on their ability to continue to function while they are in treatment. Stage I considerations of safety and stability must be paramount. In spite of this there may be times when the therapist-patient who is otherwise functioning well professionally reaches a point of crisis as past material is being uncovered. The judicious use of additional sessions and/

or medication may be helpful on a short-term basis. Although hospitalization is an option, we have never had to employ it.

Therapists with dissociative conditions experience dissociative phenomena more frequently than other therapists in the therapeutic situation; nonetheless, it is our experience that, when they are properly treated and have resolved their own trauma issues, they may become highly attuned to their countertransference responses and able to utilize their transient symptomatology to understand more about what is happening in the transference. We share Dolan's (1991) view about therapists who have experienced trauma: There are both problems and assets attached to the therapist's having been a trauma victim. The problems consist of less than optimum functioning in the therapist role before she has resolved her own trauma issues; the assets include increased sensitivity and capacity to understand what the patient is talking about. The therapist has a professional obligation to keep physically and mentally healthy in order to provide a model for healthy living for her patients, many of whom have had no role models within their families.

DIFFERENCES IN SKILL DEVELOPMENT AMONG HYPNOTHERAPISTS

The beginning hypnotherapist frequently feels overwhelmed by the demands of working with patients with dissociative conditions. The additional stresses of confronting countertransference phenomena of the magnitude of secondary PTSD or discovering that she herself has significant personal difficulties that have come from her own traumatization may seem just too much. She may decide that working with these disorders is not for her (Kluft, 1989). In many cases, the hypnotherapist's skill level may be a contributing factor to therapy stalemates.

Some therapists may benefit from awareness of the developmental process, in which the therapist moves through stages of increasing expertise, from "neophyte" to "mastery" to "expert," as has been described by Hyde and Weinberg (1991). Awareness of the signs of these stages, as well as their pitfalls, can be useful to the developing therapist, who can sense her place in a larger community of therapists. For example, the neophyte may be more prone to secondary PTSD symptoms, may feel more isolated, and may become angry more frequently. Neophytes often feel anxious and overwhelmed by what they hear, feel indispensable, and are tempted to push the limits of usual therapeutic boundaries. Therapists in the mastery phase are more comfortable exploring their own countertransference reactions and more capable of role definition. In this phase the therapist can tolerate the loss of the patient and not blame herself for it. There is more emphasis on the therapist's own creativity and her faith in the ability of the patient's internal system to discern what it truly needs for healing. On the other hand, therapists in the mastery phase may push their patients too fast, lead the patient instead of following, and become self-righteous and competitive. Therapists who have reached the expert phase have seen and treated many varied cases and can distinguish with relative ease between countertransference and projective identification. They are involved in teaching, supervision, and consultation; they publish in their field and gain recognition from their colleagues. "Experts" must beware of grandiosity and competitive feelings. There is a danger of exhaustion, both emotional and physical, from attempting to meet multiple demands.

Family Systems Issues

Other obstacles to the treatment of dissociative patients may involve family systems issues. Many therapists who work with dissociative patients have been trained in family therapy and recognize it as a significant treatment modality. Within family systems models the entire family is thought of as containing the difficulties, rather the individual symptomatic member who has presented as the patient, and treatment is addressed to the family unit instead of the individual patient. Bowen (Kerr & Bowen, 1988) has theorized that each family possesses its own ego, which family members share. While healthy growth and differentiation of a family member may strengthen the family ego, in some instances it threatens the stability of the unit. Family members may struggle to prevent any change within the family structure. In some families the healing of one member may be accompanied by the decompensation of another.

Many therapists with strong family therapy orientations feel they should do family therapy with their dissociative patients (Putnam, 1989). We believe, however, that there are many special circumstances that may make family therapy undesirable. Much of this hinges upon two issues. The first is whether the trauma has occurred within the family or has been external to the family. The second involves the amount of openness to self-revelation and change a family that has hosted internal traumatization demonstrates.

When the trauma has been extrafamilial, family therapy can become a powerful instrument for healing (Figley, 1988). It is important that the family therapy be conducted by a therapist other than the therapist who is treating the dissociative patient. The family therapist can help the family alter communications by changing unwritten rules and stereotyped roles. Self-disclosure can lead each family member to share how trauma in one of its members has affected them, and the family can understand the trauma better when it is recapitulated within the family therapy setting. Figley (1988) has based his version of a corrective emotional experience for the family on Horowitz's (1976, 1986) belief that it is through creating new belief systems or "realities" about the causes and meanings of traumatic event that healing occurs. Figley calls this reframing the *healing theory*. This is a stage in the therapy of the family comparable to stage III and early stage IV of our SARI model.

If a family with internal trauma is ready to face its own abusive behaviors, then family therapy can be valuable. Such families can also find education and support from attending various branches of Families United, a support group that extends itself to victims, perpetrators, and other family members.

Many families in which internal traumatization has occurred are not inclined to deal honestly with the intrafamilial abuse. It is not surprising that post-traumatic and regressive symptoms may flare when the patient has contact with abusers (Kluft, 1983) or those who failed to protect her within her family. Family therapy is contraindicated under these circumstances. Therapeutic efforts can be directed to protecting the patient from family encounters and helping members of the family to obtain therapy on their own.

ATTEMPTS TO SABOTAGE THERAPY BY THE FAMILY OF ORIGIN

Although salient psychodynamic factors with the families of origin of patients with dissociative conditions have been described (Allison, 1974; Greaves, 1980; Kluft, 1984a, 1984b; Kluft, Braun, & Sachs, 1984), little has been reported about successful work with these families when internal traumatization has occurred. Therapeutic interventions with such families are often wished for both by the patient and the therapist; in fact, successful family interventions can become the object of fantasies on the part of the patient and, countertransferentially, of the therapist. A family therapy session may be imagined as the golden opportunity for the patient to confront family members for their wrongdoing and/or discover "what really happened" (Putnam, 1989, p. 266).

At times family interventions can be made with siblings or other family members who were not involved in producing or condoning abuse. However, it must be remembered that an essential part of the family pathology in many instances centers around secrecy and denial that the family has united to preserve. The dissociative patient may be viewed as disloyal, a troublemaker, and often a liar, or misled by the therapist. This latter allegation has been fueled by the recent strenuous efforts of the False Memory Syndrome Foundation. Such muddying of the waters may make it difficult for the patient to hold her own truth. To the extent that any objective evidence for trauma produced within the situation may exist, another family dynamic frequently seen is one which maintains that it was the patient's fault. Thus, the family, which was not able to protect and support the patient at the time of internal traumatization (Dolan, 1991), continues to demonstrate the same damaging patterns.

In most cases the main responsibility of the therapist is to help the patient learn to protect herself from the abusive family and to separate from it. Often contact with the family means contact with the abuser, and crises frequently erupt under these circumstances (Kluft, 1983). One reason for this is that ego states may not have matured sufficiently to experience power within the situation. Another involves the frequent presence within the family of a situation known as "pseudomutuality" (Wynne, Rykoff, Day, & Hirsch, 1958). This dynamic, originally observed in families of schizophrenics, also occurs in the families of dissociative patients. Where pseudomutuality exists within families, individual identity and separateness are sacrificed so that family members can continue to play certain roles, which are intended to preserve the appearance of uniformity within the family. These mechanisms are quite difficult to alter, inasmuch as they are completely unconscious.

Kluft (1983) has noted the "pseudonormal veneer" observed in certain families of MPD patients and has cautioned that contact or even anticipated contact with abusers or certain other members of the family can precipitate crises and major regressions within the patient. The patient and therapist may find themselves in troubled waters, as certain ego states may continue to do that very thing which is harmful to them, i.e., seek out the company of their abusers.

The therapist should experience no amazement at attempts, sometimes drastic, on the part of the family to sabotage the therapy. Boundary violations, as evidenced by intrusive phone calls and letters to the therapist, attempts to retraumatize the patient, guilt-inducing communications with the patient, and even the threat of legal action against the therapist, occur from time to time. When families display such signs of destructive pathology or offer evidence of experienced suffering, we recommend treatment for them with another therapist and apart from the patient. It is not at all unusual for families that are financially supporting treatment to suddenly announce that they will no longer do so; it is advisable to discuss with patients who are being financially supported the possibility that their support could be withdrawn, and to formulate an alternative plan for continuing therapy. Some dissociative patients are not able to recover until they have permanently separated from family members. Ritterman (1983) has suggested that for some patients "person-ectomies" must be conducted to this end, and Dolan (1991) has suggested the usefulness of ritual "imaginary funerals" for intransigent family members who victimized patient.

Some patients may be able to deal with their families at much later stages of therapy. For example, one of my (CF) patients, Emma, had been in psychotherapy for nine years in another part of the country. She moved back to California to enter therapy nearer to her mother's home. Shortly after this she was able to tell her mother for the first time that she was angry with her for not protecting her when she was a child exposed to the horrors attached to her father's alcoholic acting-out. She had helplessly witnessed this as a small child without any adult support. When her mother made a grudging semi-apology, Emma was able to realize her mother's limitations, which had resulted in Emma becoming her own parent. She was now able to see and accept this as a positive comment on her own strength and ability. This proved to be a turning point for her.

THERAPEUTIC INTERVENTIONS FOR SPOUSES

Clinicians working with MPD (DID) patients (Panos, Panos, & Allred, 1990; Sachs, 1986; Williams, 1991) and PTSD patients (Figley, 1988) have reported on the need for work with the spouses of their patients. The spouse of the dissociative patient may find herself having to deal with two kinds of difficulties. One centers around the need to understand what is happening in her partner and how to deal with it appropriately; the other involves her own psychopathology and its impact upon her dissociative partner and any children in the family. We divide the needs of the spouse into three categories: educational, inevitable emotional reactions, and therapy addressed to major pathology in the spouse.

Educational Interventions with the Spouse

Dissociative conditions are understood by our patients' spouses to greatly varying degrees. Spouses often require considerable educational help understanding the nature of the patient's disorder and finding out what their role may be in assisting the treatment process.

Education may extend to what the goals of the treatment process are, how long it might last, how the medications employed work, what their side effects are, and how to spot an emerging crisis. The spouse needs to learn how to set limits for tolerated behavior and to be clear about any issues of dangerousness. Specifically, education aims to help the spouse in her overt reactions to dissociative behavior, different ego states, etc., and to increase her sensitivity and communications skills concerning the ways in which post-traumatic reactions may affect intimacy, sexuality, etc.

A somewhat novel and controversial approach (which we do not employ) is Barker's (1993) technique of training the spouses of MPD patients to be co-therapists. This training enables the spouse to understand more about dissociation and the treatment process, how to deal with or not interact with certain alters, how to manage medication in the home, how to handle suicidal behavior, etc. Barker's position is that if the spouse needs individual therapy this should be done, as should any needed marital counseling, by another therapist.

Inevitable Emotional Reactions of the Spouse

The spouse should have ongoing therapeutic contact for help with her own emotional reactions to what is going on with the patient. How does she feel when the dissociated patient misperceives her as an abuser, awakens in the middle of the night screaming, makes conflicting demands, or doesn't want to join her in recreational activities? It is our experience that many spouses tend to be quite caretaking and masochistic and often struggle against getting therapy for themselves. The question arises about who should see the spouse (Williams, 1992). Although some therapists feel comfortable seeing both partners, we feel this creates boundary and probable transference problems. We recommend meeting with the spouse and the patient once or twice so that therapist and spouse can become acquainted. This can be invaluable should the spouse's assistance be needed in an crisis situation. After this, however, the spouse should be referred to a colleague with knowledge of the hypnotic treatment of dissociative disorders. If family therapy is to be conducted (Figley, 1988), it should not be done by the patient's primary therapist.

While therapy for the spouse facilitates the therapy of dissociative patients (Panos, Panos, & Allred, 1990), not all spouses are ready to enter therapy; in fact, considerable resistance may be encountered. Frequently the resistance is voiced in financial terms. The therapist has to work with this and other resistances in an attempt to maximize treatment possibilities for the patient. In some geographical areas there are various support groups for spouses and significant others of abuse victims. We strongly encourage group support when it is available.

Treatment of Major Pathology in the Spouse

Some families have more than their share of troubles. From time to time we encounter dissociative patients who have partners with significant and often disruptive emotional illness. These partners may be, for example, frankly psychotic (bipolar more often than schizophrenic) or substance abusers, batterers, or pedophiles. It may be impossible to stabilize the patient until some major change has taken place within the family environment. The spouse may require hospitalization, medication, 12-step work, and other support groups. Ongoing therapy for this partner is mandatory if safety and stability are to exist for the patient, and situations of danger must be addressed. The patient may have to become involved in 12-step support groups such as Alanon or

Narcanon if the spouse is abusing alcohol or drugs. If the partner is abusing the children, the therapist will employ the appropriate legal channels.

THERAPEUTIC INTERVENTION FOR THE CHILDREN

Diagnostic interviews with the children of patients with dissociative conditions leave little doubt that dissociative disorders in an adult family member produce significant family problems. The children may live in an atmosphere of terror or hypervigilance caused by the effects of the parent's trauma-based dissociation (Figley, 1988). They may feel they have to walk on eggs to avoid precipitating dissociative behavior in this parent, and may experience great confusion if a parent switches to other ego states. It is common to hear from adults who were reared by dissociative parents that they never knew whom they would encounter when they came home each day.

Children of dissociative patients should be checked for dissociative pathology of their own, including childhood MPD (DID). Should MPD be discovered, a careful search for the source of the abuse must be conducted, as the child cannot recover until the abuse has ceased (Kluft, 1986). It is the better part of wisdom that the children of all patients with overwhelming dissociative symptoms should be checked. They may require therapeutic intervention in a family and/or individual setting for help with inevitable emotional sequelae to living in the family with a symptomatic parent.

WHEN THERAPEUTIC SUCCESS IS A THREAT TO FAMILY MEMBERS

Patients who are improving, who have resolved many of their childhood abuse memory experiences and developmental problems, and who are moving successfully into integration may be assaulted by considerable family acting-out. Its purpose is to get the patient to return to her original role within the family, thus maintaining the family homeostasis. It is almost uncanny how family members will emerge, sometimes apparently from nowhere, in these roles as protectors of "the way things were." We have seen an assortment of such activities. They include the sudden and "coincidental" development of serious physical illness in one or more family members, psychotic or other disturbed behavior, paranoid allegations, threats to the therapist, and major guilt-producing maneuvers. Commonly, our patients are not strong enough to maintain their gains in a family treatment situation where they would have to deal with their abusers.

The Bowen (Kerr & Bowen, 1988) model of family therapy provides for one motivated family member to engage in family therapy. We have found that hypnosis is valuable in helping these patients do family therapy internally. Internal declarations, questionings, and confrontations with family members can occur. Increased use of the imagination in trance can sometimes lead to greater understanding of multifactorial transgenerational factors. Ego-strengthening and hypnotic reinforcement of assertiveness techniques with imagined or remembered family members can also be useful. We encourage our patients to take up these family issues with their ego states while they are in trance. It is not unusual for them to find within the internal family hitherto unrecognized sources of strength for dealing with the external family.

Another effective way of treating family dissonance is through therapy with the internal family of ego states. An extension of the concept of internal therapy with an imagined family is that of each individual containing within herself, among her ego states, a microcosm of her external family structure and dynamics. We have often observed dramatic changes take place in family structure and dynamics of our patients when growth and change have occurred in their internal family of ego states. Family pathology can mirror a powerful symptomatic dissociative patient's internal strife and chaos, and vice versa. It is dramatic to see corresponding subsidence of quarreling and bickering among family members when internal quarrels and squabbles among ego states have been resolved.

What about Forgiveness?

Dissociative patients who have been victims of internal family trauma must often face the resolution of family issues by themselves. Most perpetrators do not even admit the abuse, let alone ask for forgiveness. Our patients and their ego states frequently go through long periods of wishing to revenge themselves upon their abusers; countertransferentially, we may find ourselves joining their fantasies. According to Herman (1992), the revenge fantasy is driven by an urge for catharsis and a need for a sense of power that can overcome feelings of extreme helplessness in the face of the abuse. Within such fantasies a role reversal has occurred, and the victim has become the perpetrator (Herman, 1992). When these fantasies are repeated over and over again, they do not empower the patient; to the contrary, they cause her to begin to feel like a monster. As Herman has pointed out, combat veterans who have acted out their revenge fantasies have never been cured of their PTSD by this kind of activity.

Our goal in exploring forgiveness with dissociative patients is to help them assume responsibility for the kind of family relationships they want to have at the present time. We help them understand that the range of family relatedness can range from choosing to have no relationship or contact at all, to learning ways of communicating about current needs without knowing or confronting all that happened in the past, to handling confrontations about past hurts and working through related issues together.

For example, a patient who was just beginning to uncover and deal with sexual abuse by her father complained that she did not know how to act when she visited her parents and feared that she would have to wait a long time to find out exactly what happened so that she could confront them and have a more "honest" relationship. I (MP) pointed out to her that she needed to decide how she could be more honest with her parents about issues that were current in her life now, rather than wishing for some dramatic, magical change in the future, when she imagined she might know the "whole truth" of her childhood. She decided to confront her parents about their attitudes toward her current boyfriend and was astonished to discover that they were far more supportive of her than she feared. Once patients are able to take responsibility for defining current relationships, they are often better able to separate unrealistic childlike wishes from obtainable adult needs, and to move on with their grieving process. Their movement along the continuum of family relatedness may shift during this process and we encourage them to continue to keep an open mind.

Much as all healthy individuals must let go of their parents in order to complete the important developmental tasks of leaving home, developing their own values, and establishing their own object relations, the traumatized patient must learn to let go of childlike attachments to those who abused her and those who failed to protect her from abuse, neglect, and abandonment. In letting go, the patient must realize that she will never "get even" or "receive justice." When she is able to do this and go through what Herman (1992) calls "traumatic mourning," she can transform revenge into "righteous indignation." Patients often attempt to avoid this critical step in their recoveries through both internal and external maneuvers. Internally, they may grasp at forgiveness as a solution that will keep them from experiencing revenge fantasies. Externally, they may become embroiled in legal maneuvers designed to make the perpetrator or someone who symbolizes him/her "pay" (Herman, 1992; Putnam, 1989).

Case Example: Jack

Jack had dropped out of treatment in a flight into health. Subsequently, he visited some sites of childhood abuse, and in that geographical area he was injured in a traffic accident. He instituted a lawsuit for intentional infliction of emotional damage over this injury and then sought further therapy (not to mention assistance with his legal case). He told me (CF), "I've done a lot of suffering in my life, and someone's going to pay for it." He also stated that he wished to reenter treatment. I asked him to relinquish the suit so that he could get on with resolving his significant dissociative problems and childhood trauma in a therapeutic way. He was unwilling to do this; instead he saw treatment as something that would help him win this lawsuit, whose purpose was to compensate him for all the sufferings attendant upon his childhood abuse. I indicated that I would like to help him achieve treatment goals of personal rather than monetary value. I told him that I thought the suit was yet another way of avoiding the inevitable pain and grief of trauma that he would eventually need to face and that it would interfere with his therapeutic work.

Jack would not give up the lawsuit and was angry that I did not see things the way he and his attorney saw them. I was unwilling to see him in therapy under these circumstances, although I offered to see him again once the legal situation had been resolved or dropped. I explained that I was reluctant to attempt to conduct therapy in an atmosphere designed to circumvent it.

The therapist can be tempted to collude with the patient's internal or external avoidance mechanisms. Our patients may never be able to "forgive" abusers in any sentimental or intentional way. We are satisfied with their being able to go through "traumatic mourning" for the damage that has been done to them by family members, for the pain they have endured, and the limitations they have had to face in their lives. We attempt to assist with an understanding of why abusing family members acted as they did. This is part of reframing and giving a new meaning to traumatic memory material, which is essential to its release for proper integration. We focus upon helping the patient become more self-loving and generative, and we accept that she may never reach a sentimental forgiveness toward those who have harmed her.

12

REENACTMENTS OF TRAUMA

Trauma victims tend to relive the original trauma in various ways, often becoming retraumatized or retraumatizing in the process (Goodwin, 1990; Terr, 1991; van der Kolk, 1989). Unwanted aspects of the trauma may return as physical sensations, intrusive images or nightmares, hypnagogic experiences, behavioral reenactments, or some combination of these. Trauma reenactments can result in harm to others in the form of family violence and sexual abuse; self-destructive acts such as self-starving, bulimia, and cutting; and revictimization. Both psychological and physiological factors have been suggested as contributing to this phenomenon.

Psychological Factors

There is something "uncanny" about traumatic reenactments. Regardless of the level of conscious awareness that accompanies them, they seem to have a quality of complete involuntariness and driven tenacity (Herman, 1992). Although traumatic reenactments offer opportunity for learning and mastery, they also provoke intense emotional distress, which can lead to retraumatization responses. Below we review a variety of psychological explanations of traumatic reenactments, including Freud's repetition compulsion theory and social attachment theory.

REPETITION COMPULSION THEORY

There is some evidence to suggest that of the three main categories of posttraumatic symptoms—repetition, avoidance, and hyperalertness—repetition may be the clearest and best indicator of childhood psychic trauma (Terr, 1990). Janet (1911) wrote about how traumatized patients become fixed on the trauma. Janet pointed out that, because these individuals are unable to make sense of the source of their terror, they have great difficulty in assimilat-

250

ing subsequent experiences, as if their personality development had stopped at a certain point. Freud (1896, 1920) came to similar conclusions. Originally, Freud (1914) described the repetition compulsion as an activity in which remembering the original traumatic situation is replaced by behavioral reenactment. Later, Freud (1920) suggested that traumatic repetition was an attempt to overcome feelings of helplessness about the experience and to achieve mastery over it by moving from a passive to an active position.

Fenichel (1939/1953) noted that the repetition and search for mastery continue because the fear still remains. Janet (1919) wrote of the need to "assimilate" and "liquidate" traumatic experience, which, when accomplished, results in a feeling of "triumph" (p. 603). This indicates Janet's belief that recovery from traumatic helplessness involves the restoration of efficacy and power through continued attempts at adaptation (Herman, 1992).

Related to this issue is Horowitz's "*completion principle*" or *information-processing model*. Horowitz (1986) postulated that the brain has intrinsic capacity to update continually the inner schemata of self and the world. When these inner schemata are shattered through trauma, unassimilated traumatic experiences are stored in a special kind of "active memory," which lies outside normal experience and therefore cannot be matched with the individual's existing cognitive schema (Horowitz, 1979). The results are an "information overload" of trauma-related ideas, affects, sensations, and images that cannot be integrated with the self, along with an inability to process new information. Denial, numbing and other defensive maneuvers are used to keep traumatic information unconscious. However, because of the active memory's "intrinsic tendency to repeat the representation of contents" (Horowitz, 1986, p. 93), the traumatic information becomes conscious at times as part of the process of information-processing. This information may take the form of intrusive flashbacks, repetitive nightmares, unwanted thoughts and feelings, and may lead to partial or complete reexperiences (van der Hart et al., 1993). Theoretically, such intrusive psychic material continues to enter consciousness until the traumatic information is fully processed (Peterson, Prout, & Schwarz, 1991). Trauma resolution occurs when a new mental schema is developed that contains the understanding of what happened, or when reality and cognitive schemas match.

Beahrs (1990) has explored the effects of "*trauma-driven*" *behavior*. This kind of behavior consists of two components, which often work against each other and contribute to the persistence of post-traumatic conditions. *Avoidance behavior* can become an organizing force for the personality, creating a "false self" whose function is to keep the trauma material at bay; this is usually coupled with *reenactment behavior* that episodically recreates the trauma. Reenactment behavior may stimulate sufficient ongoing rehearsal and practice to result in the development of coping skills that can be used in "real" emergencies. However, the disadvantages of such behaviors can be far more significant than the benefits. Beahrs (1990) conceptualizes traumatic experiences as an "emotional ball and chain" (p. 19), which may restrict individual personality development throughout the life cycle and lead to transgenerational perpetuation of the trauma.

SOCIAL ATTACHMENT THEORY

Social attachment has also been shown to play an important role in explaining traumatic reenactment and the abilities to deal with external threat. Van der Kolk (1989) has pointed out that the presence of familiar caregivers helps children modulate their physiologic arousal. In the absence of a primary caregiver, children may experience extremes of under- and overarousal that are physiologically aversive and disorganizing (Finkelhor & Brown, 1985). If the caregiver is abusive, children are likely to become hyperaroused. And when the individuals who are needed as sources of safety and nurturance become simultaneously the source of danger, children attempt to reestablish some sense of safety by blaming themselves (van der Kolk, 1989) or becoming fearfully attached and anxiously obedient (Cicchetti, 1984).

Sudden, uncontrollable loss of attachment bonds appears to be important in the development of post-traumatic stress reactions (Krystal, 1978; Lindy, 1987; van der Kolk, 1985). Severe external threat and exposure to extreme terror can result in intense clinging and attachment behavior in both children and adults, as they attempt to return to physiological and psychological calm. When usual social sources of comfort are unavailable, trauma victims may turn toward their tormentors. Adults as well as children may develop strong emotional ties to those who intermittently harass, beat, and threaten them (Bowlby, 1969; Finkelhor & Brown, 1885; Kempe & Kempe, 1978). Walker (1979) has described the operation of intermittent reinforcement patterns in such relationships. In child abuse and battering situations, this mechanism is accentuated by extreme contrasts of terror followed by submission and reconciliation. Such intermittent negative reinforcement can strengthen the attachment bonds between victim and perpetrator.

Individuals who are exposed to early violence, abuse, or neglect seem to develop vulnerability to subsequent traumatic bonding. Males may tend to be hyperaggressive, while females fail to protect themselves and their offspring against danger. Trauma victims of both sexes observe the chronic helplessness of their parents' alternating outbursts of affection and violence and learn that they themselves have no control (van der Kolk, 1989). As adults, they hope to repair the past by exemplary behavior in their relationships (Frieze, 1983; Krugman, 1987; Walker, 1979). When this fails, they may return to earlier coping mechanisms, such as self-blame, numbing through emotional withdrawal or drugs and alcohol, and violence directed toward the self or the other—all of which sets the stage for a repetition of the early trauma and a "return of the repressed" (Ainsworth, 1967; Freize, 1983; van der Kolk, 1987c).

Biological Factors

Other reasons for traumatic reenactment seem to originate within the biological response to trauma. Several variables are considered in this section, including state-dependent learning, inescapable shock reactions, endogenous opioid responses and addiction to trauma.

STATE-DEPENDENT LEARNING

Many scientific studies have validated the operation of state-dependent memory and learning (Rossi, 1993a; see Chapter 1.) For example, what has been learned under the influence of a particular drug tends to become dissociated and seemingly lost until a return of the state similar to the one in which the memory was stored (Eich, 1980). Hilgard (1977), as well as Milton Erickson (1974/1980), viewed dissociation as being in the same class of psychophysiological phenomena as state-dependent memory and learning; thus, memories can be isolated from consciousness and each other because of different available information (Hilgard, 1977).

During states of heightened autonomic arousal, which occur in response to trauma, memory "tracks" are laid down that powerfully influence later behaviors and perceptions of events. In traumatized individuals, visual and motoric reliving experiences, such as nightmares, flashbacks, and reenactments, are generally preceded by increased central nervous system arousal (Delaney, Tussi, & Gold, 1983). Reactivation of state-dependent memory "tracks" may help to explain why current stress is experienced as a return of past trauma (van der Kolk, 1989).

INESCAPABLE SHOCK REACTIONS

Chronic hyperarousal in response to new challenges is found in animals exposed to inescapable shock (Anisman, Ritch, & Sklar, 1981). This chronic hyperarousal results in heightened norepinephrine levels with widespread behavioral and physiological effects (van der Kolk, 1989). This is not the result of the shock itself but of an accompanying learned helplessness syndrome (Maier & Seligman, 1967). Additional biological reactions include a decrease in the animal's capacity to initiate a response, inhibition of the organism's capacity to modulate the extent of the arousal, and an analgesic response, mediated by endogenous opioids (Peterson, Prout, & Schwarz, 1991).

Humans who have been subjected to overwhelming trauma respond physiologically much like animals who have been exposed to inescapable shock
situations (Grinker & Spiegel, 1945; van der Kolk, Greenberg, & Boyd,
1985). There is a secretion of opiod peptides, known as enkephalins, which
produce analgesia, reduce anxiety, and seem to have antidepressant and tran-
quilizing actions (Vereby, Volavka, & Clouet, 1978).

ENDOGENOUS OPIOID RESPONSES AND ADDICTION TO TRAUMA

Research has shown that high levels of stress, including social stress (Miczek,
Thompson, & Shuster, 1982), can activate opioid systems. Van der Kolk
(1985, 1989) has suggested that the calming and pleasurable effects of these
internal opioids may lead trauma victims to seek out subsequent traumatic
situations in order to obtain psychobiological relief. Thus, an addictive cycle
of retraumatization and trauma-seeking behavior can develop.

In humans, elevations of enkephalins and beta endorphins have been
found following a large variety of stressors, resulting in stress-induced analgesia (Janal, Colt, & Clark, 1984). Van der Kolk (1989), for example, reported
that Vietnam veterans diagnosed with PTSD experienced a 30% subjective
reduction in pain, equivalent to an injection of 8 mg of morphine, following
the viewing of a combat movie. This research suggests that even in individuals
traumatized as adults, re-exposure to situations reminiscent of the trauma
may evoke an endogenous opioid response similar to that in animals exposed
to mild shock following an inescapable shock situation. Re-exposure to traumatic stress may therefore have the same effect as temporary application of
artificial opioids, providing similar relief from anxiety (Gold, Pottash, &
Sweeney, 1982; van der Kolk, 1989). It is not clear, however, how this type
of relief might compare with anxiety reduction achieved through exposure to
neutral or positive stimuli.

Other research has shown that infants are helped to modulate physiologic
arousal through the presence of a primary attachment figure, who helps to
provide a balance between soothing and stimulation. In the absence of this
figure, infants may experience disorganizing extremes of under- and overarousal (Reite, Short, & Seiler, 1978, 1981). Van der Kolk (1989) has hypothesized that this soothing and arousal process may be mediated by various
neurotransmitter systems, including endogenous opioids. Since childhood
abuse and trauma may precipitate a long-term vulnerability to hyperarousal,
these individuals may require much higher external stimulation of the endogenous opioid system for self-soothing than those whose internal opioid systems are activated by responses based on good early attachment experiences
(van der Kolk, 1989). Thus, traumatized individuals may attempt to neutralize their hyperarousal through a variety of addictive behaviors, including

compulsive re-exposure to situations reminiscent of the original traumatic one.

We have found that individuals who were traumatized during very early stages of development may require medication to mitigate this response. Other patients are able to use self-hypnosis to modulate CNS arousal patterns, as illustrated in the following case example.

Case Example: Roberto

Roberto, a 24-year-old dissociative patient, was self-referred to me (MP) for hypnotic treatment of a variety of anxiety symptoms. Initially, his complaints centered around the appearance of intrusive images, which consisted of vivid scenes where he was castrated, mutilated, and killed in a variety of ways. Through Ego-State Therapy approaches (see Chapter 4), we identified "Dracula," an ego state responsible for creating these gruesome mental pictures, and after numerous sessions of interventions with "Dracula" and other relevant ego states, the images abated, along with feelings of fear, panic, and shame.

As Roberto's therapy progressed, he revealed that he had coped with these symptoms previously through the use of alcohol, marijuana, pornography, and compulsive masturbation and exercise. After we discussed his cycles of hyperarousal, I suggested self-hypnosis and meditation to modulate his tendency toward overstimulation. After several weeks, he reported that the use of progressive relaxation, along with self-suggestions and cognitive cues, was consistently producing a calming effect. At present, he is even able to tolerate movies with violent scenes, which he has had to avoid for years because of their retraumatizing effects. Roberto has also mastered personal autohypnotic approaches to deal with a variety of external triggers, which has resulted in more consistent emotional responses throughout his daily life.

Trauma Reenactments in Therapy

Van der Kolk (1989) has written that the extensive behavioral, emotional, physiologic, and neuroendocrinologic repetitions of trauma cause a great degree of individual and social suffering. Part of the therapist's role in the treatment of trauma is to recognize and, over time, to identify and interpret various kinds of traumatic reenactments for the patient (Blank, 1985, 1989), so that he may gain conscious control over the unbidden reenactments. Because such reenactments can be subtle and highly symbolic, even experienced therapists may fail to detect them. The following section explores the nature of reenactments that occur outside of therapy sessions and within the therapy hour and methods of working with this material.

Traumatic reenactments in the patient's everyday life are often embedded in therapy material that is presented routinely by the patient in the therapy hour. In some cases, because such reenactments are undramatic and unmeaningful to the patient, they are omitted in his communications. Often the therapist must discover such material by exploring actively how the patient spends his time outside the therapy hour—that is, by inquiring about personal relationships, work situations, and leisure activities, with a particular focus on repetitive personal or interpersonal conflicts (Parson, 1988).

ASSESSMENT OF TRAUMATIC REENACTMENTS IN THE PATIENT'S OUTSIDE EXPERIENCES

With patients who have been subjected to violence, the therapist must assess whether there is aggressive or antisocial acting-out toward themselves, other people (especially children), or objects. Self-destructive acts, including self-mutilation, biting, burning, and cutting, are common in adults abused as children. It is important to understand and explore with the patient the paradoxical nature of many self-injury behaviors. Although the injury is real and sometimes dangerous, the intent may be to help the patient with self-regulation (Waites, 1993). For example, self-cutting can be an attempt to relieve intolerable inner pressures or to produce pain that heightens awareness and reassures the patient that he is still alive and capable of feeling. Other behaviors may induce numbness or anesthesia that dulls intolerable feelings. Self-abusive behaviors can also be symbolic reenactments of childhood abuse experiences; for example, cutting and mutilation can be reenactments of ritualized abuse, or reminders of physical abuse, neglect, or invasive caretaking (Miller, 1994). The therapist must assess the underlying motivation or intention of self-injury; if aimed at suicide, he must provide for the patient's safety. If, on the other hand, such behaviors are attempts at containing and moderating suicidal urges by reassuring the patient of his control over his body (Waites, 1993), the patient must be helped to find less destructive alternatives for self-regulation and self-soothing. More is written about this in Chapter 13.

A common outlet among those who have experienced physical abuse by parents is harsh punishment or abuse of their own children (McCann & Pearlman, 1990). In working with patients with this kind of history who have children, the therapist can inquire as to which behaviors result in discipline, what specific discipline approaches that are used, and what the results of disciplinary actions are, particularly whether any injuries have ever been sustained. The therapist must be aware that revelations of such aggressive or abusive behavior may often be accompanied by shame and guilt, and join with the part of the patient who wants to stop the abuse in understanding such behaviors empathically. If the patient is a complex dissociative disorder patient or has MPD, he may have no conscious knowledge of abusive behaviors, since such activity may be under the direction and control of a hostile alter or ego state, who is unknown to the greater personality. Obviously, the therapist must work to provide protection for the children and to elicit the patient's full cooperation in accomplishing this goal.

Another indication of traumatic reenactment may be symptoms of anxiety, including panic, hyperarousal, somatic disturbances, and intrusive imagery or thoughts. These responses must be explored in terms of their possible connections to past traumatic experiences and to current triggers in the patient's everyday life. Somatic disturbances are particularly problematic. As Terr (1990) has suggested, repeated body sensations may mimic the physical sensations that originally were connected with trauma. The non-medical therapist, in particular, must confirm that proper medical consultation has been sought to rule out organic causes for persistent symptoms, and that the patient is receiving ongoing preventive services such as regular physical examinations and dental care. On the other hand, it is essential that the therapist convey an attitude of interest and curiosity about somatic complaints, rather than imply that they are outside the concerns of psychotherapy (McCann & Pearlman, 1990).

For patients who suffer from alexithymia, a major disturbance in affective and symbolic functioning, there may be additional considerations. Alexithymia involves impaired ability to identify and utilize emotional states (Krystal, 1988). The emotional reactions of these patients are mostly distressing somatic responses that arise from undifferentiated, incomplete emotional states and an inability for reflective self-awareness. Alexithymic patients sometimes learn to compensate for this deficiency through the use of social clues and logic to infer what they "should" be feeling. Since this condition is found, to varying degrees, in traumatized individuals (Krystal, 1988), alexithymia may be part of the clinical picture for many dissociative patients. Because of their impaired ability to identify and differentiate emotional states through "talking" therapy, it may be necessary to provide additional preparation during the first stage of treatment to teach these patients how to connect physiological reactions with emotional states. The somatic experiencing model (see Chapter 7) can be particularly useful in this regard, as can the use of journal writing, artwork, and other less verbal approaches.

Interpersonal reenactments often include a tendency toward revictimization, as discussed above; Kluft (1990c) has termed this the "sitting duck" syndrome. Decreased self-trust and impaired ability to make self-protective judgments can result in "blind spots" for abusive or exploitive relationships.

Dissociative defenses may cloud awareness in interpersonal situations, leading to confusion, withdrawal, and discontinuous experiences with others (Kluft, 1990c). Further, many patients hold deeply ingrained beliefs that abusive, neglectful, or exploitative attachments are the norm, having learned these patterns from childhood experiences. Coupled with repetition and reenactment tendencies, and with biological predispositions to seek out traumatic situations to modulate high arousal levels, are feelings of learned helplessness, lack of control over life circumstances, and deep despair and hopelessness. All of these factors leave the traumatized individual vulnerable to those who might offer a sense of control or authority, who offer the promise of gratifying dependency needs, and who may, at least initially, serve as a "self-object" to stabilize a shaky sense of self (Kluft, 1990c).

Gently challenging these patterns and helping the patient to develop a stronger sense of self, including the ability to establish appropriate interpersonal boundaries and make self-protective decisions, is an important aspect of treating dissociative conditions and reversing tendencies toward revictimization (McCann & Pearlman, 1990). Individuals who demonstrate a high level of traumatic reenactment in their everyday lives may be quite destabilized. For these patients, it is important to focus extensively on stage I tasks (see Chapter 5) before actively connecting behavioral, emotional, and sensory patterns to specific traumatic events.

Sexual dysfunction may also be an area of interpersonal traumatic reenactment. There is extensive evidence for impaired sexual functioning among victims of childhood sexual abuse, rape, domestic violence, and combat (Becker, Skinner, Abel, & Cichon, 1986; Feldman-Summers, Gordon, & Meagher, 1979; Garte, 1986; Stark & Flitcraft, 1981). Issues may include fear of sex, arousal dysfunction, and decreased sexual satisfaction. Often patients will not reveal these difficulties unless the therapist explores them in an open, matter-of-fact way. Specific issues to be explored by the therapist include frequency of sexual contact; degree of satisfaction; arousal level; nature of sexual interactions; thoughts, feelings, and fantasies that accompany arousal; and any concerns the patient may have about his sexual functioning (McCann & Pearlman, 1990).

It is also important to determine whether particular difficulties are specific to certain sexual partners, sexual activities, or contexts, or are generalized to all sexual experiences. For example, one dissociative patient told me (MP) early in treatment that she and her husband enjoyed frequent, satisfying sex. It wasn't until after incest material had surfaced later in the therapy that she disclosed that almost all her sexual fantasies were related to her uncle and that she could only make love in a very ritualized manner that excluded several specific sexual behaviors with which she was intensely uncomfortable. In order to utilize these kinds of clues in making effective connections to early abuse experiences, it may be very important to obtain a detailed sexual history as part of the intake process and to explore unique meanings and experiences related to certain sexual behaviors and activities for that individual.

TRAUMATIC REENACTMENTS AS ATTACHMENT AND DETACHMENT ISSUES

In addition to sadistic, invasive, ritualistic, and humiliating experiences reported by dissociative patients, trauma related to parents' failure to respond may profoundly influence the development of dissociative pathology (Barach, 1991). This type of trauma, consisting both of parental failure to protect the child from the trauma and of parental tendencies to dissociate or otherwise detach emotionally, can eventually cause a corresponding detachment in the child. The child's reactive detachment can eventually lead to reliance on dissociation as a response to more "active" abuse. Barach (1991) suggests that such detachment protects the abused child from crying out for help and discovering that he is alone. The abused child has long learned not to expect help from mother because of her ongoing emotional detachment.

These attachment disturbances are likely to be reflected in the kinds of attachment patterns that are reenacted by the dissociative patient within the therapeutic relationship. Early in treatment, when the patient is flooded with signals that indicate the possibility of danger, the need for an attachment figure is strong. Thus, emergency phone calls, requests for extra sessions, or insistence on hospitalization can be reflective of attachment needs that are elicited by fear. Alternatively, patients can defend against their attachment needs by cancelling appointments, initiating self-destructive behaviors, or threatening to drop out of therapy.

Attachment-seeking behavior on the part of the patient can readily elicit caretaking behavior on the part of the therapist. Tendencies of MPD (DID) and other dissociative patients to violate the therapist's boundaries in an attempt to meet attachment needs have usually been understood as transference reenactment of abuse and early traumatic experiences of violation (Loewenstein, 1993); they may also be seen, however, as a reactivation of transference attachment behavior (Barach, 1991).

On the positive side, this kind of reenactment may fuel the patient's hope that the original trauma can be corrected–that is, that this time he will not be abandoned. Thus, attachment reenactment experiences raise the possibility that the patient may eventually develop internal security in attachment and will not need to detach (or dissociate). On the negative side, the patient may view the therapist's attempts at empathic neutrality as unresponsive or as a real abandonment. Expressions of dissociative anger to therapist neutrality can provoke detachment or retaliation from the therapist, further compounding the reenactment (Barach, 1991).

This attachment dilemma for both patient and therapist may parallel Herman's (1992) assessment of the classic therapeutic bind in the treatment of trauma. The therapist must create a balance between approaching the traumatic material and risking the patient's fear of invasion, exploitation, or voyeurism, or avoiding the trauma and risking feelings of neglect and abandonment. If the therapist confronts the patient's attachment-seeking behavior, or plays into it, the patient may feel invaded or pushed to move "too close"; if the therapist does not respond in appropriately gratifying ways to these attempts to attach or detach, the patient may feel real abandonment.

Case Example: Barry

Barry, a 42-year-old musician, was referred to me (MP) for hypnotherapy for post-traumatic symptoms he believed related to sexual and physical abuse by his father. During the first two sessions of history-taking and initial assessment, Barry found it very difficult to look at me while he was talking. In exploring this reaction, he stated his fear that I could "see right through him," that he would have no protection from my knowing about all the pain inside him. When I suggested that it might be interesting for him to experiment with finding out what it was like when he connected with me more fully, and then to compare that experience with purposeful disconnection through losing eye contact, Barry replied that he did not believe he was ready for that. He continued to make little direct eye contact with me, except when he was laughing defensively.

In a later session, although Barry had agreed to the ground-rules and policies stated during the initial phone interview and again during the first session, he became quite upset with my policy of handling insurance forms and billing statements during the first few minutes of the last session of every month. He insisted that he had to have a form filled out and signed by me at every session. This demand persisted even though he had checked with his insurance company and had determined that this would not greatly facilitate his reimbursement process. As we explored his strong feelings about this issue following a phone call in which he had threatened to cancel his appointment and perhaps to terminate therapy, I gently wondered whether he might feel better cared for by me if I attended to the forms each time we met. Barry replied, "You know, I really don't know how to get you to care about me. I can tell that I can't manipulate you like I tried to do with my father. At least with him I knew that sometimes what I did would work. With you, I don't know whether anything I do will work. I feel really lost and vulnerable."

This case illustrates some of the attachment disturbances reenacted by the dissociative patient in therapy. Barry demonstrated a tendency to detach in the face of his fear of invasion and letting me get "too close"; yet at the same time he appeared driven by a desperate wish to experience attachment through my caring about him in a way he could tolerate.

The development of a secure, safe therapeutic relationship appears to be essential in providing a context within which to explore the realities of the past and to interrupt current internal and social isolation that keeps traumatized individuals stuck in repetitive patterns (van der Kolk, 1989). Therefore, attention to attachment phenomena and the development of secure attachment bonds with the therapist is an important therapeutic task.

Trauma and Addiction

By the time they enter treatment, many dissociative patients have developed habitual patterns of trauma-seeking behavior coupled with a variety of addictive behaviors, such as alcohol and drug abuse, eating issues, and compulsive acting-out, as an attempt to neutralize their hyperarousal and anxiety levels. Carnes (1991, 1993) has summarized the evidence of a strong relationship between addiction and post-traumatic conditions, including the finding that the more severe the sexual and physical abuse in childhood, the more addictions developed in adulthood. He has suggested that careful exploration of addictive patterns can reflect how the individual was abused as a child; for example, patterns of compulsive abstinence may reflect deprivation, while extreme excesses may indicate excessive intimate boundary violations or other dynamics.

Dissociative patients with acute addictive patterns must be helped to bring these issues under control before exploring the underlying trauma. Often, stopping compulsive behavioral extremes, whether in eating, use of chemicals, or sex, will begin to remove blocks to traumatic memory material. Failure to achieve stability in recovery from addictive behavior before exploring underlying traumatic experiences can result in relapse and rapid decompensation. Even when stability has been achieved through sobriety, the addict who is exploring trauma requires additional safety in the form of frequent checks of the effectiveness of relapse prevention plans (Carnes, 1993). Since working with trauma can raise anxiety and trigger relapse, careful monitoring of the patient's ongoing addictive behaviors is essential before, during, and following sessions where trauma is explored. Carnes (1993) also points out that such patients may develop "new" addictions during the course of traumatic exploration, which can serve the same function as a relapse from a previous addiction.

Dissociative patients who do not demonstrate common addictions, such as eating disorders, chemical dependency, and sexually addictive behavior, often reenact trauma by seeking out or otherwise recreating forms of traumatic stress, which serves a similar purpose of achieving psychobiological relief from post-traumatic hyperarousal states. Such patients may engage in high-risk behaviors, obsess about attractions to people who have been hurtful in the past or who have the tendency to be hurtful or exploitive in relationships, overwork to avoid self-connection, or require excessive stimulation in the form of dangerous, violent, or pornographic movies or reading material. These individuals persist in such behaviors, despite insight and awareness that continuing to do so has overwhelmingly negative consequences.

We have found that dealing with the addictive aspects of trauma requires a balance between the more directive, confrontive interventions used in the addiction field and the permissive focus on self-empowerment that is an inherent part of working in the field of trauma. At times we are quite directive with patients, teaching them about the connections between addiction and trauma, the psychobiological aspects of the trauma response (especially the role of endogenous opioids), the cycles of multiple addictions and relapse prevention, and the concepts of traumatic bonding and systemic repetition (Carnes, 1993). We confront addictive behaviors, focus on sobriety, recovery, and stabilization of non-addictive patterns, and teach alternative strategies, such as the use of self-hypnosis for anxiety reduction and substitution of positive internal resources for addictive gratification patterns. Finally, we insist that our patients demonstrate ongoing stability in modulating their daily anxiety and arousal levels in healthy ways. If this is not occurring, we are prepared to change the course of therapy to provide an intensive focus on this goal until the patient can achieve it. Such a direct approach is balanced with communications of our inherent respect for the patient's own timing and ways of moving through these issues. We also employ the utilization principle to remind ourselves and the patient that addictive aspects of trauma give us additional opportunities to discover more about how he was traumatized and what his deeper needs may be.

Addiction to Trauma in the Therapist

Like their patients, many therapists become "addicted" to the exploration of traumatic material, experiencing a certain "high" or type of satisfaction that comes from abreaction of traumatic experiences and colluding with the patient's attempts to pursue the opioid relief that can follow such experiences at the expense of achieving ongoing stability and empowerment.

It is inevitable that many of those entering the mental health fields will have experienced early trauma, especially sexual abuse, and may have developed dissociative disorders. In addition to therapists who themselves suffer from trauma-based conditions, there is evidence to suggest that every therapist who works with traumatized individuals may experience some form of traumatic symptoms. It is not clear whether such responses can be attributed to properties of the "dissociative transference field" (Loewenstein, 1993), or whether they are a type of "vicarious traumatization" (McCann & Pearlman, 1990).

Trauma responses in the therapist, like those in the patient, can manifest in various types of addictive and trauma-driven patterns. An example of this is the therapist's intense investment in or even "addiction" to the role of rescuer, which can lead to boundary violations with the therapist gratifying the patient's regressive needs for longer sessions, excessive phone contact, or "emergency" caretaking. The therapist may feel empowered by the patient's dependency and end up undermining his attempts to take charge of his own life. Such behavior greatly compromises the patient's ability to resolve his own struggles internally (Comstock, 1991).

The best antidotes to such addictive responses in the therapist are the use of an effective support system and adequate methods for self-regulation. Whether the therapist is a neophyte or an expert, we believe that the therapist who works hypnotherapeutically with dissociative patients should either have had or be in the process of obtaining personal psychotherapy. Further, we recommend that therapy be accomplished with a therapist who, all other things being equal, possesses hypnotherapeutic skills. This therapist should also be in the ongoing, lifelong process of obtaining further training. Supervision and peer supervision, study groups, and supervision groups are essential for the further development of the therapist. Each of the authors conducts supervision groups for therapists who treat dissociative conditions, and we are impressed by the growth and development which they can stimulate.

There must be available other human resources for the therapist, however. We cannot tell our patients to "get a life" if we do not have lives ourselves. Therapists are often compelled to do their healing work by virtue of their family dynamics and early life experiences; however, we will not do it well if it is all there is for us. Our family lives and warm affectionate connections help make us better therapists. So do our interests in the arts, our own further personal expressiveness and creativity, our activities in the community, including the global community, our relationships with nature, and healthy excitement, play, and fun. Connections with other therapists, with our communities, with our private passions and playfulness, and with nature provide us with possibilities for transforming the residue of the pain and stress we experience as we walk with our trauma patients into something within us that is part of the healing forces of the universe: not just another set of techniques, not scrambling to arrive at another level of expertise as a therapist, but becoming more generative and spiritual people. If we fail to keep our connections with the wellsprings of life, we may well fall into pools of pathology and become ineffective people as well as ineffective therapists.

Revictimization

One of the significant effects of trauma reenactments or repetitions is the revictimization of traumatized individuals. Available data suggest that victims of childhood sexual abuse, for example, are much more likely than nonvictims to suffer sexual revictimization, both inside and outside of the family (Russell, 1986; Walker, 1985). Kluft (1990c) has summarized reports indicating that those who have experienced childhood sexual abuse are differentially vulnerable to rape after age 18 (Craine et al., 1988), to masochistic behavior (Katlan, 1973; Kaufman, Peck, & Tagiuri, 1954; Summit & Kryso, 1978), to involvement with abusive men (Briere, 1984; Russell, 1986), to participation in prostitution (Harlan, Rodgers, & Slattery, 1981; Silbert & Pines, 1981), to substance abuse (Herman, 1981; Peters, 1976), to becoming psychiatric inpatients (Bryer et al., 1987; Enslie & Rosenfeld, 1983), and to chronic institutionalization (Beck & van der Kolk, 1987; Sansonnet-Hayden et al., 1987).

Russell (1986) found that few women who had experienced childhood incest made a conscious connection between their early victimization and their subsequent experiences of drug abuse, prostitution, and suicide attempts. Nearly twice as many women in her study with a history of incest reported incidents of rape or attempted rape after the age of 14 as non-abused women, and twice as many reported later physical violence in their marriages. Victims of father-daughter incest in this study were four times as likely as non-incest victims to be solicited for pornography.

Perhaps even more significantly, Russell (1986) reported that more than twice as many female victims of incest reported unwanted sexual advances by an unrelated authority figure, such as teacher, therapist, or clergyman. Kluft (1990c) has also shown that the woman who has experienced incest is differentially vulnerable to sexual misuse by mental health professionals.

SEXUAL EXPLOITATION BY THERAPISTS

Many experts have observed the reenactment dynamics involved in patient-therapist sex (De Young, 1981; Feldman-Summers & Jones, 1984; Marmor, 1972; Pope & Bouhoutsos, 1986; Stone, 1976). One of the largest studies to date, conducted by Kluft (1990c), presented a study of 12 of his patients who had experienced sexual exploitation by former therapists. Data indicated that these patients had seen an average of 6.9 therapists and had received an average of 4.5 diagnoses each. One of his findings was that each victim of therapist-patient sexual exploitation had not only been an incest victim, but had also had full sexual intercourse with the abuser. In each case, the incest had persisted over a number of months and, in most cases, years. These 12 patients reported sexual contact with a total of 23 prior therapists (or 28% of the total therapists seen); 17 of these therapists had full intercourse with the patient subjects in the study. Of the 23 perpetrators, 22 began sexual behaviors while the therapy was in progress, and in most cases continued throughout the therapy.

In Kluft's study, there was some corroboration in nine of the 12 cases. This is consistent with findings by Coons and Milstein (1986), who were able to document 85% of the abuse accusations toward former therapists by 20 MPD patients. Such findings dispel the notion that such allegations by patients are largely fantasies or distortions.

Kluft (1990c) concluded from his investigations that the patients in his study suffered from "sitting duck syndrome," a "condition of heightened vulnerability to revictimization due to the conjunction of severe multiple symptoms and traits, dysfunctional individual dynamics, pathologic object relations and family dynamics, and deformation of the observing ego/debased cognition" (p. 278). These factors appear to combine in such a way that the patient comes to "accept as normative, familiar, and even necessary and/or desirable, situations and relationships that most would perceive as dangerous and exploitive, and attribute to herself responsibility for the actions of those who have taken steps to exploit her" (Kluft, 1990c, p. 283). There are no data to suggest that this syndrome is specific to incest victims, and since most traumatized individuals exhibit evidence of the clusters of characteristics listed above, it is likely that the "sitting duck" syndrome can be generalized to many patients who exhibit "divided self" difficulties.

What is the therapist's role in such dynamics? De Young (1981) has speculated that the incest victim may be perceived by the therapist as dangerously attractive and, having been deflowered, as "damaged goods" no longer deserving respect or protection. Pope and Bouhoutsos (1986) point out that the incest victim presents the therapist with a "pliable, often pathetically naive, needy patient who will not tell and will not blame the therapist, but who will frequently remain in the therapeutic relationship for years, paying for the damage and feeling guilty for causing the inevitable abuse and neglect by the therapist" (p. 53).

Without adequate management of transference and countertransference reactions, sexualized or seductive behavior on the part of the patient may be misinterpreted and misused by the therapist. For example, the therapist might begin to rationalize that a sexual encounter would facilitate therapy by providing a corrective experience, that the patient is obviously demonstrating the need for a different kind of therapeutic attention, or that certain types of sexual attention would demonstrate to the patient that he is desirable and help with low self-esteem. Such rationalizations by the therapist often resemble those used by the original perpetrators of sexual abuse (Courtois, 1988). These kinds of therapeutic violations breach the core intent of the professional relationship: providing a safe connection based on the patient's needs, rather than attending to the professional's needs through a misuse of power (Peterson, 1992).

Kluft (1989) has also conducted investigations of therapists who seek consultation in being "overwhelmed" by their MPD patients. Among his findings was the profile of the therapist who may be treating an MPD patient at a time of great personal stress; in this context, the therapist may begin to invest the patient with inappropriate importance and to bring his own personal issues into the treatment. Such behaviors may result in a projection of the therapist's own issues onto the patient, followed by attempts to heal himself through the patient and to "love the patient/self into health" (Kluft, 1989, p. 245). This dynamic may help to explain how several psychiatrists in Kluft's study began to develop sexualized relationships with MPD patients at times when they were going through difficult divorces, and how other sexualized relationships can develop in therapy.

OTHER TYPES OF RETRAUMATIZATION BY THE THERAPIST

Courtois (1988), among others, has written about a type of "privileged voyeurism" that can occur in therapists who treat those who experienced childhood sexual abuse. In general terms, the therapist uses the patient to satisfy curiosity about deviant, abnormal, or forbidden experiences. In more specific forms of voyeurism, the therapist may fixate on specific details that interest or stimulate him, such as intimate and humiliating aspects of sexual, physical, or ritual abuse, to the exclusion of other relevant therapeutic issues.

In an attempt to gratify his own dependency needs, the "needy" therapist may take advantage of the traumatized individual's learned helplessness, predisposition to enter the caretaker role, and hunger for special attention. This type of therapist makes a role reversal so that the patient becomes the caretaker and the professional relationship is structured according to the therapist's needs (Peterson, 1992). Jacqueline, who has a childhood history of emotional abuse and neglect, recently entered therapy with me (MP) and reported experiences of exploitation with both of her previous therapists. Her first therapist persuaded Jacqueline to share her expertise in jewelry making and later terminated the therapy arrangement to enter into a business partnership; subsequently, Jacqueline lost several major accounts to her former therapist, who broke off the partnership to work on her own. She ended her second therapy experience when her therapist denounced her for refusing to keep an appointment that the therapist insisted they schedule on Thanksgiving Day. "How will I pay my rent this month if you don't come?" the former therapist wailed. Jacqueline and patients like her have only a vague sense that they are being mistreated. They have come to accept as normal and predictable their experiences of disempowerment and disconnection from others (Herman, 1992).

Another important source of retraumatization for the dissociative patient may lie in the therapist's inability to pace the therapy properly. The patient then becomes overwhelmed by traumatic material and retraumatized in the process of exploring early painful experiences. The therapist must help the patient to maintain a sense of fairly constant safety, both within the therapy setting and in her outside life, throughout therapy. Therapy approaches, including hypnosis, should be focused so that the dissociative patient can provide himself with a consistently available safe haven, titrate the intensity of his internal experiences, and continue the ongoing work of treatment (Willliams, 1993).

Failure to provide balance in structuring an often chaotic course of treatment can make therapy a retraumatizing experience of being overwhelmed and trapped in the past, rather than a growthful experience of moving forward into a more promising future. There is no substitute for ongoing training and supervision and the formation of a good support system for the therapist. Careful attention to the boundaries of therapy provides the best protection against excessive, unmanageable transference and countertransference reactions and reenactments.

13

EMERGENCIES, CRISES, AND SPECIAL PROBLEMS

We are aware of therapists who carry beepers with them so that they may be apprised of any state of emergency in their dissociative or borderline patients, of others who put in a great deal of telephone time in the evenings in the hope of averting emergencies, and of still others who report and discuss frequent emergencies within their case loads.

We seldom are confronted with emergencies with our patients. There are probably several reasons for this. The most important is that we attempt to anticipate and avert possible emergencies by working with material within therapy sessions, making necessary contracts, and arranging for appropriate medication. The second factor is that neither of us finds emergencies desirable or thrilling. We feel that therapists should have within their lives topics of more interest than their patients' latest escapades or cliffhangers. Undoubtedly this attitude is conveyed automatically and unconsciously throughout the treatment process. What interests us with our patients is the therapeutic work at hand.

In spite of the best laid plans, crises do occur from time to time, and Braun (1986), in fact, has found dissociative disorder patients to be more inclined to them. Each of us has a different pattern of availability to our patients outside of therapy sessions. Both will be described in the spirit that there is no single correct way to deal with these matters, but rather that the therapist needs to find a way that is respectful of her own boundaries. One of us (MP) is available by phone to patients at specific times between sessions by prearranged appointment. The other (CF) has open telephone hours at home every morning from 7 a.m. until 9 a.m. Any contact outside of our arranged telephone hours is reserved for life-or-death emergencies. We have encountered very few of these.

Threats of Homicide, Suicide, and Self-Destructive Behavior

True emergencies involve homicidal or suicidal drive, dangerous self-mutilation, unmanageable confusion caused by rapid switching, or the ascendancy of a psychotic ego state. Methods used to contain them include increased frequency of sessions; introduction, change, or increase in medication; renegotiation of contracts; and, in extreme cases, full or partial hospitalization. We have seldom arranged for our patients to be hospitalized; however, neither of us will hesitate to act in this direction if the emergency cannot be otherwise contained or resolved. The hospital is the ultimate stage I ensurer. Some patients may need this kind of external provision of safety when other attempts have failed or when the patient is not able to cooperate with medication, contracts, etc.

Working with Destructive or Malevolent Ego States

Many crisis situations among patients with dissociative conditions arise from the activities of malevolent, hostile, or destructive ego states. The therapist may be sorely tempted to violate the fundamental principles of Ego-State Therapy when she first encounters a destructive or malevolent ego state. These states have also been called such things as "demonic alters" and "persecutor states." Although they may directly threaten the therapist or others with harm, more commonly it is the patient who is the victim of the malevolent state. Malevolent states often produce painful and dangerous symptoms, including but not limited to obsessions, internal "horror shows," panic attacks, self-mutilation, alcohol and drug abuse, destructive public outbursts, negative job behavior, legal problems, perilous sexual acting-out, suicidal preoccupations and attempts, and physical harm to others. Their primary function is usually one of protection, although this is not always readily apparent (Beahrs, 1982; Watkins & Watkins, 1988).

Frequently the patient expresses wishes that such an alter might be destroyed in the process of therapy; unfortunately, certain therapists share this viewpoint. An extreme version of this is the view that malevolent or demonic alters are created by satanic abusers, are "of Satan," and must be cast out through exorcism (Friesen, 1991). In another version of modern-day exorcism therapists find a rationale in terms of object relations theory for using exorcism with malevolent ego states (Hill & Goodwin, 1993). We believe that therapeutic approaches aimed at casting out destructive ego states offer poor models for other, weaker ego states concerning the nature of therapy, and may engender competitions among ego states with the therapist about who is worthy to survive, which could endanger the therapist, the patient, or both.

The key to working with these threatening and disrupting states is understanding that *they also want to help the greater personality.* Like every other ego
state they are adaptive. Many of them serve as protectors who have identified
with their abusers. Behind the doors they now guard are the forgotten pain
and degradation of past trauma and abuse. Some of them help by producing
the predictable "worst" symptoms in the patient's life as punishment. An ego
state may tell the therapist: "I am her fate. She can never escape me. She
deserves what she gets. She is bad." What is not stated or initially conceived
by the part is what worse thing would happen if this part were not helping
the patient by punishing her. The self-mutilating ego state may have an
additional function of physiological help, mobilizing endorphins to help anes-
thetize against internal pain.

Each destructive ego state has its own purpose or mission. Several types of
malevolent ego states exist (Beahrs, 1982; Frederick, 1994b), and the therapist has to validate each of them. Some ego states are clear about belonging to
the greater personality; we call these "functionaries" (Frederick, 1994d; Reagor & Connors, 1993). Functionary malevolent ego states may harbor tremendous fear about their ultimate fates if they give up their harmful functions
(Watkins & Watkins, 1988) and must be reassured that they can become
free to assume new and possibly more interesting roles within the greater
personality.

Other ego states, which have come into existence during abusive programming of either a formal or an informal nature, may believe that they are the
property of the abuser rather than of the greater personality of the individual.
These hostile alters can be placed under a general category titled "janissaries."
Like the janissaries of the Ottoman Empire, they are fiercely loyal to their
masters and prepared to battle to the death. The critical task in working with
this type of malevolent ego state is helping them to understand that they
really do not belong to the abuser, that they came to help the greater personality deal with the overwhelming programming abuse. The therapist must
ultimately convince them that they are true members of the internal family of
selves. Once this step has been achieved, the therapeutic alliance can be used
to help the ego state recall and, if necessary, to abreact in a controlled fashion
the abuse situation in which it agreed to accept its job assignment. Like
"functionaries," the "janissaries" require reassurance that they will not have to
perish in order to stop the destructive behavior.

Finally, some malevolent ego states are quite delusional about themselves,
thinking that they are God, the Devil, or some kind of demon or spirit. These
are often quite threatening in their speech and occasionally in their behavior
toward therapists. As Janet noted, the Devil is always susceptible to vanity
(Ellenberger, 1970). Repeated attempts by the therapist to converse with

such ego states can lead to a formation of a therapeutic alliance and an opportunity to change the false beliefs.

The fate of malevolent ego states in therapy is interesting. Those that are filled with rage must ultimately have these feelings shared by other parts of the internal family. As Watkins and Watkins (1988) have noted, all malevolent ego states are child parts in disguise. With the steady utilization of the therapeutic alliance, they can be transformed into co-therapists (Frederick, 1994b; Watkins & Watkins, 1988). Quite often they become strong positive internal healers and extremely loving members of the system.

Working with malevolent ego states, one must keep in mind the need for safety and *protection*. "Since no amount of validation or rapport can assist a patient who is either dead or sentenced to life imprisonment, protection must take priority over validation in real life crises. Actually, even when forcefully and strenuously opposed, protection is usually interpreted correctly as validation by some important part-self that had up to that point not been given adequate attention . . . validation and protection go hand in hand" (Beahrs, 1982, p. 114).

Therapeutic Moves for Safety

THE SAFETY OF THE PATIENT: STAGE I OF THE SARI MODEL

The patient's suicidal potential must be evaluated, as must her potential for other self-harm. She may, for example, become involved in criminal activity, contract AIDS or other STDs, become pregnant, or create serious health problems with alcohol or drugs. As we shall discuss in Chapter 14, medication can temporarily buy time and safety, but only if the patient's behavior is consonant with her being able to take medication safely. When destructive ego states jeopardize the patient's safety, further movement in treatment is impossible until safety is established. The therapist may attempt to work with the ego state in ways described to no avail, and destructive ego states may not be willing or able to make a "no harm" contract with the therapist. At these times hospitalization can be life-saving.

Case Example: Mattie

Mattie was a 13-year-old female who had run away from home many times. She was on probation and had been referred to a therapist for evaluation and treatment. The therapist noted that Mattie had substance abuse problems and such severe memory difficulties that, although she frequently got into serious physical fights with other girls, she only remembered the beginning of the fights. She never recalled what went on after that. She also complained of suicidal thoughts and impulses, and had attempted suicide in the past. She was experiencing mood swings, and she also complained of panic attacks. The therapist referred her to me (CF) for evaluation concerning diagnosis and medication.

The patient was accompanied to her session by her mother, who told me that Mattie had thrown a knife at her 11-year-old sister that morning. I saw Mattie alone first. She confirmed the information her therapist had given me, and also confided that she used marijuana every day. She asked me not to let her mother know this. Mattie also told me that she was aware of two personalities that sat on her shoulders and that one of them kept telling her to kill herself.

Later in the session I asked Mattie's mother to join us. Mattie assured her mother that there was no way that she would remain under what her mother described as her "constant supervision" in her home and school. She became inappropriate and delusional about the matter. While Mattie was declaring that she would never take medication, her mother, who viewed medication as her daughter's salvation, implored me to place her daughter on medication. She assured me that Mattie would be closely supervised by her and by her teachers.

I explained to Mattie and her mother that medication was not a wise choice at this time for several reasons. One was that it did not seem that Mattie could take it safely, with her general admitted drug and alcohol use, not to mention her refusal to take medication and her plans to run away from home. Moreover, in spite of her mother's guarantees, there was no possibility of true supervision in the home in view of the patient's refusal to cooperate with this and her history of fighting and running away. An additional reason for not immediately giving her medication was her need for a neurological workup to rule out possible seizure states.

I telephoned Mattie's therapist after I had seen her and explained to her that neither the patient nor her family was in a position of safety at this time. There was serious potential for homicide as well as suicide and other dangers to Mattie and her family. I recommended immediate hospitalization in a dissociative disorders inpatient unit.

In situations where there is no perceived threat to safety, the therapist can proceed to activate the hostile, destructive ego state and begin communication. Asking what the state likes to be called and approximately how old the patient was when it came to help her will probably yield some interchange, as these states will often argue that they did not come to help. The therapist must stay the course and insist that helping is the nature of all ego states, but that perhaps this part could just tell the therapist what was going on when it arrived on the scene, etc. At some point the therapist will find a way, using the cooperation principle and the yes-set, as well as direct and indirect sugges-tion, to further communication.

THE SAFETY OF THE THERAPIST

Although most threats made against the therapist by malevolent alters are seri-ous only in that they intend to frighten the therapist away from sensitive mate-rial, some malevolent alters do pose genuine threats to the physical safety of the therapist. Therapists who work with dissociative disorder patients can be harmed physically and in other ways that can be potentially damaging to them professionally (Comstock & Vickery, 1993; Frederick, 1994c; Reagor, 1993). The therapist who often works with individuals who have been severely dam-aged and with ego states that are in primitive transferences must carefully evalu-ate any threats made to her by destructive alters from historical, cognitive, and counter-response/countertransference perspectives. If the therapist decides that there is a possibility that she is in physical danger, appropriate measures for self-protection must be taken. These include but are not limited to having someone else in the room with the patient for therapy sessions or having ses-sions take place where they can be observed at a distance (Comstock & Vickery, 1993; Frederick, 1994c), the use of medication, and hospitalization of the pa-tient. When patients are not agreeable to joining the therapist in making ther-apy safe for both of them, therapy is at a serious impasse.

Therapists may also be at legal risk, and occasionally therapists may endan-ger both the patient and/or themselves because of their own unresolved countertransference issues (see Chapter 11). Another danger to the therapist is that certain patients may endanger the therapist through false allegations and complaints. Careful documentation, as well as audio or videotaping the sessions, provided they are obtained with the consent of the patient, should be considered as protective moves for the therapist (Comstock & Vickery, 1993; Frederick, 1994c).

In California recently, the father of a patient received a $500,000 award from her therapists who he alleged had used hypnosis and "truth serum" to produce false memories of incestuous abuse. This legal decision should make therapists aware of the dangers of seeing family members and significant oth-ers unless they are willing to sign releases (satisfactory to the therapist's attor-ney) to the effect that they are only there to give information and are not there as patients, as well as contracts (similarly satisfactory to the therapist's attorney) to maintain confidentiality about what is discussed.

Our position about the "truth" or meaning of memories continues to be that it is not something the therapist *can* produce, inasmuch as the difficult task of assigning truth or falsity to material produced in therapy belongs to the patient alone.

Case Example: Joe

Joe was a brilliant dentist who was in treatment with me (CF) for multiple personality disorder. During a hypnotherapy session several alters became vocally upset, stating that they had revealed too many secrets about various kinds of abuse in situations which had apparently been ritualized.

Suddenly, a new voice, one I had never heard before, stated firmly and distinctly, "Your life is in immediate danger." At this point I rose from my chair and left the office. Joe slowly followed me, went to the parking lot, and lit a cigarette (a switching mechanism for him). We arranged for him to telephone me that evening.

Joe assured me over the telephone that he wanted to ensure my safety and that he would take whatever measures I thought necessary. He was highly motivated to continue his treatment, as he had become aware of how badly his multiplicity had interfered with his ability to sustain intimate relationships with women.

Joe was a high school wrestling champion, and once, when restrained after some surgery, he had become wild and done bodily harm to a hospital orderly. Joe agreed to have two muscular, male psychiatric technicians present at our therapy sessions, and he requested full upper body restraint, which was supplied for him and which he wore during sessions. We met for six double-length weekly sessions. During these sessions the material concerning the warning was explored and resolved. The patient made a great deal of progress and was able to be seen alone and without body restraint again.

The Role of Contracts

Contracts can be made with both the greater personality and with individual ego states over a wide range of issues, including lateness for appointments, missing appointments, proper regulation of medication, abstinence from substances, attendance at 12-step meetings, the assumption of the responsibility for self-care through the use of self-hypnosis, and securing proper medical care.

Contracts can also be useful treatment tools in facilitating work with malevolent ego states. They appeal to such ego states because they validate them (Beahrs, 1982) and indicate respect. In keeping with the cooperation principle, the therapist deals with what is important to the ego state in a positive way so that the power to harm is transformed at first into the power to warn, or if necessary to restrain, and later into the power to help.

The inherent value of the contract lies in its potential for facilitating safety by setting limits and establishing responsibility. Contracts that call upon an ego state to speak for all the other ego states may "force" co-consciousness and protect against homicide and suicide (Braun, 1986). The therapeutic alliance is simultaneously strengthened. Braun's contract with MPD patients is a model for clinicians working with destructive alters. It attempts to close the loopholes for destructive-acting out. However, useful as they can be with many patients, contracts may never be the ultimate mechanism for providing safety. Whenever they are made with malevolent ego states, other ego states should be consulted about the internal status of the family of selves and their estimate of the reliability of the destructive ego state. Their willingness to cooperate with the contract should be discovered. The therapist also needs to tune in to her own internal estimate of the matter to determine whether she feels the contract will provide safety. If the answer is a strong intuitive "No," hospitalization or some other method of securing safety should be considered, as some ego states, like some individuals, may lie.

In our opinion the most effective contracts are negotiated, elaborated, and renegotiated bit by bit, beginning with the early stages of therapy. They are established with each ego state as it is recognized and communicated with in treatment. While we agree with Braun that they are essential to progress, our emphasis is on early, clear contracts about the business of therapy. Later in therapy it may be important to have more formal, even written, contracts as certain ego states emerge. By that time the spirit of contract-making or agreements will already permeate the therapeutic atmosphere.

We use a modification of Braun's contract with destructive ego states that are involved in behavior that could physically endanger them or others. Contracts of this type must be negotiated with every ego state. We find it useful to review the content of the contract with the patient before hypnosis is used. In trance, other ego states are engaged in negotiations about the terms of a contract. Contracts may be time-limited; however, when these are made, it is vital to renegotiate them in a timely way.

Case Example: Fred

Fred, now 49, had had extended contact with many therapists over the years. As an adolescent, he made a suicide attempt with "all the drugs in the medicine cabinet." He told me (CF) that he had suicidal fantasies, but was certain he could control them. However, during a business trip, he acted out, spent a lot of money, and developed a fantasy that he would spend all his money on illicit pleasures in a distant city, and there kill himself when all the money was gone.

One day he reported to me that on the previous morning, and without any earlier plan, he had sat in his garage with the car engine running for an hour. He felt as if he were watching, rather than carrying out, this behavior. He also revealed for the first time that he had always had a lifelong assumption that suicide was an omnipresent option. He could tell therapists what he thought they "wanted to hear" on the topic, but he retained his suicide option internally.

We discussed hospitalization. There were substantive financial problems: Fred had no health insurance and would only be kept for several days in a public facility. Further, the relevant psychological problems were with the ego state, Nicky, who had initiated both the suicidal fantasies and the attempt. Fred was interested in a plan that would involve both a change in his medication and a "no harm" contract. I reviewed a contract with him, and he found it acceptable. The contract (which was written and dated) said:

> I agree that I will not harm myself or anyone else, externally or internally, directly or indirectly, accidentally or on purpose. This agreement will remain in effect until July 18, 1994. I agree to renegotiate it before its expiration date.

In hypnosis, the ego state, Nicky, was activated; although he produced many suicidal fantasies for the patient, he disclaimed total responsibility for the attempt. There was another ego state, usually completely concealed, that had kept Fred in his garaged car with the engine running. This ego state was willing to communicate with finger signals and then to speak. He said he had no name; he had come to get Fred out of his depression. I told him that we had the same goal, but that I thought my methods would produce a better outcome. After more discussion, Nicky and the nameless ego state agreed to sign the contract. After they had done this, I invited Fred to open his eyes and sign it as well.

After the trance was formally terminated, Fred showed me the contract. It had been signed by him and by Nicky. The nameless ego state had signed as "Mr. X." In subsequent sessions, the patient reported a rolling away of the depressive feelings and suicidal thoughts. He was able to make another business trip with no harmful consequences.

Current work continues with a renegotiation of the contract, with the insertion of a clause that will have to do with an agreement that less destructive ego states, as well as destructive ones, will immediately communicate a need for help if Mr. X. or any other ego state initiates self-destructive activities. Fred and I are also working on what really makes suicide a viable alternative or not. This is a breakthrough for him, as we have discovered that suicide is an option he always held closely – as his parachute. The difference for him now is that he has hope that he will find different, positive solutions for his problems.

In Fred's case, a written contract was used to emphasize the gravity of the matter as well as to get two destructive ego states to become motorically involved in committing to it. Contracts to communicate about self-destructive impulses may be crucial factors for certain patients who are struggling with addictions, self-mutilation, or "fatal attractions."

Establishing the Therapeutic Alliance

The therapist will discover eventually that there is something that she and the malevolent state can share as a treatment goal. However, this will probably only happen after the therapist has begun to *validate* (Beahrs, 1982) the destructive ego state, to resonate (Watkins, 1978) with the feelings of the part, and to understand some of its needs. This act of respectful recognition often captures the attention of malevolent ego states, who then become curious about the therapist and what, exactly, she wants. It is necessary for the therapist to communicate that she shares a general goal with the ego state in wanting something of value for the state itself, for the patient, and for the internal system. Utilizing the cooperation principle, the therapist may be able to move from the malevolent ego state's form of "therapy" for the patient to her own proposals for goals the ego state can join in attaining. Beahrs (1982) has suggested that the therapist may have to find strategies to *neutralize* totally recalcitrant destructive ego states should the above approaches fail.

Case Example: Susanna

Susanna, a patient with multiple personality disorder (DID), operated with tremendous clinical efficiency as a nurse in an intensive care unit. This was done to the detriment of her relationships with fellow professionals, whose imperfections she viewed with intolerance. The patient was in trouble at work because of her verbal abusiveness toward fellow workers, and as this escalated she was in danger of losing her job and the income that supported her therapy.

In a hypnotherapy session an ego state named "Bitch" was activated. Her function was to get things done for the entire internal system through the force of her strength. She was in tremendous denial about how much she was jeopardizing Susanna's job and how her behavior was hurting the feelings of Susanna's friends and causing them to become wary of her. She believed that if she didn't behave in this way, the other alters would never get anything of importance done. She vigorously explained to me (CF) what powerless wimps they were.

I told Bitch that they certainly appeared to have taken a back seat in the assertiveness department, but that possibly she could help them grow stronger. I suggested that she might discover that she had something to learn from them. For example, they might be able to help her learn how to get touch with her fearful and insecure feelings. At this point Bitch burst into tears: "Nobody ever cares about what I feel! I just have to do all this work. . . . Nobody cares if I get tired!! I want a rest!"

I told Bitch that her feelings were very important and that she was certainly entitled to some rest. In this way we began to share some treatment goals. I persuaded Bitch to step back and allow Susanna to deal with fellow professionals at work. In spite of her initial trepidations, she finally agreed to try this.

Bitch's permitting Susanna to handle things at work turned out to be successful. Susanna was able to repair old relationships, and she began to make friends with her peers at work for the first time. Since Bitch was not so strenuously engaged with Susanna's work situation, therapeutic work could be aimed at understanding Bitch's tears. They were connected with serious childhood abuse which Bitch, of all the ego states, was the first to recall.

In our experience work with malevolent or destructive alters is fruitful in the construction of strong therapeutic alliances with powerful parts of the personality, which then become strong co-therapists. These ego states undergo profound transformation during the therapeutic process and not uncommonly come to display loving attitudes toward the rest of the system.

Clinical Management: When to Hospitalize

Clinical management of emergencies and dangerousness must be individualized. From our standpoint the most meaningful work therapists can do in this area is preventive. Therapists who encounter frequent emergencies in their practices need to take a close look at what is going on within themselves and consider consultation and supervision.

This is not to say that real emergencies do not occur. When they do, the therapist must mobilize both her own and her patients' inner resources to resolve the situation. Brief hospitalization may be necessary. We advise therapists who like ourselves work exclusively in outpatient settings to be prepared ahead of time by locating a good inpatient unit that will do short-term inpatient crisis management and coordinate the patient's release from the hospital back into outpatient treatment with the therapist. Non-medical therapists must locate a competent psychiatrist to medicate when necessary, since appropriate medication can play an important role in emergency prevention.

There are certain patients who can best be treated in inpatient dissociative disorder units over longer periods of time. These are patients who develop an unresolvable pattern of emergencies or who may be seriously endangering themselves socially and physically in both acute and chronic ways. Dissociative patients are not able to receive what they need over the long-term in ordinary acute psychiatric units or in many general psychiatric partial hospitalization arrangements. The need for specialized inpatient and partial hospitalization services for those few patients who are unable to resolve their difficulties on an outpatient basis should not be underestimated.

Hypnotic Crisis Techniques

One of the many advantages of the use of hypnosis in the treatment of dissociative conditions is the ability of certain techniques to help the patient who is in crisis. Nothing could be more illustrative of the power of hypnotic technique than the dramatic positive results obtained when hypnosis is used on an emergency basis with burn patients (Ewin, 1978). The hypnotic suggestions made by this burn surgeon allowed the body responses of inflammation to be modified in his patients.

Hypnosis has been used successfully with medical emergencies and crises, and Rossi and Cheek (1990) have outlined a specific plan for approaching the critically ill with direct suggestions. They also utilize ideodynamic healing (Rossi & Cheek, 1988, 1990) with critically ill patients. Both Rossi and Cheek (1990) and Wright (1990) recommend the utilization of spontaneous trance in emergency and other acute situations.

Kluft (1983) has identified crises as states of disequilibrium created by "some pressure or event" that offer both dangers of worsening and occasions for growth. The restoration of equilibrium, according to Kluft, involves the "balancing factors" (Aguilera, Messick, & Farrell, 1970) of accurate perception of what has occurred, supports existing within the situation, and the patient's coping mechanisms. He regards crises as times when creativity and novelty may be introduced into the situation by the therapist. Kluft (1983) believes that MPD patients are predisposed to crises for a variety of reasons; among them are their inability to have clear perceptions about the nature of events, their lack of a supportive environment because of their continued entanglement with dysfunctional relationships, and their compromised coping mechanisms.

Kluft (1983, 1989) has recommended a variety of techniques for dealing with crises in MPD patients. Among them are reassurance and ego-strengthening, allowing alters to ventilate their feelings, making contact with any intruding alters in co-presence crises, the use of internal dialogue and writing tasks, "horse trading" and diplomacy, deep trance, putting certain alters to sleep, making contracts, direct suggestion, and hypnotic time distortion. Although hypnotic techniques may be sufficient for the management of crisis situations, Kluft (1983) advises that some situations will not yield to them and must be managed additionally with medication and/or hospitalization.

Torem, Gilbertson, and Kemp (1990) have reported the successful use of future-oriented guided imagery with suicidal MPD patients, and Frederick and Phillips (1992) have employed projective/evocative hypnotic age progressions as interventions with acute psychosomatic conditions. We continue to use hypnotic age progressions as crisis intervention techniques with our dissociative patients, as we have found them to be ego-strengthening, integrating, and prognostic (Phillips & Frederick, 1992). Of particular value is their prognostic feature, which is helpful in the evaluation of the patient's status after other crisis intervention techniques have been used. We utilize a number of Kluft's (1983) techniques, and we also place emphasis on ego-strengthening with individual ego states (Frederick & McNeal, 1993). Ericksonian ego-strengthening can be interwoven throughout the therapeutic intervention. Within the therapeutic session, the therapist can provide seeding and intersperse and embed suggestions.

Like Kluft we may also employ limited age regression, abreactions, revivifications, etc., when indicated. The art of utilizing hypnotic techniques in crisis situations begins with an attempt to discover the cause of the crisis. In evaluating the patient and the internal family, it is recommended that the least intrusive techniques be used. Evaluation and ego-strengthening may go hand in hand with hypnotic age progressions (Phillips & Frederick, 1992).

Substance Abuse and Other Destructive Behaviors

Substance abuse is not compatible with psychotherapy. It is one of the most frequently encountered negative defensive moves in therapy. Many patients with such problems tend to conceal or minimize them. We often see patients who have been self-medicating with alcohol and drugs. Appropriate psychotropic medication cannot be safely instituted when the patient is drinking to excess or using drugs. Consequently we insist that patients who present with such problems or develop them during the course of therapy enter 12-step or similar programs and actively participate in them. For many patients this is a stage I task requiring considerable time to complete. Until the patient is engaged in a 12-step program, neither hypnotic exploration nor appropriate medication can be initiated.

We are prepared to encounter considerable and prolonged resistance to changing this destructively comforting way of dealing with post-traumatic stress symptoms and depression. We are often told that we are narrow-minded, that we exaggerate the importance of the problem, or most commonly, that if only we would do the hypnoanalytic work, the substance abuse would disappear. This is not a negotiable issue from our viewpoint. Occasionally, we may refer a patient for inpatient detoxification and drug and alcohol therapy.

Other types of behaviors may be as destructive as drug and alcohol abuse. Gambling and sexual addictions, overspending, and other addictions, for example, can also be utilized by the patient as ways of acting out dissociated conflicts that must come under control during stage I of treatment. It must be remembered that many addictive behaviors are manifestations of bipolar disorders.

What about Mind Control and Ritual Abuse?

Ritual abuse and mind control programming are topics of intense debate within the field today. There seem to be two major camps: those therapists and scientific investigators who believe that cult abuse and mind control are quite common and that most ritual abuse victims are still in contact with the cult (Gould & Graham-Costain, 1990; Neswald, 1992), and those who believe that these are urban myths whose existence has never been established but whose emergence is within historical traditions of mass hysteria (Ellis, 1992; Victor, 1992). The middle ground where we stand is well described by Hammond (1993)–that some patients who claim ritualized abuse have indeed been victims of such activity. Some clinicians do not believe that cult abuse occurs in most patients who allege it; nevertheless, they claim that they find it possible to work with these patients, just as they work with patients alleging UFO abduction. These therapists assume that the patients' material is metaphoric or symbolic of other kinds of trauma and abuse. In such cases it is essential that the therapist keep her beliefs to herself and allow the patient to discover her own truth.

We have found that a knowledge of the symptoms of ritualistic abuse and the programming techniques utilized (Reagor & Connors, 1993; Neswald, 1992; Young, unpublished) can be extremely useful in working with patients whose clinical picture suggests evidence of such experiences. These patients often respond paradoxically in treatment. As one patient told the author (CF), "The better it gets, the worse it gets." It is not within the purview of this work to undertake rationales and explanations for treating victims of cult abuse. We recommend specialized training through the International Society for the Study of Dissociation (formerly ISSMPD) or its affiliates in the hypnotherapeutic treatment of ritual abuse victims for therapists who wish to undertake identification of these patients and uncovering work with them. Training in the field raises the incidence of identification of such patients by therapists (Bucky & Dalenberg, 1992). Issues of informed consent (Young, unpublished) are of great significance here, as treatment usually brings enormous disruption of the status quo for the patient.

Other Crises, Deaths, Natural Catastrophes, and Losses

Our patients may well encounter the crisis situations of ordinary life while they are in treatment. It is also not uncommon for patients to enter treatment after the occurrence of a life event that has triggered symptoms from earlier trauma. The presenting clinical pictures for this latter group may vary from overt PTSD to such syndromes as pathological grief.

The therapist must be sensitive to the feelings of patients who have experienced real-life issues brought on by death and divorce, acute terminal illness in the family, and a diagnosis of terminal or other serious illness in the patient. All the psychodynamic and hypnotherapeutic knowledge in the world is no substitute for the therapist's concern as a human being. Greenson (1967) points out that neophyte therapists may overlook the impact of intercurrent events on patients in their attempts to remain "analytical." It is true that the therapist must remain in her role and not transgress boundaries; however, this does not mean that the therapist should continue to push for childhood memory material when the patient is grieving about the finality of a divorce or the death of a child.

In terms of the SARI model, the intervening life crisis has temporarily placed the patient in stage I. The immediate tasks of therapy are to deal with pressing issues of fear, grief, and confusion. When the patient is in stages II, III, and IV, the therapist may have to work with individual ego states around these issues. It is usually only later, and only if it is relevant, that the therapist and patient are able to identify connections between the life crisis event and other underlying feelings engendered. Occasionally a patient may see the connection immediately, and when this happens, the therapist must be alert for signs of an emergency requiring more vigorous intervention. At times such maneuvers as more frequent sessions, medication, and certain support groups may be called for immediately.

14

MOBILIZING EXTERNAL RESOURCES

Fortunately, our patients live in a world of modern therapies, and there is an abundance of external resources available to them. They include psychotropic medication, body oriented therapies such as bodywork and acupuncture, selected kinds of family and group therapies, support groups, and vocational counseling. We encourage our patients to expand their horizons and become involved in appropriate ancillary therapies that will be helpful to them.

For patients who are unable to find the kind of structure required to ensure their safety and stability as outpatients, psychiatric hospitalization, partial hospitalization, and residential treatment programs are also available resources.

The Use of Medication

Medication, properly used with dissociative patients, is a therapeutic asset of inestimable value. It may provide a way of alleviating useless pain and suffering, and it may facilitate the therapeutic process by helping the patient gain stage I goals of safety and stability, maintain control and mastery during uncovering and reassociation, bring more energy to the treatment process, and manage overwhelming depression, rage, and mania.

Some therapists hesitate to introduce medication into the treatment process because of concern that it may hinder it. This is an apprehension that has been present since the introduction of the major tranquilizers and antidepressant medications. It is based on the concept that all neurotic behavior is purposeful and directed toward eventual solution and mastery of the underlying problems. From this standpoint the introduction of medication would interfere with the psychological healing process by lulling the mind through the medium of the body.

Roth (1982, 1988) has addressed the flaw in this kind of thinking. "From a philosophical and empirical standpoint the dichotomy between psychology and biology–mind and body–is untenable" (p. 40). Clinical syndromes such as obsessive compulsive disorder, panic disorder, and agoraphobia that were once thought to be purely psychological have been discovered to have strong biological and hereditary components as well. Each instance of one of these disorders may represent within a patient the unique braiding of the biological and the psychological (Frederick, 1990, 1993c). With Roth (1988), we recommend that clinicians view post-traumatic stress disorder patients from "an integrated psychobiological viewpoint" (p. 40).

Both psychotherapeutic and psychosocial interventions may help move the system toward homeostasis; however, many symptoms are maladaptive and appear to serve no good purpose. Patients' thinking can become distorted from its problem-solving function into obsessionalism, or can become blocked, faulty, and stultified by depression. Within the affective realm, overwhelming anxiety can also paralyze problem-solving functions, and depression may deprive the patient of sufficient energy to address his concerns or may lead to social withdrawal, self-destructive behavior, and suicidal acting-out. Hypomanic or manic symptomatology, unmitigated rages, and rapid uncontrolled switching of ego states may endanger the patient or others.

There are times when treatment with psychotropic drugs "can be an essential part of treatment, the omission of which can be construed as maltreatment" (Roth, 1988, p. 41). We recommend medication for symptoms that interfere with the patient's safety or that of others or which are so maladaptive that they interfere with the course of treatment. One of the authors is a non-medical psychotherapist; the other is a psychiatrist. Regardless of one's ability to legally prescribe medication, the first discussion of this issue must come from the therapist. The discussion the non-medical therapist will have with the patient may lead to a referral to a competent psychiatrist who is familiar with medication issues involving dissociative patients. We do not encourage the medication of dissociative patients by non-psychiatric physicians. The medical therapist has two choices: one is to refer the patient to a colleague for medication, thus avoiding some clouding of the transference; the other is to undertake prescribing and monitoring any psychotropic medication himself as part of the treatment process.

These are, fortunately, the days of informed consent. This means that the patient needs to have an opportunity to hear why medication might be helpful and what the alternatives might be should he reject medication. The choice belongs to the patient and should be decided within the atmosphere of the therapeutic alliance. An authoritarian approach to medication considerations would probably represent a replay of abuser/victim within the countertransference and transference. Heavy-handed authoritarian approaches threaten the patient with a loss of mastery and are anti-therapeutic, whereas a cooperative approach to medication enhances the therapeutic alliance (Herman, 1992).

Certain caveats apply when patients are evaluated for medication. One is that many dissociative patients have had a number of experiences with psychotropic medications in the past. They have often been undiagnosed and improperly treated (Ross, 1989), and they may have had bad experiences with and/or become dependent on various sleeping pills, as well as minor tranquilizers with side effects of habituation and/or depression. They may have received major tranquilizers or certain mood elevators whose side effects have made them hallucinate or feel crazy. Additionally, many dissociative patients have been self-medicating with alcohol, over-the-counter drugs, and street drugs, as well as "borrowed" medication from friends or family members. A number of them are heavy substance abusers who need to become involved in Alcoholics Anonymous or Narcotics Anonymous before they can be safely medicated at all. Consequently, it is necessary to get good medical and drug and alcohol histories.

The prescribing physician may discover that he is under pressure to undermedicate, overmedicate, or simply use the wrong medication. The pros and cons of medicating must be carefully considered. Some patients require special precautions—for example, the ill or elderly patient (Roth, 1988). When the patient's psychological symptoms are producing so much stress that serious physical consequences might ensue, e.g., coronary infarction or ischemia, arrythmias, respiratory crises, or cerebral vascular accidents, anti-anxiety medications should be introduced rapidly. On the other hand, patients with suicidal drive or previous medication misuse patterns may need to have medication changed, withheld, or limited in quantity. To be truly therapeutic, the employment of medication with all patients in psychotherapy must be done on a highly individualized basis and with the patient's involvement.

One significant rationale for the use of medications with dissociative patients rests on their usefulness in helping the patient stop focusing on the past when his symptoms were created, and achieve a focus on the present when they are being dealt with. According to van der Kolk (1994), PTSD symptoms such as "hyperarousal, intrusive reliving, numbing, and dissociation" must be treated as part of helping the patient distinguish between the present and the traumatic past before other therapeutic issues can be addressed. In his review of the literature van der Kolk (1994) noted that "practically every class of psychoactive medication" has been shown to be helpful with these symptoms; nevertheless, van der Kolk's studies of fluoxetine (Prozac) show that it has a high range of efficacy along the entire spectrum of PTSD symptoms and works faster than other antidepressants. The art of medicating the patient lies in discovering what medication or combination of medications is best for the particular patient at a particular time.

There are some special considerations that apply to MPD (DID) patients. Putnam (1989) has noted that MPD patients appear to be more inclined to develop side effects to their medications. When medications are utilized with MPD patients, the prescribing physician should be aware that different alters may well have different sensitivities to medications. An NIMH study revealed that 46% of therapists surveyed reported observing this phenomenon (Putnam et al., 1986). On an anecdotal basis I (CF) have noted that dissociative patients may have different sensitivities across ego states and some unusual responses to medication.

However, there is evidence (Putnam & Loewenstein, 1993) that medication, particularly antidepressant and anxiolytic medication, can play a significant positive role in the treatment of MPD as "moderately helpful" adjuncts. For more detail about specific issues relevant to the medication of MPD patients the reader is referred to Barkin, Braun, and Kluft (1986), Putnam (1989), and Ross (1989).

Medications are used for symptomatic treatment in dissociative patients. There are no medications available to "cure" dissociative conditions. The prescribing physician is referred to the *Clinical Guide to Psychopharmacology* (Schatzberg & Cole, 1986), as well as to the *Physician's Desk Reference*, for detailed information on side effects and interactions of the drugs discussed here.

There are, in general, three classes of antidepressant medications: polycyclic antidepressants, which are often called tricyclic antidepressants (TCAs); selective serotonin reuptake inhibitors (SSRIs); and monoamine oxidase inhibitors (MAOIs). Each class has clinical advantages and disadvantages. The tricyclic antidepressants may produce a host of anticholinergic side effects, such as urinary retention, orthostatic hypotension with compensatory tachycardia, dry mouth, constipation, drowsiness, dizziness, and cardiac arrhythmias. Many of them tend to be sedating. The serotonin reuptake inhibitors may produce agitation, headaches, gastrointestinal symptoms, and drowsiness (if the latter occurs, the patient switches the dosage time from the morning to the evening). The monoamine oxidase inhibitors may produce malignant hypertension when combined internally with other medications or with foods rich in the amino acid tyramine (aged cheese, beer, sardines, chicken livers, etc.).

There is a dual rationale for using antidepressants with dissociative patients. First, they can have a direct effect on the symptoms of PTSD that may paralyze the patient so that he is unable to participate in psychotherapy. Second, many dissociative patients present with signs and symptoms of depression. Indeed, refractory depression in patients who have not responded to many antidepressants should lift the index of suspicion for the presence of dissociative disorder. When the depression is interfering with stage I necessities of safety and stability or the ability to work on stage I or II tasks, antidepressant medication should be considered. We recommend that the medication regime be kept as safe and as simple as possible. Ross (1989) has found antidepressants generally unhelpful in his work with MPD patients. This has not been our experience, nor that of Putnam and Loewenstein (1993). Mindful of the possibility of suicidal acting-out, I (CF) tend to avoid tricyclic antidepressants whenever possible and use, instead, the available selective serotonin reuptake inhibitors fluoxetine (Prozac), sertaline (Zoloft), and paroxetine (Paxil).

It may be wise to start the patient at half the recommended initial dosage so that immediate side effects can be identified and managed without the patient's becoming overwhelmed by them. I reassure patients that some side effects may be transient, disappearing in a few days, and that if side effects persist at this or higher doses the medication will be changed. We have observed that many dissociative patients' depressive symptoms do not resolve on standard doses of medication; in fact, the dosage may have to be two, three, or even four times the average dose. When dosages of this size are used, blood levels and necessary medical monitoring for certain patients are recommended.

Some patients are unable to take any of the selective serotonin reuptake inhibitors because of their side effects (fluoxetine, for example, must be discontinued in approximately 15% of the patients started on it because of side effects) and must be managed on tricyclic antidepressants such as amitriptyline, doxepin, and nortriptyline. Significant anxiety and sleep disturbance during the night can often be controlled by a combination of a serotonin reuptake antagonist and a tricyclic antidepressant, the latter to be taken in the evening. Monoamine oxidase inhibitors may be needed for a small handful of patients, who are unable to take any of the other classes of antidepressant medication. They are generally avoided because of the need for diet restriction and the utmost caution with regard to interaction with other medications, as well as the inability to combine them with polycyclic antidepressants and the difficulty of switching from this kind of antidepressant medication to another class (a two-week period of no antidepressant medication, during which the monoamine oxidase inhibitor is allowed to leave the system, is recommended before a polycyclic antidepressant can be used).

Antidepressant medications usually improve the physical signs of depression, such as disturbances in sleep, eating patterns, energy and activity levels, and sexual drive. They also help with memory and concentration and lift or at least mitigate depressed affect. Thinking becomes more energetic and optimistic. Like other patients, dissociative patients may experience an increase in suicidal ideation and drive as their depressions improve, and due caution should be observed in this phase of treatment.

The major hazards that may occur with antidepressant medication, in addition to drug-interaction problems, are drug overdosage, increased suicidal ideation during the recovery period, and activation of manic symptoms in certain patients. Patients who develop mania may be undiagnosed bipolar patients or may have a manic ego state that has become activated by the medication. In most of these cases the medication is discontinued and the mania treated with appropriate anti-mania medications. In some instances the patient may be able to continue to take the antidepressant if it is appropriately "covered" with an anti-mania medication such as carbamazepine (Tegretol), divalproex (Depakote), or lithium carbonate.

ANTI-ANXIETY MEDICATIONS

Some of our patients show agitation as part of their depressive pictures and require other types of medication in concert with the antidepressant medication. Most patients carry definite levels of anxiety and may be subject to panic attacks as well. Anxiety symptoms and panic attacks may associated with flashbacks, emerging memories, or external triggers that remind the patient of traumatic events. We deal with anxiety and panic symptoms with several classes of medication. The first is the minor tranquilizers, benzodiazepines. Their disadvantages include availability for suicide attempts, habituation, and with some minor tranquilizers, particularly lorazepam and diazepam, symptoms of depression.

Among the minor tranquilizers, clonazepam (Klonopin) appears to be the most useful for dissociative disorder patients. It has little tendency to cause psychological addiction and has no unwanted depressive side effects. It can be used in small doses (0.25 mg twice daily) or considerably larger ones (1-2 mg four times a day) as the needs of the patients demand. Loewenstein, Hornstein, and Farber (1990) have favorably reported on its use in the treatment of post-traumatic stress symptoms in MPD patients. We do not advocate the prolonged use of high doses of clonazepam. When the management of anxiety requires persistent high doses, it is usually preferable to use a class of medication more powerful in its ability to control anxiety and panic. There are some patients who do not respond favorably to clonazepam (Klonopin) and may require and be able to tolerate lorazepam (Ativan) or diazepam (Valium). However, usually the opposite is true. Many patients enter treatment medicated with these latter two drugs and can be switched to clonazepam with ease. They usually report that its effects are subjectively experienced as "more natural."

At times minor tranquilizers or anxiolytics do not control anxiety or panic symptoms adequately, and antidepressant medication must be added to the therapeutic regime. Sometimes even this does not control overwhelming anxiety. Several options remain. One is introduction of carbamazepine (Tegretol) or divalproex (Depakote). These drugs are powerful anticonvulsants that are also used to control symptoms of bipolar disorder. With PTSD and many other dissociative patients, including MPDs, these medications act as powerful anxiolytics. They afford the patient enough calmness and sense of control to focus on therapeutic issues. It is necessary to follow blood levels (valproic acid levels in the case of divalproex) if they are used for more than an "as needed" bedtime dose for otherwise insuperable insomnia. At one time (Barkin, Braun & Kluft, 1986) carbamazepine was used with caution because serious side effects, including agranulocytosis, were feared. Blood counts were obtained frequently. Today experience has shown us that the incidence of side effects is quite low, and it suffices to educate the patient about some of the signs of agranulocytosis and to make suitable inquiries during medication checkups. Although a patient may develop idiosyncratic ataxia to carbamazepine, ataxia and vertigo are usually found to be associated with blood levels in excess of the therapeutic range. Many patients who are not comfortable with the side effects of carbamazepine are able to tolerate divalproex (Depakote) well. Although screening for hepatic difficulties is recommended in the *Physician's Desk Reference* (1994), divalproex's difficulties with hepatotoxicity are usually relegated to children. Divalproex-induced liver damage in adults, even adults with hepatitis B, is rare and idiosyncratic.

Occasionally patients respond to none of these medication but do well on lithium carbonate. Are these patients bipolar? Certainly, some are. An individual with a bipolar diathesis is not immune to trauma and dissociation. There are dissociative patients who may benefit from short- or medium-term lithium carbonate therapy and then be able to discontinue it.

MEDICATIONS FOR THE CONTROL OF VIOLENCE AND PSYCHOTIC SYMPTOMS

Carbamazepine, divalproex, and lithium carbonate can often control transient psychotic symptoms, including delusions and hallucinations. Each of these medications may control rages and violent impulses in dissociative patients. At times, lithium carbonate may have to be used in combination with carbamazepine and divalproex.

There is always an exception to prove the rule. Clinicians who work with dissociative patients do not generally like to use major tranquilizers. These drugs are experienced by most dissociative patients as unsatisfactory, and they may produce the serious temporary side effects of extrapyramidal symptoms and permanent side effects of tardive dyskinesia. Nevertheless, there are times when only a major tranquilizer or neuroleptic can control psychotic behavior, rages, or violence toward others. Risperidone (Risperdal) shows promise as an agent that produces fewer extrapyramidal symptoms and does not cause the patient to feel "drugged."

OTHER USEFUL MEDICATIONS

Hypnotic medications, which are useful in the inpatient setting, are not recommended for outpatients. They are habituating, fail to deal with any underlying depression, and are frequently subject to abuse. Tolerance to these medications develops and the dosage needs may escalate.

For a few patients verapamil hydrochloride (Calan SR), a medication used for the treatment of hypertension and in the treatment of bipolar disorder, may alleviate crippling anxiety or explosiveness when carbamazepine (Tegretol), divalproex (Depakote), and lithium carbonate have failed.

Both propanolol and clonidine have been found useful for PTSD symptoms (van der Kolk, 1994). Barkin, Kluft, and Braun (1986) called attention to their experimental use of beta adrenergic receptor blocking drugs such as propranolol and the alpha adrenergic agonist clonidine for the control of extremes of anxiety and hyperactivity in MPD patients. Braun (1990) has continued studying the effects of these medications with dissociative disorder patients and has found that they can complement the benzodiazepines. Sometimes used in ultrahigh doses, they are experimental and are suitable primarily for inpatient settings where they can be administered under close supervision.

CHANGING MEDICATION NEEDS

The clinical interests of the patient are served when medication is used in concert with psychotherapy and regulated on an individual basis. This kind of regulation of medication recognizes that the needs of the patient will probably vary according to what is going on in therapy. If the therapist is non-medical, a close working relationship with the prescribing psychiatrist is essential.

Ideally, a patient would take no, one, or at the most two medications.

This may not turn out to be the case, as we deal with such a wide range of symptoms within our dissociative population. We do not do inpatient work, and in most instances are not eager to get our patients into the inpatient track. This may mean that at times our patients are taking a number of medications at the same time (e.g., serotonin reuptake inhibitor, tricyclic antidepressant, clonazepine, carbamazepine). We have not found this to present serious obstacles in terms of drug interactions, unendurable side effects, or the process of therapy itself. Inevitably, as patients renegotiate and integrate, the number of medications they are taking and the size of the dosages usually can be reduced, often dramatically. A gradual reduction in dosage is recommended as the reasonable way to end the medication phase of treatment. This is a way of avoiding rebound effects from rapid drug removal, and it enables both patient and clinician to watch for the emergence of untoward symptoms. The patient needs the support of both therapist and medicating psychiatrist as he may have to apply new techniques (e.g., self-hypnosis) to cope with symptoms that emerge as the medication is withdrawn.

Very occasionally the treatment of a patient who is receiving medication may reach a plateau or even come to a standstill. When no clear-cut psychodynamic reasons for this are apparent, the question of whether the patient is receiving too much medication for where he is in his treatment must be addressed. Some indications that this is the case are the failure of new material to emerge in trance or through dreams, the patient's drawing "blanks" in trance, or frustrated expressions from the patient that "nothing is happening." The possibility of a judicious reduction in medication for the purpose of allowing the internal system to "wake up" can be discussed with the patient. The patient must be reassured that recurring symptoms will not be ignored, but that he may be able to note how much stronger he has become and that he will be able to tolerate symptoms better now in the interests of furthering his psychotherapy. Another sign indicating that the patient requires less medication at a given stage of treatment is the emergence of side effects and blood levels higher than usual on dosages that have not previously been associated with these phenomena.

The medication situation could move in the other direction as well. A patient who has been doing extremely well symptomatically and has been taking little or no medication might become flooded with memories, flashbacks, and symptoms. His stage I needs might not be manageable with ego-strengthening, self-hypnotic techniques, and the utilization of support systems. For this patient an increase in medication or the introduction of medication is indicated.

Stopping the medication can be a big event for the patient. At times it is viewed with apprehension, even fear. An important external support, which has possibly also been a transitional object, is about to be removed. Further, this represents success as well as increased maturity, both of which can be threatening. The cessation of medication has to be done within the therapeutic alliance as a mutual decision. The patient can be reassured that nothing arbitrary will be done, that he will have a great deal of control over when and how medications are stopped, and that if he really needs medications in the future they can be reinstituted. Patients who are fearful may require many techniques other than medication appropriate to stage I, such as ego-strengthening, direct and indirect hypnotic suggestions, and ideodynamic healing. It is usually helpful to work with available ego states around this medication issue. The ability to stop medication is, in and of itself, ego-strengthening.

Not every patient is fearful of stopping the medication, and many patients cut down and stop on their own, eventually offering to the therapist as well as to themselves the gift of not having to depend on these physical resources. Patients should be encouraged to discuss all proposed medication changes for several reasons: (1) They may tend to push themselves prematurely in reducing medication; (2) because of their arbitrary changes in medication they may present with behavior and material in their therapy sessions that the therapist cannot place into the proper perspective; (3) arbitrary changes in medication dosages by the patient indicate his failure to utilize the therapeutic alliance properly.

Health Care Problems in Dissociative Patients

Medication of the dissociative patient should not be done in the absence of an appropriate physical examination by a licensed physician as well as any appropriate laboratory procedures. Many medical conditions mimic psychiatric disorders in their manifestations. For example, hypothyroidism can produce depression and a clinical picture that features dulling and blunting of affective responses, and patients with pheochromocytoma (a tumor of the medulla of the adrenal gland that excretes epinephrine and norepinephrine) can appear in the therapist's office requesting help for anxiety and panic attacks.

Further, patients in therapy need to have ordinary, ongoing, medical check-ups and attention when appropriate. Somatic symptoms may emerge during therapy, and without responsible and responsive medical backup it may be impossible to know if they are connected with the therapeutic work or caused by significant organic disease. Dissociative patients may also have a problem about "borrowing" their friends' medications or getting medication from friends who are health care professionals. Cooperation with a plan that includes an adult approach to medical care may often become a goal to be worked for in therapy with dissociative patients, as many of them fear examinations, procedures, and even transient contact with medical personnel. There are four important reasons for this, according to Courtois (1988):

1. Patients who are abuse survivors may have had medical experiences in which even obvious signs of abuse failed to bring identification and proper diagnosis of their trauma problems.

2. Somatic manifestations of their abuse symptoms have often been mistreated.

3. Misdiagnosis as well as a lack of understanding of trauma patients' difficulties have led to insensitivity in medical treatment. Trauma patients may be viewed as "crocks," malingerers, and "untreatables."

4. Medical personnel, at times, may abuse or retraumatize patients.

We have observed that many of the problem behaviors noted by Courtois (1988) appear to be the result of traumatic countertransference. Significant traumatic transferences in our patients are also frequently involved. Moreover, the situation may be somewhat complicated, since adult aspects of the patient's personality may clearly understand the need for appropriate medical care, while child ego states may be terrified of the doctor, the examining room, and the needles. Therapeutic work with ego states, as well as with the transference nature of the problem, can be instrumental in removing obstacles to appropriate medical care.

Sodium Amytal and Sodium Brevital Interviews

Sodium amytal and sodium brevital interviews should be done only in an inpatient setting or in an outpatient setting that is part of a hospital or psychiatric health facility. There is a danger of respiratory paralysis as the result of too rapid administration (di Vito, 1993). We strongly discourage therapists from conducting such interviews on an outpatient basis. Ross (1989) has compared the sodium amytal interview with a battering ram used to gain entry where such entry has been resisted. We realize that there are some (Ray et al., 1993) who believe that patients who were drugged at the time of certain kinds of trauma associated with programming can only retrieve information through amytal or similar kinds of interviews. This is a debatable point, as it is not clear that the state specificity achieved by sodium amytal cannot be achieved with hypnosis, time, and a good plan of treatment. Additional dangers of addiction to the drug by certain ego states have been reported (di Vito, 1993; Ross, 1989). Finally, no evidence exists that material obtained with any of the "truth serums" is necessarily accurate. As Ross (1989) has cautioned, "Patients can lie, confabulate, get lost in fantasy, and distort their memories under sodium amytal, just as under verbal hypnosis" (p. 286).

Body-Oriented Therapies

One of the most challenging aspects of treatment with dissociative patients is finding effective ways of reestablishing, or in some cases establishing for the first time, a positive connection between these individuals and their bodies. Achieving this connection can serve several positive functions. First, a positive body identification can increase self-esteem, self-awareness, and the ability to be sensuous and sexual in healthy, meaningful ways (Dolan, 1991). Secondly, such a connection can increase the dissociative patient's ability to monitor important emotional and somatic feelings so that he can decrease nontherapeutic dissociation. This in turn can lead to a decrease in self-abusive behaviors such as self-mutilation and bulimic purging, as these patients begin to develop the desire to care for and protect their bodies. Further, a focus on the body as part of the total healing process can help to free the mind from obsessive thoughts and intrusive recall and lead to a more centered sense of self (Merwin & Smith-Kurtz, 1988).

This section reviews several approaches to body-oriented therapy, including professional bodywork, massage, and EMDR (eye movement desensitization and reprocessing). It is important to note that for many dissociative patients various kinds of body-oriented therapy are initially too threatening. Therapeutic touch can be frightening and confusing; it may trigger intense somatic material that may be related to traumatic experiences that neither patient or body therapist are prepared to deal with. Especially at the beginning of treatment, many patients benefit from more self-paced activities, such as group Feldenkrais exercises, yoga, aerobics, physical exercise classes, and self-massage. When they are better integrated they can make the transition to more formal bodywork and massage therapies. Generally speaking, more intrusive forms of bodywork, such as Rolfing, bioenergetics, Reichian therapy, primitive breath work, and deep tissue massage, should be avoided by dissociative patients during early stages of treatment. EMDR work with dissociative patients involves similar cautions, which will be discussed in more detail below.

PROFESSIONAL BODYWORK AND MASSAGE

Professional body practitioners have become increasingly sensitive to the needs of dissociative patients. Many have pointed out the importance of bodywork and massage in integrating traumatic experiences in the body, as well as teaching post-traumatic patients how to set physical boundaries and how to be more connected with the physical self (Rochman, 1993). Also, working through sensations of numbing or dissociation can often be facilitated with careful use of therapeutic touch.

Technique is often not as important as therapist sensitivity to individual needs. Davis (1993) has pointed out the necessity of working very slowly: "It is better to touch one toe with a survivor [of childhood abuse] being present and integrated than to do deep tissue work and have the survivor split off" (p. 23). She suggests that bodyworkers encourage such patients to explore freely the kinds of touch that feel helpful, rather than attempting to fit into any kind of prescribed treatment program. It is very important that patients with a history of abuse and trauma be allowed to define the level of disrobing and draping, body areas that will be touched and not touched, and depth of touch that is used. Patient feedback should be elicited often and used to shape the bodywork process. If these guidelines are not followed by the bodywork or massage practitioner, the patient runs the risk of retraumatization.

Many psychotherapists are justifiably concerned about bodyworkers attempting to provide therapy without adequate training. I (MP) had the unfortunate experience of having a dissociative patient referred by her friend to a massage therapist and lay hypnotist who claimed expertise in the area of sexual abuse. During the first session, Susan, the patient, became flooded with feelings and sensations and was in the bodyworker's office for two and a half hours before she was able to leave. In talking about the session, Susan described the bodyworker's attempts to conduct hypnotic "inner child" work along with the massage, in a manner that was in conflict with the hypnotherapeutic work she and I had been doing. With Susan's permission, I called the bodyworker and discussed our differing roles, suggesting that she focus on the use of massage to help Susan connect with her body in a positive way and to tolerate and eventually appreciate appropriate, *non*sexual touch. I requested that she refrain from using hypnosis, since it was proving confusing to Susan. At her next session, however, the bodyworker appeared to ignore our discussion. Susan was again overwhelmed with emotional and physical feelings related to her incest experiences, which the bodyworker attempted to work with through hypnotic "inner child" work. She was in the bodyworker's office for over three hours. With my subsequent support, she decided to terminate bodywork. In making this decision, Susan commented, "I need to work with a professional who has much better boundaries. I was actually falling apart instead of moving forward."

For these and related reasons, we insist that bodyworkers and massage therapists who see our patients work in consultation with us to coordinate treatment and provide clear boundary structure. Many professionals who train bodyworkers recommend that bodywork clients with a history of trauma or abuse have a therapist to consult with when they begin massage or bodywork therapy, so that somatic experiences can be integrated into the therapy process (Rochman, 1993), a practice we wholeheartedly endorse. When referring patients to bodyworkers, we make sure that these practitioners have experience in working with dissociative patients and with issues related to trauma and abuse. For many patients, it may be helpful to schedule bodywork or massage sessions closely preceding psychotherapy appointments whenever possible, so that elicited material can be worked with by the psychotherapist and more immediately integrated into ongoing therapy.

ROSEN METHOD BODYWORK

Rosen Method Bodywork is an approach to body therapy developed by Marion Rosen. We have found the Rosen method to be a helpful adjunct to psychotherapy for many of our patients, primarily because of its gentle, non-intrusive techniques and its focus on emotional and verbal experience, as well as somatic and sensory aspects. We have chosen to feature the Rosen method as a prototype here.

Principles of Rosen bodywork may overlap with other types of body therapy, such as Reiki body therapy. Careful screening is used to determine the appropriateness of Rosen bodywork for a particular patient, including assessment of his current support system, tolerance for touch, chemical dependency, mental stability and self-abuse behavior, and willingness to initiate psychotherapy as needed. Rosen workers do not recommend work with a patient who is suicidal, unable to cope with everyday life, or overwhelmed by traumatic material—unless that patient is also in psychotherapy (Bailey, 1992; Winn, 1988). Clarification of bodywork boundaries is important, and may involve specifying the body therapist's role as nonsexual, outlining exactly what will happen before, during, and after each session, and reminding the patient that he is in charge of deciding how much clothing to wear and what areas of the body are to be touched or not touched. Additionally, Rosen workers are trained to allow patients to express and release feelings related to past trauma rather than "fixing" or resolving them, and to encourage self-pacing in all aspects of the bodywork process (Bailey, 1992; Winn, 1988).

EYE MOVEMENT DESENSITIZATION AND REPROCESSING (EMDR)

Eye movement desensitization and reprocessing (EMDR) is a procedure developed by Francine Shapiro (1989a) for the treatment of post-traumatic stress disorder and related anxiety. This approach involves eliciting sequences of "large-magnitude, rhythmic saccadic eye movements" (Boore, 1993, p. 41). These eye movements are considered to have a biological effect on recalled traumata, approximating the rapid eye movements (REM) that occur naturally in sleep (Boore, 1993).

Eye movements are elicited while the patient holds in mind the most critical visual, cognitive, emotional, and somatic aspects of a traumatic memory that triggers current anxiety. Shapiro has reported data which suggest that EMDR can produce a lasting reduction of anxiety, changes in the cognitive assessment of the memory, and cessation of such symptoms as flashbacks, intrusive thoughts, and sleep disturbance (Shapiro, 1989a, 1989b, 1991).

Proponents of this approach claim that EMDR results in profound and lasting relief from the effects of trauma, including rape, combat, and natural disaster, in one to three sessions (Boore, 1993; Shapiro, 1989a, 1989b, 1991). In addition to providing rapid reduction of anxiety-related symptoms, EMDR has been reported to elicit repressed material untouched by years of psychotherapy, including hypnotherapeutic age regression (Boore, 1993; L. Wildwind, personal communication, 1993). Furthermore, with historic traumas, as opposed to recent traumatic experiences, rapid generalization of desensitization and reprocessing effects appears to occur to all aspects of the target incident and to various related memories, even when one specific aspect of a single traumatic incident is treated (Shapiro, 1991). With recent traumas, each important aspect of the event needs to be processed in order to get corresponding results.

Others have reported additional benefits of EMDR in work with dissociative patients and have claimed similar positive results with non-dissociative patients in the exploration and processing of targeted traumatic memories (Wildwind, 1993).

Critics have claimed, however, that dissociative patients may decompensate more rapidly than with other treatment methods since effects are so rapid and often unpredictable. Many have noted that clinicians with little training or experience working with traumatized individuals have used EMDR as a "quick cookbook" approach to treatment, a practice Shapiro denounces. Recently, she (1993a) has clarified special guidelines for the use of EMDR with dissociative patients. These include: using appropriate screening for dissociative disorders before attempting EMDR with patients; having specialized training in dissociative disorders and the intermediate EMDR training before using EMDR with this population; and using EMDR protocols designated for dissociative disorders and MPD.

Shapiro (1993b) has suggested that EMDR differs from hypnosis in several ways: Hypnosis usually involves complete processing of the entire event while

EMDR does not require full scanning of the entire event and moves to resolution much more rapidly; EMDR is more generative and can lead to positive cognitions, imagery, affect, and associations without therapist suggestions; EMDR gives more control to the patient; and EMDR is less intrusive than hypnosis.

Our clinical experience does not support these claims. Rather, we have found hypnotic approaches to be equally rapid, generative, non-intrusive, and effective in the processing and resolving traumatic memories using the guidelines we have suggested in this book. In addition, we have found that hypnosis can give subjects and clinician a different sense of control, since hypnotic approaches offer the advantage of focusing on a particular task or therapeutic goal and following through to its completion, in contrast to the somewhat unpredictable nature of EMDR sessions with dissociative patients. For example, hypnotic approaches can access specific aspects of a traumatic event, such as only the time before the trauma or only the visual aspects without the emotional/sensory aspects. We believe that this affords a sense of mastery, as well as helping dissociative patients create internal boundaries. We agree, however, with the assessment that EMDR may facilitate less dependency on therapist suggestion. Perhaps the ideal use of EMDR involves its synthesis with hypnotic and other effective therapy approaches in the hands of experienced, well-trained clinicians (Wildwind, 1993).

If EMDR is used with dissociative patients, we firmly endorse the adoption of guidelines and cautions established by Shapiro and her staff. We present EMDR as an experimental approach, explaining that it is a new, unproven technique which has been helpful to some individuals, and that we do not know how the patient will respond. We may use it as an adjunct technique for certain patients, carefully monitoring the results. If we, or the patient, are uncomfortable with the results, we go back to the use of other techniques. We also consider updated training in this modality a must, since procedures are modified continually as more data are collected. For example, the recent use of EMDR sets with a positive target image to promote ego-strengthening is an approach we have found useful with some patients. The publication of anticipated replication and new research results with EMDR are needed to support its acceptance into more mainstream use.

OTHER BODY-ORIENTED THERAPIES

We consider the physical dimension to be an important part of post-traumatic therapy. Helping patients to include physical activity in their everyday routines is essential for the discharge of tension and the maintenance of positive well-being. Instead of rigorous or compulsive programs, we recommend naturalistic approaches such as walking further than usual to do errands, taking stairs instead of elevators, and perhaps gentle stretching or yoga exercises. Whenever possible, we support whatever body approaches fit the patient's interests, readiness, and lifestyle, with the exception of intrusive approaches early in treatment. We remind our patients that regular physical activity helps the mind shift away from rational, problem-solving activity, a type of quieting that may also help to reduce depressive and anxiety symptoms.

Emphasizing the physical dimension also helps to put the patient in charge of his own body and allows him to reclaim its positive energy. Occasionally, we refer patients for movement therapy, a structured approach providing gentle opportunities for body connection through basic movement tasks. For patients under the care of medical professionals such as chiropractors, acupuncturists, naturopathic doctors, physicians, and physical therapists, it is important to support the patient's compliance and cooperation with various health care procedures. Acupuncture may give specific symptomatic relief for current symptoms of anxiety and depression to patients who are unable to take various psychotropic medications because of their sensitivity to side effects.

Regular consultation between therapist and medical professionals is essential to coordinate treatment and prevent splitting and manipulation. Many dissociative patients have neglected their bodies for years, fearing loss of control and avoiding intrusive physical examinations, which may place their health at risk. When appropriate, making referrals to sensitive, competent professionals for medical attention and health-care needs and working through psychological issues that arise is an important therapist role.

For individuals who are socially isolated, becoming involved in more organized physical activity, such as low-impact aerobics classes, slow-pitch softball and other sports, gyms and health clubs, and dance classes can provide naturally occurring social contact in a relatively safe and defined setting (Merwin & Smith-Kurtz, 1988). For those with fears of entering a social world, these settings provide structured opportunities to meet other people.

DEVELOPING BODY AWARENESS

We frequently encounter patients who have great difficulty connecting with body sensations. For many, the dissociative defenses that help to protect them from the pain of past trauma also separate them from the normal, pleasurable sensations of the present. For some, severe dissociative responses precipitate terrifying states of fugue, depersonalization, and derealization that make the process of establishing body awareness even more problematic.

Regardless of how the patient's divided self is manifest in a broken body/ mind connection, reconnecting body and mind is an important therapeutic task. Often, the primary fear behind an inability to feel emotional and body feelings is further loss of control. It is helpful to explore all concerns and fears about connecting with and expressing body feelings, asking the patient to imagine, describe, write about, or draw what it would be like to connect fully with somatic and emotional feelings. Whatever the patient imagines often can be used to generate a safe environment for body awareness. For example, if the patient imagines an exploding volcano or nuclear bomb, the therapist can reassure him that such an image can be utilized as a signal to alert patient and therapist of the need for slowing, stopping, or containing any experience of body awareness. The therapist must convey an attitude of confidence that these needs for control can be met with ongoing practice and good communication between therapist and patient.

The next step is often to explain to the patient the process and benefits of simple body focusing (Gendlin, 1981). Here, the patient is simply helped to turn his awareness inward, with eyes open or closed, as he focuses on different areas of the body. In extreme cases of dissociation, this may begin with asking the patient to notice any differences in sensation when he is in a standing vs. sitting position, progressing to more specific distinctions, such as those between upper and lower body areas, or arms and legs, or right arm and left arm. If the patient has body integrity problems or developmental issues of object constancy and permanence, the therapist can remind him throughout that, even though he is aware of differences such as heavy and light in these body areas, these are all part of him and belong within his whole "body self." Similar suggestions to promote body integrity and body boundaries (Baker, 1994) can be interspersed in focusing activities as needed.

Once the patient has mastered the process of general body focusing, the therapist may direct him to begin to identify specific body sensations related to emotional responses. At first this may be a complex process, as the highly dissociated patient has few clear clues as to where in the body his emotions are located. A good place to begin is with some general emotional reaction that the patient is aware of, such as anger or sadness. The patient can be helped to do a "body scan" to identify sensations in various parts of the body, beginning with the head and continuing on to the feet, noting various body feelings along the way. As Simonds (1994) points out, for the dissociative patient who tends to be flooded with feelings and sensations, this process helps to differentiate sensations that have become overly generalized (or overcoupled, from the SIBAM standpoint). If appropriate, an additional step can be added where the patient puts his hands over the body location of a particular sensation, and breathes into the areas until images form. Eventually, the patient will develop enough awareness to be able to identify and connect emotional reactions with body sensations on a routine basis in therapy sessions as well as in everyday life situations, a practice that provides much more information, a sense of empowerment, and many more choices.

Simonds (1994) has added several more activities as part of her five-step process. Once the patient has learned to (1) pay attention to body sensations that accompany feelings and (2) can find the body location, Simonds suggests that the individual (3) clarify feelings and sensations by describing them in detail or by drawing a picture of the feelings in the body. This is followed by (4) exploration, with the patient associating to sensations, words, and/or drawings and, if appropriate, (5) learning to make connections with relevant past experiences and processing those.

Our approaches are similar to hers. We prefer to switch to the somatic experiencing (SIBAM) model once the patient has mastered the steps of attending to and locating body sensations that accompany emotional feelings. Through self-paced focusing and tracking, sensations and affects that are disconnected or dissociated can be reconnected, and those that are overcoupled or overly generalized can be differentiated. Although the somatic experiencing approach generally leads naturally to past experiences that may be trauma-related, the therapist can also use a somatic or affect bridge to explore connections with the past as appropriate. Artwork can be used to facilitate clarification throughout all of the activities described in this section and may serve to help the patient further develop the "body felt sense" (Simonds, 1994) and a feeling of body identity and wholeness.

Social Interventions

In his famous *Devotion* John Donne reminded us that just as every funeral bell tolls for all of us, we are all intimately interconnected with other people. Our patients do not live in vacuums or only exist when they enter our offices. Each one brings to us problems that have been the result of a vast interplay among many forces, including personal biology inherited from a multitude of people stretching back into time, psychosocial systems such as the family, and the sociopolitical conditions of their times. Aristotle pointed some of this out in his succinct statement, "Man is a social animal."

In the second half of the 20th century social approaches to psychological problems have blossomed. We have seen the emergence of family and group psychotherapies, of community psychiatry and partial hospitalization, and of self-help and support groups. As we foster independence in our patients, we recognize their need for healthy interdependence within their families and other social groups and for the feedback social interactions can provide. These interactions are particularly valuable since dissociative difficulties split off parts of one's internal world and are then reflected in the external world. The internal changes that occur with reassociation can be helped by external healings and reassociations in families, therapeutic groups, and therapeutic communities.

GROUP THERAPY

Since marital and family therapies are discussed in Chapter 11, let us turn here to group therapy. Group therapy is a term attributed to Moreno's invention in 1931 (Shaffer & Galinsky, 1974). It is neither a new concept nor one confined to Western culture. Asclepiad priests at Epidauros often had their patients gather in the mornings to discuss and interpret one another's dreams and nocturnal experiences, and the Far Eastern tribe known as the Senoi also has a long tradition of group dream interpretation.

Group therapy has long been recognized as one of the most effective forms of treatment for many people (Bion, 1959; Foulkes, 1965). Groups may be homogenous (same diagnosis, age, sex, etc.) or heterogeneous (different sexes, ages, diagnoses). There are many kinds of groups into which patients may enter. Among them are process groups in which the group itself is considered to be the patient and all interpretations are directed toward understanding that process. These groups are usually conducted by co-therapists. Another form of group work might be called individual therapy within a group setting. In this situation each group member receives individual attention from the group leaders and from other members of the group. Groups can be created around certain kinds of performance, psychodrama, movement therapy, or art therapy groups. Groups may also be task-oriented and dedicated to improving socialization, communication, or cooperation. Groups can be composed of other groups, as in family group therapy, in which several families work together, or in couples group therapy.

Process-oriented analytic group psychotherapy is usually employed as the sole method of treatment for its patients, and for this reason may not be suitable for many dissociative patients. A patient's participation in such a group could be confusing to him and to his individual therapist, especially in view of the strong transference reactions that often appear in this kind of group work. Other kinds of groups are probably more suitable while the patient is in hypnotherapy for the primary dissociative symptoms. Analytic group psychotherapy could be an excellent choice for patients who are post-integration and need further work on personality problems. Group therapists can address the needs of patients in the way they set up various aspects of the group structure and goals.

Patients who have available to them art and movement therapy groups are often encouraged to participate in them if the group therapists are willing to communicate and cooperate with the primary therapist. This is also true for task-oriented group work, for example, relaxation and meditation training, or social skills and assertiveness training. For the same reasons we discourage process group work, we tend to discourage patients from becoming involved in groups in which there is individual therapy within the group setting, unless this is their primary mode of treatment.

Heterogeneous and Homogeneous Group Psychotherapy
with Dissociative Patients

Attempts at heterogeneous group therapy with MPD patients have not been promising (Caul, 1984; Caul, Sachs, & Braun, 1986; Frederick et al., 1994; Putnam, 1989). Some attempts have been reported as disastrous. Such patients disrupt the group process in much the same way as actively manic patients do. They demand attention, hog group time, and baffle group members with their switches. Caul (1984) reported hostility between MPD and non-MPD patients in heterogeneous groups. The effects of the heterogeneous group on MPD patients have been observed to be as disastrous as their effects upon the group.

Caul, Sachs, and Braun (1986) recommend that all their MPD group therapy patients be in individual therapy as well and, with Coons and Bradley (1985), have suggested Yalom's (1975) here-and-now approach for group work with MPD patients. This combination appears to minimize what could be disrupting memories and abreaction within the group and to emphasize strengthening of the group ego as well as the egos of the group members, while maintaining observation of group process as a goal. This kind of group structure takes stage I issues of safety and stability into consideration. Braun's (1993) recommendation of task-oriented groups in inpatient settings appears to be aimed at similar goals.

It is probable that the issue with MPD patients in heterogeneous groups has little or nothing to do with their diagnoses and much more to do with their levels of functioning (Caul, Sachs, & Braun, 1986) and stages of treatment. This is also true of groups with other kinds of trauma victims (Herman, 1992). High functioning dissociative patients can function in either homogenous or in heterogeneous groups, but lower functioning patients are not appropriate for heterogeneous groups. Herman (1992) has a deep understanding of the relationship between the kind of group work that is appropriate and each patient's progress toward recovery. According to her, group work is particularly helpful for trauma victims. It substitutes support and bonding for feelings of being alone and different, and it enables the patient to recognize the universal elements in his experiences and difficulties. She has found that group experiences have the power to neutralize feelings of isolation, shame, dehumanization, and degradation, and to replace them with affirmation, a sense of belonging, a restoration of the individual's humanity, and an appreciation of his ability to have survived his experiences.

"The solidarity of a group provides the strongest protection against terror and despair, and the strongest antidote to traumatic experience" (Herman, 1992, p. 215).

According to Herman, patients who are coping with safety issues do better in open-ended, homogenous groups where the structure is in the didactic or teaching/learning mode, the time orientation is in the present, little conflict is present, and the goals involve self-help. Twelve-step groups would be a paradigm for this type, although certain other kinds of task-oriented groups could also serve these purposes. Patients who are ready to extend their explorations of internal memory material and to confront trauma are, in Herman's model, best helped in homogenous, time-limited groups whose goals involve, specifically, the uncovering of trauma. Presumably these patients would be of sufficiently high level of function to handle such a group. Strong, active group leaders who have a plan for the group and will not permit useless and traumatic confrontations or traumatizing marathons of memory experience recovery are necessary for the success of these groups. The group members would all need to be trauma survivors. Herman and Schatzow (1984) have found that the group's time-limited nature and an emphasis on the personal goals of each member are significant elements in its success. Only during the final stages of treatment does Herman recommend the patient moving into a heterogeneous, open-ended psychotherapy group where work concentrates on interpersonal issues.

We would caution therapists about the presence of hazardous groups devoted to "inner child" work. Group leaders who blanket ego states with this single definition may work in conflict with the therapist. The patient, at best, may experience conflict; at worst, he could enter a crisis.

The general rules and principles for conducting groups also apply to those for dissociative patients. We strongly advocate co-therapists for group work. This not only increases safety for the therapist, who does not have to carry the burden of all the group transferences alone, but also helps in the identification and resolution of countertransference issues. Ideally, there should be co-therapists of each sex; however, if this is not possible, the group will tend to assign to one co-therapist "masculine" transferences and to the other "feminine" transferences. It is the experience of many group therapists that this is a quite workable arrangement. The co-therapists have additional functions within the group. They model the cooperation of two people for group members, a cooperation which is quite different in nature from the "united front" of the internally traumatizing family; they also establish the group contract, which includes such things as the times and lengths of sessions, how many absences are permitted, confidentiality for group members, abstinence from social contact outside the group, the kind of the work to be done within the group (day-to-day issues, feelings, history/memories, abreactions, etc.), and the goals of the group. Also included are such matters as what constitutes unacceptable group behavior, what is the relationship of any individual therapy to the group, and, if group treatment is the sole method of treatment, what should be done about any emerging crises (Frederick et al., 1994). Maximum size for therapy groups in general is eight members, and all patients should be screened by both co-therapists for appropriateness of placement, as well as willingness and ability to abide by group rules before beginning with the group.

I (CF) have supervised group therapy, which is the major form of psychotherapy for dissociative patients in a public mental health system clinic where I have consulted. In these groups patients may move from present concerns and safety issues (stage I), to emerging memories (stage II), their resolution (stage III), and into the integration phase (stage IV), as the maturity levels of the group and of its members grow. Other important elements of the treatment plan for these group members are access to appropriate psychotropic medication and careful medication monitoring, the availability of a limited number of individual sessions when crises occur, access to an inpatient psychiatric unit, and teamwork among the group therapists, the medicating outpatient psychiatrist, and the inpatient psychiatrist.

Support Groups

Support groups can be significant as the patient learns to find support and accept caring in the world. They tend to be organized for individuals who have certain kinds of histories, concerns, or distresses in common. Our patients often attend support groups for those who have suffered similar trauma, such as Adults Molested As Children and Incest Survivors Anonymous. Support groups exist for Vietnam veterans, the Holocaust victims and their children, individuals who have been abused in cults, people with multiple personality disorder, and those who suffer from obsessive compulsive disorder. The therapist needs to listen with his third ear for any antitherapeutic trends in a given group. They are not common but do require identification and working-through.

This is the era of the self-help group. The Alcoholics Anonymous 12-step program achieved success for some people with drinking problems that conventional medicine and psychology were not able to achieve. Its success has resulted in the formation of many varieties of 12-step programs, each addressing certain kinds of problems. Patients who abuse alcohol and drugs usually need active participation in Alcoholics Anonymous or Narcotics Anonymous. We encourage patients participating in these 12-step programs to attend meetings frequently, become involved, and get sponsors (individuals who have some seniority in the program and who can help them work it more effectively). Frequently our patients benefit from such programs as Co-dependency Anonymous, Adult Children of Alcoholics, Overeaters Anonymous, or Gamblers Anonymous. We will discuss other aspects of 12-step programs in Chapter 15.

There are some viable alternatives to 12-step programs. As we shall discuss in Chapter 15, some of our patients have difficulty with anything that refers to God. The 12-step programs utilize the concept of a Higher Power to which one must ultimately turn over one's addictions and compulsions. For some patients this concept is repugnant or even frightening, even when it is explained that the "Higher Power" can be anything the patient's belief system can accept, such as the right side of the brain. Other patients object to what they perceive as hidden sexism in the 12-step programs. Women for Sobriety objects to the A. A. concept of needing to humble oneself, feeling that women have been humbled too much as it is. There are also Rational Recovery groups, which do not invoke a higher power.

There is probably no end to the kinds of community support groups available. Patients with suicidal preoccupations, as well as those who are addicted to crisis calls, might find 24-hour-a-day hotlines helpful until they have achieved greater stability. Groups within churches and affinity groups can also be strong sources of support.

HOSPITALIZATION, PARTIAL HOSPITALIZATION, AND RESIDENTIAL TREATMENT SERVICES

Hospitalization is recommended for patients who are unable to achieve stage I goals of safety and stability because of acting-out, dangerous switching, legal risks, inability to meet most therapy appointments or to comply with a needed medication regime, as well as for patients with other complicating Axis I diagnoses who cannot be regulated on an outpatient basis. Hospitalization may also be necessary for disorganized patients who have continued contact with abusing cults.

A good general psychiatric unit may well be able to deal with intercurrent suicidal or homicidal issues or other Axis I considerations on a fairly short-term basis; however, there is no substitute for a well-run dissociative disorders hospital or unit, where the staff has training and experience necessary for working with the dissociative disorders. Patients with uncontrollable dangerous switching, those who are too disorganized to meet appointments, and patients who are embroiled in ongoing cult contact are good candidates for inpatient stabilization.

Partial hospitalization may be a viable and preferable alternative to full, 24-hour-a-day hospitalization (Frankel & Conners, 1993). Partial hospitalization may obviate the need for full hospital residence or may be the next step after such a hospitalization. The advantages to partial hospitalization are many: The all too obvious one is that it is more affordable than a full inpatient stay. More importantly, the secondary symptoms of dependence and institutionalization tend to be avoided in partial settings, as well as the maintenance and encouragement of strong community ties and involvement. The focus of partial hospitalization is outward, to the eventual integration of the patient with his community.

Certain residential programs with less intensive staffing patterns than full-fledged day treatment or night treatment programs may be used to continue the work of partial hospitalization. Residential programs also offer ancillary services, such as occupational therapy, art and music therapy, and vocational guidance.

VOCATIONAL COUNSELING AND TRAINING

Work is a fundamental human activity. Freud placed the ability to work with the ability to love as the most important goals of maturity. Since the symptoms of pathological dissociation can impair the ability of the individual in the work arena, it is not surprising that dissociative patients present with extremely varied relationships to work. We encounter patients with serious dissociative problems who are doing extremely well in their jobs, while other dissociative patients are not able to hold any kind of employment. In between these two extremes are many variations.

Work is one of the most underrated avenues of ego-strengthening, consolidation, and change for many recovering patients. The damage caused by trauma and dissociation to the realization of educational and vocational potential cannot be measured, although it is worthy of serious consideration (Murphy, 1993). Cognitive and emotional arrests, as well as rapid switching, flashbacks, depression, and anxiety symptoms, often make it impossible for dissociative patients to consider, seek, or complete educational goals commensurate with their abilities. Often their poor sense of identities has prevented them from knowing what their interests might be; consequently, if they are employed, they may be in the wrong kind of work or unable to function well because of the job setting.

With recovery comes hope of maturity in the area of work, hopefully fulfilling work. The selection of the right vocational counselor is crucial. In addition to good standard training, the counselor who works with our patients must have some understanding of the dissociative process, dissociative symptoms, the signs and symptoms of PTSD and of multiplicity. This counselor must also know something about the effects of the medications commonly used with our patients. Finally, he must be willing to communicate with the referring therapist during the rehabilitative process.

Vocational preparation and performance exist on several tiers (Sachs, 1986). Once the patient is sufficiently functional in society again, he may need help with reentry into an old job category. Although this reentry will probably be frightening at first, it fosters independence, helps self-esteem, and brings in income. If the patient has no job skills, he might begin with a simple unskilled, low-pressure job. Certain patients must begin on the first rung of the ladder with volunteer work, which gives them the opportunity to develop promptness, reliability, and other good work habits. An evaluation of abilities and skills will help the patient identify where he wants to go in the job market at a later date and where to obtain necessary education and training.

When vocational evaluation and training are needed, the evaluation should occur as soon as the patient is able to tolerate it. This is often in stage III of treatment. Admittedly, some patients in stage III may construe this as an unnecessary pressure. However, it presents many patients with a powerful expectation that there really is a future for them. Patients are encouraged rather than driven to an investigation of their abilities and possibly unsuspected interests. Early evaluation also means planning of a program that can be slow and cautious, with lots of room for trial-and-error and essential ongoing feedback from the patient. Measured rehabilitation leaves room for failures or therapeutic regressions, without a pervasive sense of defeat. The danger of overwhelming dissociative patients with too much too fast is a genuine one.

15

SPIRITUALITY AND THE GENERATIVE SELF

We frequently see patients whose emotional immaturity has inhibited their spiritual development and alienated them from the acknowledgment of their own spiritual experiences. As part of their search for the meaning of traumatic experiences, many dissociative patients reexamine their spiritual beliefs. In those who have felt religious beliefs to be a basic part of their identity, spirituality may become quite disrupted. Questions about why God allowed traumatic events to occur, and even about whether God exists, are likely to surface. Those who did not relate to any sense of spirituality before confronting traumatic events may experience profound emptiness and meaninglessness as they struggle to make sense of life.

One of the most significant barriers for both patient and therapist in the realm of the spiritual is semantic–the lyrics of spirituality may seem dead indeed, although the music is alive and vibrant. We affirm the meaning of their spiritual experiences, just as we affirm the meanings of their memories as parts of their own truth (see Chapters 1, 6).

Spiritual Development and Personality Development

We have found it valuable to correlate the tasks of psychological development, as described by Erik Erikson (1950, 1964, 1980), in tandem with the stages of spiritual development as outlined by the paleontologist, priest, and philosopher, Pierre Teilhard de Chardin (1964, 1969, 1966/1973). Teilhard de Chardin believed that spiritual evolution occurs within each of us as an innate call to participate in the evolution of the life on our planet, and in the evolution of the consciousness of the human race. Such participation in the evolutionary process was termed *worship* by Teilhard de Chardin. This stage of human development may be accompanied by great risk of pain and loss, even loss of life, but it features operating at a new level of consciousness, one that is filled with *joy*.

THE EVOLUTION OF HAPPINESS

We are often privileged to see psychological and spiritual growth occur within our patients. Although we speak about stages as if they must follow one another, we frequently observe non-linear movement. For example, reaching out to give to the community (the third stage of happiness presented below) can enhance self-esteem (the first stage).

For Teilhard de Chardin, "happiness," which can also be conceptualized as self-realization, could be achieved if a few principles were followed. One principle, which will be appreciated by ego-state therapists, is " . . . unification of self within our own self" (Teilhard de Chardin, 1966/1973, p. 50). The second principle is establishment of unity with one's fellow kind. The final principle involves subordination of one's life to some life greater than one's own. Although this may be perceived as the divine, it is not necessarily so.

The First Stage of Happiness

Happiness in Teilhard de Chardin's system occurs with the successful development of various stages of personalization. This means that happiness is a spiritual quality that can be found first in the individual's development of her own talents, capacities, sensitivities, and self-esteem. From the framework of Erik Erikson, the individual would have to achieve basic trust (vs. mistrust), autonomy (vs. shame and doubt), initiative (vs. guilt), and industry (vs. inferiority), in order to have taken fully that first Teilhardian step in becoming a person. For many of our patients and/or their ego states, basic trust is developed for the first time in therapy. For this to occur, both the paranoid and depressed positions (Klein, Heiman, & Money-Kyrle, 1957) must be relinquished and defensiveness in intimate relations forgone. The infant learns to trust the adequate "mother" to feed and love her.

When the development of basic trust has been thwarted by trauma, there are often accompanying spiritual manifestations, as the individual cannot love a self which never fully existed. When this occurs, lack of trust for self, other human beings, and divine beings is commonly seen, as the person may remain stuck in developmental arrests that fail to validate reality and cannot provide adequate self-soothing and organization.

Another possible outcome of arrest at this stage is the emergence of militant atheism and the fear of approaching any concept of the divine whatsoever. Philosophically, atheism is as logically indefensible as proofs of the existence of God. The passion with which militant atheists pursue their faith appears to be a defense against vulnerability to the mysteriousness of the divine, and when we hear it in our consulting rooms, we are alerted to the presence of basic trust issues. Another spiritual expression of a lack of basic trust is a pervasive indifference to all "cosmic" or spiritual issues. These simply play, the patient thinks, no part in her life.

We would be naive, indeed, to think that our patients could be totally lacking in basic trust. Without some trust they would not have been able to take the risk of entering therapy. We often see mixtures of developmental/ psychological and spiritual patterns. At times our patients appear to have developed just enough to get along in many of the major life tasks, but not enough to withstand the onslaught of symptoms that have been building up for years. They regress both psychologically and spiritually. The following case example will orient the reader to such a situation and to how we might deal with the spiritual/developmental issue in a therapeutic way.

Case Example: Patsy

Patsy was an assembly-line worker who had sustained an industrial injury that necessitated several surgical interventions; she was left with severe physical limitations and a chronic pain syndrome. She developed an overwhelming major depression as a response to her physical difficulties, her forced inactivity, and the ongoing pain. She entered treatment with me (CF) in order to obtain relief from her depression and to learn how to manage the physical pain she experienced.

It was soon apparent that Patsy had a dissociative disorder. She experienced memory loss, and she displayed a great deal of "switching," which she experienced as mood swings. In the first phase of her treatment her motivation was inadequate. She missed many appointments, and she looked to medication as the major source of relief. Her treatment was interrupted because the covering insurance company refused to pay for her psychotherapy.

After an interval of seven months, Patsy had straightened out her problems with the insurance company and reentered treatment; she was extremely depressed. This time she was open to hypnotic exploration and made a strong effort to keep her appointments; she also began to utilize self-hypnosis at home for the control of pain. Soon Patsy began to retrieve memories of childhood abuse by her mother and older sister in her hypnotherapy sessions. As her therapy progressed, her memory for her childhood expanded dramatically, and she came to realize that her mother had been frequently either cold or angry with her. Her only sources of love, Patsy concluded, had come from her father and from his family, especially her paternal grandmother to whom she was sent every summer.

Patsy was a wife and mother. Although she loved her husband and her son deeply, she had regressed so much that she was not able to show it as much as she once had. This was complicated further by the fact that some of her immature ego states wanted any "reaching out" to come from others.

I looked for evidences of love in Patsy's life as her therapy proceeded, and I discovered many. Patsy loved nature. In hypnosis she went to a remote, peaceful place in the Sierra mountains, where she loved to camp in the summer. She loved her animals; indeed, Patsy always traveled with one of her dogs, Trapper. If Patsy stopped to get a hamburger, a cookie, or a milkshake, she always gave Trapper half.

Patsy, isolated from most of the world in her depression, followed the adventures of the human race from television news stories. I discovered that she was involved emotionally with many people who were in suffering and pain throughout the world though she would never know them personally. Eventually we learned that Patsy "switched" to an angry ego state every time she felt overwhelmed by feelings of pity or sympathy for others: a needy neighbor child, a wounded animal, her own narcissistic sister who lived an empty life.

With time, Patsy began to help out at her son's school one afternoon a week; eventually she volunteered at a drug prevention program's weekly fund raising dinner. As she reclaimed the stage of her psychological/spiritual development that expanded her sense of community, her own damaged self-esteem began to rise.

Patsy's primary task in therapy is to learn how to accept herself as lovable and to love herself directly. The manifestations of love for her husband and son, animals (especially Trapper), and nature provided me with clues that she had functioned well at this level earlier in her life and would do so again once her trauma issues and depression had been resolved. She has already become involved in reaching beyond her immediate loves in the direction of expressing her love for the human race.

Patsy has probably never considered herself a spiritual person. She devoted no energy to formal religion, and she would probably be shocked to hear anyone describe her volunteer work with school or the drug program as worship. In Patsy's case her slow but steady developmental progress in therapy has been accompanied by a cosmic spiritual development, which can be discerned in her deep connections with nature, with her dog, her family, the multitudes of people in the world whose concerns are hers but who will never see her or know about her, and the people in her own community.

The Second Stage of Happiness

For Teilhard de Chardin as well as for Erik Erikson, physical and psychological union with another human being in intimacy and love also brings happiness. In both schema the individual develops a clear identity and rejects isolation by successfully reaching out for intimacy and union.

Developmental deficiencies in these and earlier stages may be expressed spiritually through beliefs in a childlike God who is paranoid, capriciously punishing, and who offers a life plan that is totally safe as long as there is no disobedience or "sinning." This God does not inspire humans to love, to create, to feel unity with nature, the "biosphere," or the cosmos, or to meet challenges. He is a God of the Rules, and he is a God of the Past. The concept of God immanent dwelling within each person as a principle and energy of growth is completely missing. Since any sense of unity with the planet or the cosmos is missing, another manifestation of arrest at this stage may be environmental callousness.

In our experience passage through this stage of development within therapy usually changes the individual's spiritual orientation, although, as we shall see later, the semantics surrounding the patient's spiritual activities may cloud their true nature from her.

Case Example: Billy

Billy was a 33-year-old pastoral counselor who had been raised in a strict fundamentalist tradition, which he still embraced. He entered therapy with me (CF) because he had many psychosomatic complaints, including severe migraine headaches, genitourinary problems, and an irritable bowel syndrome. He was also extremely accident-prone.

Billy had obtained his postgraduate education in the behavioral sciences at a Christian institution. His parents derogated his work as a therapist, and they never missed an opportunity to let Billy know that all his patients really needed to get better was the right kind of faith in God. Sometimes they sent him literature oriented to this point of view. In spite of his parents' doctrinaire, literalist approach to spirituality, Billy was not merely "religious." He was truly spiritual. He enjoyed nature, beauty, other people, his work, and his family. He was a non-judgmental person, and his own personal brand of religious fundamentalism emphasized love for others.

In the course of his therapy Billy retrieved memories suggestive of having been sexually molested by his father when he was a little boy. His experiences with his own ego states and his professional training in the area of dissociative disorders led Billy to conclude that his father had a dissociative disorder, probably MPD, and that he probably had no conscious memory of having molested him.

Billy was overcome with feelings of revulsion and rage for his father. Child ego states varied in the way they felt about him. Some were terrified and wanted nothing to do with him; some were furious; and some yearned for more of that kind of closeness with him. There were ego states who produced physical difficulties and accidents in order to punish him for his childhood sexual activity with his father, which was, they assured him, "wrong" and totally his fault.

Billy's therapy was stormy at times, since the ego states were engaged in a civil war about the resolution of the abuse issues as well as other significant conflicts in Billy's life. Billy was no longer able to speak with his father because he had become overwhelmed with feelings; he knew that his father would never be able discuss his experiences with him and would shroud himself in righteous indignation. His withdrawal from his parents caused a family upset of the greatest magnitude.

After several years of therapy, the warring of the ego states came to an end, integration of the ego states was occurring, and Billy began to enter the termination phase of therapy. This was accompanied by a strengthening of his own boundaries as a counselor, the development of appropriate assertiveness, and his finally being able to experience traumatic grief (Herman, 1992) about his lost, smashed childhood and the lifetime of symptoms he had endured. He also began to evaluate his fundamentalist religion.

Billy and his wife began to attend services at more "liberal" churches, and Billy became both critical and concerned about his older brother's rigid fundamentalism. He had overheard his nephew telling another child that *Snow White* was "of Satan." He began to drop remaining elements of fear from his concept of God, and he was beginning to think about doing some writing and teaching in his profession. From Erik Erikson's standpoint he had released guilt, anxiety, and identity diffusion, while developing initiative and a clear identity. His intimacy with his wife had become more adult in nature, as he no longer required so much attention. With this new freedom he was becoming more generative and had entered Teilhard de Chardin's third stage of happiness, in which he was able to worship joyfully with his entire life, unencumbered by the restraints of guilt and fear and the other limitations his earlier fundamentalism had imposed upon him.

The Third Stage of Happiness

The third stage of happiness for Teilhard de Chardin, *worship*, or participation in the evolutionary process, requires the successful resolution of Erik Erikson's stages of *generativity vs. stagnation* and *integrity vs. despair*. Generativity is a broad term referring to the production of something more than genital pleasures and animal comfort from one's achievement of an identity and the establishment of intimacy. For many this will be primarily their children. Others may seek generativity or additional generativity though such activities as artistic creativity, exploration, science, service to others, and worship. De Chardin liked to talk about the pilots who carried the mail in the United States years ago. At great risk to themselves (for many died) they were compelled to soar out generatively into the universe to further its progress (Teilhard de Chardin, 1966/73).

The rewards of generativity considered as such are not enough for Teilhard de Chardin; for him their greatest value is that they connect us with the continuing energy of the evolutionary process and allow us to be co-creators with the divine. Inherent are not only matters which belong to generativity, but also those which affect the person's sense of integrity in the face of the world's pain and suffering.

Within this context we would see Mother Theresa, Chagall, the astronauts, Ignatius of Loyola, and Alexander Fleming as generative people. We would also see as generative the father who runs a Brownie troop, the couple that rescues injured wildlife, the group that meets weekly to solve ecological problems, or the patient Patsy, described above, who gives her time to her son's school and to a drug program even though she is often seriously depressed. From the Teilhardian viewpoint, which we share, these activities are spiritual as well as generative.

Case Example: Samuel

Samuel had come to the end of his rope. He had battled cancer against all odds for several years. His doctors had called him "the miracle man" because of his successful tenacity. He came to see me (CF) because he was in great pain, and he wanted hypnotic help with pain control. Samuel was a scientist and writer, an overprotective father and husband.

Samuel was easily able to become free of pain in my office. However, he could not maintain this at home, nor could he successfully utilize self-hypnosis for pain control. Curious about what this might mean, we conducted ego-state exploration of the matter. Several ego states told me that Samuel had split off from himself the knowledge that he had cranial lesions which he knew would be untreatable at this time. In other words, he had dissociated his scientific knowledge about what was going on within him. The ego states continued the pain in the hope that it might cause him to pay attention to the most serious aspects of his life.

The reason for Samuel's denial, the ego states informed me, was that Samuel was so involved in caring for others. He worried about what would happen to his wife and children and to his scientific co-workers when he was gone. He could not admit that he was going to die soon because he could not conceive of their being able to manage without his help. Samuel had been an extremely generative man in terms of his contributions to his family and to the scientific community. Where would he find the strength not to despair in his last days when he felt that only he stood between people he loved and chaos?

I had a session with Samuel devoted to a review of these issues. We considered what really would happen when he was gone, how his wife and daughters would manage, and how his co-workers would cope. We also reviewed his life, and in the reviewing he was able to acknowledge and experience pride both in his contributions to the ongoing process of life and in his own creativity. He was also able to take pride in the strengths of the people he loved—the strengths that his self-division had previously kept him from exploring. Samuel brought an end to his dividedness. He was in Teilhard de Chardin's third stage of happiness, and within Erik Erikson's schema he had achieved integrity over despair.

Samuel died just a few weeks later. Although there is no indication that he viewed himself as a spiritual person, his life was characterized by great generativity, and his death characterized by profound integrity. I perceived him as someone who was involved in worship without being aware of it.

The Generative Self

We have suggested earlier in this chapter that engaging in the process of worship or participation in the evolutionary process requires the successful completion of Erikson's stage of *generativity vs. stagnation*. Generativity involves the achievement of a personal identity and the establishment of intimacy and creativity. In many ways, everything in this book is aimed toward the development of a generative self, capable of creative expression, integrity, healthy intimate relationships, and ongoing growth.

THE GENERATIVE SELF IN THE HYPNOTHERAPEUTIC RELATIONSHIP

In our clinical experience, hypnosis is one of the most effective ways of enhancing and promoting the development of the dissociative patient's generative self. Gilligan (1985) has pointed out that Milton Erickson had the special ability "to convey that *each of us is one of a kind*, though we all share a deep common unity" (p. 197). Erickson appeared to view generativity as "that vital sense of the beingness of the self [that] is often overlooked" (Erickson, 1962/1980, p. 345). The principles of Ericksonian hypnosis suggest that even if a person is dissociated or disconnected at functional levels, her "unconscious autonomy" (Gilligan, 1985, p. 208) can always generate whatever is needed for integration and growth. Hypnotic experience can be used as an opportunity for the subject to return to her deep self to rebalance her personality system and allow this generative autonomy to develop resources suitable for current needs (Gilligan, 1985, p. 209).

In the hypnotic relationship, an interpersonal trance state forms within which the patient's state of generative autonomy can be expressed and utilized. We share Gilligan's (1990) belief that this can best be accomplished through cooperative generativity by both therapist and subject; this allows solutions and changes to arise from the integrity of the relationship, rather than from the self of the therapist.

Our view of therapy suggests that the hypnotherapist, as well as the patient, needs to be willing to use her generative self. This requires the use of a receptive, participatory posture, an orientation to future possibility instead of toward the past, a focus on resources rather than deficits, and an interest in solutions rather than problems (Gilligan, 1990). In practical terms, this involves aligning with the patient's deepest, generative self, rather than with her primary diagnosis of PTSD or multiple personality disorder. Within this context, the therapist must accept and make room for the individual patient's dominant self-view, such as trauma survivor or sexually abused, helpless victim. The therapist must then be able to help generate or expand beyond this conscious, claimed identity to non-dominant, less conscious descriptions and identities of this person. This might include wondering what a patient is like when she's not being depressed, traumatized, or "stuck." Finally, the generative therapist will find ways of acknowledging and utilizing the understanding that both she and the patient are engaged in something "bigger" than either of them can define (Gilligan, 1994), which is, from our point of view, what generativity is all about.

True Spirituality: Rising above Dead Words

"Words, words, words"
Shakespeare, *Hamlet*, II, ii.

Spiritual interests are often rejected in our time because they carry the devitalized language and concepts of our childhood, and because they have often been sentimentalized (Fox, 1978). Nevertheless, they remain universal issues. Jung (1928/1971) even attributed the discovery of psychology as an outgrowth of our search for understanding of our spiritual natures. He believed that one of psychology's greatest achievements would be the solution of the relationship of the microcosm to the macrocosm.

As therapists we have the privileged opportunity to support our patients as they look beyond empty and outmoded religious concepts and words into the vitality of their own spiritual experiences. Matthew Fox (1988) has suggested that religion, with its "cult of personality," may interfere with true worship; he has reminded us that Native Americans and aboriginal people "do not worship anthropocentrically, they worship as citizens of a universe — a living, teeming, moving, diverse, sacred universe" (Fox, 1988, p. 213). He suggests that all worship be set within a cosmological context, and further recognizes ritual as playing an important role in accomplishing the ancient task of linking the microcosm with the macrocosm (Jung, 1928).

For our dissociative patients this ritual often means that they can connect with the cosmos spiritually in a way that they could never connect with a childlike God who resembles the abuser, and they can touch their deepest spiritual sources through a reverent appreciation of their own evolution as human beings. The integration of ego states frequently makes it much easier for our patients to conceive of integration with the cosmos. For our more fundamentalist patients integration may mean a reframing of the fundamentalist concept of the creation from a static happening that took place seven days in the distant past into a rich and dynamic process in which they actively participate and to which they contribute as holy people.

When our patients are able to resolve traumatic memories and reconnect with their own bodies, they are able to worship with those bodies in many ways: in rituals, dance, movement, and sexuality: "Eros belongs at the heart of worship . . . " (Fox, 1988, p. 218). They are able to reclaim their birthrights to their own holy bodies. This reclaiming can be on the level of affect and proprioception. The integrating patient who gets up early just to watch the sun rise is not only participating in a living metaphor (Dolan, 1991) but also having a spiritual experience she may not have been told about in Sunday school. We have also noticed that when our patients' lives are no longer permeated with the ugliness of abuse and trauma, they can become free enough to play, and they can connect with the playfulness of the cosmos.

It is not uncommon for some of our patients to seek new forms of worship. Those reared in Western traditions may turn to Eastern religions, and Jews may become Christians, and Christians, Jews. Many will experience the freedom to explore ancient rituals of native people or to create their own rituals. There will always be those who will not seek formal worship. The proof of their spirituality can be found in the joy of their increasing generativity. True self-realization in our opinion is not narcissistic; on the contrary, it may be cosmic (Teilhard de Chardin, 1964, 1969, 1966/1973), and peak experiences are frequently manifestations of worship, as we discuss below in the section on "Communicating About Spirituality."

Resolving Obstacles to Spiritual Development

Spiritual crises can shatter important frames of reference, including basic safety (a sense of being protected by God), trust (belief in the constancy of God or goodness in the universe), and intimacy (an ability to feel connection to a higher power beyond the self) (McCann & Pearlman, 1990). We believe that it is very important to initiate discussions of spirituality as part of the therapy process. Patients often do not bring up this topic themselves for several reasons: They may not believe that spirituality is an appropriate topic for psychotherapy; they may be concerned that the therapist has a different belief system, and so understandably want to avoid having their own beliefs challenged or misunderstood; they may feel comfortable discussing this topic only with clergy from their own religious background—in this latter case we may refer to a trained pastoral counselor or to a chaplain or clergy with sensitivity to issues of childhood trauma and abuse.

Whatever the nature of the therapist's spiritual beliefs, the willingness to explore and share the patient's struggle with deep, difficult spiritual issues can be one of the most meaningful aspects of the healing process. The sections below present some ways of helping dissociative patients resolve common obstacles to spiritual development.

WORKING THROUGH EMOTIONAL BARRIERS

A major barrier to spiritual development for our patients arises from some of the emotional feelings that are part of the trauma response. Blame is a prime example. Traumatized individuals have often coped by blaming themselves for what happened to them and, later on, by blaming those who activated the trauma or who failed to protect them from the trauma. Muller (1992) points out that the current tendency to claim identity through the "name" of the source of individual pain, such as "incest survivor," "rape victim," "child of an alcoholic," may be underscoring the assumption that pain is a mistake and should never have happened, rather than leading to acceptance of the reality of suffering as a thread in the fabric of life. Because pain is so uncomfortable, the illusion of comfort is sought in the explanation for the cause of personal suffering. In their insistence on determining who is responsible for the injustice of their pain, however, many individuals may be actually increasing their attachment to pain of the past and avoiding the personal experience of pain, which can lead to acceptance, growth, and spiritual awakening.

One way of breaking through the "blame" barrier is to help the traumatized patient to set aside the question of "why"—Why did this happen? Why didn't someone see what was happening and stop it? Why do others have it so much easier than I do? This often frees her to be directly in touch with her inner pain, to grieve it, and to become open to new possibilities of the present and future. Through guided experiences designed to help her simply to become aware of how she experiences the pain of the past in a given moment, the patient can learn to confront many of her limiting beliefs about pain, such as the impossibility of surviving it. At best, these kinds of experiences can lead ultimately to the letting go and resolution of childhood pain:

> Examining what we feel, not analyzing why, we discover the labyrinthine patterns of our grief and unfinished business. . . . That which has seemed so untouchable in the past is cradled in the arms of forgiveness and compassion, and the armoring begins to melt. (Levine, 1987, p. 103)

Fear is another emotion that is a central part of the trauma response and often blocks spiritual growth. For those raised in an atmosphere of betrayal, lies, unpredictability, and confusion, there is a sense of danger that permeates every moment. Because this terror is beyond the control of the traumatized individual, complex coping strategies become necessary. Often these individuals attempt to control the environment, including the people, around them. Some learn to deny their own feelings in order to keep surroundings predictable; others disown themselves as the cause of problems and become whomever they believe others want them to be. Out of fear and desperation, these individuals have learned to cultivate an emotional and spiritual dishonesty in order to protect themselves from further harm (Muller, 1992). Such pervasive fear is a big stumbling block to the development of spiritual faith. As Muller (1992) points out, faith is a centering response, a search for one's true nature, for the divine spirit within. Fearful preoccupation with danger often keeps the trauma survivor from learning that true safety is not the absence of danger and pain, but the presence of something that transcends those negative experiences.

An important therapeutic task is to help the patient learn to make the important determination, as Muller has suggested, of knowing "when the war is over" (1992, p. 22) – that is, when there is real danger and when it is safe to feel safe. One way of doing this is to teach the patient to experience fear *without* danger – that is, to begin to recognize fear as a signal that can alert her to the possibility that something requires her attention (Muller, 1992). For example, something in her body may be off balance, someone at work may have said something that day that was upsetting, or maybe she's overtired and not getting enough sleep and needs to attend to that. Jack Kornfield (1993), a psychologist and respected teacher of Buddhism, has indicated that the presence of fear may even be a sign of growth, a moment in which the individual is about to open to something bigger than the world she usually experiences. Arnold Mindell (1985, p. 37) has suggested that this kind of fear occurs when the individual reaches an "edge" between what is known and therefore claimed as a part of the self and what is yet unknown and about to be revealed.

The utilization approach, along with other techniques that provide inner safety in the present, can help the dissociative patient learn, as she monitors her own fear process, that she has a distorted sense of danger based on past feelings when there was real danger (Dolan, 1991). Such a process also allows her to learn about fear as a signal that can expand her self-awareness and lead to responses that truly are self-protective and enhancing, rather than to those that are reactive and self-limiting.

The emotional barrier of shame is a particularly challenging one in working with traumatized individuals. The sense of unworthiness and humiliation that accompanies shame makes it difficult for the individual to believe that she can be accepted, loved, and cared about by an intangible power, when those most intimately connected to her demonstrated their loathing and contempt in such powerful ways. Individuals who are preoccupied with feelings of unworthiness often suffer from "toxic shame" (Goldberg, 1991; Nathanson, 1992). Healthy shame, or humility, can be a motivation for self-improvement; reminders that more knowledge of self and others is needed to live in a full, positive way can generate a willingness to openly examine and do something constructive about bothersome behaviors (Goldberg, 1991). Toxic shame, however, can leave the patient with the belief that she is flawed and defective, unworthy of love or intimacy. Such a state of toxic shame makes it virtually impossible to connect in healthy, sustaining ways with God or any other being.

One of the most effective methods of intervention for shame issues is ego-state therapy. We are able to help the patient identify the internal "shamers," the ego states that are perpetuating her shame, often through the voices of parental introjects who were abusive and neglectful (see the case example of Barbara in Chapter 7). Once they are identified, these ego states are helped to build a therapeutic alliance, to identify their strengths and liabilities, and to work toward harmony and cooperation with the greater personality. This can result in more positive feelings about the self, as well as an emerging sense of possibility from a power beyond herself.

Developing Contemporary Perceptions of God

In addition to trauma-based beliefs and emotions, outdated childhood perceptions of God can block adult spiritual development. Gorsuch (1990) points out that "false" images of God are frequently brought from childhood into adult life. For many individuals who have grown up in dysfunctional, trauma-prone families, God was seen from the child's eyes as an enemy, a giant source of punishment, a terrifying presence "who desires nothing but to shape us up with bizarre rules and impossible demands" (Gorsuch, 1990, p. 25). It seems likely that such negative perceptions of God are modeled from the child's experiences of parent figures and taken in as unchanging parental introjects, which later prevent new, positive information from being assimilated into the child's developing schemas.

Another variation of this phenomenon is the unrealistic view of God as an "ultimate fixer in the sky" (May, 1988, p. 13). In this case, the individual has the hope of turning over a defective self to God, who can offer what her parents never could: comfort, restoration of wholeness, and protection from all pain and suffering. Of course, when such expectations are inevitably dashed, God joins the ranks of others who have disappointed and betrayed her.

As part of exploring spirituality during the therapy process, we believe it is important to help our patients identify their outdated beliefs about God. Usually, these are based on abusive or neglectful parental introjects that limit or prohibit the individual's current explorations of the deeper self. First, we may ask our patients to consider what holds them back from seeking God in their present lives and to make a list of their awarenesses. Such lists may include:

- "I'm not sure that God exists. How can I trust something that I can't see or experience directly?"
- "I might have to give up everything that I enjoy, and that is precious little as it is."
- "I might become so spiritual that my friends would laugh at me or even leave me."
- "What if God lets me down or disappoints me? I've had enough of that in my life."

- "I might change and then I wouldn't know who I am. I don't want to lose control over the me I already know."

Such concerns reflect some of the basic issues of the dissociative patient: fears of betrayal, loss, invasion, disappointment, and inability to trust. We help our patients to identify the past source of these beliefs and then invite them to generate new ones by considering whether they have ever encountered the "true God" in any of their life experiences. They are asked to write down their reactions before, during, and after any such experiences. Some of the common answers we receive include memories of spectacular sunrises or other natural phenomena, experiences of pregnancy or childbirth, encounters with individuals considered wise or truly spiritual, and experiences of formal meditation or spiritual retreat. We then help our patients "mine" their answers to discover what they already know in many different ways about the divine and the Holy, and to claim these as the beginnings of their current understandings about God. The final step is to encourage our patients to expand and deepen these "knowings" by creating spiritual awareness in their everyday lives. More will be written about this in the section below on "Promoting Experiences of Spiritual Growth during Therapy."

This three-step process developed by Gorsuch (1990) can be modified by having the patient complete steps one and two while in a state of hypnosis. We have found, however, that some dissociative patients are so intimidated by the idea of approaching God that they prefer the greater privacy and control afforded by writing. This task can also be completed at home as part of journaling or therapeutic writing assignments and brought in to share when the patient is ready.

ADDICTION ISSUES AND SPIRITUALITY

Addiction and compulsive behaviors have been discussed as the sequelae of traumatic responses in Chapter 12. Van der Kolk (1987c) has speculated that the biological release of opioids that occurs as part of the trauma response actually precipitates addiction to traumatic stress, as well as other types of addictions. Although the development of addictions is a complex issue, most experts agree that the function of addictive behaviors is to help the traumatized individual survive the pain of dissociated trauma experiences through numbing, self-medication, defending against shame, and distraction (Courtois, 1988).

May (1988) has pointed out that individuals who are preoccupied with addictions learn to displace their inherent longings for God onto addictive activities and behaviors. The addiction cycle eventually replaces the natural freedom to search for deeper satisfaction, meaning, and love in life. May

(1988) also suggests that interior spaciousness, which is necessary for communion with God, may be threatening to the addicted individual because the empty space allows repressed feelings and thoughts back into awareness. For the trauma survivor, this can be particularly problematic, since much of the emerging material may be related to trauma experiences. Thus, the traumatized individual, like the addicted one, learns to avoid experiences of internal quieting at all costs.

An important role of the therapist here is to facilitate the discovery of deeper and more lasting ways of satisfying various needs than can be offered by the addicting agent—whether it be food, sex, drugs, alcohol, work, exercise, or shopping. May (1991) suggests that the basic requirement for finding this satisfaction is to enter states of being or emptiness that allow for deeper connections with the inner and higher self. Although many dissociative patients are terrified of inner quieting because of what may enter their awareness, they can be helped to have neutral, and gradually more positive, experiences of inner attunement through simple, nonthreatening exercises and directives.

One approach is to ask patients to become aware of the moments of space that occur naturally in their lives (May, 1991). These may include quiet time with the newspaper and coffee in the morning, a daily walk with the dog, or a few minutes of unexpected free time after completing a work task. The patient is instructed first just to notice these times and make a mental or written list of them. Next, she is asked to notice whether there might be any of these natural times that already exist that could be expanded, or perhaps enjoyed a bit more completely. She is then asked to consider whether any of these are spaces that she would usually try to "fill" somehow through drinking, television, eating, or compulsive thoughts. We invite her to experiment with staying present and quietly aware for a few moments before moving to distract or numb herself. Exercises such as this one can help even the most fearful patient begin to develop mastery over the process of inner quieting; they can be expanded through more formal experiences of centering, self-hypnosis, meditation, types of prayer, chanting, or yoga. Ego-state therapy can also be useful in identifying and resolving inner conflicts related to inner quieting experiences.

Twelve-Step Programs

Many dissociative patients benefit greatly from the support of organized self-help groups. Their advantages include widespread availability, provisions for crisis contact and peer counseling, and the lack of fees. Regardless of their spiritual orientations, however, most individuals who attend these meetings experience conflicts. Some are relieved to discover within the 12-step structure the concept of a caring, loving God who does not blame or judge them for their difficulties in the ways they have learned to blame themselves. Others, however, feel pressured to take on the beliefs they hear presented at meetings. Still others resent the concept of their situation as an "illness" that requires acknowledgment of the helplessness they are hoping to shed.

Several of the "steps," especially those related to the spiritual principles of the program, also pose problems in light of the traumatized individual's belief system. "Letting go" of one's own will and surrendering to a higher power can be very difficult for those who believe that they have been abandoned by a cruel or uncaring God (Courtois, 1988). Others have problems with the requirement that each individual take responsibility for what happened in the past and forgive others in order to be free of anger and resentment. Fortunately, there are materials available now that acknowledge these issues and help to modify 12-step principles, particularly for those who have been abused.

We tell our patients that any resistances or obstacles that arise in 12-step programs are important and that we will explore and resolve them together. Often, experiences in these groups provide invaluable insights into the issues that limit a patient's spiritual beliefs and development, and promote opportunities to examine them in light of her early childhood experiences. Working through such issues can deepen the impact of therapy and provide openings for development of "generative self" capacities.

Promoting Experiences of Spiritual Growth during Therapy

We are deeply committed to helping our patients develop spirituality in the sense of its Latin root, "spiritus," meaning breath, life, alive (Merwin & Smith-Kurtz, 1988). We believe that spirituality involves the state of being fully alive, of having a sense of belonging to the universe, a deep appreciation of nature, an openness to surprise in each moment (D. Steindl-Rast, personal communication, 1993). David Steindl-Rast, psychologist and Benedictine monk, has written that prayer involves "communicating with your full self, with all there is, with God. Which is the real prayer, the Psalms or the watering of your African violets? . . . Through prayerfulness, every activity can and should become prayer" (1984, pp. 40–52). Our goal, then, is to help patients develop this full communication with "all that there is" throughout the fabric of their everyday lives.

COMMUNICATING ABOUT SPIRITUALITY

Connecting with God can be a semantic issue. As Steindl-Rast has suggested, "Don't talk to people about God. That will just put them off. Talk about joy, a sense of belonging. If people learn to experience these things, to celebrate them in life, then they will have a spiritual experience" (1993). He has identified spirituality as containing three aspects: a sense of belonging, a doctrine or set of beliefs about belonging, and ritual to celebrate belonging. These elements belong to all religions, but patients can incorporate them into their lives without ever participating in a formal church.

A helpful framework for understanding this approach to spirituality is the work on "peak experience" conducted by Abraham Maslow. Maslow (1970) has written that: "The experiences of the holy, the sacred, the divine, of awe, . . . of surrender, of mystery, of . . . thanksgiving, gratitude, . . . if they happen at all, tend to be confined to a single day of the week, to happen under one roof only of one kind of structure only. . . . 'Religionizing' only one part of life secularizes the rest of it" (p. 31). He has identified the "core-religious experience" as a "transcendent" or "peak experience," which he believes is the essence or universal nucleus of every known religion (p. 19). Maslow (1970, pp. 59–68) has defined several characteristics of the naturalistic peak experience, which are virtually the same as mystical or religious experiences:

1. The universe is perceived as a whole and the individual perceives her place in it.
2. Perception shifts so that figure and ground are less sharply differentiated. Things are perceived as equally important rather than in hierarchy.
3. The cognition of being becomes more detached. The individual can look on nature as it truly exists in and for itself, not as if it is put there to serve human purposes.
4. Perception becomes relatively ego-transcending and unselfish.
5. The peak experience is felt as a self-validating moment with its own intrinsic value.
6. There is a very characteristic disorientation in time and space, or even the lack of consciousness of time and space. This state is like experiencing universality and eternity.
7. The world is seen only as beautiful, good, desirable, and hopeful. The world is accepted and understood; evil is also accepted and understood and seen in perspective as necessary, inevitable, as having its own place as well.

"Mining" our patients' life experience to find these peak experiences is an important part of discussing spirituality. If they are unable to recall any moments of this kind on their own, we discuss with them their various experiences of nature, times when they felt they were their "best self," experiences of unexpected pleasant surprises, or times when they found themselves filled with unaccountable gratitude. Sometimes we "prime the pump" by giving metaphorical examples, such as the delight of a small child who finds a shiny quarter, the joyous surprise of finding a new rose that blooms suddenly after a dark time of cold and frost, or a card that comes unexpectedly in the mail from a friend who had not written for many years and had been presumed lost forever.

We follow Steindl-Rast's (1993) guidelines to developing spirituality by helping patients define a new sense of belonging that transcends the past, based on current experiences of belonging to the universe. This can be cultivated by helping patients explore the world of nature through their senses. For example, we might suggest a ten-minute nature walk in a location of their choice. We ask them to look at every flower and every blade of grass, listen to every sound, smell every smell, feel every sensation that is available in those moments. We might ask them to add a meaningful phrase as a meditation following each sensory awareness, such as "And this is God too" (Gorsuch, 1993). Such experiences expand a sense of belongingness and incorporate some of Maslow's elements of the peak experience.

Once the patient begins to experience a sense of belonging, we might ask her to redefine her beliefs about whatever word she uses to indicate God (the source, higher power, higher self, or the universe), along with her understanding of her place in the world around her. Finally, we help her develop rituals for celebrating and expressing gratitude for this new sense of belonging. Such rituals may include a short meditation before meals, a brief statement of thanks for one *new* thing each day (Steindl-Rast, 1993), daily journaling on the subject of celebrating life, or a party or candle-lighting ceremony that celebrates the person's new spiritual identity. This last step of celebrating gratefulness is essential to the spiritual process. As Steindl-Rast writes, "The root of joy is gratefulness. We tend to misunderstand the link between joy and gratefulness. We notice that joyful people are grateful and suppose that they are grateful for their joy. But the reverse is true: their joy springs from gratefulness" (1984, p. 204).

HYPNOSIS AND SPIRITUALITY

Another way of communicating about and fostering spirituality is to incorporate the patient's newly emerging spiritual growth into hypnotic experiences. Benson (1979, 1984) has recommended utilizing the individual's spiritual beliefs to augment the positive results of relaxation. One way of doing this is by asking the individual to develop an inner focus on a word that is spiritually meaningful. This may include a phrase such as "I belong to God," a line from the Bible or another spiritual teaching, or a meaningful word or phrase. Such an approach can be used to initiate a quiet, focused meditation or prayer, or to enhance and deepen part of a hypnotic induction.

We also utilize the patient's spiritual or religious symbols as a part of various hypnotic experiences. For example, if a patient already has inner spiritual guides, we may suggest using them as a resource of safety and stabilization when initiating age regression experiences back to disturbing traumatic material. Or, if an individual has strong Christian beliefs, we may incorporate these in healing imagery experiences, for example, using her image of Jesus as a resource to take on a healing journey back to the past to learn about forgiveness, if that is what she believes would be helpful to her. Many patients experience the ego-strengthening technique, *inner strength* (McNeal & Frederick, 1993), transpersonally—as an aspect of the divine within, or as a force, or some manifestation of grace, sent by the divine. Many patients have reported their perceptions of inner strength as crucial experiences in their spiritual awareness and growth. As patients learn to develop healthy dependency upon what they can experience with the *inner strength* and *inner love* techniques (Frederick, 1994a) internally, they are well on the road to the development of a healthy dependency upon God. In ego-state therapy, we have suggested that various ego states go on "spiritual retreats" or "journeys" in order to learn about spiritual matters such as love or forgiveness. These experiences have been very successful, though we are never sure what has actually happened. The patient and relevant ego states invariably experiences such assignments as important and beneficial.

One "internal mother" ego state was asked to go on such a journey after complaining for weeks that her life was worthless and she herself was an "empty shell"; unless her son, the patient, made her happiness the primary focus of his life, she was filled with grief and despair. After returning from her "spiritual retreat," she decided to build a greenhouse and planned a magnificent garden, which was to become her life's work. Whenever she was activated after that time, she could be found puttering happily among pots and flower beds, and was able to develop a fully supportive relationship with her "son."

Certainly, when spiritual symbols or resources appear spontaneously during hypnotic experiences, we validate these as being as important as any other resource, if not more so, and encourage their utilization within therapy sessions as well as in the patient's everyday life. As always, our purpose is to affirm the patient's experience, regardless of our own belief systems.

The centerpiece of our model and the essence of our philosophy is that patients can and should be strengthened during the course of therapy. Identifying and helping the patient to access spiritual strength is one way of contributing to this general process. Spiritual strength can and should be connected with strengths found in other realms: emotional, physical, creative, relational, the community, and the world at large.

REFERENCES

Abraham, S., & Beaumont, P. J. V. (1982). Varieties of psychosexual experiences and patients with anorexia nervosa. *International Journal of Eating Disorders, 1*, 10-19.

Abse, W. (1966). *Hysteria and related mntal disorders: An approach to psychological medicine*. Bristol: John Wright & Sons.

Adler, G. (1985). *Borderline psychopathology and its treatment*. New York: Jason Aronson.

Aguilera, D., Messick, J., & Farrell, M. (1970). *Crisis intervention*. St. Louis: C. V. Mosby.

Ainsworth, M. D. S. (1967). *Infant care and the growth of attachment*. Baltimore: Johns Hopkins University Press.

Allison, R. B. (1974). A guide to parents: How to raise your daughter to have multiple personalities. *Family Therapy, 1*, 83-88.

Alman, B. M., & Lambrou, P. (1992). *Self-hypnosis: The complete manual for health and self-change* (2nd ed.). New York: Brunner/Mazel.

Alon, N. (1985). An Ericksonian approach to the treatment of chronic posttraumatic stress disorder patients. In J. Zeig (Ed.), *Ericksonian psychotherapy* (Vol. 2): *Clinical applications* (pp. 307-326). New York: Brunner/Mazel.

American Psychiatric Association (1980). *A psychiatric glossary* (5th ed.). Washington, DC: Author.

American Psychiatric Association (1994). *Diagnostic and Statistical Manual, Fourth Edition*. Washington, DC: American Psychiatric Press.

Anisman, H. L., Ritch, M., & Sklar, L. S. (1981). Noradrenergic and dopaminergic interactions in escape behavior. *Psychopharmacology, 74*, 263-268.

Assagioli, R. (1965). *Psychosynthesis: A collection of basic writings*. New York: Viking.

Ayalon, O. (1983). Coping with terrorism. In D. Meichenbaum & M. Jaremko (Eds.), *Stress reduction and prevention*. New York: Plenum.

Azima, H., & Wittkower, E. (1956). Gratifications of basic needs in schizophrenia. *Psychiatry, 19*, 121-129.

Bailey, K. (1992). Therapeutic massage with survivors of abuse. *Massage Therapy Journal, Summer*, 79-120.

Baker, E. L. (1981). An hypnotherapeutic approach to enhance object relatedness in psychotic patients. *International Journal of Clinical and Experimental Hypnosis, 29* (2), 136-137.

329

Baker, E. L. (1983a). Resistance in hypnotherapy of primitive states: Its meaning and management. *International Journal of Clinical and Experimental Hypnosis, 31*, 82–89.

Baker, E. L. (1983b). The use of hypnotic techniques with psychotics. *American Journal of Clinical Hypnosis, 25*, 283–288.

Baker, E. L. (1985). Ego psychology and hypnosis: Contemporary theory and practice. *Psychotherapy in Private Practice, 3*, 115–122.

Baker, E. L. (1994, March). *The therapist as transitional object in intensive hypnotherapy.* Paper presented at the annual meeting of the American Society of Clinical Hypnosis, Philadelphia.

Baker, H. S., & Baker, M. N. (1987). Kohut's self psychology: An overview. *American Journal of Psychiatry, 144*, 1–8.

Balint, M. (1979). *The basic fault: Therapeutic aspects of regression.* New York: Brunner/ Mazel.

Bandler, L. C. (1978). *They lived happily ever after.* Cupertino, CA: Meta Publications.

Banyai, E. I., Meszaros, I., & Csokay, L. (1982). *Interaction between hypnotist and subject: A social psychophysiological approach.* Paper presented at the International Congress of Hypnosis and Psychosomatic Medicine, Glasgow, Scotland.

Barach, P. M. (1991). Multiple personality disorder as an attachment disorder. *Dissociation, 4*(3), 117–123.

Barber, J. (1980). Hypnosis and the unhypnotizable. *American Journal of Clinical Hypnosis, 23*, 4–9.

Barber, T. X., & Wilson, S. C. (1978/79). The Barber suggestibility scale and the creative imagination scale: Experimental and clinical applications. *American Journal of Clinical Hypnosis, 21*, 85.

Barker, M. A. (1993, April). *Use of the spouse as co-therapist.* Presented at the sixth annual Western Clinical Conference on Multiple Personality and Dissociation, Irvine, CA.

Barkin, R., Braun, B. G., & Kluft, R. P. (1986). The dilemma of drug therapy for multiple personality disorder. In B. G. Braun (Ed.), *The treatment of multiple personality disorder* (pp. 159–174). Washington, DC: American Psychiatric Press.

Bass, E., & Davis, L. (1988). *The courage to heal: A guide for women survivors of child sexual abuse.* New York: Harper & Row.

Beahrs, J. O. (1982). *Unity and multiplicity.* New York: Brunner/Mazel,

Beahrs, J. O. (1990). The evolution of post-traumatic behaviors: Three hypotheses. *Dissociation, 3*, 13–20.

Beahrs, J. O. (1993, October). *Dissociative identity disorder: Adaptive deception of self and others.* Paper presented at the 24th Annual Meeting of the American Academy of Psychiatry and the Law, San Antonio, TX.

Beck, J. C., & van der Kolk, B. A. (1987). Reports of childhood incest and current behavior of chronically hospitalized psychotic women. *American Journal of Psychiatry, 144*, 1426–1430.

Becker, J. V., Skinner, L. J., Abel, G. G., & Cichon, J. (1986). Level of postassault sexual functioning in rape and incest victims. *Archives of Sexual Behavior, 15*, 37–49.

Bellak, L., Harvich, M., & Gedeman, H. (1973). *Ego functions in schizophrenics, neurotics and normals.* New York: Wiley.

Benson, H. (1979). *The relaxation response.* New York: Morrow.

Benson, H. (1984). *Beyond the relaxation response.* New York: Morrow.

Bentzen, M., Jarinaes, E., & Levine, P. (1993). *The body self in psychotherapy: A psycho-motoric approach to developmental psychology*. Unpublished manuscript.

Berne, E. (1961). *Transactional analysis in psychotherapy*. New York: Grove Press.

Bernhardt, P. (1992). *Somatic approaches to traumatic shock*. Unpublished manuscript.

Bernstein, E. M., & Putnam, F. (1986). Development, reliability, and validity of a dissociation scale. *Journal of Nervous and Mental Disease, 174*, 727-735.

Binet, A. (1977a). *Alterations of personality*. Washington: University Publications of America. (Original work published 1896).

Binet, A. (1977b). *On double consciousness*. Washington: University Publications of America. (Original work published 1890).

Bion, W. R. (1959). *Experiences in groups*. New York: Basic Books.

Bion, W. R. (1967/1984). *Second thoughts: selected papers on pycho-analysis*. New York: Jason Aronson.

Blank, A.S. (1985). The unconscious flashback to the war in Vietnam veterans. In S. M. Sonnenberg, A. S. Blank, & J. A. Talbot (Eds.), *Stress and recovery of Vietnam veterans*. Washington, DC: American Psychiatric Press.

Blank, A. S. (1989, June). *Principles of psychotherapeutic treatment of PTSD in war veterans*. Paper presented at Psychobiological Aspects of Catastrophic Trauma, New Haven, CT.

Bliss, E. L. (1986). *Multiple personality, allied disorders, and hypnosis*. New York: Guilford.

Boor, M. (1982). The multiple personality epidemic. *Journal of Nervcous and Mental Diseases, 170*, 302-304.

Boore, J. (1993). EMDR–a new procedure. *The California Therapist, May/June*, 40-42.

Bower, G. H. (1981). Mood and memory. *American Psychologist, 36*, 129-148.

Bowers, K. S., & Hilgard, E. R. (1988). Some complexities in understanding memory. In H. M. Pettinati (Ed.), *Hypnosis and memory*. New York: Guilford.

Bowlby, J. (1969). *Attachment and loss, Vol. I: Attachment*. New York: Basic Books.

Boyer, B. L., & Giovacchini, P. L. (1967). *Psychoanalytic treatment of characterological and schizophrenic disorders*. New York: Science House.

Braun, B. G. (1980). Hypnosis for multiple personalties. In H. Wain (Ed.), *Clinical hypnosis in medicine*. Chicago: Year Book Medical.

Braun, B. G. (1984). Uses of hypnosis with multiple personalities. *Psychiatric Annals, 14*, 34-40.

Braun, B. G. (1986). Issues in the psychotherapy of multiple personality disorder. In B. G. Braun (Ed.), *Treatment of multiple personality disorder* (pp. 1-28). Washington, DC: American Psychiatric Press.

Braun, B. G. (1988a). The BASK model of dissociation. *Dissociation, 1*(1), 4-23.

Braun, B. G.(1988b). The BASK model of dissociation: Part II–Treatment. *Dissociation, 1*(2), 16-23.

Braun, B. G. (1990). Unusual medication regimens in the treatment of dissociative disorder patients: Part I: Noradrenergic agents. *Dissociation, 3*(3), 144-150.

Braun, B. G. (1993). Aids to the treatment of multiple personality disorder on a general psychiatric inpatient unit. In R. P. Kluft & C. Fine (Eds.), *Clinical perspectives on multiple personality disorder* (pp. 155-175). Washington, DC: American Psychiatric Press.

Braun, B. G., & Sachs, R. G. (1985). The development of multiple personality disorder: Predisposing, precipitating, and perpetuating factors. In R. P. Kluft (Ed.), *The childhood antecedents of multiple personality*. Washington, DC: American Psychiatric Press.

Brende, J. O. (1985). The use of hypnosis in post-traumatic conditions. In W. E. Kelly (Ed.), *Post-traumatic stress disorder and the war veteran patient* (pp. 193–210). New York: Brunner/Mazel.

Brende, J. O., & Benedict, B. D. (1980). The Vietnam combat delayed stress syndrome: Hypnotherapy of "dissociative symptoms." *American Journal of Clinical Hypnosis, 23*, 34–40.

Bresler, D. E. (1990). Meeting an inner adviser. In D. C. Hammond (Ed.), *Handbook of hypnotic suggestions and metaphors* (pp. 318–320). New York: Norton.

Breuer, J., & Freud, S. (1893–1895). Studies on hysteria. In J. Strachey (Ed. & Trans.), *The standard edition of the complete psychological works of Sigmund Freud*, Vol. 2. New York: Norton.

Briere, J. (1984, April). *The long-term effects of childhood sexual abuse: Defining a post-sexual abuse syndrome*. Paper presented at the Third National Conference on the Sexual Victimization of Children, Washington, DC.

Briere, J. (1992). *Child abuse trauma: Theory and treatment of the lasting effects*. Newbury Park: Sage.

Brown, D. P., Forte, M., Rich, P., & Epstein, G. (1982–83). Phenomenological differences among self hypnosis, mindfulness meditation, and imaging. *Imagination, Cognition, and Personality, 2*, 291–309.

Brown, D. P., & Fromm, E. (1986). *Hypnotherapy and hypnoanalysis*. Hillsdale, NJ: Erlbaum.

Bryer, J. B., Nelson, B. A., Miller, J. B., et al. (1987). Childhood sexual and physical abuse as factors in adult psychiatric illness. *American Journal of Psychiatry, 144*, 1426–1430.

Buber, M. (1976). *I and thou*. New York: Scribner's.

Bucky, S., & Dalenberg, C. (1992). The relationship between training of mental health professionals and the reporting of ritual abuse and multiple personality disorder symptomatology. *Journal of Psychology and Theology, 20*, 233–238.

Calnan, R. D. (1977). Hypnotherapeutic ego-strengthening. *Australian Journal of Clinical Hypnosis, 5*, 105–118.

Calof, D. L. (1991). Protecting the therapeutic framework. *Treating Abuse Today, 1*(3), 10.

Carich, P. A. (1986). Contraindications to using hypnosis. In B. Zilbergeld, M. G. Edelstien & D. L. Araoz (Eds.), *Hypnosis questions and answers*. New York: Norton.

Carnes, P. J. (1991). *Don't call it love*. New York: Bantam.

Carnes, P. J. (1993). Addiction and post-traumatic stress: The convergence of victims' realities. *Treating Abuse Today, 3*(3), 5–11.

Caul, D. (1984). Group and videotape techniques for multiple personality. *Psychiatric Annals, 14*, 43–50.

Caul, D., Sachs, R. G., & Braun, B. G. (1986). Group therapy in treatment of multiple personality disorder. In B. G. Braun (Ed.), *The treatment of multiple personality disorder* (pp.145–156). Washington, DC: American Psychiatric Press.

Cheek, D. B. (1994). *Hypnosis: The application of ideomotor techniques*. Boston: Allyn & Bacon.

Cheek, D. B., & LeCron, L. M. (1968). *Clinical hypnotherapy*. New York: Grune & Stratton.

Chu, J.A. (1988). Ten traps for therapists in the treatment of trauma survivors. *Dissociation, 1*(4), 24–32.

Cicchetti, D. (1984). The emergence of developmental psychopathology. *Child Development, 55,* 1–7.

Clary, W. F., Burstin, K. S., & Carpenter, J. S. (1984). Multiple personality and borderline personality disorder. *Psychiatric Clinics of North America, 7,* 69–87.

Cohen, S. B. (1982, May). *Clinical uses of measures of hypnotizability.* Paper presented to the American Psychiatric Association, Dallas, TX.

Combs, G., & Freedman, J. (1990). *Symbol, story, and ceremony: Using metaphor in individual and family therapy.* New York: Norton.

Comstock, C. M. (1991). Countertransference and the suicidal multiple personality disorder patient. *Dissociation, 4*(1), 25–35.

Comstock, C. M., & Vickery, D. (1993). The therapist as victim: A preliminary discussion. *Dissociation, 5*(3), 155–158.

Coons, P. M. (1980). Multiple personality: Diagnostic considerations. *Journal of Clinical Psychiatry, 41,* 330–336.

Coons, P. M. (1984). The differential diagnosis of multiple personality. *Psychiatric Clinics of North America, 7,* 51–65.

Coons, P. M. (1986). Treatment progress in 20 patients with multiple personality disorder. *Journal of Nervous and Mental Disorders, 176,* 715–721.

Coons, P. M., & Bradley, K. (1985). Group psychotherapy with multiple personality patients. *Journal of Nervous and Mental Disease, 173,* 515–521.

Coons, P. M., & Milstein, V. (1986). Psychosexual disturbances in multiple personality: Characteristics, etiology, treatment. *Journal of Clinical Psychiatry, 47,* 106–110.

Courtois, C. A. (1988). *Healing the incest wound: Adult survivors in therapy.* New York: Norton.

Courtois, C. A. (1991). Theory, sequencing, and strategy in treating adult survivors. *New Directions for Mental Health Services, 51,* 47–60.

Crabtree, A. (1992). Dissociation and memory: A two-hundred-year perspective. *Dissociation, 5*(3), 150–154.

Craik, F. I. M., & Lockhart, R. S. (1972). Levels of processing: A framework for memory research. *Journal of Verbal Learning and Verbal Behavior, 11,* 671–684.

Craine, L. S., Henson, C. E., Colliver, J. A., et al. (1988). Prevalence of a history of sexual abuse among female psychiatric patients in a state hospital system. *Hospital and Community Psychiatry, 39,* 300–304.

Crasilneck, H. B., & Hall, J. A. (1975). *Clinical hypnosis: Principles and applications.* New York: Grune & Stratton.

Danieli, Y. (1984). Psychotherapists' participation in the conspiracy of silence about the holocaust. *Psychoanalytic Psychology, 1,* 23–42.

Davis, L. (1993). In S. Rochman, Massage therapy for survivors of childhood sexual abuse. *Massage, 43,* 25.

Delaney, R., Tussi, D., & Gold, P. E. (1983). Long-term potentiation as a neurophysiological analog of memory. *Pharmacology of Biochemical Behavior, 18,* 137–139.

De Shazer, S. (1978). Brief hypnotherapy of two sexual dysfunctions: The crystal ball technique. *American Journal of Clinical Hypnosis, 20,* 203–208.

De Shazer, S. (1985). *Keys to solution in brief therapy.* New York: Norton.

De Shazer, S. (1988). *Clues: Investigating solutions in brief therapy.* New York: Norton.

De Young, M. (1981). Case reports: The sexual exploitation of incest victims by health professionals. *Victimology, 6,* 92–101.

Diamond, M. J. (1980). The client-as-hypnotist: Furthering hypnotherapeutic change. *International Journal of Clinical and Experimental Hypnosis, 28*(3), 197–207.

Diamond, M. J. (1983, August). *Reflections on the interactive nature of the hypnotic experience: On the relational dimensions of hypnosis.* Presented at the 91st Annual Convention of the American Psychological Association, Anaheim, CA.

Diamond, M. J. (1984). It takes two to tango: Some thoughts on the neglected importance of the hypnotist in an interactive hypnotherapeutic relationship. *American Journal of Clinical Hypnosis, 27*(1), 3–13.

Diamond, M. J. (1986). The interactional basis of hypnotic experience: On the relational dimensions of hypnosis. *International Journal of Clinical and Experimental Hypnosis, 35,* 95–113.

Dimond, R. E. (1981). Hypnotic treatment of a kidney dialysis patient. *American Journal of Clinical Hypnosis, 23,* 284–288.

Di Vito, R. A. (1993). Use of amytal interviews in the treatment of an extremely complex case of multiple personality disorder. In R. P. Kluft & C. Fine (Eds.), *Clinical perspectives on multiple personality disorder* (pp. 227–240). Washington, DC: American Psychiatric Press.

Dolan, Y. M. (1985). *A path with a heart: Ericksonian utilization with resistant and chronic clients.* New York: Brunner/Mazel.

Dolan, Y. M. (1991). *Resolving sexual abuse.* New York: Norton.

Dubois, P. (1904). *The psychic treatment of mental disorders.* New York: Funk & Wagnall.

Edelstien, M. G. (1981). *Trauma, trance, and transformation.* New York: Brunner/ Mazel.

Edelstien, M. G. (1990). *Symptom analysis: A method of brief therapy.* New York: Norton.

Eich, J. E. (1980). The cue-dependent nature of state dependent retrieval. *Memory and Cognition, 8,* 157–168.

Elkind, S. N. (1992). *Resolving impasses in therapeutic relationships.* New York: Guilford.

Ellenberger, H. (1970). *The discovery of the unconscious.* New York: Basic Books.

Ellis, B. (1992). Satanic ritual abuse and legend ostentation. *Journal of Psychology and Theology, 20,* 274–277.

Enslie, G. J., & Rosenfeld, A. (1983). Incest reported by children and adolescents hospitalized for severe psychiatric problems. *American Journal of Psychiatry, 140,* 708–710.

Erickson, M. H. (1945/1980). Hypnotic techniques for the therapy of acute psychiatric disturbances in war. *American Journal of Psychiatry, 101,* 668–672. Reprinted in E. L. Rossi (Ed.), *The collected papers of Milton H. Erickson on hypnosis,* Vol IV (pp. 28–34).

Erickson, M. H. (1952). Deep hypnosis and its induction. In L. M. LeCron (Ed.), *Experimental hypnosis.* New York: Macmillan.

Erickson, M. H. (1954). Pseudo-orientation in time as a hypnotherapeutic procedure. *Journal of Clinical and Experimental Hypnosis, 2,* 261–283.

Erickson, M. H. (1959). Further clinical techniques of hypnosis: Utilization techniques. *Journal of the American Society of Clinical Hypnosis, 2,* 3–21.

Erickson, M. H. (1961/1980). Historical note on the hand levitation and other ideomotor techniques. In E. Rossi (Ed.), *The collected papers of Milton Erickson on hypnosis: The nature of hypnosis and suggestion,* Vol. I (pp. 135–138). New York: Irvington.

Erickson, M. H. (1962/1980). Basic psychological problems in hypnotic research. In

E. L. Rossi (Ed.), *The collected papers of Milton H. Erickson on hypnosis*, Vol. II (pp. 340–350). New York: Irvington.

Erickson, M. H. (1964). The "surprise" and "my-friend-John" techniques of hypnosis: Minimal cues and natural field experimentation. *American Journal of Clinical Hypnosis, 6*, 293–307.

Erickson, M. H. (1965). The use of symptoms as an integral part of therapy. *American Journal of Clinical Hypnosis, 8*, 57–65.

Erickson, M. H., (1966). The interspersal hypnotic technique for symptom correction and pain control. *American Journal of Clinical Hypnosis, 8*, 198–209.

Erickson, M. H. (1970/1980). Hypnosis: Its renascence as a treatment modality. In E. L. Rossi (Ed.), *The collected papers of Milton H. Erickson on hypnosis*, Vol. IV (pp. 52–75). New York: Irvington.

Erickson, M. H. (1974/1980). Varieties of hypnotic amnesia. In E. Rossi (Ed.), *The collected papers of Milton H. Erickson on hypnosis*, Vol. III (pp. 71–90). New York: Irvington.

Erickson, M. H. (1986). Mind-body communication in hypnosis. In E. L. Rossi & M. O. Ryan (Eds.), *The seminars, workshops, and lectures of Milton H. Erickson*, Vol. III. New York: Irvington.

Erickson, M. H., & Kubie, L. (1939). The permanent relief of an obsessional phobia by means of communications with an unsuspected dual personality. *Psychoanalytic Quarterly, 8*, 471–509.

Erickson, M. H., & Kubie, L. S. (1940). The translation of the cryptic automatic writing of one hypnotic subject by another in a trancelike dissociated state. *Psychoanalytic Quarterly, 9*, 51–63.

Erickson, M. H., & Rossi, E. L. (1976). Two level communication and the microdynamics of trance and suggestion. *American Journal of Clinical Hypnosis, 18*, 153–171.

Erickson, M. H., & Rossi, E. L. (1977). Autohypnotic experiences of Milton H. Erickson, MD. *American Journal of Clinical Hypnosis, 20*, 36–54.

Erickson, M. H., & Rossi, E. L. (1979). *Hypnotherapy: An exploratory case book*. New York: Irvington.

Erickson, M. H., & Rossi, E. L. (1980). The February man: Facilitating new identity in hypnosis. In E. L. Rossi (Ed.), *The collected papers of Milton H. Erickson on hypnosis:*, Vol. IV (pp. 525–542). New York: Irvington.

Erickson, M. H., & Rossi, E. (1981). *Experiencing hypnosis: Therapeutic approaches to altered states*. New York: Irvington.

Erickson, M. H., & Rossi, E. L. (1989). *The February man: Evolving consciousness and identity in hypnotherapy*. New York: Brunner/Mazel.

Erickson, M. H., Rossi, E. L., & Rossi, S. I. (1976). *Hypnotic realities*. New York: Irvington.

Erikson, E. H. (1950). *Childhood and society*. New York: Norton.

Erikson, E. H. (1964). *Insight and responsibility*. New York: Norton.

Erikson, E. H. (1980). *Identity and the life cycle*. New York: Norton.

Ewin, D. M. (1978). Clinical use of hypnosis for attenuation of burn depth. In F. H. Frankel & H. S. Zamansky (Eds.), *Hypnosis at its bicentennial*. New York: Plenum.

Fairbank, J. A., De Good, D. E., & Jenkins, C. W. (1981). Behavioral treatment of a persistent post-traumatic response. *Journal of Behavioral Therapy and Experimental Psychiatry, 12*(4), 321–324.

False Memory Syndrome Foundation, 3401 Market Street, Suite 30, Philadelphia, PA, 19114.

Federn, P. (1952). *Ego psychology and the psychoses*. New York: Basic Books.

Feldman-Summers, S., Gordon, P. E., & Meagher, J. R. (1979). The impact of rape on sexual satisfaction. *Journal of Abnormal Psychology, 88*, 101–105.

Feldman-Summers, S., & Jones, G. (1984). Psychological impacts of sexual contact between therapists or other health care practitioners and their clients. *Journal of Consulting and Clinical Psychology, 52*, 1054–1061.

Fenichel, O. (1939/1953). The counter-phobic attitude. In *The collected papers of Otto Fenichel*, Vol. 2 (pp. 163–173). New York: Norton.

Fenichel, O. (1941). *Problems of psychoanalytic technique*. New York: The Psychoanalytic Quarterly.

Ferenczi, S. (1950). Silence is golden. In *Further contributions to the theory and technique of psychoanalysis*. London: Hogarth Press.

Figley, C. R. (1988). Post-traumatic family therapy. In F. M. Ochberg (Ed.), *Post-traumatic therapy and victims of violence* (pp. 85–109). New York: Brunner/Mazel.

Fine, C. (1990). The cognitive sequelae of incest. In R. P. Kluft (Ed.), *Incest-related syndromes of adult psychopathology* (pp. 161–182). Washington, DC: American Psychiatric Press.

Fine, C. (1993) A tactical integrationist perspective on the treatment of multiple personality disorder. In R. P. Kluft & C. Fine (Eds.), *Clinical perspectives on multiple personality disorder* (pp. 135–153). Washington, DC: American Psychiatric Press.

Fine, C., & Comstock, C. (1989). Completion of cognitive schema and affective realms through temporary blending of personalities. In B. G. Braun (Ed.), *Dissociative disorders, 1989–Proceedings of the Sixth International Conference on Multiple Personality/Dissociative States*. Chicago: Rush University.

Fink, D. (1993). Observations on the role of transitional objects and transitional phenomena in patients with multiple personality disorder. In R. P. Kluft & C. Fine (Eds.), *Clinical perspectives on multiple personality disorder* (pp. 241–251). Washington, DC: American Psychiatric Press.

Finkelhor, D., & Brown, A. (1985). The traumatic impact of child sexual abuse. *American Journal of Orthopsychiatry, 55*, 530–541.

Fish-Murray, C. C., Koby, E. V., & van der Kolk, B. A. (1987). Evolving ideas: The effect of abuse on children's thought. In B. A. van der Kolk (Ed.), *Psychological trauma*. Washington, DC: American Psychiatric Press.

Fisher, C. (1945). Amnestic states and the war neuroses: The psychogenesis of fugues. *Psychoanalytic Quarterly, 14*, 437–468.

Foulkes, S. H. (1965). *Therapeutic group analysis*. New York: International Universities Press.

Fox, M. (1978). On desentimentalizing spirituality. *Spirituality Today, 30*, 64–76.

Fox, M. (1988). *The coming of the cosmic Christ*. San Francisco: Harper & Row.

Frankel, A. S., & Connors, K. J. (1993, April). *Day treatment: The best of both worlds*. Presented at the sixth annual Western Clinical Conference on Multiple Personality and Dissociation, Irvine, CA.

Frankel, F. H. (1990). Hypnotizability and dissociation. *American Journal of Psychiatry, 147*, 823–829.

Frederick, C. (1990, March). *The rapid treatment of obsessive compulsive disorder with ego state therapy: A case study*. Presented at the annual meeting of the American Society of Clinical Hypnosis, Orlando, FL.

Frederick, C. (1992, April). *Bringing up baby: A developmental approach to the management and maturation of child ego states*. Presented at the annual meeting of the American Society of Clinical Hypnosis, Las Vegas.

Frederick, C. (1993a). Pools and wellings: The resolution of refractory intermittent depression with ego-state therapy. *Hypnos, 20,* 221–228.

Frederick, C. (1993b). Mind over matter: Ego-strengthening techniques for GP's. Part I. *Scottish Medicine, 13,* 14.

Frederick, C. (1993c, March). *Who's afraid of the big bad wolf: Ego-state therapy for panic disorder with and without agoraphobia.* Presented at the annual meeting of the American Society of Clinical Hypnosis, New Orleans.

Frederick, C. (1994a, March). *When weight means wait: The hypnotherapeutic treatment of eating disorders induced by PTSD.* Paper presented at the annual meeting of the American Society of Clinical Hypnosis, Philadelphia.

Frederick, C. (1994b, March). *Functionaries, janissaries, and daemons: Some approaches to the management of malevolent ego states.* Presented at the annual meeting of the American Society of Clinical Hypnosis, Philadelphia.

Frederick, C. (1994c, March). *The safety of the therapist: Aspects of the hypnotherapeutic relationship.* Paper presented at the annual meeting of the American Society of Clinical Hypnosis, Philadelphia.

Frederick, C. (1994d). Silent partners: The hypnotherapeutic relationship with non-verbal ego states. *Hypnos, 21,* 141–149 .

Frederick, C., & Kim, S. (1993). Heidi and the little girl: The creation of helpful ego states for the management of performance anxiety. *Hypnos, 20,* 49–58.

Frederick, C., & McNeal, S. (1993). From strength to strength: Inner strength with immature ego states. *American Journal of Clinical Hypnosis, 35,* 250–256.

Frederick, C., & Phillips, M. (1992). The use of hypnotic age progressions as interventions with acute psychosomatic conditions. *American Journal of Clinical Hypnosis, 35,* 89–98.

Frederick, C., Scopelli, R., Van Auken, P., & Sorum, J. (1994, March). *MPD on a budget: Treating severe dissociative disorders in a public outpatient clinic.* Presented at the annual meeting of the American Society of Clinical Hypnosis, Philadelphia.

Freud, A. (1969). Comments on trauma. In *The writings of Anna Freud,* Vol. 5, *1956–1965. Research at the Hampstead Child Therapy Clinic and other papers.* New York: International Universities Press.

Freud, S. (1896). The aetiology of hysteria. In J. Strachey (Ed. & Trans.), *The standard edition of the complete psychological works of Sigmund Freud,* Vol. 3. New York: Norton.

Freud, S. (1910). The future prospects of psycho-analytic therapy. In J. Strachey (Ed. & Trans.), *The standard edition of the complete psychological works of Sigmund Freud,* Vol. 11 (pp. 139–151). New York: Norton.

Freud, S. (1912). The dynamics of transference. In J. Strachey (Ed. & Trans.), *The standard edition of the complete psychological works of Sigmund Freud,* Vol. 12 (pp. 97–108). New York: Norton.

Freud, S. (1913). On beginning the treatment. In J. Strachey (Ed. & Trans.), *The standard edition of the complete psychological works of Sigmund Freud,* Vol. 12 (pp. 121–144). New York: Norton.

Freud, S. (1914). Remembering, repeating, and working-through. In J. Strachey (Ed. & Trans.), *The standard edition of the complete psychologial works of Sigmund Freud,* Vol. 12 (pp.145–156). New York: Norton.

Freud, S. (1920). Beyond the pleasure principle. In J. Strachey (Ed. & Trans.), *The standard edition of the complete psychological works of Sigmund Freud,* Vol. 18 (pp. 3–64). New York: Norton.

Freud, S. (1923/1961). Two encyclopedia articles. In J. Strachey (Ed. & Trans.), *The standard edition of the complete psychological works of Sigmund Freud*, Vol. 18 (pp. 235–259). New York: Norton.

Freud, S. (1933). New introductory lectures on psychoanalysis. In J. Strachey (Ed. and Trans.), *The standard edition of the complete psychological works of Sigmund Freud*, Vol. 22 (pp. 3–182). New York: Norton.

Freud, S. (1937). Analysis terminable and interminable. In J. Strachey (Ed. & Trans.), *The standard edition of the complete psychological works of Sigmund Freud*, Vol. 23 (pp. 216–253). New York: Norton.

Friesen, J. G. (1991). *Uncovering the mystery of MPD*. San Bernardino, CA: Here's Life Publishers.

Frieze, I. (1983). Investigating the causes and consequences of marital rape. *Journal of Women, Culture and Society, 8*, 532–553.

Fromm, E. (1970). Age regression with unexpected reappearance of a repressed childhood language. *Journal of Clinical and Experimental Hypnosis, 18*, 79–88.

Fromm, E. (1979a). An ego psychological theory of altered states of consciousness. *International Journal of Clinical and Experimental Hypnosis, 25*, 372.

Fromm, E. (1979b). The nature of hypnosis and other states of consciousness: An ego-psychological theory. In E. Fromm & R.E. Shor (Eds.), *Hypnosis: Developments in research and new perspectives*, 2nd ed. (pp. 81–103). New York: Adline-Atherton.

Fromm, E. (1984). The theory and practice of hypnoanalysis. In W. C. Wester & A. H. Smith (Eds.), *Clinical hypnosis: A multidisciplinary approach*. Philadelphia: Lippincott.

Fromm-Reichmann, F. (1950). *Principles of intensive psychotherapy*. Chicago: University of Chicago Press.

Ganaway, G. K. (1989). Historical versus narrative truth: Clarifying the role of exogenous trauma in the etiology of MPD and its variants. *Dissociation, 2*(4), 205–220.

Gannon, J. P. (1993). False memory syndrome: How do we come to know what is true? *San Francisco Psychologist, July*, 5–7.

Gardner, G. G. (1976). Hypnosis and mastery: Clinical contributions and directions for research. *International Journal of Clinical and Experimental Hypnosis, 24*, 202–214.

Garte, S. H. (1986). *Sexuality and intimacy in Vietnam veterans with post-traumatic stress disorder (PTSD)*. Unpublished manuscript.

Gendlin, E. T. (1981). *Focusing*. New York: Bantam.

Gelinas, D. (1983). The persistent negative effects of incest. *Psychiatry, 46*, 312–342.

Gil, E. (1988). *Treatment of adult survivors of childhood abuse*. Walnut Creek, CA: Launch Press.

Gil, E. (1991). *Healing power of play: Working with abused children*. New York: Guilford.

Gill, M. M. (1982). *Analysis of transference, Vol. I: Theory and technique*. New York: International Universities Press.

Gill, M. M., & Brenman, M. (1959). *Hypnosis and related states*. New York: International Universities Press.

Gilligan, S. (1985). Generative autonomy: Principles for an Ericksonian hypnotherapy. In J. Zeig (Ed.), *Ericksonian psychotherapy, Vol. I: Structures* (pp. 196–239). New York: Brunner/Mazel.

Gilligan, S. (1987). *Therapeutic trances: The cooperation principle in Ericksonian hypnotherapy*. New York: Brunner/Mazel.

Gilligan, S. (1990). Co-evolution of primary process in brief therapy. In J. Zeig & S.

Gilligan, (Eds.), *Brief therapy: myths, methods, and metaphors* (pp. 359–377). New York: Brunner/Mazel.

Gilligan, S. (1993). Therapeutic rituals: Passages into new identities. In S. Gilligan & R. Price (Eds.), *Therapeutic conversations* (pp. 237–253). New York: Norton.

Gilligan, S. (1994). The fight against fundamentalism: Searching for soul in Erickson's legacy. In J. Zeig (Ed.), *Ericksonian psychotherapy.* New York: Brunner/Mazel.

Glover, E. (1955). *The technique of psycho-analysis.* New York: International Universities Press.

Gold, M., Pottash, A. C., & Sweeney, D. (1982). Antimanic, anti-depressant and antipanic effects of opiates: Clinical neuroanatomical and biochemical evidence. *Annals of the New York Academy of Science, 398,* 140–150.

Goldberg, C. (1991). *Understanding shame.* Northvale, NJ: Jason Aronson.

Goodman, W. K., McDougle, C. J., & Price, L. H. (1992). Pharmacotherapy of obsessive compulsive disorder. *The Journal of Clinical Psychiatry, 53,* 29–37.

Goodwin, J. M. (1980). The etiology of combat-related post-traumatic stress disorders. In T. Williams (Ed.), *Posttraumatic stress disorders of the Vietnam veteran* (pp. 1–23). Cincinnati: Disabled American Veterans.

Goodwin, J. M. (1990). Applying to adult incest victims what we have learned from victimized children. In R. P. Kluft (Ed.), *Incest-related syndromes of adult psychopathology* (pp. 55–74). Washington, DC: American Psychiatric Press.

Goodwin, J. M. (Ed.) (1993). *Rediscovering childhood trauma: Historical casebook and clinical applications.* Washington, DC: American Psychiatric Press.

Goodwin, J. M., & Attias, R. (1993). Eating disorders in survivors of multimodal childhood abuse. In R. P. Kluft & C. Fine (Eds.), *Clinical perspectives on multiple personality disorder* (pp. 327–341). Washington, DC: American Psychiatric Press.

Goodwin, J. M., Cheeves, K., & Connell, V. (1988). Defining a syndrome of severe symptoms in survivors of extreme incestuous abuse. *Dissociation, 1,* 11–16.

Gorsuch, J. (1990). *An invitation to the spiritual journey.* New York: Paulist Press.

Gorsuch, J. (1993, May). *What draws us to God? What holds us back?* A guided spiritual retreat.

Gould, C., & Graham-Costain, V. (1990, November). *Play therapy with ritually abused children.* Presented at the seventh International Conference on Multiple Personality and Dissociative States, Chicago.

Greaves, G. B. (1980). Multiple personality: 165 years after Mary Reynolds. *Journal of Nervous and Mental Disease, 168,* 577–596.

Greaves, G. B. (1988). Common errors in the treatment of multiple personality disorder. *Dissociation, 1*(1), 61–66.

Greenberg, M. S., & van der Kolk, B. A. (1987). Retrieval and integration of traumatic memories with the "painting cure." In B. A. van der Kolk (Ed.), *Psychological trauma* (pp. 191–216). Washington, DC: American Psychiatric Press.

Greenson, R. R. (1961). On silence and the sounds of the analytic hour. *Journal of the American Psychoanalytic Association, 9,* 79–84.

Greenson, R. R. (1967). *The technique and practice of psychoanalysis.* Vol. I. New York: International Universities Press.

Grellert, E. A. (1992). Sources of countertransference in the treatment of MPD for never-multiple and once-multiple therapists. *Treating Abuse Today, 2*(1), 5–8.

Grinder, J., & Bandler, R. (1981). *Trance-formations: Neuro-linguistic programming and the structure of hypnosis.* Moab, UT: Real People Press.

Grinker, R. R., & Spiegel, J. P. (1945). *War neuroses.* Philadelphia: Blakiston.

Grove, D. J., & Panzer, B. I. (1989). *Resolving traumatic memories. Metaphors and symbols in psychotherapy.* New York: Irvington.

Grunhaus, L. (1988). Clinical and psychobiological characteristics of simultaneous panic disorder and major depression. *American Journal of Psychiatry, 145,* 1214–1221.

Gunderson, J. (1984). *Borderline personality disorder.* Washington, DC: American Psychiatric Press.

Guze, H. (1956). The involvement of the hypnotist in the hypnotic session. *Journal of Clinical and Experimental Hypnosis, 4,* 61–68.

Haberman, M. A. (1990). Suggestions for simple and social phobias. In D. C. Hammond (Ed.), *Handbook of hypnotic suggestions and metaphors* (pp. 178–180). New York: Norton.

Hall, R. C., Le Cann, A. F., & Schoolar, J. C. (1978). Amobarbital treatment of multiple personality. *Journal of Nervous and Mental Disease, 166,* 666–670.

Hammond, D. C. (1990a). Formulating hypnotic and posthypnotic suggestions. In D. C. Hammond (Ed.), *Handbook of hypnotic suggestions and metaphors* (pp. 11–44). New York: Norton.

Hammond, D. C. (1990b). *Handbook of hypnotic suggestions and metaphors.* New York: Norton.

Hammond, D. C. (1993). False memories, misrepresentations, and ritual abuse. *American Society of Clinical Hypnosis Newsletter, 34,* 3.

Harlan, S., Rodgers, L., & Slattery, B. (1981). *Male and female adolescent prostitutes: Huckleberry House sexual minority youth services project.* Washington, DC: Youth Development Bureau, U.S. Department of Human Services.

Hartland, J. (1965). The value of "ego strengthening" procedures prior to direct symptom removal under hypnosis. *American Journal of Clinical Hypnosis, 8,* 89–93.

Hartland, J. (1971). Further observations on the use of ego-strengthening techniques. *American Journal of Clinical Hypnosis, 14,* 1–8.

Hartmann, H. (1961). *Ego psychology and the problems of adaptation.* New York: International Universities Press.

Hartmann, H. (1965). *Essays on ego psychology.* New York: International Universities Press.

Havens, R. (1986). Posthypnotic predetermination of therapeutic progress. *American Journal of Clinical Hypnosis, 26,* 78–83.

Hearn, G. (1978). *Susceptibility and the process of social interaction in the hypnotic context.* Unpublished B.A. Honours Thesis, University of Queensland, St. Lucia, Queensland, Australia.

Hedges, L. (1992). *Interpreting the counter-transference.* Northvale, NJ: Jason Aronson.

Herman, J. L. (1981). *Father-daughter incest.* Cambridge, MA: Harvard University Press.

Herman, J. L. (1992). *Trauma and recovery.* New York: Basic Books.

Herman, J. L., Russell, E. H., & Troki, K. (1986). Long-term effects of incestuous abuse in childhood. *American Journal of Psychiatry, 143,* 1293–1296.

Herman, J. L., & Schatzow, E. (1984). Time-limited group therapy for women with a history of incest. *International Journal of Group Psychotherapy, 34,* 605–616.

Herman, J. L., & Schatzow, E. (1987). Recovery and verification of memories of childhood sexual trauma. *Psychoanalytic Psychology, 4,* 1–14.

Herzog, A. (1984). On multiple personality: Comments on diagnosis and therapy. *International Journal of Clinical and Experimental Hypnosis, 22,* 216–233.

Hilgard, E. R. (1965). *Hypnotic susceptibility*. New York: Harcourt, Brace & World.

Hilgard, E. R. (1971). Hypnosis and childlikeness. In J. P. Hill (Ed.), *Minnesota symposium on child psychology*, Vol. V (pp. 29–51). Minneapolis: University of Minnesota Press.

Hilgard, E. R. (1973). A neodissociation interpretation of pain reduction in hypnosis. *Psychological Review, 80*, 396–411.

Hilgard, E. R. (1977). *Divided consciousness: Multiple controls in human thought and action*. New York: Wiley.

Hilgard, E. R. (1984). The hidden observer and multiple personality. *International Journal of Clinical and Experimental Hypnosis, 32*, 248–253

Hill, S., & Goodwin, J. M. (1993). Freud's notes on a seventeenth-century case of demonic possession: Understanding the uses of exorcism. In J. M. Goodwin (Ed.), *Rediscovering childhood trauma* (pp. 45–63). Washington, DC: American Psychiatric Press.

Horevitz, R. P. (1983). Hypnosis for multiple personality disorder: A framework for beginning. *American Journal of Clinical Hypnosis, 26*, 138–145.

Horevitz, R. P., & Braun, B. G. (1984). Are multiple personalities borderline? In B. G. Braun (Ed.). Symposium on multiple personality. *Psychiatric Clinics of North America, 7*, 69–87.

Horner, A. J. (1984). *Object relations and the developing ego in therapy*. Northvale, NJ: Jason Aronson.

Horowitz, M. J. (1973). Phase-oriented treatment of stress response syndromes. *American Journal of Psychotherapy, 27*, 506–515.

Horowitz, M. J. (1974). Stress response syndromes: Character style and dynamic psychotherapy. *Archives of General Psychiatry, 31*, 768–781.

Horowitz, M. J. (1976). *Stress response syndromes*. Northvale, NJ: Jason Aronson.

Horowitz, M. J. (1979). Psychological response to serious life events. In V. Hamilton & D. M. Warburton (Eds.), *Human stress and cognition*. New York: Wiley.

Horowitz, M. J. (1986). *Stress response syndromes*, 2nd ed. New York: Jason Aronson.

Horowitz, M. J., Wilner, N., Kaltreider, N., & Alvarez, M. A. (1980). Signs and symptoms of posttraumatic stress disorder. *Archives of General Psychiatry, 37*, 85–92.

Hull, C. L. (1933). *Hypnosis and suggestibility*. New York: Appleton-Century-Crofts.

Hyde, R., & Weinberg, D. (1991). The process of the MPD therapist and the use of the study grup. *Dissociation, 14*(2), 105–108.

Jacobson, E. (1964). *Anxiety and tension control*. Philadelphia: Lippincott.

Jaffe, R. (1968). Dissociative phenomena in concentration camp inmates. *International Journal of Psychoanalysis, 49*, 310–312.

James, B. (1989). *Treating traumatized children: New insights and creative intervention*. Lexington, MA: Lexington Books.

James, W. (1889). Automatic writing. *Proceedings of the American Society for Psychical Research, 1*, 548–564.

James, W. (1890/1983). *The principles of psychology*. Cambridge: Harvard University Press.

Janal, M. N., Colt, E. W. D., & Clark, W. C. (1984). Pain sensitivity, mood and plasma endocrine levels in man following long-distance running: Effects of naloxone. *Pain, 19*, 13–25.

Janet, P. (1887). L'anesthesie systematisee et la dissociation des phenomenes psychologiques. *Revue philosophique, 23*, 449–472.

Janet, P. (1907). *The major symptoms of hysteria*. New York: Macmillan.

Janet, P. (1911). *The mental state of hystericals*. Paris: Alcan.

Janet, P. (1919). *Psychological healing*, Vol. 1. New York: Macmillan.

Janet, P. (1926). *Les states de l'evolution psychologique*. Paris: Chaline-Maloine.

Janoff-Bulman, R., & Frieze, I. H. (1983). A theoretical perspective for understanding reactions to victimization. *Journal of Social Issues, 39*(2), 1–17.

Jehu, D., Klassen, C., & Gazan, M. (1985). Cognitive restructuring of distorted beliefs associated with childhood sexual abuse. *Journal of Social Work and Human Sexuality, 4*, 49–69.

Jencks, B. (1984). Using the patient's breathing rhythm. In W. C. Wester & A. H. Smith (Eds.), *Clinical hypnosis: A multidisciplinary approach* (pp. 29–41). Philadelphia: Lippincott.

Jung, C. G. (1964). *Man and his symbols*. Garden City, NY: Doubleday.

Jung, C. G. (1928/1971). The spiritual problem of modern man. In J. Campbell (Ed.), *The portable Jung*, Part II (pp. 456–479). New York: Viking.

Jung, C. G. (1969). A review of the complex theory. In *Collected works, Vol. 8. The structure and dynamics of the psyche*. Princeton: Princeton University Press.

Katlan, A. (1973). Children who were raped. In Ruth Eissler et al. (Eds.), *The psychoanalytic study of the child*, Vol. 28 (pp. 208–224). New Haven, CT: Yale University Press.

Kaufman, L., Peck, A., & Tagiuri, C. (1954). The family constellation and overt incestuous relations between father and daughter. *American Journal of Orthopsychiatry, 24*, 266–279.

Keane, T. M., & Kaloupek, D. G. (1982). Imaginal flooding in the treatment of a posttraumatic stress disorder. *Journal of Consulting and Clinical Psychology, 550*(1), 138–140.

Kemp, K., Gilbertson, A. D., & Torem, M. (1988). The differential diagnosis of multiple personality disorder from borderline personality disorder. *Dissociation, 1*, 41–46.

Kempe, R. S., & Kempe, C. H. (1978). *Child abuse*. Cambridge, MA: Harvard University Press.

Kernberg, O. (1984). *Severe personality disorders: Psychotherapeutic strategies*. New Haven: Yale University Press.

Kerr, M., & Bowen, M. (1988). *Family evaluation*. New York: Norton.

Khan, M. M. R. (1963). Silence as communication. *Bulletin of the Menninger Clinic, 27*, 300–317.

Klein, M., Heiman, P., & Money-Kyrle, R. (Eds.), (1957). *New directions in psychoanalysis*. New York: Basic Books.

Kleinhauz, M., & Beran, B. (1981). Misuses of hypnosis: A medical emergency and its treatment. *International Journal of Clinical and Experimental Hypnosis, 29*, 148–161.

Kline, M. V. (1968). Sensory hypnoanalysis. *International Journal of Clinical and Experimental Hypnosis, 16*, 85–100.

Kluft, R. P. (1982). Varieties of hypnotic intervention in the treatment of multiple personality. *American Journal of Clinical Hypnosis, 24*, 230–240.

Kluft, R. P. (1983). Hypnotherapeutic crisis intervention in multiple personality. *American Journal of Clinical Hypnosis, 26*, 73–83.

Kluft, R. P. (1984a). Aspects of the treatment of multiple personality disorder. *Psychiatric Annals, 14*, 51–55.

Kluft, R. P. (1984b). Treatment of multiple personality disorder: A study of 33 cases. *Psychiatric Clinics of North America, 7,* 9–29.

Kluft, R. P. (1985a). *The childhood antecedents of multiple personality disorder.* Washington, DC: American Psychiatric Press.

Kluft, R. P. (1985b). Childhood multiple personality disorder: Predictors, clinical findings, and treatment results. In R. P. Kluft (Ed.), *The childhood antecedents of multiple personality disorder* (pp. 167–196). Washington, DC: American Psychiatric Press.

Kluft, R. P. (1985c). The treatment of multiple personality disorder (MPD): Current concepts. In F. F. Flach (Ed.), *Directions in psychiatry.* New York: Hatherleigh.

Kluft, R. P. (1986). Treating children who have multiple personality disorder. In B. G. Braun (Ed.), *Treatment of multiple personality disorder* (pp. 79–105). Washington, DC: American Psychiatric Press.

Kluft, R. P. (1988). The dissociative disorders. In J. A. Talbott, R. E. Hales, & S. C. Yudofsky (Eds.), *The American Psychiatric Press textbook of psychiatry* (pp. 557–584). Washington, DC: American Psychiatric Press.

Kluft, R. P. (1989). Playing for time: Temporizing techniques in the treatment of multiple personality disorder. *American Journal of Clinical Hypnosis, 32,* 90–98.

Kluft, R. P. (1990a). An abreactive technique. In D. C. Hammond (Ed.), *Handbook of hypnotic suggestions and metaphors* (pp. 526–527). New York: Norton.

Kluft, R. P. (1990b). *The diagnosis and treatment of multiple personality disorder.* Workshop presented at the annual scientific meeting of the American Society of Clinical Hypnosis, Orlando, FL.

Kluft, R. P. (1990c). Incest and subsequent revictimization. In R. P. Kluft (Ed.), *Incest-related syndromes of adult psychopathology.* Washington, DC: American Psychiatric Press.

Kluft, R. P. (1991). Invited discussion of "bandaging a 'broken heart': Hypnoplay therapy in the treatment of multiple personality disorder." *American Journal of Clinical Hypnosis, 34*(1), 15–17.

Kluft, R. P. (1993a). Clinical approaches to the integration of multiple personalities. In R. P. Kluft & C. Fine (Eds.), *Clinical perspectives on multiple personality disorder* (pp. 101–133). Washington, DC: American Psychiatric Press.

Kluft, R. P. (1993b). The initial stages of psychotherapy in the treatment of multiple personality disorder patients. *Dissociation, 6*(2/3), 145–161.

Kluft, R. P., Braun, B. G., & Sachs, R. (1984). Multiple personality, intrafamilial abuse and family psychiatry. *International Journal of Family Psychiatry, 5,* 283–301.

Kohut, H. (1984). *How does analysis cure?* Chicago: University of Chicago Press.

Kornfield, J. (1993). *A path with heart: A guide through the perils and promises of spiritual life.* New York: Bantam.

Kroger, W. S. (1977). *Clinical and experimental hypnosis.* Philadelphia: Lippincott.

Kroger, W. S., & Fezler, W. D. (1976). *Hypnosis and behavior modification: Imagery and conditioning.* Philadelphia: Lippincott.

Kroll, J. (1993). *PTSD/Borderlines in therapy: Finding the balance.* New York: Norton.

Krugman, S. (1987). Trauma and the family: Perspectives on the intergenerational transmission of violence. In B. A. van der Kolk (Ed.), *Psychological trauma.* Washington, DC: American Psychiatric Press.

Krystal, H. (1968). *Massive psychic trauma.* New York: International Universities Press.

Krystal, H. (1978). Trauma and affects. In Albert J. Solnit et al. (Eds.), *The psychoanalytic study of the child*, Vol. 33 (pp. 81–116). New Haven, CT: Yale University Press.

Krystal, H. (1988). *Integration and self-healing: Affect, trauma, alexithymia*. Hillsdale, NJ: Erlbaum.

Krystal, H., & Niederland,W. G. (1968). Clinical observations on the survivor syndrome. In H. Krystal (Ed.), *Massive psychic trauma*. New York: International Universities Press.

Lagache, D. (1953). Some aspects of transference. *International Journal of Psycho-Analysis, 34*, 1–10.

Langs, R. (1977). *The therapeutic interaction: A synthesis*. New York: Jason Aronson.

Langs, R. (1980). *Interactions: The realm of transference and countertransference*. New York: Jason Aronson.

Langs, R. (1988). *A primer of psychotherapy*. New York: Irvington.

Lankton, S. (1980). *Practical magic*. Cupertino, CA: Meta Publications.

Lankton, S. (1992, December). *Strategies for trauma resolution*. Workshop presented at the fifth International Congress on Ericksonian Approaches to Hypnosis and Psychotherapy. Phoenix, AZ.

Lankton, S., & Lankton, C. (1983). *The answer within: A clinical framework for Ericksonian hypnotherapy*. New York: Brunner/Mazel.

Lankton, S., & Lankton, C. (1987). *Enchantment and intervention*. New York: Brunner/Mazel.

Laurence, J. R., & Perry, C. (1983). Hypnotically created memory among highly hypnotizeable subjects. *Science, 222*, 523–524.

Lazar, B. S., & Dempster, C. R. (1984). Operator variables in successful hypnotherapy. *International Journal of Clinical and Experimental Hypnosis, 32*, 28–40.

Lehrer, M. (1986). How much complexity and indirection are necessary? In B. Zilbergeld, M. G. Edelstien, & D. L. Araoz (Eds.), *Hypnosis questions and answers*. New York: Norton.

Leuner, H. (1977). Guided affective imagery: An account of its development. *Journal of Mental Health, 1*, 73–92.

Levine, P. (1991). The body as healer: A revisioning of trauma and anxiety. In M. Sheets-Johnstone (Ed.), *Giving the body its due* (pp. 85–108). Stonybrook, NY: State University of New York Press.

Levine, P. (1994). *Encountering the tiger: How the body heals trauma*. Lyons, CO: Ergos Institute Press.

Levine, S. (1987). *Healing into life and death*. New York: Anchor/Doubleday.

Levitan, A. A., & Jevne, R. (1987). Patients fearful of hypnosis. In B. Zilbergeld, M. G. Edelstien, & D. Araoz (Eds.), *Hypnosis questions and answers*. New York: Norton.

Lindner, H. (1960). The shared neurosis: Hypnotist and subject. *International Journal of Clinical and Experimental Hypnosis, 8*, 61–70.

Lindy, J. (1987). *Vietnam: A casebook*. New York: Brunner/Mazel.

Lister, E. D. (1982). Forced silence: A neglected dimension of trauma. *American Journal of Psychiatry, 139*, 872–876.

Loewenstein, R. J. (1993). Posttraumatic and dissociative aspects of transference and countertransference in the treatment of multiple personality disorder. In R. P. Kluft & C. G. Fine (Eds.), *Clinical perspectives on multiple personality disorder* (pp. 51–86). Washington, DC: American Psychiatric Press.

Loewenstein, R. J., Hornstein, N., & Farber, B. (1990). Open trial of clonazepam in the treatment of posttraumatic stress symptoms in MPD. *Dissociation, 3,* 22–30.

Loftus, E. F. (1979). *Eyewitness testimony.* Cambridge, MA: Harvard University Press.

Loftus, E. F. (1993) The reality of repressed memories. *American Psychologist, 48*(5), 518–537.

Loftus, E. F., Miller, D. G., & Burns, H. J. (1978). Semantic integration of verbal information into a visual memory. *Journal of Experimental Psychology: Human Learning and Memory, 4* , 19–31.

Loftus, E. F., & Zanni, G. (1975). Eyewitness testimony: The influence of the wording of a question. *Bulletin of the Psychonomic Society, 5,* 86–88.

Maier, S. F., & Seligman, M. E. P. (1976). Learned helplessness: Theory and evidence. *Journal of Experimental Psychology, 105,* 3–46.

Mann, H. (1986). Describing hypnosis to patients. In B. Zilbergeld, M. G. Edelstien, & D. Araoz, (Eds.), *Hypnosis questions and answers.* New York: Norton

Marmer, S. S. (1980). Psychoanalysis of multiple personality disorder. *International Journal of Psychoanalysis, 61,* 439–459.

Marmor, J. (1972). Sexual acting-out in psychotherapy. *American Journal of Psychoanalysis, 32,* 3–8.

Maslow, A. H. (1970). *Religions, values, and peak-experiences.* New York: Penguin.

Masterson, J. (1981). *The narcissistic and borderline disorders: A developmental approach.* New York: Brunner/Mazel.

May, G. G. (1988). *Addiction and grace: Love and spirituality in the healing of addictions.* San Francisco: Harper & Row.

May, G. G. (1991). *The awakened heart: Opening yourself to the love you need.* San Francisco: Harper & Row.

McCaffrey, R. J., & Fairbank, J. A. (1985). Behavioral assessment and treatment of accident-related posttraumatic stress disorder: Two case studies. *Behavior Therapy, 16,* 406–416.

McCann, I. L., & Pearlman, L. A. (1990). *Psychological trauma and the adult survivor: Theory, therapy, and transformation.* New York: Brunner/Mazel.

McDougall, J. (1979). Primitive communication and the use of countertransference. In L. Epstein & A. Feiner (Eds.), *Countertransference.* New York: Jason Aronson.

McMahon, E. (1986). Creative self-mothering. In B. Zilbergeld, M. G. Edelstien, & D. Araoz (Eds.), *Hypnosis questions and answers* (pp. 150–155). New York: Norton.

McNeal, S., & Frederick, C. (1993). Inner strength and other techniques for ego-strengthening. *American Journal of Clinical Hypnosis, 35,* 170–178.

McNeal, S., & Frederick, C. (1994, March). *Internal self-soothing: Other implications of "inner strength" with ego states.* Paper presented at the annual meeting of the American Society of Clinical Hypnosis, Philadelphia.

Meares, A. (1957). *Hypnography: A study of the therapeutic use of hypnotic painting.* Springfield, IL: Thomas.

Merwin, M. R., & Smith-Kurtz, B. (1988). Healing of the whole person. In F. M. Ochberg (Ed.), *Post-traumatic therapy and victims of violence* (pp. 57–82). New York: Brunner/Mazel.

Miczek, K. A., Thompson, M. L., & Shuster, L. (1982). Opioid-like analgesia in defeated mice. *Science, 215,* 1520–1522.

Miller, A. (1981). *Prisoners of childhood: The drama of the gifted child and the search for the true self.* New York: Basic Books.

Miller, A. (1984). *Thou shalt not be aware: Society's betrayal of the child.* New York: Farrar, Straus, & Giroux.

Miller, A. (1986). Hypnotherapy in a case of dissociated incest. *International Journal of Clinical and Experimental Hypnosis, 34,* 13–28.

Miller, D. (1994). *Women who hurt themselves: A book of hope and understanding.* New York: Basic Books.

Mills, J. C., & Crowley, R. J. (1986). *Therapeutic metaphors for children and the child within.* New York: Brunner/Mazel.

Mindell, A. (1985). *Working with the dreaming body.* London: Arkana.

Monane, M., Leichter, D., & Lewis, D. O. (1984). Physical abuse in psychiatrically hospitalized children and adolescents. *Journal of the American Academy of Child Psychiatry, 23,* 653–658.

Muller, W. (1992). *Legacy of the heart: The spiritual advantages of a painful childhood.* New York: Simon & Schuster.

Murphy, P. (1993). *Making the connections: Women, work, and abuse.* Orlando, FL: Paul M. Deutsch.

Murray-Jobsis, J. (1984). Hypnosis with severely disturbed patients. In W. C. Wester & A. H. Smith (Eds.), *Clinical hypnosis: A multidisciplinary approach* (pp. 368–404). Philadelphia: Lippincott.

Murray-Jobsis, J. (1985). Exploring the schizophrenic experience with the use of hypnosis. *American Journal of Clinical Hypnosis, 28,* 34–42.

Murray-Jobsis, J. (1990a). Renurturing: Forming positive sense of identity and bonding. In D. C. Hammond (Ed.), *Handbook of hypnotic suggestions and metaphors* (pp. 326–328). New York: Norton.

Murray-Jobsis, J. (1990b). Suggestions for creative self-mothering. In D. C. Hammond (Ed.), *Handbook of hypnotic suggestions and metaphors* (p. 328). New York: Norton.

Napier, N. J. (1993). *Getting through the day: Strategies for adults hurt as children.* New York: Norton.

Nathanson, D. L. (1992). *Shame and pride: Affect, sex, and the birth of the self.* New York: Norton.

Neswald, D. (1992, April). *Working with primal dissociative experiences in adult MPD survivors of satanic ritual abuse.* Presented at the sixth annual Western Clinical Conference on Multiple Personality and Dissociation, Costa Mesa, CA.

Newey, A. B. (1986). Ego state therapy with depression. In B. Zilbergeld, M. G. Edelstien, & D. L. Araoz (Eds.), *Hypnosis questions and answers.* New York: Norton.

Niederland, W. G. (1981). The survivor syndrome: Further observations and dimensions. *Journal of the American Psychoanalytic Association, 29*(2), 413–425.

Novaco, R. W. (1977). Stress inoculation training: A cognitive therapy for anger and its application to a case of depression. *Journal of Consulting and Clinical Psychology, 45*(4), 600–608.

Orne, M. T. (1959). The nature of hypnosis: Artifact and essence. *Journal of Abnormal Social Psychology, 58,* 277–279.

Orne, M. T., Whitehouse, W. G., Dinges, D. F., & Orne, E. C. (1988). Reconstructing memory through hypnosis: Forensic and clinical implications. In H. M. Pettinati (Ed.), *Hypnosis and memory* (pp. 21–63). New York: Guilford.

Ornstein, P., & Ornstein, A. (1976). On the continuing evaluation of psychoanalytic psychotherapy: Reflections and predictions. In *Annals of Psychoanalysis, Vol. V* (pp. 329–355). New York: International Universities Press.

Overton, D. (1978). Major theories of state-dependent learning. In B. Ho, D. Richards, & D. Chute (Eds.), *Drug discrimination and state dependent learning*. New York: Academic Press.

Panos, P. T., Panos, A., & Allred, G. H. (1990). The need for marriage therapy in the treatment of multiple personality disorder. *Dissociation, 3*(1), 10–14.

Pardell, S. S. (1950). Psychology of the hypnotist. *Psychiatric Quarterly, 24*, 483–491.

Parson, E. R. (1984). The reparation of self: Clinical and theoretical dimensions in the treatment of Vietnam combat veterans. *Journal of Contemporary Psychotherapy, 14*, 4–56.

Parson, E. R. (1988). Post-traumatic self disorders: Theoretical and practical considerations in psychotherapy of Vietnam war veterans. In J. P. Wilson, Z. Harel, & B. Kahana (Eds.), *Human adaptation to extreme stress: From the holocaust to Vietnam* (pp. 245–284). New York: Plenum Press.

Peebles, M. J. (1989). Through a glass darkly: The psychoanalytic use of hypnosis with post-traumatic stress disorder. *International Journal of Clinical and Experimental Hypnosis, 37*, 192–206.

Peebles-Kleiger, M. J. (1989). Using countertransference in the hypnosis of trauma victims: A model for turning hazard into healing. *American Journal of Psychotherapy, 48*, 518–530.

Perry, N. E. (1994). Clinical corner: The polarities of misdiagnosis. *International Society of Multiple Personality and Dissociation, 12*(2), 12–13.

Pert, C. (1981). Type 1 and type 2 opiate receptor distribution in the brain—what does it tell us? In J. Martin, S, Reichlin, & K. Bick (Eds.) *Neurosecretion and brain peptides: Advances in biochemical psychopharmacology, Vol 28* (pp. 117–131). New York: Raven Press.

Peters, J. J. (1976). Children who are victims of sexual assault and the psychology of offenders. *American Journal of Psychotherapy, 30*, 398–421.

Peterson, K. C., Prout, M. F., & Schwarz, R. A. (1991). *Post-traumatic stress disorder: A clinician's guide*. New York: Plenum Press.

Peterson, M. R. (1992). *At personal risk: Boundary violations in professional-client relationships*. New York: Norton.

Pettinati, H. M. (1988) (Ed.) *Hypnosis and memory*. New York: Guilford.

Phillips, M. (1989). Ericksonian options in redecision therapy. *Transactional Analysis Journal, 19*(2), 66–74.

Phillips, M. (1993a, March). *The high road or the low road? Using the language of cooperation to strengthen the hypnotherapeutic relationship*. Presented at the annual meeting of the American Society of Clinical Hypnosis, New Orleans.

Phillips, M. (1993b). Turning symptoms into allies: Utilization approaches with posttraumatic symptoms. *American Journal of Clinical Hypnosis, 35*(3), 179–189.

Phillips, M. (1993c). The use of ego-state therapy in the treatment of post-traumatic stress disorder. *American Journal of Clinical Hypnosis, 35*(4), 241–249.

Phillips, M. (1994, March). *Developing a positive countertransference "trance'" in treating posttraumatic patients*. Presented at the annual meeting of the American Society of Clinical Hypnosis, Philadelphia.

Phillips, M. (in press). Our bodies, our selves: Treating the somatic manifestations of trauma with ego-state therapy. *American Journal of Clinical Hypnosis*.

Phillips, M., & Frederick, C. (1991). Hypnose et syndrome "dissociatif " chez les patients chroniques. *Nervure: Journal de Psychiatrie, 4*, 30–35.

Phillips, M., & Frederick, C. (1992). The use of hypnotic age progressions as prognostic, ego-strengthening, and integrating techniques. *American Journal of Clinical Hypnosis, 35*, 90–108.

Phillips, M., & Frederick, C. (1993, March). *Decoding mystifying signals: Translating symbolic communications of elusive ego states.* Presented at the Annual Meeting of the American Society of Clinical Hypnosis, New Orleans.

Physicians' Desk Reference, 48th Edition (1994). Montvale, NY: Medical Economics Data.

Pope, K. S., & Bouhoutsos, J. C. (1986). *Sexual intimacy between therapists and patients.* New York: Praeger.

Price, D. R. (1990). Corporate headquarters of the mind. In D. C. Hammond (Ed.), *Handbook of hypnotic suggestions and metaphors* (pp. 343–346). New York: Norton.

Prince, M. (1906/1969). *The dissociation of a personality.* Westport, CT: Greenwood. (Original work published in 1906).

Putnam, F. W. (1985). Dissociation as a response to extreme trauma. In R.P. Kluft (Ed.), *The childhood antecedents of multiple personality.* Washington, DC: American Psychiatric Press.

Putnam, F. W. (1989). *Diagnosis and treatment of multiple personality disorder.* New York: Guilford.

Putnam, F. W., Guroff, J. J., Silberman, E. K., Barban, L., & Post, R. M. (1986). The clinical phenomenology of multiple personality disorder: A review of 100 recent cases. *Journal of Clinical Psychiatry, 47*, 285–293.

Putnam, F. W., & Loewenstein, R. J. (1993). Treatment of multiple personality disorder: A survey of current practices. *American Journal of Psychiatry, 150*(7), 1048–1052.

Racker, H. (1957). The meanings and uses of countertransference. *Psychoanalytic Quarterly, 26*, 303–357.

Raginsky, B. (1967). Rapid regression to the oral and anal levels through sensory hypnoplasty. *International Journal of Clinical and Experimental Hypnosis, 15*, 19–30.

Rappaport, D. (1959). Introduction. A historical survey of psychoanalytic ego psychology: Identity and the life cycle. *Psychological Issues, 1*, 1–17.

Ray, S., Reagor, P. A., Del Real, F., Wong, P., Huggins, S., & Kohl, K. (1993, April). *Medication-assisted interviews with structure MPD.* Presented at the sixth annual Western Clinical Conference on Multiple Personality and Dissociation, Irvine, CA.

Reagor, P. A. (1993, April). *Sabotage of the therapeutic relationship: A tape by a healing patient.* Presented at the sixth annual Western Clinical Conference on Multiple Personality and Dissociation, Irvine, CA.

Reagor, P. A., & Connors, K. (1993, April). *Mind control and psychotherapy: Advanced issues and strategies.* Presented at the sixth annual Western Clinical Conference on Multiple Personality and Dissociation, Irvine, CA.

Reite, M., Short, R., & Seiler, C. (1978). Physiological correlates of separation in surrogate-reared infants: A study in altered attachment bonds. *Developmental Psychobiology, 11*, 427–435.

Reite, M., Short, R., & Seiler, C. (1981). Attachment, loss, and depression. *Journal of Child Psychology and Psychiatry, 22*, 141–169.

Reyher, J. (1977). Spontaneous visual imagery: Implications for psychoanalysis, psychopathology, and psychotherapy. *Journal of Mental Imagery, 2*, 253–274.

Ritterman, M. (1983). *Using hypnosis in family therapy.* San Francisco: Jossey–Bass.

Rochman, S. (1993). Massage therapy for survivors of childhood sexual abuse. *Massage, 43*, 22–28.

Rosen, H., & Bartemeier, L. (1961). Hypnosis in medical practice. *Journal of the American Medical Association, 75,* 128.

Rosen, H., & Myers, H. J. (1947). Abreaction in the military setting. *Archives of Neurology and Psychiatry, 57,* 161–172.

Rosen, J. N. (1962). *Direct analytic therapy.* New York: Grune & Stratton.

Rosenfeld, H. A. (1966). *Psychotic states, A psycho-analytical approach.* New York: International Universities Press.

Ross, C. J. (1989). *Multiple personality disorder.* New York: Wiley.

Ross, C. J. (1994, April). Presidential message. *ISSMP&D Newsletter,* 1–2.

Ross, C. J., & Anderson, G. (1988). Phenomenological overlap of multiple personality disorder and obsessive-compulsive disorder. *Journal of Nervous and Mental Disease, 176,* 295–299.

Ross, C. J., Heber, S., Norton, G. R., & Anderson, G. (1989). Differences between multiple personality disorder and other diagnostic groups on structured interview. *Journal of Nervous and Mental Disease, 179,* 487–491.

Rossi, E. L. (1993a). *The psychobiology of mind-body healing: New concepts of therapeutic hypnosis (Revised edition).* New York: Norton.

Rossi, E. L. (1993b, April). *Basic approaches to mind-body healing: 1,2,3 fail-safe methods.* Presented at the sixth annual Western Clinical Conference on Multiple Personality and Dissociation, Irvine, CA.

Rossi, E. L., & Cheek, D. B. (1988). *Mind-body therapy: Ideodynamic healing in hypnosis.* New York: Norton.

Rossi, E. L. & Cheek, D. B. (1990). Direct suggestions in emergencies with the critically ill. In D. C. Hammond (Ed.), *Handbook of hypnotic suggestions and metaphors* (pp.233–234). New York: Norton.

Rossman, M. L. (1987). *Healing yourself: A step-by-step program for better health through imagery.* New York: Walker.

Roth, W. T. (1982). The meaning of stress. In F. M. Ochberg & D. A. Soskis (Eds.), *Victims of terrorism.* Boulder, CO: Westview Press.

Roth, W. T (1988). The role of medication in post-traumatic therapy. In F. M. Ochberg (Ed.), *Post-traumatic therapy and victims of violence* (pp. 39–56). New York: Brunner/Mazel.

Russell, D. (1986). *The secret trauma.* New York: Basic Books.

Sachs, R. G. (1986). The adjunctive role of social support systems in the treatment of multiple personality disorder. In B. G. Braun (Ed.), *The treatment of multiple personality disorder* (pp. 159–174). Washington, DC: American Psychiatric Press.

Sachs, R. G., & Braun, B. A. (1986). The use of sand worlds with the MPD patient. In B. G. Braun (Ed.), *Dissociative disorders 1986: Proceedings of the third International Conference on Multiple Personality/Dissociative States.* Chicago: Rush University.

Sachs, R. G., & Peterson, J. A. (1993). *Processing memories retrieved by trauma victims and survivors: A primer for therapists.* Tyler, TX: Family Violence and Sexual Assault Institute.

Sachs, R. G., & Peterson, J. A. (1994). *Processing memories retrieved by trauma victims and survivors: A primer for therapists.* Tyler, TX: Family Violence & Sexual Assault Institute.

Salzman, L., & Thaler, F. H. (1981). Obsessive compulsive disorders: A review of the literature. *American Journal of Psychiatry, 138,* 286–296.

Sansonnet-Hayden, H., Haley, G., Marriage, K., et al. (1987). Sexual abuse and psychopathology in hospitalized adolescents. *Journal of the American Academy of Child Psychiatry, 26,* 753–757.

Scagnelli, J. (1972). Hypnotherapy with psychotic and borderline patients: The use of trance by patient and therapist. *American Journal of Clinical Hypnosis, 22,* 164–169.

Scagnelli, J. (1976). Hypnotherapy with schizophrenic and borderline patients. *American Journal of Clinical Hypnosis, 19,* 33–38.

Scagnelli-Jobsis, J. (1982). Hypnosis with psychotic patients: A review of the literature and presentation of a clinical framework. *American Journal of Clinical Hypnosis, 25,* 33–45.

Schatzberg, A. F., & Cole, J. O. (1986). *Clinical guide to psychopharmacology.* Washington, DC: American Psychiatric Press.

Schetky, D. H. (1990). A review of the literature on the long-term effects of childhood sexual abuse. In R.P. Kluft (Ed.), *Incest-related syndromes of adult psychopathology* (pp. 35–54). Washington, DC: American Psychiatric Press.

Schwing, G. (1940). *A way to the soul of the mentally ill.* New York: International Universities Press.

Searles, H. F. (1960). *The nonhuman environment in normal development and schizophrenia.* New York: International Universities Press.

Searles, H. F. (1965). *Collected papers on schizophrenia and selected topics.* New York: International Universities Press.

Sechehaye, M. A. (1947). *Symbolic realization.* New York: International Universities Press.

Seligman, M. E. P. (1975). *Helplessness: On depression, development and death.* San Francisco: Freeman.

Sgroi, S. (1989). Stages of recovery for adult survivors of child sexual abuse. In S. Sgroi (Ed.), *Vulnerable populations, Vol. II* (pp. 11–130). Lexington, MA: D. C. Heath.

Shaffer, J. & Galinsky, M. D. (1974). *Models of group therapy and sensitivity training,* Englewood, NJ: Prentice-Hall.

Shapiro, F. (1989a). Efficacy of the eye movement desensitization procedure in the treatment of traumatic memories. *Journal of Traumatic Stress, 2,* 199–223.

Shapiro, F. (1989b). Eye movement desensitization procedure: A new treatment for the post traumatic stress disorder. *Journal of Behavior Therapy and Experimental Psychiatry, 20,* 211–217.

Shapiro, F. (1991). Eye movement desensitization and reprocessing procedure: From EMD to EMD/R–A new treatment model for anxiety and related traumata. *The Behavior Therapist, 14,* 133–135.

Shapiro, F. (1993a). In S. Thomson, An interview with Francine Shapiro, Part I. *Treating Abuse Today, 3*(2), pp. 26–33.

Shapiro, F. (1993b). *1993 update and cautions.* Unpublished newsletter.

Shapiro, M. K. (1988). *Second childhood: Hypnoplay therapy with age-regressed adults.* New York: Norton.

Sheehan, P. W., & McConkey, K. M. (1982). *Hypnosis and experience: The exploration of phenomena and process.* Hillsdale, NJ: Erlbaum.

Shor, R. E. (1959). Hypnosis and the concept of generalized reality orientation. *American Journal of Psychotherapy, 13,* 582–602.

Shor, R. E. (1979). A phenomenological method for the measurement of variables important to an understanding of the nature of hypnosis. In E. Fromm & R. E. Shor (Eds.), *Hypnosis: Developments in research and new perspectives (2nd rev. ed.)* (pp. 105–135). New York: Aldine.

Silbert, M., & Pines, A. (1981). Sexual abuse as an antecedent to prostitution. *Child Abuse and Neglect, 5*, 407–411.

Silver, S. M., & Kelly, W. E. (1985). Hypnotherapy of post-traumatic stress disorder in combat veterans from WW II and Vietnam. In W. E. Kelly (Ed.), *Post-traumatic stress disorder and the war veteran patient* (pp. 43–53). New York: Brunner/Mazel.

Simonds, S. L. (1994). *Bridging the silence*. New York: Norton.

Singer, J. S. (1974). *Imagery and daydream methods in psychotherapy and behavior modification*. New York: Academic Press.

Smith, A.H. (1984). Sources of efficacy in the hypnotic relationship–An object relations approach. In W. C. Wester & A. H. Smith, (Eds.), *Clinical hypnosis: A multidisciplinary approach* (pp. 85–114). Philadelphia: Lippincott.

Spanos, N. P. (1982). Hypnotic behavior: A cognitive, social, psychological perspective. *Research Communications in Psychology, Psychiatry, and Behavior, 7*, 199–213.

Spence, D. P. (1982). *Narrative truth and historical truth: Meaning and interpretation in psychoanalysis*. New York: Norton.

Spiegel, D. (1981). Vietnam grief work using hypnosis. *American Journal of Clinical Hypnosis, 24*(1), 33–40.

Spiegel, D. (1986). Dissociating damage. *American Journal of Clinical Hypnosis, 29*, 123–130.

Spiegel, D. (1988). Dissociation and hypnosis in post-traumatic stress disorders. *Journal of Traumatic Stress, 1*, 17–33.

Spiegel, D. (1990). Trauma, dissociation, and hypnosis. In R. P. Kluft (Ed.), *Incest-related syndromes of adult psychopathology* (pp. 247–262). Washington, DC: American Psychiatric Press.

Spiegel, D. (1991). Invited discussion of "Bandaging a 'broken heart': Hypnoplay therapy in the treatment of multiple personality disorder." *American Journal of Clinical Hypnosis, 34*(1), 19–20.

Spiegel, D. (1993). Multiple posttraumatic personality disorder. In R. P. Kluft & C. G. Fine (Eds.), *Clinical perspectives on multiple personality disorder* (pp. 87–100). Washington, DC: American Psychiatric Press.

Spiegel, D., & Fink, R. (1979). Hysterical psychosis and hypnotizability. *American Journal of Psychiatry, 136*, 777–781.

Spiegel, H. (1972). An eye-roll test for hypnotizability. *American Journal of Clinical Hypnosis, 15*, 25–28.

Spiegel, H., & Spiegel, D. (1978). *Trance and treatment: Clinical uses of hypnosis*. New York: Basic Books.

Stanton, H. E. (1979). Increasing internal control through hypnotic ego-enhancement. *Australian Journal of Clinical and Experimental Hypnosis, 7*, 219–223.

Stanton, H. E. (1989). Ego-enhancement: A five-step approach. *American Journal of Clinical Hypnosis, 31*, 192–1989.

Stanton, H. E. (1990). Ego-enhancement: A five-step approach. In D. C. Hammond (Ed.), *Handbook of hypnotic suggestions and metaphors*. New York: Norton.

Stark, E., & Flitcraft, A. H. (1981). *Wife abuse in a medical setting: An introduction for health personnel (Monograph No. 7)*. Washington, DC: Office of Domestic Violence.

Steindl-Rast, D. (1984). *Gratefulness, the heart of prayer: An approach to life in fullness*. New York: Paulist Press.

Sterba, R. F. (1929). The dynamics of the dissolution of the transference resistance. *Psychoanalytic Quarterly, 9*, 363–379.

Sterba, R. F. (1934). The fate of the ego in analytic therapy. *International Journal of Psychoanalysis, 15*, 117–126.

Stone, M. (1976). Boundary violations between therapist and patient. *Psychiatric Annals, 6*, 670–676.

Stutman, R. K., & Bliss, E. L. (1985). Posttraumatic stress disorder: Hypnotizability and imagery. *American Journal of Psychiatry, 112*, 741–743.

Summit, R. C., & Kryso, J. A. (1978). Sexual abuse of children: A clinical spectrum. *American Journal of Orthopsychiatry, 48*, 237–251.

Teilhard de Chardin, P. (1964). *The future of man*. New York: Harper & Row.

Teilhard de Chardin, P. (1969). *Human energy*. New York: Harcourt, Brace, Jovanovich.

Teilhard de Chardin, P. (1966/1973). *On happiness*. London: Collins.

Terr, L. (1990). *Too scared to cry: Psychic trauma in childhood*. New York: Basic Books.

Terr, L. (1991). Childhood traumas: An outline and overview. *The American Journal of Psychiatry, 148*, 10–20.

Terr, L. (1994). *Unchained memories: True stories of traumatic memories, lost and found*. New York: Basic Books.

Thames, L. (1984, September). *Limit setting and behavioral contracting with the client with multiple personality disorder*. Paper presented at the first International Meeting on Multiple Personality and Dissociative Disorders, Chicago.

Torem, M. (1984, September). *Anorexia nervosa and multiple dissociated ego states*. Presented at the first International Conference on Multiple Personality and Dissociated States, Chicago.

Torem, M. (1986). Dissociative states presenting as an eating disorder. *American Journal of Clinical Hypnosis, 29*, 137–142.

Torem, M. (1987). Ego state therapy for eating disorders. *American Journal of Clinical Hypnosis, 30*, 94–103.

Torem, M. (1992). "Back from the future": A powerful age-progression technique. *American Journal of Clinical Hypnosis, 35*, 81–88.

Torem, M. (1993a). Eating disorders in patients with multiple personality disorder. In R. P. Kluft & C. Fine (Eds.), *Clinical perspectives on multiple personality disorder*. Washington, DC: American Psychiatric Press.

Torem, M. (1993b). Therapeutic writing as a form of ego-state therapy. *American Journal of Clinical Hypnosis, 35*(4), 267–276.

Torem, M. (1994, March). *Ego state graphotherapy*. Paper presented at the annual meeting of the American Society of Clinical Hypnosis, Philadelphia.

Torem, M., Gilbertson, A., & Kemp, K. (1990). *Future oriented guided imagery as a crisis intervention technique in the treatment of suicidal multiple personality disorder patients*. Presented at the annual meeting of the American Society of Clinical Hypnosis. Orlando, FL.

Tulving, E. (1972). Episodic and semantic memory. In E. Tulving & W. Donaldson (Eds.), *Organization of memory* (pp. 381–403). New York: McGraw-Hill.

Turner, S. M., Bidel, D. C., & Nathan, R. S. (1985). Biological factors in obsessive-compulsive disorders. *Psychological Bulletin, 97*, 430–450.

Udolf, R. (1981). *Handbook of hypnosis for professionals*. New York: Van Nostrand Reinhold.

Van der Hart, O., & Brown, P. (1992). Abreaction re-evaluated. *Dissociation, 5*(3), 127–140.

Van der Hart, O., Brown, P., & van der Kolk, B. (1989). Pierre Janet's psychological treatment of post-traumatic stress. *Journal of Traumatic Stress, 2*(4), 379–395.

Van der Hart, O., Steele, K., Boon, S., & Brown, P. (1993). The treatment of traumatic memories: Synthesis, realization, and integration. *Dissociation, 6*(2/3), 162–180.

Van der Kolk, B. A. (1985). Adolescent vulnerability to post-traumatic stress disorder. *Psychiatry, 48*, 365–370.

Van der Kolk, B. A. (Ed.) (1987a). *The psychobiology of the trauma response: Psychological trauma.* Washington, DC: American Psychiatric Press.

Van der Kolk, B. A. (1987b). The drug treatment of PTSD. *Journal of the Affective Disorders, 13*, 203–213.

Van der Kolk, B. A. (1987c). The psychological consequences of overwhelming life experiences. In B. A. van der Kolk (Ed.), *Psychological trauma* (pp. 1–30). Washington, DC: American Psychiatric Press.

Van der Kolk, B. A. (1989). The compulsion to repeat the trauma: Re-enactment, revictimization, and masochism. *Psychiatric Clinics of North America, 12*(2), 389–411.

Van der Kolk, B. A. (1994). The body keeps the score: Memory and the evolving psychobiology of posttraumatic stress. *Harvard Review of Psychiatry, 1*, 253–265.

Van der Kolk, B. A., & Greenberg, M. S. (1987). The psychobiology of the trauma response: Hyperarousal, constriction, and addiction to traumatic reexposure. In B. A. van der Kolk (Ed.), *Psychological trauma* (pp. 63–88). Washington, DC: American Psychiatric Press.

Van der Kolk, B. A., Greenberg, M. S., & Boyd, H. (1985). Inescapable shock, neurotransmitters and addiction to trauma. Towards a psychobiology of post traumatic stress. *Biological Psychiatry, 20*, 314–325.

Vereby, K., Volavka, J., & Clouet, D. (1978). Endorphins in psychiatry. *Archives of General Psychiatry, 35*, 877–888.

Veronen, L. J., & Kilpatrick, D. G. (1983). Stress management for rape victims. In D. Meichenbaum & M. Jerenko (Eds.), *Stress reduction and prevention.* New York: Plenum Press.

Victor, J. S. (1992). Ritual abuse and the moral crusade against satanism. *Journal of Psychology and Theology, 20*, 248–253.

Waites, E. (1993). *Trauma and survival: Post-traumatic and dissociative disorders in women.* New York: Norton.

Walker, L. (1979). *The battered woman.* New York: Harper & Row.

Walker, L. (1985). The battered woman syndrome study. In D. Finkelhor, R. J. Gelles, G. T. Hotaling, & M. A. Straus (Eds.), *The dark side of families* (pp. 31–48). Beverly Hills, CA: Sage.

Wallas, L. (1985). *Stories for the third ear.* New York: Norton.

Watkins, H. H. (1980). The silent abreaction. *International Journal of Clinical and Experimental Hypnosis, 23*(2), 101–113.

Watkins, H. H. (1990). Hypnotherapeutic technique for the reduction of guilt: The door of forgiveness. In D. C. Hammond (Ed.), *Handbook of hypnotic suggestions and metaphors* (pp. 312–313). New York: Norton.

Watkins, J. G. (1949). *Hypnotherapy of war neuroses.* New York: Ronald Press.

Watkins, J. G. (1963). Transference aspects of the hypnotic relationship. In M.V. Kline (Ed.), *Clinical correlations of experimental hypnosis.* Springfield, IL: Thomas.

Watkins, J. G. (1971). The affect bridge: A hypnoanalytic technique. *International Journal of Clinical and Experimental Hypnosis, 19*, 21–27.

Watkins, J. G. (1978). *The therapeutic self.* New York: Human Sciences Press.

Watkins, J. G. (1987). *The practice of clinical hypnosis. Volume I: Hypnotherapeutic techniques.* New York: Irvington.

Watkins, J. G. (1990). Watkins' affect or somatic bridge. In D. C. Hammond (Ed.), *Handbook of hypnotic suggestions and metaphors* (pp. 523–524). New York: Norton.

Watkins, J. G. (1992). *The practice of clinical hypnosis, Vol. II: Hypnoanalytic techniques.* New York: Irvington.

Watkins, J. G., & Watkins, H. H. (1979). The theory and practice of ego-state therapy. In H. Grayson (Ed.), *Short term approaches to psychotherapy* (pp. 176–220). New York: Wiley.

Watkins, J. G., & Watkins, H. H. (1984). Hazards to the therapist in the treatment of multiple personalities. In B. G. Braun (Ed.), *Symposium on multiple personality, The Psychiatric Clinics of North America, 7*, 111–119.

Watkins, J. G., & Watkins, H. H. (1988). The management of malevolent ego states in multiple personality disorder. *Dissociation, 1*, 67–71.

Watkins, J. G., & Watkins, H. H. (1991). Hypnosis and ego-state therapy. In P. A. Keller & S. R. Heyman (Eds.), *Innovations in clinical practice, Vol. 10* (pp. 23–37). Sarasota, FL: Professional Resources Exchange.

Watzlawick, P., Weakland, J., & Fisch, R. (1974). *Change: Principles of problem formation and problem resolution.* New York: Norton.

Weitzenhoffer, A. M. (1957). *General techniques of hypnotism.* New York: Grune & Stratton.

Weitzenhoffer, A. M., & Hilgard, E. R. (1959). *Stanford hypnotic susceptibility scales, Forms A and B.* Palo Alto, CA: Consulting Psychologists Press.

Wester, W. C. (1984). Preparing the patient. In W. C. Wester & A. H. Smith (Eds.), *Clinical hypnosis: A multidisciplinary approach.* Philadelphia: Lippincott.

Wester, W. C., & Smith, A. H. (Eds.) (1984). *Clinical hypnosis: A multidisciplinary approach.* Philadephia: Lippincott.

Whitaker, C., & Malone, T. (1981). *The roots of psychotherapy.* New York: Brunner/Mazel.

Williams, L. M. (1992). Adult memories of childhood abuse: Preliminary findings from a longitudinal study. *The Advisor, 5*(3), 19–21.

Williams, M. B. (1991). Clinical work with families of multiple personality patients: Assessment and issues for practice. *Dissociation, 4*, 192–198.

Williams, M. B. (1993). Establishing safety in survivors of severe sexual abuse in post-traumatic stress therapy, Part III. *Treating Abuse Today, 3*(3), 13–15.

Winn, R. (1988). Working with incest survivors. Part I: When is Rosen method appropriate? *RMPA Views, 2*, August/September, p. 3.

Winnicott, D. W. (1949). Hate in the countertransference. *International Journal of Psycho-analysis, 30*, 69–75.

Winnicott, D. W. (1965a). Ego integration in child development. In *Maturational processes and the facilitating environment* (pp. 140–152). New York: International Universities Press.

Winnicott, D. W. (1965b). The theory of the parent-infant relationship. In *Maturational processes and the facilitating environment* (pp. 37–55). New York: International Universities Press.

Wolf, E. S. (1988). *Treating the self: Elements of clinical self psychology.* New York: Guilford.

Wright, M. E. (1990). Suggestions for use of spontaneous trances in emergency situations. In D.C. Hammond (Ed.) *Handbook of hypnotic suggestions and metaphors* (pp. 234–235). New York: Norton.

Wright, M. E., & Wright, B.A. (1987). *Clinical practice of hypnotherapy.* New York: Guilford.

Wynne, L. C., Rykoff, I. M., Day, J., & Hirsch, S. I. (1958). Pseudomutuality in the family relations of schizophrenics. *Psychiatry, 21,* 205–220.

Yalom, I. D. (1975). *The theory and practice of psychotherapy* (2nd ed.). New York: Basic Books.

Yapko, M. D. (1986). What is Ericksonian hypnosis? In B. Zilbergeld, M. G. Edelstien, & D. L. Araoz (Eds.), *Hypnosis: questions and answers* (pp. 223–231). New York: Norton.

Yapko, M. D. (1990). *Trancework: An introduction to the practice of clinical hypnosis.* New York: Brunner/Mazel.

Yapko, M. D. (1992, December). *Memories of the future: Regression and suggestions of abuse.* Paper presented at the fifth International Congress on Ericksonian Approaches to Hypnosis and Psychotherapy, Phoenix, AZ.

Young, W. C. *Recognition and treatment of survivors reporting ritual abuse.* Unpublished manuscript.

Zeig, J. K. (Ed.) (1980). *A teaching seminar with Milton H. Erickson.* New York: Brunner/Mazel.

Zeig, J. K. (1986). Motivating patients to follow prescriptions. In B. Zilbergeld, M. G. Edelstien & D. L. Araoz (Eds.), *Hypnosis questions and answers* (pp. 252–254). New York: Norton.

Zilbergeld, B., & Hammond, D. C. (1988). The use of hypnosis in treating desire problems. In S. R. Leiblum & R. C. Rosen (Eds.), *Sexual desire disorders* (pp. 192–225). New York: Guilford.

Zilboorg, G., & Henry, G. W. (1941). *A history of medical psychology.* New York: Norton.

Index

357